AF881491

The Cambridge Companion to

Gender and the Law

To what extent is the legal subject gendered? Using illustrative examples from a range of jurisdictions and thematically organised chapters, this volume offers a comprehensive consideration of this question. With a systematic, accessible approach, it argues that law and gender work to co-produce the legal subject. Cumulatively, the volume's chapters provide a systematic evaluation of the key facets of the legal subject: the corporeal, the functional and the communal. Exploring aspects of the legal subject from the ways in which it is sexed and sexualised to its national and familial dimensions, this volume develops a complete account of the various processes through which legal orders produce gendered subjects. Across its chapters, each theoretically ambitious in its own right, this volume outlines how the law not only acts on the social world, but genders it.

Stéphanie Hennette Vauchez is Professor of Public Law at the Paris Nanterre University, Director of the CREDOF (*Centre d'études et de recherches sur les droits fondamentaux*) and senior member of the Institut universitaire de France. Her research focuses on conceptual issues of equality and human rights law. She has authored, co-authored and co-edited numerous journal articles, monographs and volumes. Her most recent publications include *How to Democratize Europe* (2019) and *Droits de l'Homme et libertés fondamentales* (2022).

Ruth Rubio-Marín is Professor of Constitutional Law at the University of Seville, Adjunct Professor at the School of Transnational Governance of the European University Institute, Florence, and Director of the UNIA UNESCO Chair in Human Rights and Interculturalism. Her research focuses on comparative constitutionalism, law and gender, immigration and citizenship, as well as transitional justice. Her most recent publications include *Gender Parity and Multicultural Feminism: Towards a New Synthesis* (2018), *Women as Constitution Makers: Case Studies from the New Democratic Era* (2019) and *Global Gender Constitutionalism and Women's Citizenship: A Struggle for Transformative Inclusion* (2022).

Cambridge Companions to Law

Cambridge Companions to Law offers thought-provoking introductions to different legal disciplines, invaluable to both the student and the scholar. Edited by world-leading academics, each offers a collection of essays which both map out the subject and allow the reader to delve deeper. Critical and enlightening, the Companions library represents legal scholarship at its best.

The Cambridge Companion to European Union Private Law
Edited by Christian Twigg-Flesner

The Cambridge Companion to International Law
Edited by James Crawford and Martti Koskenniemi

The Cambridge Companion to Comparative Law
Edited by Mauro Bussani and Ugo Mattei

The Cambridge Companion to Human Rights Law
Edited by Conor Gearty and Costas Douzinas

The Cambridge Companion to Public Law
Edited by Mark Elliott and David Feldman

The Cambridge Companion to International Criminal Law
Edited by William A. Schabas

The Cambridge Companion to Natural Law Jurisprudence
Edited by George Duke and Robert P. George

The Cambridge Companion to Comparative Family Law
Edited by Shazia Choudhry and Jonathan Herring

The Cambridge Companion to Comparative Constitutional Law
Edited by Roger Masterman and Robert Schütze

The Cambridge Companion to the First Amendment and Religious Liberty
Edited by Michael D. Breidenbach and Owen Anderson

The Cambridge Companion to the Philosophy of Law
Edited by John Tasioulas

The Cambridge Companion to Legal Positivism
Edited by Torben Spaak and Patricia Mindus

The Cambridge Companion to Hugo Grotius
Edited by Randall Lesaffer and Janne E. Nijman

The Cambridge Companion to International Arbitration
Edited by Chin Leng Lim

The Cambridge Companion to Business & Human Rights Law
Edited by Ilias Bantekas and Michael Stein

The Cambridge Companion to International Organizations Law
Edited by Jan Klabbers

The Cambridge Companion to Gender and the Law
Edited by Stéphanie Hennette Vauchez and Ruth Rubio-Marín

The Cambridge Companion to

Gender and the Law

Edited by

Stéphanie Hennette Vauchez
Paris Nanterre University

Ruth Rubio-Marín
University of Seville

CAMBRIDGE
UNIVERSITY PRESS

CAMBRIDGE
UNIVERSITY PRESS

Shaftesbury Road, Cambridge cb2 8ea, United Kingdom

One Liberty Plaza, 20th Floor, New York, NY 10006, USA

477 Williamstown Road, Port Melbourne, VIC 3207, Australia

314–321, 3rd Floor, Plot 3, Splendor Forum, Jasola District Centre, New Delhi – 110025, India

103 Penang Road, #05–06/07, Visioncrest Commercial, Singapore 238467

Cambridge University Press is part of Cambridge University Press & Assessment, a department of the University of Cambridge.

We share the University's mission to contribute to society through the pursuit of education, learning and research at the highest international levels of excellence.

www.cambridge.org
Information on this title: www.cambridge.org/9781108499248
DOI: 10.1017/9781108634069

© Cambridge University Press & Assessment 2023

This publication is in copyright. Subject to statutory exception and to the provisions of relevant collective licensing agreements, no reproduction of any part may take place without the written permission of Cambridge University Press & Assessment.

First published 2023

A catalogue record for this publication is available from the British Library.

Library of Congress Cataloging-in-Publication Data
Names: Hennette-Vauchez, Stéphanie, editor. | Rubio-Marín, Ruth, editor.
Title: The Cambridge companion to gender and the law / edited by Stéphanie Hennette Vauchez, Université Paris Nanterre; Ruth Rubio-Marín, Universidad de Sevilla.
Description: Cambridge, United Kingdom ; New York, NY : Cambridge University Press, 2022. | Series: Cambridge companions to law | Includes bibliographical references and index.
Identifiers: LCCN 2022041527 (print) | LCCN 2022041528 (ebook) | ISBN 9781108499248 (hardback) | ISBN 9781108713306 (paperback) | ISBN 9781108634069 (epub)
Subjects: LCSH: Gender identity–Law and legislation. | Sex discrimination–Law and legislation. | Women–Legal status, laws, etc.
Classification: LCC K3243 .C37 2022 (print) | LCC K3243 (ebook) | DDC 342.08/78–dc23/eng/20221031
LC record available at https://lccn.loc.gov/2022041527
LC ebook record available at https://lccn.loc.gov/2022041528

ISBN 978-1-108-49924-8 Hardback
ISBN 978-1-108-71330-6 Paperback

Cambridge University Press & Assessment has no responsibility for the persistence or accuracy of URLs for external or third-party internet websites referred to in this publication and does not guarantee that any content on such websites is, or will remain, accurate or appropriate.

The Cambridge Companion to

Gender and the Law

Edited by

Stéphanie Hennette Vauchez
Paris Nanterre University

Ruth Rubio-Marín
University of Seville

CAMBRIDGE
UNIVERSITY PRESS

CAMBRIDGE
UNIVERSITY PRESS

Shaftesbury Road, Cambridge cb2 8ea, United Kingdom

One Liberty Plaza, 20th Floor, New York, NY 10006, USA

477 Williamstown Road, Port Melbourne, VIC 3207, Australia

314–321, 3rd Floor, Plot 3, Splendor Forum, Jasola District Centre, New Delhi – 110025, India

103 Penang Road, #05–06/07, Visioncrest Commercial, Singapore 238467

Cambridge University Press is part of Cambridge University Press & Assessment, a department of the University of Cambridge.

We share the University's mission to contribute to society through the pursuit of education, learning and research at the highest international levels of excellence.

www.cambridge.org
Information on this title: www.cambridge.org/9781108499248
DOI: 10.1017/9781108634069

© Cambridge University Press & Assessment 2023

This publication is in copyright. Subject to statutory exception and to the provisions of relevant collective licensing agreements, no reproduction of any part may take place without the written permission of Cambridge University Press & Assessment.

First published 2023

A catalogue record for this publication is available from the British Library.

Library of Congress Cataloging-in-Publication Data
Names: Hennette-Vauchez, Stéphanie, editor. | Rubio-Marín, Ruth, editor.
Title: The Cambridge companion to gender and the law / edited by Stéphanie Hennette Vauchez, Université Paris Nanterre; Ruth Rubio-Marín, Universidad de Sevilla.
Description: Cambridge, United Kingdom ; New York, NY : Cambridge University Press, 2022. | Series: Cambridge companions to law | Includes bibliographical references and index.
Identifiers: LCCN 2022041527 (print) | LCCN 2022041528 (ebook) | ISBN 9781108499248 (hardback) | ISBN 9781108713306 (paperback) | ISBN 9781108634069 (epub)
Subjects: LCSH: Gender identity–Law and legislation. | Sex discrimination–Law and legislation. | Women–Legal status, laws, etc.
Classification: LCC K3243 .C37 2022 (print) | LCC K3243 (ebook) | DDC 342.08/78–dc23/eng/20221031
LC record available at https://lccn.loc.gov/2022041527
LC ebook record available at https://lccn.loc.gov/2022041528

ISBN 978-1-108-49924-8 Hardback
ISBN 978-1-108-71330-6 Paperback

Cambridge University Press & Assessment has no responsibility for the persistence or accuracy of URLs for external or third-party internet websites referred to in this publication and does not guarantee that any content on such websites is, or will remain, accurate or appropriate.

Contents

Part III Communities

Contributors

Márcia Nina Bernardes is Associate Professor of Law (PUC-Rio), Coordinator of the Human Rights Center (PUC-Rio), JSD (NYU School of Law), and a member of Red ALAS (Latin-American Network of Feminist Jurists). Bernardes' scholarship intersects gender, feminism, decoloniality and law. Her latest publication discusses the struggle against domestic violence in Brazil from a subaltern perspective. Her ongoing project focuses on the discussion on the possibility of feminist judgments from an anti-racist and decolonial perspective.

Marie-Xavière Catto is an assistant professor in public law at University of Paris I Pantheon-Sorbonne. Her research focuses on the limits of the economic use of the human body, bioethics, and issues of procreation and gender bicategorization from a feminist critical legal perspective. Her publications include *Le principe d'indisponibilité du corps humain, limite de l'usage économique du corps* (LGDJ, 2018) and *La bicatégorisation de sexe: Entre droit, normes sociales et sciences biomédicales* (co-edited with Julie Mazaleigue-Labaste, Mare et Martin, 2021).

Joanne Conaghan is Professor of Law at the University of Bristol. She has written extensively on issues relating to law and gender, across a range of legal sub-fields including labour law. She is author of *Law and Gender* (Oxford University Press, 2013).

Joanna N. Erdman is a Professor and the inaugural MacBain Chair in Health Law and Policy at the Schulich School of Law, Dalhousie University, Nova Scotia. Her research focuses on sexual and reproductive health and human rights in a transnational context. She has also acted as an intervener before various courts and international bodies. She holds a JD from the University of Toronto and an LLM from Harvard Law School, and has completed a fellowship at Yale Law School.

Stéphanie Hennette Vauchez is Professor of Public Law at Paris Nanterre University, a senior member of the Institut universitaire de France and the director of the CREDOF (Centre de recherches et d'études sur les droits fondamentaux). She has also served as a postdoctoral Fulbright Fellow at Northwestern University Law School (USA), a Marie Curie Fellow at the European University Institute (Italy) and a Law & Public Affairs Fellow at Princeton University. Her research focuses on conceptual issues of equality and human rights law. After working on bioethics for a decade, her interests turned to law and gender with particular attention to issues of religious pluralism (religious freedom and non-discrimination) as well as security issues (terrorism and states of emergency). Professor Hennette Vauchez has published extensively in all these fields. She is the author and co-author of one of the most prominent manuals of human rights law in France and a noted essay on states of emergency. She is also the co-editor of three volumes that are major francophone references on the study of gender and law: *La loi & le genre: Etudes critiques de droit français* (Ed. du CNRS, 2014); *Ce que le genre fait au droit* (Dalloz, 2013); and *Genre et droit: Ressources pédagogiques* (Dalloz, 2016).

Jonathan Herring is the DM Wolf-Clarendon Fellow in Law at Exeter College and Professor of Law at the Faculty of Law, University of Oxford. He has written extensively on issues around family law, medical law and ethics, care law and criminal law. His books include *Law through the Life Course* (Bristol University Press, 2021); *Law and the Relational Self* (Cambridge University Press, 2019); *Vulnerable Adults and the Law* (Oxford University Press, 2015); *Caring and the Law* (Hart, 2013); *Older People and the Law* (Oxford University Press, 2009); and (with Shazia Choudhry) *European Human Rights and Family Law* (Hart, 2010).

Sofia Martins is a writer, editor and researcher working at the intersection of government policy, human rights and artistic production. Her research on Brazilian cinema during the dictatorship, Amazonian development and its impact on human rights, and South American literature and history has won multiple awards, including the Mellon Mays Undergraduate Research Fellowship, and presentations at multiple conferences. In 2019, she was Columbia University's Valedictorian. Her scholarship on the Amazon secured Columbia's Doctorow Fellowship for a Masters program at the University of Oxford, which she completed in 2020.

Melissa Murray is the Frederick I. and Grace Stokes Professor of Law and Faculty Director of the Birnbaum Women's Leadership Network at NYU School of Law, and a leading expert in the fields of constitutional law, reproductive rights and justice, family law and criminal law. Prior to joining the NYU Law faculty, Murray was a professor at the University of California, Berkeley Law, and, from March 2016 to June 2017, served as interim dean of Berkeley Law. Murray's research has been published in *Harvard Law Review*, *Yale Law Journal* and *Columbia Law Review*, among other leading law reviews, and she regularly provides commentary for a number of lay publications, including the *Washington Post* and the *New York Times*.

Fernanda G. Nicola is Professor at the Washington College of Law, American University, where she directs the Program on International Organizations Law and Development. Her research and teaching interests are in comparative law, transnational legal theory and constitutional law. She received her PhD from Trento University and her SJD degree from Harvard Law School, where she was the recipient of the Mancini Prize in European Law. Professor Nicola has written on comparative family law, interspousal torts and gender in development policy in her forthcoming book *Misuses of Comparative Law in International Development*.

Stefano Osella is a Postdoctoral Research Fellow at Bocconi University, Department of Legal Studies, in Milan (Italy). He is also a Research Partner at the Max Planck Institute for Social Anthropology, Department of Law and Anthropology, in Halle (Saale), Germany. Previously, Stefano was Postdoctoral Global Fellow at the New York University School of Law. He obtained a doctorate in law with a specialization in public comparative law from the European University Institute, Florence. Stefano's research focuses on how constitutional and human rights represent and construct gender diversity, an area in which he has published several peer-reviewed articles. Methodologically, Stefano combines comparative law, queer theory and anthropology.

Kim Rubenstein is Professor in the Faculty of Business, Government and Law at the University of Canberra. A graduate of the University of Melbourne and Harvard University, she is Australia's leading expert on citizenship, and on law's intersection with broader normative notions of citizenship as membership and participation. This led to her scholarship around gender and public law, including legal work and oral history work around women lawyers' contributions in the public sphere. She was the Director of the Centre for International and Public law at the ANU from 2006 to 2015 and the Inaugural Convener of the ANU Gender Institute from 2011 to 2012. She is a Fellow of the Australian Academy of Law and the Australia Academy of Social Sciences.

Ruth Rubio-Marín is Professor at the School of Transnational Governance (STG), where she leads the work of gender governance. She is Professor of Constitutional Law at the University of Seville, as well as member of faculty of the Hauser Global Law School Program at New York University. Her research represents an attempt to understand how public law creates categories of inclusion and exclusion around different axes including gender, citizenship, nationality and ethnicity. Methodologically, she combines law and political theory.

Ann Shalleck is Professor of Law and Carrington Shields Scholar, American University, Washington College of Law, where she directs the Women and the Law Program. Her writing, research and teaching interests encompass family law, feminist theory, narrative theory, and clinical legal education. She coauthored *Transforming the Education of Lawyers: The Theory and Practice of Clinical Pedagogy* and *Lawyers and Clients: Critical Issues in Interviewing and Counseling.* The Women and the Law Program offers specialized courses on gender and the law, has a Gender Justice Clinic, integrates gender-related issues throughout the curriculum, organizes scholarly workshops, conducts projects on gender justice, and offers an LLM in Gender, International and Comparative Law.

Michael Thomson is Professor of Law at the University of Technology Sydney and the University of Leeds. His research interests span the fields of health law, children's rights, and legal and political theory. He has written on the legal regulation of reproduction, non-therapeutic interventions on children, and social and political theories that centre the body as a means of rearticulating the responsibilities of the state. His current work explores the role of law in addressing health inequalities. Recent publications include: 'A Capabilities Approach to Best Interests Assessments', *Legal Studies* (2021); 'Conscience, Abortion, and Jurisdiction', *Oxford Journal of Legal Studies* (2020) (with S. McGuinness); and *A Jurisprudence of the Body* (edited with C. Dietz and M. Travis, Palgrave, 2020).

Melissa Murray is the Frederick I. and Grace Stokes Professor of Law and Faculty Director of the Birnbaum Women's Leadership Network at NYU School of Law, and a leading expert in the fields of constitutional law, reproductive rights and justice, family law and criminal law. Prior to joining the NYU Law faculty, Murray was a professor at the University of California, Berkeley Law, and, from March 2016 to June 2017, served as interim dean of Berkeley Law. Murray's research has been published in *Harvard Law Review*, *Yale Law Journal* and *Columbia Law Review*, among other leading law reviews, and she regularly provides commentary for a number of lay publications, including the *Washington Post* and the *New York Times.*

Fernanda G. Nicola is Professor at the Washington College of Law, American University, where she directs the Program on International Organizations Law and Development. Her research and teaching interests are in comparative law, transnational legal theory and constitutional law. She received her PhD from Trento University and her SJD degree from Harvard Law School, where she was the recipient of the Mancini Prize in European Law. Professor Nicola has written on comparative family law, interspousal torts and gender in development policy in her forthcoming book *Misuses of Comparative Law in International Development.*

Stefano Osella is a Postdoctoral Research Fellow at Bocconi University, Department of Legal Studies, in Milan (Italy). He is also a Research Partner at the Max Planck Institute for Social Anthropology, Department of Law and Anthropology, in Halle (Saale), Germany. Previously, Stefano was Postdoctoral Global Fellow at the New York University School of Law. He obtained a doctorate in law with a specialization in public comparative law from the European University Institute, Florence. Stefano's research focuses on how constitutional and human rights represent and construct gender diversity, an area in which he has published several peer-reviewed articles. Methodologically, Stefano combines comparative law, queer theory and anthropology.

Kim Rubenstein is Professor in the Faculty of Business, Government and Law at the University of Canberra. A graduate of the University of Melbourne and Harvard University, she is Australia's leading expert on citizenship, and on law's intersection with broader normative notions of citizenship as membership and participation. This led to her scholarship around gender and public law, including legal work and oral history work around women lawyers' contributions in the public sphere. She was the Director of the Centre for International and Public law at the ANU from 2006 to 2015 and the Inaugural Convener of the ANU Gender Institute from 2011 to 2012. She is a Fellow of the Australian Academy of Law and the Australia Academy of Social Sciences.

Ruth Rubio-Marín is Professor at the School of Transnational Governance (STG), where she leads the work of gender governance. She is Professor of Constitutional Law at the University of Seville, as well as member of faculty of the Hauser Global Law School Program at New York University. Her research represents an attempt to understand how public law creates categories of inclusion and exclusion around different axes including gender, citizenship, nationality and ethnicity. Methodologically, she combines law and political theory.

Ann Shalleck is Professor of Law and Carrington Shields Scholar, American University, Washington College of Law, where she directs the Women and the Law Program. Her writing, research and teaching interests encompass family law, feminist theory, narrative theory, and clinical legal education. She coauthored *Transforming the Education of Lawyers: The Theory and Practice of Clinical Pedagogy* and *Lawyers and Clients: Critical Issues in Interviewing and Counseling*. The Women and the Law Program offers specialized courses on gender and the law, has a Gender Justice Clinic, integrates gender-related issues throughout the curriculum, organizes scholarly workshops, conducts projects on gender justice, and offers an LLM in Gender, International and Comparative Law.

Michael Thomson is Professor of Law at the University of Technology Sydney and the University of Leeds. His research interests span the fields of health law, children's rights, and legal and political theory. He has written on the legal regulation of reproduction, non-therapeutic interventions on children, and social and political theories that centre the body as a means of rearticulating the responsibilities of the state. His current work explores the role of law in addressing health inequalities. Recent publications include: 'A Capabilities Approach to Best Interests Assessments', *Legal Studies* (2021); 'Conscience, Abortion, and Jurisdiction', *Oxford Journal of Legal Studies* (2020) (with S. McGuinness); and *A Jurisprudence of the Body* (edited with C. Dietz and M. Travis, Palgrave, 2020).

Melany Toombs is a lawyer and researcher who loves thinking and writing about the law using creative, interdisciplinary approaches. She was previously named Global Winner in the Law category of the Global Undergraduate Awards for her work on colonial law and Islamic architecture in Spain, and awarded the ANU Gender Institute Honours Thesis Prize for her examination of women's sanctuary spaces and witchcraft in Morocco. A former legal associate in the Federal Circuit and Family Court of Australia, Melany currently works as a family lawyer in Canberra. Melany is a keen advocate for women's participation in academic, sporting and faith-based communities and dedicates all she does to God.

Introduction

From Law and Gender to Law as Gender – The Legal Subject and the Co-production Hypothesis

Stéphanie Hennette Vauchez and Ruth Rubio-Marín

In terms of gender equality, law is a fundamentally ambivalent artefact. It can certainly be a vector for progressive change, as documented in several of the contributions in this volume. Indeed, law has played a crucial role in many decisive battles and victories for gender equality globally, from the extension of political franchise to all those that were initially excluded therefrom (such as women, racialized minorities, servants, dependants, etc.),[1] to the more contemporary steps in the confirmation of a principle of equality among sexual orientations, gender identities,[2] family arrangements and so on. Accompanying a number of social and political struggles, law has helped tackle forms of discrimination and exclusion that were once entrenched in law and channelled claims of equal recognition and equality of opportunities relevant to the dignitarian, redistributive and participatory dimensions of equality.[3]

Conversely, law can also entrench profound inequalities – including gender inequality. Indeed, law has a long (and unfinished) history of doing exactly that, for it is also inevitably an instrument of power. Feminist legal scholars have largely documented and analysed the numerous ways in which legal rules and concepts have consolidated inequality between the sexes,[4] from the denial of political franchise to unequal civil and marital status as well as criminal protection. Formal differentiations between the sexes which underlie patriarchal legal orders are not fully in the past either. As Melanie Toombs and Kim Rubenstein remind us in Chapter 8, in 2019, twenty-five states still upheld laws with patrilineal rules of nationality transmission. Women are impeded from passing on their

[1] Hennette Vauchez and Rubio Marin, Chapter 10 in this volume.

[2] Catto and Osella, Chapter 1 in this volume.

[3] N. Fraser, *Fortunes of Feminism: From State-Managed Capitalism to Neoliberal Crisis* (New York: Verso Books, 2013).

[4] See, for example, C. Smart, *Feminism and the Power of Law* (New York: Routledge, 1989).

nationality to their children, either on an equal basis with men or altogether, because they are perceived as part of a male household and lacking independent citizenship status. These rules coexist with norms of 'marital denaturalization', still present in twenty-five countries today, which perceive women's allegiance to the state as mediated through marriage in the understanding that, when a woman marries a foreigner, she leaves her former identity behind or she betrays the home state through marriage to a non-citizen.

As the concept of gender gained traction and increasingly came to be read as one part of a much larger matrix of power dynamics and inequality (in conjunction with race, class, religion, geography, disability, etc.), feminist studies broadened their scope. They now confirm the paradoxical compatibility between formal legal proclamations of 'gender or sex equality' as a general overarching principle, an axiom in liberal democratic orders, and massively unequal outcomes in their concrete operation as testimony to the law's severe shortcomings. Women and other social groups that were historically deprived of political rights remain massively under-represented in key political decision-making arenas decades and sometimes centuries after gaining the franchise. Moreover, the striking down of racial segregation in countries where it was once legally enshrined, such as the United States or South Africa, has been unable to overcome the de facto segregation which in many ways continues to exclude racially oppressed groups from certain residential areas, educational and professional opportunities, and institutions of power. More generally, a number of important human rights – from the right to education to that of religious freedom or privacy rights – continue to be unevenly enjoyed by individuals (notably depending on their gender, race, class, ability and/or other factors), in spite of them being universally recognized.

1. Law Perpetuating and Legitimizing Gender Inequality

Time and again, law at the service of power has shown its capacity to metamorphosize in a process labelled 'preservation through transformation',[5] which allows for the emergence of new legal doctrines

[5] R. B. Siegel, 'The Rule of Love: Wife Beating as Prerogative and Privacy' (1996) 105 *Yale Law Journal* 2117–2207 at 2178–2187.

able to restrain the effects of legislation intended to overcome inequalities and, as critical race and gender scholars have shown, maintain the unequal gender and racial status quo. Law routinely expresses itself through rules and concepts that in fact perpetuate (or aggravate) inequality, even when sex-based classifications are avoided. This volume provides many examples of formally neutral legal norms that nonetheless produce enduringly and consistently unequal results, both in hermeneutical and empirical terms. Despite many affirmations to the contrary, gender-blind legal rules seem not to be blind at all, but one-eyed at best.[6]

Gender bias is often hidden behind general legal concepts and technical legal rules that may appear gender neutral in principle. In terms of general legal concepts, several chapters in this volume testify to their ambivalence. For example, in her chapter on the procreational subject (Chapter 6), Joanna Erdman highlights the ways in which the concept of 'reproductive rights' remains tied to female bodies (and thereby to the female sex) in international human rights law, and thus perpetuates the invisibilization of all other reproductive bodies, as well as the cognitive suppression of the bodies of those women who do not match 'essential womanhood'. As far as technical legal rules are concerned, labour law provides us with numerous examples. Minimum hours thresholds governing access to employment protection, or labour collectivism shaped after the manufacturing model and equal pay standards which require establishing comparisons to workers employed in the same establishment, account for much of the marginalization and segregation of women in the employment market, and the precariousness of their position in it.[7] Legal requirements in citizenship tests that do not take into account higher levels of women's illiteracy or poverty when setting fees, such as knowledge and language tests, have gendered consequences too, as do migration rules that make circular migration difficult, since this impedes migrant women from travelling back and forth to fulfil care responsibilities back home.[8] In Chapter 1, Catto and Osella tellingly document the ways in which the legal rules pertaining to sexual identity, as well as the legal requirement that every individual's sex be defined at birth, have played in most parts of the world:

[6] S. Hennette Vauchez, M. Pichard and D. Roman (eds.), *La loi & le genre, Etudes critiques de droit français* (Paris: CNRS Éditions, 2014).

[7] Conaghan, Chapter 5 in this volume.

[8] Toombs and Rubenstein, Chapter 8 in this volume.

Not only have they caused the erasure (intersex individuals) or containment (trans individuals) of physical and psychological variations in 'sex', they have also legitimized and even led to the requirement of medical practices (reassignment surgery) that would have otherwise been qualified as unacceptable violations of physical integrity.

Other examples in this volume point to the limits of many of the traditionally crafted legal remedies in tackling the roots of discrimination, or its intersectional nature, even while trying to compensate for some of its effects, or in overcoming law's territorially bounded scope in a globalized world. In Chapter 7, on the caring subject, Herring mentions the possibility of moving towards the concept of family responsibilities discrimination, rather than a broadly conceived notion of sex-based discrimination or measures to assist *women* with reconciling work and family, as a way to ensure that law does not further entrench existing gender roles while looking for remedies. The contemporary debate about extending maternity leaves versus advancing towards joint adoption of paternity/maternity leaves and gender-neutral parental leaves, which he also mentions, raises similar concerns. The possibility that all these remedies might still be insufficient to compensate for the current care labour shortage in advanced democracies leads to the phenomenon of the global care chain, showing how deficiencies in national regulatory systems are likely to have spill-over effects beyond national borders, entrenching existing socio-economic, gender and racial gaps across the globe as a result. Moreover, the phenomenon by which legal rules fail to apply fully and universally to all individuals appears repeatedly throughout the volume, making the call for intersectional analysis all the more compelling: Family law tends to either fail to protect or play out adversely for those poor, coloured, unmarried or otherwise nonconforming individuals;[9] legal regimes pertaining to the protection of women against domestic violence seem to effectively operate along the lines of pre-existing and untouched hierarchies of race and class.[10] Labour law is also filled with legal loopholes that have gendered and racialized impacts. Several of our authors remind us that the lived realities of domestic workers provide a good example of the collusion of law with structures of sexism and racism: These workers traditionally fell outside the scope of employment protection and thus

[9] Nicola and Shalleck, Chapter 9 in this volume.

[10] Bernardes and Martins, Chapter 3 in this volume.

remain uncovered by several forms of protection, such as those provided by working time and minimum wage laws, with particularly exploitative effects on live-ins.

Beyond instances where the law fails to correct gender inequality, this volume confirms that it can even legitimize it by affirming domains of legal exemption and drawing up legal exceptions in ways that entrench gendered social arrangements and gender bias. The inconceivability of marital rape in many legal systems until well into the twentieth century is a case in point: In the United Kingdom, Australia, France and the United States, it was not until the 1990s that courts and legislators reversed the principle according to which marriage conferred a right on husbands to force intercourse upon their wives, thus de facto proclaiming the family and the marital context as a domain in which protections against sexual violence against women did not apply (see also Murray, Chapter 4 in this volume). Between 1999 and 2008, the Italian Corte di Cassazione formulated the 'blue jeans exemption', refusing to find legal instances of rape whenever the victim was wearing blue jeans, based on the notion that 'it is nearly impossible to slip off tight jeans even partly without the active collaboration of the person who is wearing them'.[11] In many countries, marriage after rape continues to shield the perpetrator from liability for the aggression. In other words, the legal institution of marriage has been legally constructed to legitimize sexual violence.

2. Gender Theory and (In)Equality

The varied, complex and at times erratic ways in which both gender equality and gender inequality occur as the result or the effect of legal rules are now well documented. They are further echoed in the immensely sophisticated theoretical and epistemological discussion which is ongoing in feminist legal theory and, more generally, in all scholarship that looks at law from the perspective of gender. The topic of law and gender (in)equality has indeed generated a vast body of literature that is uniquely variegated in its theoretical underpinnings and orientations, including

[11] Cass., sez. III, 6 nov. 1998, n. 1636. B. Faedi, 'Rape, Blue Jeans, and Judicial Developments in Italy' (2009) 16 *Columbia Journal of European Law Online* 13–18.

liberal,[12] materialist,[13] radical,[14] (a variety of) postmodern,[15] and other frames, with hardly one dominant approach. In fact, scholars concerned with gender equality strongly differ in their opinions on the very identification of the best intellectual tools to shed light on the intersectional forms of oppression and subordination that women continue to be subject to. While some have called for a break with feminism,[16] others claim that feminist fundamentalism[17] is the key. Others still see more contemporary concepts and debates, such as those opened up by the perspective of intersectionality,[18] not as a disavowal of feminism but rather as a mostly welcome paradigmatic shift enabling new and mostly complementary angles of analysis.[19]

To a certain extent, the fundamental affirmation which brings together much of this astonishingly rich, sophisticated and variegated literature is that law reproduces gendered outcomes when acting upon already gendered social facts. Be it in constitutional law, contract law, land law, family law, international law, human rights law, labour law or basically any domain regulated by law, one of the accomplishments of feminist legal theory and gendered studies of law has been to establish the various ways in which law operates as a tool of perpetuation, aggravation and

[12] M. Wollstonecraft, *A Vindication of the Rights of Woman* [1792] (New York: Knopf, 1992); H. Taylor Mill, 'Enfranchisement of Women', in A. S. Rossi (ed.), *Essays on Sex Equality* (Chicago, IL: University of Chicago Press, 1970), 89–121.

[13] C. McKinnon, *Toward a Feminist Theory of the State* (Cambridge, MA: Harvard University Press, 1989).

[14] S. Firestone, *The Dialectic of Sex: The Case for Feminist Revolution* (New York: William Morrow, 1970); M. Wittig, *The Straight Mind* (Boston, MA: Beacon Press, 1992); A. Dworkin, *Right-Wing Women* (New York: Perigee, 1978).

[15] J. Butler, *Gender Trouble: Feminism and the Subversion of Identity* (New York: Routledge, 1990); M. J. Frug, 'A Postmodern Feminist Legal Manifesto (An Unfinished Draft)' (1992) 105 *Harvard Law Review* 1045–1075; H. Cixous, *The Newly Born Woman* (Minneapolis: University of Minnesota Press, 1986).

[16] J. Halley, *Split Decisions: How and Why to Take a Break from Feminism* (Princeton, NJ: Princeton University Press, 2006).

[17] M. A. Case, 'Feminist Fundamentalism and Constitutional Citizenship' in J. Grossman and L. McClain (eds.), *Dimensions of Women's Equal Citizenship* (Cambridge: Cambridge University Press, 2009), 107.

[18] K. Crenshaw, 'Demarginalizing the Intersection of Race and Sex: A Black Feminist Critique of Antidiscrimination Doctrine, Feminist Theory and Antiracist Politics' (1989) 1 *University of Chicago Legal Forum* 139–167; S. Atrey, *Intersectional Discrimination* (Oxford: Oxford University Press, 2009).

[19] J. Conaghan, 'General Introduction', in J. Conaghan (ed.), *Feminist Legal Studies* (London: Routledge, 2009), 10.

legitimization of gender inequality as a social reality, in spite of the fact that the banning of sex-based inequality has come to be accepted as a fundamental pillar in the affirmation of their legitimacy in more and more countries.

As the examples already mentioned show, the present volume certainly supports these important findings. However, the book uses a wider gaze in seeking to examine not only 'the many ways in which law ... harms women', or other individuals that are subordinated on the grounds of gender norms for that matter, but rather 'to make sense of the many ways gender shapes law'.[20] Starting from the premise of law's claim to knowledge and truth,[21] it intends to analyse not only the social effects of legal regulation and the deficiencies of law in changing social outcomes, but also the manner in which law actually shapes the world as we understand it both cognitively and normatively. It seeks to underline the ways in which law is gender*ing*, and not only the ways in which it is gender*ed*.[22] Such an endeavour presupposes a number of epistemological clarifications. Seeking to analyse the gendered effects of law or to unearth the ways in which it is gendering are two different analytical aims that require different epistemological starting points.

3. Social Constructionism in Law and Gender

Scholarly attempts to analyse the gendered effects of a particular set of legal rules typically posit 'law' and 'gender' as two distinct orders: 'Law' is seen as the acting normative order and 'gendered effects' are measured as empirical results from pre-existing sex-specific social facts. Such efforts tend to verify the gendered dimension of law on the basis of social outcomes that are arguably (re)produced by law. For instance, data is used to support the need for parity rules: The fact that the share of women in parliamentary representation had remained roughly the same for decades was instrumental in foregrounding the critique of falsely neutral constitutional rules pertaining to political representation, and subsequently, legitimizing active measures by means of legal reform. The assessment of

[20] N. Naffine, 'In Praise of Legal Feminism' (2002) 22 *Legal Studies* 71–101 at 72.
[21] Smart, *Feminism and the Power of the Law*.
[22] J. Conaghan, *Law and Gender* (Oxford: Oxford University Press, 2013), 67.

Nelson Mandela's decision to pardon inmates who were also mothers (as opposed to fathers) relied heavily on data indicating that mothers shouldered a disproportionate share of care duties, thus justifying the differential treatment on the basis of sex by a presidential order that ultimately sought to ensure the well-being of the country's youth.[23]

The project underlying this volume seeks to complexify the epistemology of the study of the interaction between law and gender, and the relationship between the legal and the social. It seeks to further the notion that gender (in)equality is not merely social, but also normative, and that law plays a constitutive role in shaping social reality. Data alone is insufficient to measure and analyse the full extent of the ways in which gender is pervasive in the organization and operation of socio-political orders, and in the legal rules that they put in place. The social and the legal should not be treated as two fully distinct realms of operation and effect. As Conaghan argues in this volume, the convention that affirms this separation enables 'law to self-present as an autonomous repository of norms'. This in turn has certain 'consequences for how gender is mobilized and conceptualized in law'. Specifically, 'it positions gender as a *social* rather than legal category, a product of social arrangements not legal forms, [and since] gender is conceived as extraneous to law, law may comfortably acquit itself of responsibility for gender-unequal outcomes'. In her view, a view that we share,

> [If] we adopt a conceptual frame which positions law within rather than without the iterative processes contributing to the construction of the social fabric, another picture of the relation between law and gender emerges. In this alternative conception, law does not simply act upon an already gendered social world; it is already imbricated in processes by which gender roles and relations come into being and garner normative potency. Law *genders*: In conjunction with other forms of discourse, law constrains and enables gendered identities and behaviours, fashioning and refashioning distinct gendered subjectivities.[24]

The goal of this volume is thus to contribute to the scrutiny of the ways in which social norms pertaining to gender, an instrument that actually produces sex differentiation and regulation, infuse and shape legal rules

[23] *President of the Republic of South Africa and Another* v. *Hugo* (CCT11/96) [1997] ZACC 4; 1997 (6) BCLR 708; 1997 (4) SA 1 (18 April 1997).

[24] Conaghan, Chapter 5 in this volume.

and concepts. The question underlying the volume is the following: Once gender is defined as a social construct made of social norms that are often reinforced and echoed by legal norms, to what extent can law offer emancipatory options, entangled as it is in the very making of that gender order?

Since its successful establishment of the need to complement the concept of sex (biological) with that of gender (social),[25] gender theory has experienced major debates and evolutions, many of which have been sparked by the refinement of that primary differentiation. Back in the 1980s, authors such as Moira Gatens criticized the strict opposition between nature and culture implied in the affirmation of the social dimension of 'gender' as opposed to the natural dimension of sex.[26] Judith Butler later famously suggested that sex rested on social construction as well, and that gender was in fact a performance.[27] Works by historian Thomas Laqueur and biologist Ann Fausto-Sterling further uncovered the variations in the definition(s) of sex over time and in biological substance. While the former powerfully established that the definition of two sexes as both opposite and incommensurable only dates back to the eighteenth century,[28] the latter reinforced the notion that gender effectively precedes sex: '[L]e sexe d'un corps est tout simplement trop complexe. Loin de l'alternative "ou bien/ou bien", la différence est affaire de nuances'; 'apposer sur quelqu'un l'étiquette "homme" ou "femme" est une decision sociale. Le savoir scientifique peut nous aider à prendre cette décision, mais seules nos croyances sur le genre – et non la science – définissent le sexe'.[29] Other authors, such as Gayle Rubin[30] and Eve Sedgwick,[31] also

[25] A. Oakley, *Sex, Gender and Society* (Farnham: Ashgate, 1972); K. O'Donovan, *Sexual Divisions in Law* (London: Weidenfeld & Nicolson, 1985).

[26] M. Gatens, 'A Critique of the Sex/Gender Distinction', in J. Allen and P. Patton (eds.), *Beyond Marxism: Interventions after Marx* (Sydney: Intervention Publications, 1983), 143–146.

[27] Butler, *Gender Trouble.*

[28] T. Laqueur, *Making Sex: Body and Gender from Greeks to Freud* (Cambridge, MA: Harvard University Press, 1992).

[29] A. Fausto-Sterling, *Sexing the Body: Gender Politics and the Construction of Sexuality* (New York: Basic Books, 2000), 19.

[30] G. Rubin, 'Thinking Sex: Notes for a Radical Theory of the Politics of Sexuality', in C. Vance (ed.), *Pleasure and Danger* (London: Routledge & Kegan, Paul, 1984); G. Rubin, 'The Traffic in Women: Notes on the "Political Economy" of Sex', in R. Reiter (ed.), *Toward an Anthropology of Women* (New York: Monthly View Press, 1975).

[31] E. Sedgwick, *Epistemology of the Closet* (Berkeley: University of California Press, 1990).

invited reflection on the co-dependency between gender and sexuality, linking the construction of both to the notion of heteronormativity. This connection has also been highlighted by Michel Foucault,[32] Monique Wittig[33] and, perhaps most famously, Judith Butler, who argued that 'the internal coherence or unity of either gender, man or woman, thereby requires both a stable and oppositional heterosexuality. That institutional heterosexuality both requires and produces the univocity of each of the gendered terms that constitute the limit of gendered possibilities within an oppositional, binary gender system'.[34] Queer of colour critique has explored and discussed the 'race' dimension of the definition of gender and sexuality.[35] This relationship has also been explored in the field of queer anthropology, which has highlighted how gender and sexuality are situated vis-à-vis a plurality of social factors, such as class, immigrant status, race and nationality.[36] These works and many others have complexified our understanding of sex, gender and sexuality. Certainly, the issue of the ontological primacy of the social (culture) over the biological (nature) remains debated and variable. It is also a topic causing much political anxiety, for the affirmation of gender as a social construct (the core operator of social reproduction) as opposed to a natural given necessarily places it within the reach of political will, thereby shaking the foundations of many arguments opposing reform such as eternity, fate or immutability. This explains the numerous and vocal political contestations to 'gender theory',[37] many of which are central to contemporary nationalist, conservative and populist agendas.

Concerned with the identification of those processes through which *law genders*, the core research question that unites the chapters of this volume

[32] M. Foucault, *The History of Sexuality*, trans. R. Huxley, 4 vols. (New York: Vintage Books, 1990), vol. 1, 152.

[33] M. Wittig, 'The Category of Sex', in *The Straight Mind and Other Essays* (Boston, MA: Beacon Press, 1992), 2–5.

[34] Butler, *Gender Trouble*, 31.

[35] R. Ferguson, *Aberrations in Black: Toward a Queer of Color Critique* (Minneapolis: University of Minnesota Press, 2003); F. El-Tayeb, *European Others: Queering Ethnicity in Postnational Europe* (Minneapolis: University of Minnesota Press, 2011).

[36] See, for example, D. Valentine, *Imagining Transgender: An Ethnography of a Category* (Durham, NC: Duke University Press, 2007); M. F. Manalaansan IV, *Global Divas: Filipino Gay Men in the Diaspora* (Durham, NC: Duke University Press, 2003).

[37] C. Robcis, *The Law of Kinship* (Ithaca, NY: Cornell University Press, 2013); R. Kuhar and D. Paternotte (eds.), *Anti-Gender Campaigns in Europe: Mobilizing against Equality* (London: Rowman & Littlefield, 2017).

needs not address, let alone solve, the issues of the respective roles of and relationship between the social and the biological. Rather, because the project is firmly committed to the notion that law is itself a social construct, it reads legal rules and concepts as choices that are by definition autonomous from any natural necessity, and could by definition take different forms. This is of course not to say that reality, including biological reality, does not matter. Take bodies, for instance. In the same way that gender theory itself has come to acknowledge the importance of material bodies,[38] and articulate this element by means of the social construction of sex and gender, this volume pays attention to the legal construction of human bodies. For example, in Chapter 2, on the 'foetal subject', Thomson endorses theories of subjectivity that frame subjectivity formation 'as a dynamic interplay of material and representational processes in consciousness formation and knowledge generation', in contrast to theories of social constructions resulting from 'social, symbolic and linguistic practices which shape collective understandings to produce historically situated, socially embedded subjects' as well as 'theories which are reduced to material conditions which include sentient needs, desires and emotions'.[39] As he focuses on legal embodiment by looking at the foetal subject, Thomson reminds us of the need to overcome the mind/body division that has beset legal thought and practice. He calls for a historicized account of the body as 'an important site where law and gender entwine in processes that construct legal subjects',[40] and illustrates the potential of such an enterprise by focusing on changing legal understandings of the foetus and women's reproductive body at various points in time across history. Similarly, in her reflection on the 'procreational subject' (Chapter 6), Joanne Erdman uses body theory to identify some ways out of the bind of the division between bio-reductionist understandings of sex and social constructionist understandings of gender that the legal construction of reproductive rights seems to be unable to escape from.[41] In other words, this volume does not ignore the materiality of the body and its importance in the construction of gender and law as social norms. However, its focus lies

[38] J. Butler, *Bodies That Matter: On the Discursive Limits of Sex* (New York: Routledge, 2014).

[39] Thomson, Chapter 2 in this volume.

[40] Ibid.

[41] Erdman, Chapter 6 in this volume.

consistently on the meaning and significance attached to bodies rather than on the thing itself.[42]

4. The Co-production of the Legal Subject by Law and Gender

The ways in which the chapters collected in this volume comprehend the legal subject support this social constructionist epistemology. Indeed, the project starts from the premise that the legal subject, the human person that the law deals with, is not a 'natural' entity imposing its subjectivity onto legal rules and categories, but an artificially constituted one instead, and that law is a key instrument in this constitutive act. Legal persons are not a reality simply acknowledged by law; rather, they are constituted by law. This has of course been historically documented. In both Anglo-Saxon and Roman traditions, the concept of the legal person is artificial (and not natural). As a legal category, the Roman *persona* did not coincide with the actual human person: Slaves and foreigners were denied legal personality; several human persons could coexist within one single legal person, notably for matters of patrimony and inheritance. The progressive humanization of the legal category of the person has certainly blurred the lines between nature and artifice, as the right of all persons to a legal personality was increasingly established.[43] Yet this contingent evolution of the substance of legal rules has not subverted the fact that the concept of the legal person was never supposed to coincide with that of the human person. The admission of corporate entities within the category of 'legal persons' evidently establishes this disconnect. More sophisticated elements also converge in showing that 'the legal subject' remains an artificial category. As the development of biomedical law in many Western legal orders over the course of the past three or four decades has only reinforced the relevance of the Foucauldian concept of biopolitics,[44] numerous studies have established that legal rules and concepts do not protect

[42] Again, this echoes the work of Joanne Conaghan: 'Bodies are one thing and the meaning and significance we attach to them another.' Conaghan, *Law and Gender*, 178.

[43] Y. Thomas, 'Le sujet de droit, la personne et la nature: Sur la critique contemporaine du sujet de droit' (1998) 3 *Le Débat* 85–107.

[44] M. Foucault, *Il faut défendre la société* (Paris: Seuil, 1997).

'life itself',[45] but rather specific forms of life that are deemed valuable.[46] Only when they convey *bios* (political life) rather than mere *zoe* (bare life) do forms of human life enjoy full legal protection. This fact defines the ontology of law.[47] Law is not only selective in the forms of life it protects, it is also constraining. In that respect, Catto and Osella's chapter on the sexed subject powerfully establishes the legal rejection of 'unruly bodies' and the constitutive function of law with respect to the legal subject in view of its rigid insistence on making 'sex' a necessary and foundational element thereof (Chapter 1).

Therefore, law is viewed here as both instrumental and integral to gender as a normative order and the very source of the production of the legal person, and thereby the inevitably gendered dimension of the legal abstraction in this constitutive process. In order to echo these epistemological premises, all authors contributing to this volume have been invited to reflect on the hypothesis of the co-production of the legal subject by law and gender as normative orders that produce hierarchies of power and assign specific identities. The co-production hypothesis has been borrowed from the very insightful and stimulating works in the field of science and technology studies – in particular, in the work of Sheila Jasanoff. Jasanoff has developed her co-production hypothesis as a tool (a grammar) for interpreting complex phenomena of interaction. In Jasanoff's words:

> Co-production is a shorthand for the proposition that the ways in which we know and represent the world (both nature and society) are inseparable from the ways in which we choose to live in it. Knowledge and its material embodiments are at once products of social work and constitutive of forms of social life; society cannot function without knowledge any more than knowledge can exist without appropriate social supports.[48]

[45] N. Rose, *The Politics of Life Itself: Biomedicine, Power, and Subjectivity in the Twenty-First Century* (Princeton, NJ: Princeton University Press, 2007).

[46] P. Hanafin, *Conceiving Life: Reproductive Politics and the Law in Contemporary Italy* (London: Routledge, 2016); L. Marguet, *Le droit de la procréation en France et en Allemagne: étude sur la normalisation de la vie, dissertation* (Nanterre: Université Paris Nanterre, 2018); S. Hennette Vauchez, 'Human Embryos as Persons in EU Law', in L. Azoulai, S. Barbou des Places and E. Pataut (eds.), *Constructing the Person in EU Law: Rights, Roles, Identities* (Oxford: Hart Publishing, 2016), 259.

[47] On this distinction, see G. Agamben, *Homo Sacer: Sovereign Power and Bare Life* (Palo Alto, CA: Stanford University Press, 1998).

[48] S. Jasanoff (ed.), *States of Knowledge: The Co-production of Science and Social Order* (London: Routledge, 2004), 2.

She mainly applies her hypothesis to the interaction of science and the social. Here, we hypothesize that the grammar of co-production can be applied to the legal subject as simultaneously produced (e.g. co-produced) by law and gender. What is interesting in Jasanoff's approach is that she sees co-production as allowing for an interpretation of science and the social order as mutually constitutive. Saying that law and gender are mutually constitutive of the legal subject is really to echo the notion that, although the legal subject is clearly a legal artefact, law does not produce the legal subject alone. As a social construct, law interacts with other social norms (including gender norms) in order to produce the artifice that is the legal subject. The contributions reunited in this volume examine gender as one of the key normative orders that interact with law in the production of the legal subject. The perspective is historical and multifaceted.

A. The Legal Subject as Co-produced by Law and Gender: Historical Approach

The understanding of law as expressive of a gendered social order that shapes the construction of the legal subject brings to the fore the need to historicize such a construction. In fact, several of the authors in this volume precisely attend to this. In Chapter 2, on embodiment and the foetal subject, Thomson cites Sheila Jasanoff when alluding to the '"openness" of the body' as allowing it 'to respond to the various social meanings attributed to the body in its concrete historical, social, and cultural particularity'.[49] In tracing the origins of modern foetal conceptions, Thomson highlights the importance of 'the "natural" realm be[ing] subject to critical scrutiny, particularly in addressing how gender becomes naturalized within biological and biomedical discourses which then become embedded in law'.[50] Indeed, he writes that 'scientific, legal and other discourse that address the body are only intelligible in the context of historically specific understandings of gender so that epistemic claims around the body often become a battlefield where different epistemic communities compete in a process that shapes the gender order'.[51] Thomson exemplifies this claim by providing a socio-legal history of theories of quickening and the abortion regulation they have led to, as they came to be replaced in modern times

[49] Ibid., 27. [50] Thomson, Chapter 2 in this volume. [51] Ibid.

with epistemic claims formulated by an emerging medical profession that asserted its monopoly over the definition of the beginning of human life, marginalizing not only the jurisdictional competence of ecclesiastical authorities but also women's experience, knowledge and interests. This process strongly resonates with similar contemporary attempts to cut back women's reproductive rights through laws, such as the legislation recently passed in the United States known as foetal heartbeat legislation that proposes outlawing abortion once rhythmic electrical activity is medically detectable in the foetus.

A similar emphasis on historical context is placed on the working subject in Conaghan's Chapter 5, as she describes how labour law has contributed to the institutionalization and naturalization of a historically specific gender division of labour, founded 'in the social and spatial distancing of work and family' and the privileging of productive over reproductive labour taking place in the shift from feudalism to capitalism, and its predominantly wage-based, market-centred economy supporting industrialization. She explains that this shift brought about the reconfiguration of labouring practices to meet the emergent needs of industrial production and the expansion of 'production-for-exchange' and 'timed work', as opposed to 'production-for-use' and 'task-oriented work', since 'much productive work was moved out of the household and into the mills and factories, while reproductive work – feeding, caring for, and reproducing labour – continued to be performed by women' in a 'home' that was no longer acknowledged as a key economic unit. Conaghan explains that this led to 'a unitary juridical model of the wage–labour contract, with working arrangements of full-time, long-term workers in a direct and stable relationship with a single employer', a model that has confined labour law to paid work and that is 'deaf to the practicalities of domesticity, consign[ing] most women workers to the margins of paid employment to serve as a reserve of flexible labour upon whom employers could call as market demands dictated'.[52] Women are 'clustered in part-time work and in sectors of the labour market which deviate from standard working norms', 'entering and exiting employment to the rhythms of reproductive cycles', often performing care-related work that has been symbolically devalued as 'low-skilled'.[53] According to her, the end result is that, 'until

[52] Conaghan, Chapter 5 in this volume. [53] Ibid.

we confront the dependence of labour law, conceptually and normatively, formally and substantively, on a conception of work as a space into which the practical demands of family life do not normally or ideally intrude, legal solutions to gender inequality are unlikely to yield great results'.[54]

Our chapter on the political subject also includes a historical detour in order to illuminate the dynamics of the formation of the sexual contract foundational to early European political modernity as well as the more recent battles that have been fought to challenge, if not overcome it. Taking the French Revolution and its 'invention' of modern citizenship as a historical landmark, the chapter documents that women were initially only implicitly denied franchise, for reasons pertaining to profoundly gendered conceptions of the family (and family status) that were essential to the definition of the political order. Later rules rendering the denial of other political rights explicit are best interpreted as a form of backlash against women's active and public involvement in the Revolution, and their corresponding failure to conform to the nurturing and reproductive roles that they were expected to assume in the gender-specific conceptions of civic duty prevalent at the time. A comparative analysis of the evolutions that took place in women's search for political agency in a number of Western countries from the beginning of the twentieth century confirms the ambivalence of law as a tool of emancipation, for the conquest of franchise, important as it was, has been shown to have had only a limited transformative potential with respect to the public/private divide in the foundational political order that continues to rest on the original sexual contract to a large extent. Only at the turn of the twenty-first century did a new horizon dawn in political rights with the appearance of participatory parity mechanisms, which have proved to contribute more significantly to the disestablishment of gender roles – including in the private sphere – and to the definition of the political subject in less intrinsically gendered terms.

Several other chapters tie together the co-production of the legal subject by law and gender with broader historically situated considerations of state power and nation building. Joanna Erdman's Chapter 7, on the procreational subject, critically analyses international human rights law in the field of reproductive rights as 'inviting' rather than 'interrogating' state power. She claims that this is one of the perspectives that reveals the

[54] Ibid.

importance of the gendering effect of legal constructions, for the essential role of social reproduction in the affirmation of nation states largely depends on the preservation of particular methods of biological reproduction. In Chapter 9, on the familial subject, Fernanda Nicola and Ann Schelleck also echo this claim, in particular as they note that 'historically, family law has served to shape the ideology of nation states'. They further note that the phenomenon endures to this day, as revealed, e.g., in the ways in which European law continues to shield domestic legal orders from supranational influence in the family law field, thus allowing for the protection of the various arrangements of the interaction of law and gender in the production of legal families.

Finally, Chapter 1, on the sexed subject, authored by Marie-Xavière Catto and Stefano Osella, tells the diachronic and comparative tale of the affirmation and weakening of the legal equation between the individual's 'legal sex' (the birth-assigned sex) and their 'true sex'. By providing a historically informed analysis of the definitions and redefinitions of the legally relevant criteria for the definition of sex, these authors show the extent to which these were geared towards the objective of preserving the sexual binary and the correlative heteronormative definition of marriage, even at the expense of discrepancies with reality and/or severe violations of physical integrity. Their historicized account leads to the analysis of more contemporary developments that progressively allow for 'a new sexed subject' to become legally intelligible, under the influence of growing concerns for physical integrity and the recognition of a right to gender self-determination, both of which have paved the way for questioning the binary or even imagining a sexless legal subject. Here, law's role in creating and enforcing the regulatory gender apparatus is most visible.

B. The Legal Subject as Co-produced by Law and Gender: A Multifaceted Approach Steering Clear of Traditional Disciplinary Divides

Even though the legal subject is in itself a legal abstraction, which legal systems insist on defining mostly for the purpose of deciding who is granted legal agency in general terms, it hardly exists as such on the legal scene. Rather than operating with the legal subject as one uniform and stable abstraction, legal orders tend to produce different masks that the subject is to wear in different situations – when performing in various domains, developing different capabilities, exercising various activities, interacting in different communal capacities and seeking protections and/or provisions for various purposes. In this way, the political subject is defined by a set of rules (a mask) differing from that which is applicable to the same subject seeking protection from terror and violence or displaying their familial status or employment contractual relationship.

The legal subject only really exists throughout multifaceted sets of rules that are triggered by or relevant to specific situations. The authors of the current volume have been asked to reflect on these various sets of rules.

In a sense, the structure of legal systems in certain areas or bodies of law already conveys epistemological clues about the way that the legal subject is constructed. Sometimes, it is the omission of any dedicated body of law to certain forms of activities and interactions that reveals the essential elements in the machinery for such construction, hence our conscious choice not to rely on the legal disciplines as traditionally defined. The overall structure of the book is threefold. As it seeks to examine the multiple masks of the legal subject's life on the legal scene, it successively looks at the corporeal, communal and functional dimensions that they may have. Within each chapter, the various authors have focused on one specific facet of the legal subject, discussed a set of relevant themes and identified a set of theoretical aspects to be explored, as well as specific issues and legal controversies that might allow for such exploration.[55] In so doing, we steer clear of the disciplinary approach to law and the old categories that it has traditionally relied on (i.e. private/public law; labour, commerce, family, administrative, criminal, etc.), as doing so better allows us not only to underscore the (often gendered) epistemic presuppositions of such disciplinary divides, but also the gendered results of their interaction as well as the variations in disciplinary and normalizing legal instruments across time and space from one legal regime to another.

As for the disciplinary divides, in Chapter 7, on the caring subject, Herring draws attention to the fact that law has traditionally promoted a vision of the self as an 'isolated, independent, self-sufficient autonomous man', ignoring the 'reality of our vulnerable, caring, relational selves', and

[55] This volume should have included additional chapters, especially on the religious subject and the racialized subject. Pandemic-related hardship affecting several authors forced us to move forward without those.

that this has made law unfit for the 'reality of our existence in which autonomies are mixed; meaning is found in sharing experiences; and flourishing is discovered in the mingling of our lives'. Canonical disciplinary divides have also entailed the privileging of 'certain particular activities, those traditionally seen as the domain of men, and the downplaying of the importance of caring, traditionally seen as the domain of women', something that arguably accounts for the fact that care has not been perceived as deserving of a separate legal discipline and that it has also been fully ignored in the shaping of other legal disciplines, such as labour law. As Conaghan's Chapter 5, on the working subject, beautifully portrays, labour law has been shaped around concepts of space and time that have contributed 'both to the delineation of work as a distinct sphere of activity and to the incorporation of gender norms and relations within its internal order' by importing gender 'into working arrangements via the medium of these seemingly "natural", pre-discursive categories', with the result that 'the conceptual and normative significance of gender as a feature of work regulation remains largely hidden, as do the (gendered) power relations therein'.[56]

In Chapter 4, on the sexual subject, Melissa Murray asks how law constructs the sexual citizenship, or – in other words – how we as a society, and by means of legal mechanisms, 'identify those whose sexual conduct and identities as sexual beings are consistent with our notions of citizenship and the public good'. She shows that this question can only be adequately answered by assessing the regulatory regime of sexual conduct that results from the interaction of various legal branches. In particular, her chapter shows how, historically, in the Anglo-American legal tradition, a large part of the construction of sexual citizenship relied on the interplay of marital law and criminal law in ways that produced an intra-racial, monogamous, exogamous and heterosexual procreative and marital understanding of legitimate and moral sex.[57] Crimes including those of miscegenation, incest, sodomy, abortion, contraception, fornication and seduction interacted with the conditions spelled out in marriage licences to create marriage as a status relationship that mediated the expressions of legal and morally acceptable forms of sexual expression. Critically, as marriage law and criminal law have receded as drivers of sexual regulation

[56] Conaghan, Chapter 5 in this volume. [57] Murray, Chapter 4 in this volume.

over the last fifty years, Murray shows how a newer, alternative regulatory modality has gained force, in part because of the rise of the administrative state. This new modality relies upon compliance with professional codes of conduct, employment licensing, and other forms of regulation that derive from the administrative state and the proliferation of bureaucratic agencies. It thrives on indeterminate concepts – such as 'unbecoming conduct', 'improper conduct', 'disruptive conduct' or even 'consent' – which through interpretation can still act as mechanisms to import the marital sex model and to entrench the traditional sexual gender and racial stereotypes. Similarly, Fernanda Nicola and Ann Shelleck's Chapter 9, on the familial subject, breaks traditional disciplinary boundaries of 'family law'. Rejecting an all-private law approach that would uncritically endorse the family as a unit of private ordering, they firmly place the familial subject at the crossroads of state regulation and market operation. This allows them to provide a dynamic exploration of the evolution of the legal construction of the family in neoliberal times, analysing how the expansion of certain spheres of personal freedom (such as the recognition of same-sex marriage) has gone hand in hand with increased economic regulation of family life (through, for instance, the rules governing child support). Their chapter also includes reflections on the impact of employment practices and norms on family decision-making.

Beyond the articulation of legal disciplines and subdisciplines, and the intended or unintended effects of their interaction, this collection provides ample evidence on the many ways in which the central legal concepts in the various legal disciplines have been centred around gendered epistemological presuppositions. Examples abound and include the notion of *damage* for compensation purposes in civil law, which under tort law typically fails to value interference with care work equally with interference with paid work (Herring, Chapter 7); the notion of *employment*, which failed to be understood as the right to combine paid work and care (instead of care being an external interference) (Conaghan, Chapter 5); the notions of *bodily integrity* and *family privacy* developed around gendered concepts as the different regulation of male and female genital cutting practices show (Thomson, Chapter 2); the notion of *family privacy* as giving coverture to marital rape and violence (Murray, Chapter 4); the notion of *parenthood* as a biology-oriented property/status based concept rather than a care-centred approach, which would allow heteronormative fault lines to be overcome (Herring, Chapter 7). Core concepts of family law (duties, parenting, power and authority, violence) are also a case in point (Nicola and Shelleck, Chapter 9).

Yet sometimes it is the reliance of law on general, indeterminate or vague concepts, which also become rooted in the various legal disciplines, that makes law permeable to the infiltration of gender biases and stereotypes in the hermeneutic processes necessary for its implementation by judges or public officials. With regard to the construction of the national subject through nationality law, Toombs and Rubenstein (Chapter 8) show how gendered expectations have shaped what is required of a person to access citizenship or avoid citizenship removal thanks to the overreliance of indeterminate legal concepts in nationality law that include 'good moral character', 'allegiance', 'loyalty', 'national identify', 'shared values', 'national security' and 'public order'.[58] These gendered expectations have included ideas such as women as biological reproducers of the nation, women's loyalty measured in terms of romantic love, loyalty to the husband and conformity with traditional family-oriented gender roles.[59] They also intersect with prejudices associated with race, ethnicity and sexuality in constructing the national subject, as shown by the fact that the wearing of a veil in French naturalization procedures is a matter that case workers are required to record by ticking a specific box and that North African women blow-dry or straighten their hair in order to 'present well' – in an attempt to erase religious or racialized phenotypic markers.[60] Similarly, in the domain of family law, Herring (Chapter 7) reminds us of the risks of interpreting the concept of 'the best interest of the child' without sufficiently foregrounding a relational understanding of the self and hence of the relevance of caring relationships in which women invest more heavily than men.[61]

[58] Toombs and Rubenstein, Chapter 8 in this volume. [59] Ibid. [60] Ibid.
[61] Herring, Chapter 7 in this volume.

Part I

Bodies

The Sexed Subject 1

Marie-Xavière Catto and Stefano Osella

1. Introduction

In Salisbury, Connecticut, 'gender trouble' took place during a local election in 1843,[1] as the 'sex' of one voter was contested. Allegedly, the Whig Party had introduced – what was contested as – a woman into the electorate. Determining the 'sex' of the voter was necessary to judge whether the ballot could be validly cast. A medical expert was summoned. An imperforated penis and a small testicle were found. This discovery temporarily resolved the dispute, and the person was admitted to the vote. On Election Day, however, the voter was denied electoral rights. Since the 'sex'[2] of the voter was subject to further controversy, two more doctors were called in to consult. The presence of a testicle was established, thus 'legitimizing' the vote. Yet a few days later, it became known that the individual menstruated. A third examination was deemed necessary, which

This chapter offers separate works by the two authors, which should be read in conversation with each other. The introduction and conclusion have been co-authored. Marie-Xavière Catto wrote Section 2, and Stefano Osella Section 3. The sections authored by Stefano Osella largely rely on the research carried out during a Hauser Post-Doctoral Global Fellowship generously offered by the New York University School of Law. Marie-Xavière Catto wishes to express sincere thanks to Stéphanie Hennette-Vauchez for her support in writing this article in English.

[1] J. Greenberg, *Intersexuality and the Law: Why Sex Matters* (New York: NYU Press, 2012), 47.

[2] Embracing one of the central tenets of queer theory, the chapter does not distinguish between sex, as the biological and bodily dimension, and gender, as the cultural inscription upon it. J. Butler, *Gender Trouble* (New York: Routledge, 1990), 10–34. As made clear in the following, the very idea of 'sex' is deeply political. However, 'sex' is often the term used in the law to refer to the status of the individual. Furthermore, as this chapter shows, there has been a nearly constant attempt by the law to reify – on the body of the person – gender norms, and 'sexed', with its traditional and highly contested connection with the physical dimension, seems to somewhat evoke this effort to shape individual corporeality. At the same time, we may use 'sex' or 'sex/gender' to refer to the individual dimension, while 'gender' will be used to refer to the overall structure of signification.

led to the discovery of a uterus. The person, referred to as 'the hermaphrodite',[3] was concluded to have 'unduly used the right to vote'.[4] This story widely reverberated.[5] Not only had it shed light on what 'sex' was understood to be, it also hinted at the ultimate reason for gender-based rules of political franchise: What would have happened if a woman had been able to slip into the electorate? Furthermore, why should this or that specific biological characteristic be the determining factors in this case? Such 'gender troubles' were not limited to the public sphere. For example, the French Court of Cassation had to decide on the 'sex' of one of two spouses to determine the validity of their marriage in 1903. That court relied on the external appearance of genitals.

These two examples vividly portray the clash between the complexity of the human experience, and the (excessive) simplicity of socio-legal categories. They show how 'diverse' bodies and identities have (regrettably) often been perceived as a – so to say – problem to manage. Such cases also suggest that nearly constant attempts have been made to erase such diversity. A whole body of knowledge has condemned, erased, pathologized and normalized gender diversity, from antiquity – at least in what is now Europe – moving through the Middle Ages and modernity, up until today.[6]

[3] Despite the use of the term 'hermaphrodite' with a reappropriating intent by some (see C. Chase, 'Hermaphrodites with Attitude: Mapping the Emergence of Intersex Political Activism', in S. Stryker and S. Whittle (eds.), *The Transgender Studies Reader* (London: Routledge, 2006), 300), the term that is commonly used by the community and activists is 'intersex'. 'Hermaphrodite' was the term in use at the time, here reported in brackets. The first known instance of the use of the term intersex seems to be by R. B. Goldschmidt, 'Intersexuality and the Endocrine Aspect of Sex' (1917) 1 *Endocrinology* 433–456.

[4] G. Tourdes, 'Hermaphrodites (médecine légale)', in A. Dechambre and L. Lereboullet (eds.), *Dictionnaire encyclopédique des sciences médicales*, 100 vols. (Paris: G. Masson/P. Asselin, 1864–1889), vol. 13, 650.

[5] See, for example, Greenberg, *Intersexuality and the Law*, 47; E. Reis, 'Impossible Hermaphrodites: Intersex in America, 1620–1969' (2005) 92 *Journal of American History* 411–442.

[6] For Roman Law, see Y. Thomas, 'La Division des Sexes en Droit Romain', in G. Duby and M. Perrot (eds.), *Histoire des Femmes en Occident. I. L'Antiquité* (Paris: Plon, 2002), 139; Y. Thomas, 'Res, Chose et Patrimoine' (1980) 25 *Archives de Philosophie de Droit* 413–426. For European antiquity, E. Cantarella, 'L'Hermaphrodite et la Bisexualité à l'Épreuve du Droit dans l'Antiquité' (2004) 208 *Diogène* 3–15. For the Middle Ages, C. J. Nederman and J. True, 'The Third Sex: The Idea of the Hermaphrodite in Twelfth Century Europe' (1996) 6 *Journal of the History of Sexuality* 497–517. For modernity, L. Daston and K. Park, 'The Hermaphrodite and the Orders of Nature: Sexual Ambiguity in Early Modern France' (1995) 1 *GLQ A Journal of Lesbian and Gay Studies* 420–425; G. Mak, *Doubting Sex: Inscriptions, Bodies and Selves in Nineteenth-Century Hermaphrodite Case Histories* (Manchester:

These discourses that have evolved over time have constructed a new understanding and knowledge of sexual difference. They have shaped two incommensurable, universally opposite 'sexes' and 'sexed subjects'.[7]

These mechanisms have long been challenged. At least as of the 1970s, they have become the object of intense academic and social discussion. Abundant literature has developed, showing how the definition of the 'sexual' binary – the existence of two opposite, mutually attracted 'sexes' – is characterized by political considerations and power relations. In *The History of Sexuality*, Foucault rejected the notion of 'sex' as a 'natural category' that precedes political relations. On the contrary, 'sex' was reframed as an 'artificial unity' of 'anatomical elements, biological functions, conducts, sensations, and pleasures'. The 'fictitious unity' of sex 'enabled one to make use [of it] as a causal principle' to mask the interactions of power that are deployed through sexuality.[8] Famously, Butler has continued the analysis of Foucault, contesting the existence of apolitical sexed subjects altogether. In *Gender Trouble*, she argued that 'the body itself is a construction' as a 'myriad of bodies' are united under the notion of sex/gender, prior to which no body has a 'signifiable' existence. In this context, sex cannot be understood as existing before gender, but rather should be considered as a naturalized category rooted in gender itself. The binary becomes the effect of an institutional heterosexuality. The gender binary precedes the 'reading' of bodies (and genitals) and

Manchester University Press, 2012), 166. In canon law, for instance, P. Darmon, *Le Tribunal de l'Impuissance: Virilité et Defaillainces Conjugales Dans l'Ancienne France* (Paris: Seuil, 1979), 55; M. van der Lugt, 'Sex Difference in Medieval Theology and Canon Law: A Tribute to Joan Cadden' (2010) 46 *Medieval Feminist Forum* 101–121 at 110–112. As space unfortunately does not allow us to explore the history of gender/sex diversity outside the Global North, please refer to the following (non-exhaustive) publications: A. Dutta, 'Decolonizing Transgender in India: Some Reflections' (2013) 1 *Transgender Studies Quarterly* 320–337; G. Reddy, *With Respect to Sex: Negotiating Hijra Identity in South India* (Chicago, IL: University of Chicago Press, 2005); T. Boellstorff, *The Gay Archipelago: Sexuality and Nation in Indonesia* (Princeton, NJ: Princeton University Press, 2005).

7 See T. Laqueur, *Making Sex: Body and Gender from the Greeks to Freud* (Cambridge, MA: Harvard University Press 1990), 152–153.

8 M. Foucault, 'An Introduction', in *The History of Sexuality*, trans. R. Huxley, 4 vols. (New York: Vintage Books, 1990), vol. 1, 152–155.

determines their understanding.[9] The observation of difference is not the cause, but rather the consequence of the naturalizing discourse and social organization.[10]

Despite the focus on, and importance of, sexuality as an element in the construction of 'sexed' subjects, other vectors of domination – such as race or class – have played a crucial role too.[11] The political understanding of sex/gender, and arguably the 'sexed' subject, is indeed hugely indebted to black feminism, intersectionality and queer of colour critique.[12] Intersectionality in particular, 'in designating race and gender as categories that are constituted in relation to each other as well as other social differences, [is a] means for disrupting discourses of authenticity and providing alternatives to those discourses'.[13] It is not by chance that intersectional analysis has offered meaningful contribution in formulating inclusive arguments for gender-diverse and trans people.[14] This critique has been essential to paving the way for a reframing of universalist, homonormative[15] and homonationalist[16] understandings of queer identities.

[9] Butler, *Gender Trouble*, 9–12. See also D. Maffía and M. Cabral, 'Los sexos ¿Son o se hacen?', in D. Maffía (ed.), *Sexualidades Migrantes: Género y Transgénero* (Buenos Aires: Feminaria Editora, 2003), 86–87.

[10] E. Dorlin, 'Sexe, Genre et Intersexualité: La Crise Comme Régime Théorique' (2005) 18 *Raisons Politiques* 117–137.

[11] See, for example, S. Smythe, 'Black Life, Trans Study: On Black Nonbinary Method, European Trans Studies, and the Will to Institutionalization' (2021) 8 *TSQ: Transgender Studies Quarterly* 158–171; F. El-Tayeb, *European Others. Queering Ethnicity in Postnational Europe* (Minneapolis: University of Minnesota Press, 2011); D. Valentine, *Imagining Transgender: Ethnography of a Category* (New York: NYU Press, 2007); M. F. Manalansan, *Global Divas: Filipino Gay Men in the Diaspora* (Durham, NC: Duke University Press, 2003).

[12] R. A. Ferguson, 'Queer of Color Critique', *Oxford Research Encyclopedia of Literature*, 28 March 2018, http://oxfordre.com/literature/view/10.1093/acrefore/9780190201098.001.0001/acrefore-9780190201098-e-33; R. A. Ferguson, *Aberrations in Black: Toward a Queer of Color Critique* (Minneapolis: University of Minnesota Press, 2004); K. Crenshaw, 'Race, Gender and Sexual Harassment' (1991) 65 *California Law Review* 1467–1476; K. Crenshaw, 'Demarginalizing the Intersection of Race and Sex: A Black Feminist Critique of Antidiscrimination Doctrine, Feminist Theory and Antiracist Politics' (1989) 1989 *University of Chicago Legal Forum* 139–167.

[13] Ferguson, 'Queer of Color Critique', 3.

[14] E. Koyama, 'Whose Feminism Is It Anyway? The Unspoken Racism of the Trans Inclusion Debate', in S. Stryker and S. Whittle (eds.), *The Transgender Studies Reader* (London: Routledge, 2006), 698.

[15] L. Duggan, *The Twilight of Equality* (Boston, IL: Beacon Press, 2003).

[16] J. Puar, *Terrorist Assemblages: Homonationalism in Queer Times* (Durham, NC: Duke University Press, 2007).

The study of the political dimension of the 'sexed subject' went beyond the field of philosophy, encompassing a large array of studies, including in the fields of history,[17] biology[18] and anthropology.[19] The study of the political and cultural dimension of the 'sexed' subject has long been present in legal scholarship as well. As the 'Salisbury case' so vividly illustrates, law (oftentimes) relies on strict definitions of maleness and femaleness, excluding all bodies/identities that do not fit the norm. This evidently manifests where unintelligible bodies and identities are concerned. They are indeed often perceived as a problem for those social and legal organizations that are predicated on stable, 'binary' and clearly intelligible identities.[20]

This type of categorization, overwhelmingly present to this day, 'founds and maintains the gendered social order'.[21] Yet far from simply 'presupposing' the sexed subject, the law actively defines and, arguably, enforces it.[22] At the same time, however, a gradual process of contestation of the core features that define such a subject seems to be taking place. In a plurality of jurisdictions, there is a challenge to the fundamental characteristics of the 'sexed subject' upon which the binary structure of the law is based.[23] This arguably results in profound transformations of the 'sexed

[17] A. Domurat-Dreger, *Hermaphrodites and the Medical Invention of Sex* (Cambridge, MA: Harvard University Press, 1998); Laqueur, *Making Sex*.

[18] A. Fausto-Sterling, *Sexing the Body: Gender Politics and the Construction of Sexuality* (New York: Basic Books, 2000).

[19] K. Karkazis, *Fixing Sex: Intersex, Medical Authority, and Lived Experience* (Durham, NC: Duke University Press, 2008).

[20] H. Fogg Davis, *Beyond Trans. Does Gender Matter?* (New York: NYU Press, 2017); D. Spade, *Normal Life: Administrative Violence, Critical Trans Politics, and the Limits of Law* (Durham, NC: Duke University Press, 2015); A. Dutta, 'Legible Identities and Legitimate Citizens' (2013) 15 *International Feminist Journal of Politics* 494–514; P. Currah and L. J. Moore, '"We Won't Know Who You Are": Contesting Sex Designations in New York City Birth Certificates' (2009) 24 *Hypatia* 113–135.

[21] See M. Raz, 'Bicatégorisation', in J. Rennes (ed.), *Encyclopédie Critique du Genre* (Paris: La Découverte, 2016), 90; Dorlin, 'Sexe, Genre, et Intersexualité'.

[22] M.-X. Catto and J. Mazaleigue-Labaste, *La Bicatégorisation de Sexe entre Droit, Normes Sociales et Sciences Biomédicales* (Paris: Mare et Martin, 2021); S. Osella, 'Reinforcing the Binary and Disciplining the Subject: The Constitutional Right to Gender Recognition in the Italian Case Law' (2022) 20(1) *International Journal of Constitutional Law* 1–22, online; J. Repo, 'Governing Juridical Sex: Gender Recognition and the Biopolitics of Trans Sterilization in Finland' (2019) 15 *Politics and Gender* 83–106.

[23] G. Baars, 'Queer Cases Unmake Gendered Law, or, Fucking Law's Gendering Function' (2019) 45 *Australian Feminist Law Journal* 15–62.

subject', and causes (highly beneficial, from our point of view) 'gender trouble'.

In the following, we explore this two-fold dynamic. The first question to be answered in the chapter is how a 'sexed subject' is created in and by the law. To do so, Catto discusses how gender norms have been defined and 'enforced', especially for those people whose bodies and/or identities defy the accepted standards. Starting from the assignment of a legal 'sex' at birth, Catto illustrates how diversity is being erased at the earliest stages of life. Catto looks into the legal requirement of the exclusivity of the two sexes and the related 'normalization' of intersex bodies that consists in 'genital mutilations', as aimed to impose cultural norms of maleness and femaleness on 'unruly' bodies.[24] Catto subsequently explores how the definition of binary subjects is enforced later in life, with specific reference to the trans experience. She shows how an ascriptive,[25] binary and stabilized identity has been upheld, often relying on 'biologistic' and de-politicizing discourses. Yet largely constitutional and human-rights-driven evolutions are taking place in a plurality of jurisdictions. Hence, the second question addressed in the chapter is how the 'sexed subject' is changing under pressure from constitutional and human rights. Osella answers this question in the second part of the chapter. He discusses how the 'sexed subject' is being reframed in some of its fundamental assumptions – binary normativity, intelligibility, stability and anatomy – to the point of deliberating on whether a 'sexed subject' should persist in the civil status.

To present this argument, the chapter relies on a comparative and multidisciplinary method, drawing on comparative legal studies, feminist and queer theory, history, cultural studies, and anthropological and sociological literature. The discourse of nature having referred the object to a form of natural presupposition, it led to a construction of the binary based on mechanisms of private law generally analogous in the various Western systems (Section 2). The comparative method allows an analysis of the varying responses of judges to the binary being challenged, where they had

[24] We are aware that the term 'normalization' is contested by some activists as not fully reflecting the profound impact that intersex treatments may have on intersex people. In light of this critique, the term 'normalization' may be used throughout this chapter to reflect the cultural and anatomo-political rationale of intersex genital mutilations: indeed, as intended to force a bodily 'norm'. It is not in any way intended to deny or minimize the acute suffering that mutilations may cause for intersex people.

[25] J. Clarke, 'Identity and Form' (2015) 103 *California Law Review* 747–839.

to assume the mandatory nature of the standard. This normativity created questions from a fundamental rights perspective. The purpose of the comparison in Section 3 is to 'generate concepts and analytical frameworks for thinking about [primarily] constitutional [and human rights] norms and practices'. As such, focusing not on jurisdictions but rather on a few specific practices, Section 3 is intended to study 'various manifestations of and solutions to roughly analogous constitutional [and broadly legal] challenges' to analytically hone our understanding of the redefinition of the 'sexed subject'.[26] The jurisdictions selected can be seen as illustrative cases of the transformation that is occurring in the 'sexed subject' and allow for a nuanced understanding thereof. In selecting those jurisdictions, efforts have been made to add geographical diversity and to include jurisdictions less explored than others thus far.

The rest of the chapter is structured as follows. In the next section, Catto discusses the 'creation' of the 'sexed subject' through the law. It begins with the erasure of sex diversity at birth to continue with the containment of trans diversity later in life. In Section 3, Osella explores how this construction has come to be reformulated under pressure of human rights law.[27] The law is perceived to act as a tool in the hands of 'gender outlaws',[28] advocating to achieve authority over who they are, 'stealing' the role of – chiefly – medical and legal authorities. In the conclusions, the argument is summarized and further research is called for.

2. Producing Two Sexed Subjects

The sex binary was imposed for the political purpose of the juridical organization of society's reproduction according to a binary social order

[26] R. Hirschl, *Comparative Matters: The Renaissance of Comparative Constitutional Law* (Oxford: Oxford University Press 2014), 238.

[27] We are aware that intersex rights developed after the right to gender recognition for trans people. However, having decided to focus on the subject, we follow a timeline based on the subjects themselves, rather than the historical advancement of intersex and trans rights. We begin with how the subject is sexed/gendered, or whose diversity is accepted and protected, at birth: Therefore, we first explore intersex rights, which also represent the most obvious challenge to the binary construction of gender. We then discuss how the subject is sexed/gendered later in life – and here we discuss trans rights.

[28] K. Bornstein, *Gender Outlaw: On Men, Women, and the Rest of Us*. Revised and updated (New York: Vintage Books, 2016).

that defines the place of each person at birth on the basis of an examination of their genitals (Section B.1). While the original reasons for sex assignment had been largely forgotten, they reappeared in their fully normative (rather than descriptive) dimension as Western societies established formal protocols for intersex children halfway through the twentieth century (Section B.2).

A. Classifying Subjects by Sex at Birth

Sex is recorded at birth to shape the legal and social fate of each legal subject. The criterion used to assign a sex at birth was subsequently confirmed should it be called into question in marriage disputes.

Erasing most intersex conditions by registering sex at birth. The subject is sexed from the very moment of birth, according to a binary regime. All civil registers require the child's sex to be declared at birth, even though legal rules do not necessarily specify the number or nature of possible sex categories. However, until the last decade,[29] only two such categories were generally considered admissible.[30] When variations to the binary occurred, Roman, canon and ancient civil law had rules designating who was entrusted with the task of deciding the person's sex, and they specified that the determination was to be permanent. For instance, in the case of children, the decision was the parents'; in that of adults, self-identification was possible.[31] The Prussian Code (1794) had explicitly provided for the case of hermaphrodites,[32] but the German Civil Code erased the possibility in 1900: The determination of sex was assigned to doctors at a time when modern medical science denied neutral sex and

[29] See developments by Stefano Osella, Section 3.

[30] For example, in France as well as England, sex is included in registers that do not specify that only two possibilities exist (in France, by means of Art. 57 of the French Civil Code of 1804; in England, the Act for registering Births, Deaths, and Marriages in England of 17 August 1836, para. XVII). They are, however, continually interpreted in this way.

[31] M. Closson, 'Avant-propos', in M. Closson (ed.), *L'Hermaphrodite de la Renaissance aux Lumières* (Paris: Classiques Garnier, 2013), 16–17; Reis, 'Impossible Hermaphrodites', at 420; van der Lugt, 'Sex Difference', at 113.

[32] For an English translation, see G. Mak, 'Doubtful Sex in Civil Law: Nineteenth and Early Twentieth Century Proposals for Ruling Hermaphroditism' (2005) 12 *Cardozo Journal of Law & Gender* 197–212 at 202, fn. 18.

claimed to be able to accurately establish either binary sex.[33] Two phenomena in the law converge to make the legal sex stand for the 'true sex'.

The first one is the criterion used to fix sex at birth, which produces the erasure of most intersex cases. As the relevant criterion is the appearance of the child's genitalia,[34] all variations that are not perceived at first glance are not qualified as such.[35] Many intersex cases thus disappear through the criterion used (XY 'males' with a uterus, Turner 'females' who have only one X, XY 'women' with an Androgen Insensitivity Syndrome, etc.). Consequently, intersex condition counts are misrepresentative: While it is routinely affirmed that 1 child out of 4,500 is intersex,[36] statistics taking into account all intersex variations lead to a much higher estimate of around 1.7 per cent of all births.[37] This erasure hypostasizes sex. In fact, the registration at birth on the basis of the external appearance of the genitalia is deemed to say much more than that, i.e. to tell the truth about sex. Well beyond physicality, it determines status, socialization and identity, as everyone believes that the person 'is' a man or a woman. It thus becomes possible to designate women without ovaries, XY women and women without a uterus as 'women', and men with menstrual periods, a uterus or breasts etc. as 'men'. The arbitrary criterion used for the original declaration is indeed forgotten. The legally produced fiction reinforces the belief that bodies are naturally overwhelmingly binary.

The second way in which law affirms the legal sex as the true sex is by treating the intersex condition as the result of an initial error. Legal rules have always allowed for initial declarations of sex to be corrected if a mistake had been made. Intersex people have indeed benefited from this possibility of legally changing their sex if it turned out to be different to

[33] Mak, *Doubting Sex*, 132–133 and 166; Mak, 'Doubtful Sex in Civil Law', 210–211.

[34] G. W. Bartholomew, '"Hermaphrodites" and the Law' (1960) 2 *University of Malaya Law Review* 83–112 at 98. In France, the Law of 20 September 1792 required the child to be presented to the civil registrar to record the birth and for examination of the genital organs to establish the child's sex.

[35] As Jacqueline Pousson noted in 1976. J. Pousson, 'L'ambiguïté du droit face au syndrome transsexuel' (1976) 2 *Revue trimestrielle de droit civil* 263–296 at 286.

[36] I. A. Hughes et al., LWPES Consensus Group and ESPE Consensus Group, 'Consensus Statement on Management of Intersex Disorders' (2006) 91 Archives of Disease in Childhood 554–563 at 554, https://pubmed.ncbi.nlm.nih.gov/16624884/.

[37] M. Blackless et al., 'How Sexually Dimorphic Are We? Review and Synthesis' (2000) 12 *American Journal of Human Biology* 151–166 at 161. See also 'UN Free & Equal: Intersex Awareness', www.unfe.org/intersex-awareness/.

the one originally assigned. If authorized, the change had to be final as it was considered to be the correction of an error.[38] Despite some variation in the rules themselves, such legal frameworks existed in the United Kingdom,[39] France[40] and Germany.[41] In all these countries, the late revelation of intersex was likened to a clerical mistake on the birth certificate. In France, the procedure is known as 'rectification'. It has been regularly used for intersex people throughout the nineteenth, twentieth and twenty-first centuries.[42] While rectification is only possible if the birth certificate 'contains omissions or errors whose rectification does not raise any question relating to the status of persons',[43] intersex people are allowed to benefit from the procedure because it is framed as the correction of a declaration that was 'inaccurate from the outset' rather than as a legal route to sex change.[44] Of course, this leads to a major overhaul in the person's legal status, as under this legal regime the perception of finding errors led judges to 'order that in future he may wear only the clothes of men'[45] and authors to comment that, 'from being an excellent housewife,

[38] Darmon, *Le Tribunal de l'Impuissance*, 55; van der Lugt, 'Sex Difference', at 113; Closson, 'Avant-propos', 16–17. In the United States in the XVIIIth and XIXth centuries, Reis, 'Impossible Hermaphrodites', at 422 and 429.

[39] Births and Deaths Registration Act 1953, ch. 20, para. 29.3.

[40] Avis du CE du 12 Brumaire an 11, in *Recueil général des lois and des arrêts, Lois annotées, 1e série, 1789–1830* (Paris: Sirey, 1843), p. 614; Circulaire du 22 brumaire an 14, in *Recueil Sirey* (S.), 1813, vol. 2, p. 297 confirmed by Cour royale de Poitiers, 9 mai 1843 and 26 mai 1846, in S., 1846, vol. 2, p. 463.

[41] Geltung des Personenstandsgesetzes vom 6. Februar 1875 (RGBl 23), Art. 22 para. 1.33. As the BGH, 14.03.1979 – IV ZB 156/78 recalled it, para. 5, p. 7. For information on debates in Germany at that time, and the difference between the French and German approach, see Mak, 'Doubtful Sex in Civil Law', at 197–212. In 2018, the legislator created a correction procedure that is exclusively applicable to intersex people. Gesetzzur Änderung der in das Geburtenregister einzutragenden Angaben Vom 18. Dezember 2018, Art. 22 paras. 3 and 45 b.

[42] Trib. civ. de Dreux, 17 mai 1814, published and commented on by M. Worbe, 'Séance Du 16 Juin 1870' (1870) 17 *Bulletin de la Faculté de médecine de Paris* 485–486; CA Angers, 27 fév. 1846, D., 1846, II, p. 85; Trib. de Corbeil, 15 juil. 1915, La loi, 17 à 20 juil. 1915, p. 81; Trib. civ. de Soissons, 25 juil. 1945, GP, 1945, II, p. 141; CA Paris, 31 mai 1966, JCP, 1966, II, 14723 and CA Paris, 8 déc. 1967, JCP, 1968, II, 15518 bis; CA Versailles, 22 juin 2000, no. 7799–99; TGI Toulon, 7 déc. 2017, no. 17/03602, AJ Famille 2018, p. 121.

[43] Instruction générale du 21 septembre 1955 relative à l'état civil, JO du 22/09/1955, § 152, p. 9340.

[44] Ibid., 9341.

[45] Trib. civ. de Dreux, 17 mai 1814, in Worbe, 'Séance'.

he [became] a good ploughman in a very short time'.[46] The British Births and Deaths Registration Act 1953 provides that '[n]o alteration shall be made in any register of live-births'[47] but 'an error of fact or substance in any such register may be corrected by entry in the margin (without any alteration of the original entry) by the officer having the custody of the register'.[48] This procedure was successfully used by Roberta Cowell, the first trans who argued that she was an intersex in order to benefit from this procedure, and have her birth sex changed.[49] The ruling relied on the notion that variations (genetic, gonadic or genital) allow a correction as they may be considered to be errors. Judges later confirmed that 'the biological sexual constitution of an individual is fixed at birth (at the latest), and cannot be changed',[50] so that 'the only cases where the term "change of sex" is appropriate are those in which a mistake as to sex is made at birth and subsequently revealed by further medical investigation'.[51]

Confirmation of the relevance of the criterion chosen at birth in marriage disputes. In a large number of countries, the question of the definition of sex has been raised in the context of marriage. England and France for instance pursued different legal routes on this matter as the criteria for marriage validity were not the same. However, they both confirmed the relevance of the sex fixed at birth: under French law essentially to maintain the union of a cis person with an intersex; under English law, to reject the recognition of a trans wedding.

In England, the intersex issue did not give rise to litigation involving the definition of sex in the framework of marriage disputes, even though judges recalled that marriage could only be entered into by a man and a woman.[52] Variations in the individuals' sexed or reproductive system were

[46] Ibid., 487 (about a twenty-two-year-old person). For similar comments in another case (about an eighteen-year-old), see E. Lévy in Trib. de Corbeil, 15 juil. 1915, p. 81.

[47] Births and Deaths Registration Act 1953, Ch. 20, Art. 29 para. 1. Without changes since 1953.

[48] Ibid., Art. 29 para. 3.

[49] She 'became legally a woman ... at the beginning of 1951'. R. Cowell, *Roberta Cowell's Story* (New York: British Book Centre, 1954), 97. Her birth certificate is published in the printed version (between pp. 124 and 125) but is not reproduced in the pdf version.

[50] *Corbett* v. *Corbett* [1970] 2 All ER 33 [104].

[51] Ibid., [104].

[52] According to *Lindo* v. *Belisario* [1795] 1 Hag Con 216 [230], defining marriage as 'a contract according to the law of nature' that unites 'two persons of different sexes'. According to *Hyde* v. *Hyde* (1866) LR 1 P. & D. 130 [133], 'marriage, as understood in

dealt with as cases of incapacity to fulfil obligations related to marriage,[53] thus erasing the intersex question. Similar reasons explain the absence of litigation in Germany.[54] Judges were led to define the criteria of sex later, in the famous 1970 *Corbett* case, in which they affirmed that the true sex is 'fixed at birth'.[55]

By contrast, the question of the proper legal definition of sex repeatedly arose in France throughout the nineteenth century in cases where marriage had been contracted by intersex persons. After the scandals linked to the procedures of 'inspections' and 'congress' in Pre-Revolutionary France,[56] the lack of consummation was no longer a cause for the annulment of marriage.[57] Judges considered that 'the possibility of the procreation of children and carnal cohabitation is not absolutely essential to the existence of marriage'.[58] However, identical sex of both spouses did allow for an annulment. If some decisions first admitted it, implying the denial of the right to marry for any intersex person whose marriage had been annulled as they were neither a man nor a woman[59] – rules that also have been applied in other countries[60] – this issue disappeared in France after a 1903 ruling by the Court of Cassation. The requested expert testified that it was impossible to determine 'by medical diagnosis, [the] limit of malformations acceptable to belong to one sex or to be excluded from it'.[61] The court considered that, despite the absence of internal genitalia of

Christendom, may for this purpose be defined as the voluntary union for life of one man and one woman'.

53 As the judge recalled in *Corbett* v. *Corbett*, [105].

54 E. Wilhem, 'L'hermaphrodite et le droit' (1911) 26 *Revue d'anthropologie criminelle* 267–294 at 282. By this reasoning, he supports his presentation of French examples of litigation, while the other sources are German. In addition, see Mak, *Doubting Sex*.

55 *Corbett* v. *Corbett*, [106].

56 The procedures were instigated to prove the ability to consummate marriage during an impotence trial. The inspection aimed to verify that men could achieve erection; in the congress, a husband and wife were forced to attempt to copulate in front of witnesses for the judgment.

57 Darmon, *Le Tribunal de l'Impuissance*, 233.

58 Caen, 23 mars 1882, S. 1882, II, p. 108.

59 Montpellier, 8 mai 1872, S., 1872, II, p. 272; Trib. civ. d'Alais, 28 jan. 1873, D., 1882, III, p. 71.

60 A decision by the Court of Appeals of Law of South Carolina indicates that, similar to child and eunuch, hermaphrodites were not able to contract marriage, *State* v. *Barefoot*, 1845 2 Rich. 209 31 SCL 209. Family Court of Australia, *In the Marriage of C and D (falsely called C)*, 20 April 1979, 35 FLR 340, p. 344.

61 P. Brouardel, 'Malformation des organes génitaux de la femme', in *Annales d'hygiène publique et de médecine légale*, 4th ed., 4 vols. (Paris: Gabon, 1829–1922), vol. 1, 200.

one of the spouses, the marriage had been legally contracted between two persons of different sexes.[62] It thus relied on the criterion of apparent genitalia and confirmed both the validity of the determination of sex at birth and the legal existence of only two sexes. Furthermore, the hetero-normativity of the sex criterion was confirmed, as the genitals were thought to permit intercourse. French jurist Jean Carbonnier described the determination of sex at birth at first glance with fascinating simplicity, as 'scale models of the sexual union to come'.[63]

The legal erasure of intersex on medical grounds was taken to be able to establish the 'true sex', first by diagnostics and followed by surgery.

B. Standardizing Bodies to Perpetuate the Gender Order

Western legal systems yielded the determination of the definition of sex to external scientific competence. Both the law and science required that sex was to be medically assigned at birth (Section 2.B.i). The possibility of changing sex classification that initially existed for intersex people was first compromised when trans people began to claim it. As the right of trans people to undergo sex change was progressively defined and subjected to new legal requirements, the underlying reasons governing the assignment of sex at birth were unearthed. The previous *legal* gender order became an essentially *social* one that the law aims to perpetuate in sexing the subject (Section 2.B.ii).

i. From Diagnosis to Intervention: Shaping Intersex Bodies

The first operations performed on intersex people at the beginning of the nineteenth century were linked to marriage. In Germany, a person accused of being a hermaphrodite by her husband underwent surgery to 'restore ... the marriage'.[64] In the United States, a twenty-three-year-old woman without a vagina asked for an operation in order to enable penetration.

[62] Cass. civ., 6 avril 1903, *D.*, 1904, p. 395.

[63] J. Carbonniet, *Droit civil*, 2 vols. (Paris: Presses Universitaires de France, 2004), vol. 1, 497–498.

[64] In 1804, cf. U. Klöppel, 'The Lost Innocence of Hermaphrodites: Medical Reasoning on Hermaphroditism around 1800', in M. Closson (ed.), *L'Hermaphrodite de la Renaissance aux Lumières* (Paris: Classiques Garnier, 2013), 161.

In France, a twenty-one-year-old woman asked her doctor if someone in her condition could marry.[65] The question of hermaphroditism became not only a scientific but also a clinical concern when homosexuality, in its prevention and treatment, became a social obsession that doctors took on at the end of the nineteenth century.[66] In a context where some of them sought to identify physical causes of deviant sexual behaviour, the idea emerged to correct the inversion with surgery. Sapphic behaviour was attributed to conditions such as an enlarged clitoris or an ovarian hypertrophy, either of which justified the removal of these organs. 'Sexual inversion' justified testicular transplants for men.[67] Operations on intersex people, including children, became more frequent.[68] The legal erasure of intersexed people had legitimated their medical erasure. In other words, during the 1900s, the intersex question shifted 'from a legal to a clinical issue' in Europe and the United States.[69] Surgical interventions definitively inscribed the requirement of a heterosexual orientation on the bodies. 'Despite surprisingly little medical agreement on exact criteria, it became the doctors' prerogative to proclaim sex, even if their assessment contradicted how their patients had lived their lives'.[70] Until the mid-twentieth century, however, the practice functioned essentially on a case-by-case basis.[71]

This changed when the 'John Hopkins Paradigm' rapidly spread throughout the United States and Europe. It was put forth in a series of articles published in 1955 and 1956,[72] proposing a renewed understanding of intersex based on the notion that the sex of rearing, also corresponding

[65] For the United States (in 1833), see Reis, 'Impossible Hermaphrodites', at 432. For France, E. Coste, 'Conformation vicieuse des organes génitaux chez une femme. Opération' (1835) 3 *Journal des connaissances médico-chirurgicales* 276–277 at 277.

[66] As perfectly described in Foucault, *The History of Sexuality*, vol. 1, 43.

[67] For the United States, see J. Terry, *An American Obsession: Science, Medicine, and Homosexuality in Modern Society* (Chicago, IL: University of Chicago Press, 1999), 80–82; C. Matta, 'Ambiguous Bodies and Deviant Sexualities: Hermaphrodites, Homosexuality, and Surgery in the United States, 1850–1904' (2005) 48 *Perspectives in Biology and Medicine* 74–83. For France, see operations described in L. Dartigues, *Le Renouvellement de l'organisme* (Paris: Gaston Douin éditeur, 1928), 229–240.

[68] See the figures of Matta, 'Ambiguous Bodies and Deviant Sexualities', 77–78 and 82. On children, in 1849 (only based on stereotypes), 76–77.

[69] Mak, *Doubting Sex*, 166. [70] Reis, 'Impossible Hermaphrodites', at 434.

[71] A. Redick, 'What Happened at Hopkins: The Creation of the Intersex Management Protocols' (2005) 12 *Cardozo Journal of Law & Gender* 289–296 at 289–290.

[72] Five articles quoted in ibid., n 2.

to the legal sex,[73] is 'far better than any other variable'.[74] Consequently, intersex children should be operated on as soon as possible, before eighteen months of age,[75] and given an education consistent with the assigned sex. Early surgery was believed to produce a sense of self in accordance with the sex of rearing. In France, legal instructions on birth certificates were modified in 1970 to explicitly mention medical treatments to be administered in the case of sex indeterminacy.[76] Such surgical interventions are still generally performed in the European Union and beyond.[77] The sex of rearing thus determines the anatomical sex (surgically shaped). As the underpinning reason for the sex assignment, heterosexuality is logically conceived as a criterion for the success of the operations.[78] The medical and legal construction of variations of sex development as pathological disorders justifies corrections and maintains a radical distinction between the sexes in order to guarantee 'gender-consistent' education. But what is a 'gender-consistent' education if not the maintenance of the old unequal status of women and men that was previously legally compulsory and has now become a social norm? The legal and medical treatment of the intersex reflects a more global project of society: The original sex-assignment for each subject is intended to create a binary, hierarchical and heterosexual order, a project fully confirmed in the trans issue.

ii. From Refusal to Imposition: Sex as a Normative Category in Trans Identity

A change at first refused. During the first disputes involving sex reassignment of trans people, countries that admitted a procedure of sex-correction

[73] J. G. Hampson, J. Money and J. L. Hampson, 'Hermaphrodism: Recommendations Concerning Case Management' (1956) 16 *Journal of Clinical Endocrinology & Metabolism* 547–556 at 554.

[74] Ibid., at 549. [75] Redick, 'What Happened at Hopkins', at 292.

[76] Instruction générale du 19 février 1970 modifiant l'Instruction générale du 21 septembre 1955 relative à l'état civil, J.O. no. 0095, Art. 228b (added), p. 3866, which has been repeated since then.

[77] In the European Union, 'in at least 21 Member States, sex "normalizing" surgery is performed on intersex infants'. N. Pikramenou, *Intersex Rights: Living between Sexes* (Cham, Switzerland: Springer International Publishing, 2019), 140. For the other states, 39, 110, 136. In Australia, see A. Kennedy, 'Fixed at Birth: Medical and Legal Erasures of Intersex Variations' (2016) 39 *UNSW Law Journal* 813–842 at 822 and 836.

[78] A. Fausto-Sterling, 'The Five Sexes, Revisited' (2000) 19 *Sciences* 18–23 at 22; N. Ben-Asher, 'The Necessity of Sex Change: A Struggle for Intersex and Transsex Liberties' (2006) 29 *Harvard Journal of Law & Gender* 51–98 at 88.

for intersex people initially refused to allow sex change for trans people. They opposed the so-called finding and correction of errors (for intersex people) to voluntary sex reassignment (trans people). However, not all legal systems put up the same resistance: Sweden and Germany were quick to accept sex reassignment in civil status,[79] while it took much longer for France and common law countries to follow suit.

In England, disputes over the nullity of marriage because of the sex of one of the spouses being called into question emerged in cases involving trans people in the 1950s. According to the established case law, marriage was to be considered valid in cases where it could be consummated. However, it was at first denied when it involved trans people, as the High Court argued that 'the artificiality of her organ' precluded the possibility.[80] Eventually, they overturned the criterion of consummation, replacing it with that of the spouses' sex. In England, as in the United States,[81] the trans people's marriage issue was the 'first occasion on which a court in England has been called upon to decide the sex of an individual'.[82] This criterion expressed the heteronormativity of marriage, that is, 'the union of man and woman. It is the institution on which the family is built, and in which the capacity for *natural hetero-sexual intercourse* is an essential element'.[83]

While doctors indicated a plurality of elements for defining sex (chromosomes, gonads, genitals, psychological, hormonal), judges asserted that 'these criteria are, of course, relevant to, but do not necessarily decide, the legal basis of sex determination'.[84] They refused to take surgical reassignment of trans people into account, on the grounds that it was artificially obtained: '[T]he respondent's operation, therefore, cannot affect her true sex.'[85] This position was maintained until 2003 in Australia[86] and 2004 in the United Kingdom. According to the judiciary, the true sex was determined by the chromosomes, gonads and external genitalia, before any operation. In case of discrepancy

[79] We would like to thank Laurie Marguet for pointing out the relevant German decisions cited in this section.

[80] *B.* v. *B.*, 1954, 2 All ER 598 [47].

[81] J. Meyerowitz, *How Sex Changed: A History of Transsexuality in the United-States* (Cambridge, MA: Harvard University Press, 2002), 241. See, for the United States, *B.* v. *B.*, 78 Misc.2d 112 (1974) (void), *M.T.* v. *J.T.*, 140 N.J. Super. 77, 355 A.2d 204 (1976) (valid, explicitly against the Corbett case reasoning, [208].

[82] *Corbett* v. *Corbett* [1970] 2 All ER 33 [105].

[83] Ibid., [105], we stress the point.

[84] Ibid., [100].

[85] Ibid., [104, 106].

[86] *A-G (Cth)* v. *'Kevin and Jennifer'* [2003] 172 FLR 300 [309] (The Court).

between these criteria, Judge Ormond considered, as expressed in an obiter to the Corbett case, that 'the greater weight would probably be given to the genital criterion than to the other two',[87] as marriage determines the importance of sex. In other words, this legal state of affairs meant that a sex fixed at birth could not be changed, and that unions where complete heterosexual intercourse was possible could nonetheless be deemed invalid if the spouses were not of 'natural' opposing sexes.

In France, the criterion established by the Court of Cassation in 1903 was the outward appearance of the external genitalia. This criterion should have allowed trans persons whose genitalia had been operated on to change their legal sex. But a court invoked 'the principle of the inalienability of the status of individuals' as an obstacle to sex change in 1965. In the particular case, the ruling was that the applicant lacked 'the essential and natural attributes of the other sex' (genetic sex included) despite the surgery. The criterion of the appearance of the external genitalia was thus set aside.[88] In later cases, the Court of Cassation confirmed the exclusivity of the chromosomal criterion because it was supposed to be the natural sex and therefore beyond the applicants' reach, maintaining its refusal of any possibility of sex change for years.[89]

In Germany, judges also initially rejected a legal change of sex, for varying reasons.[90] In a 1971 decision, the Federal Court of Justice refused to grant an application for sex reassignment in the absence of a legislative basis for changing sex in the civil status. It recalled that 'the obvious and immutable principle of attaching a person to the alternative category "female" or "male" is a self-evident pre-condition which structures not only entire social life but also the entire legal order'.[91] In 1978, the Constitutional Court admitted sex reassignment on the grounds that its refusal infringed on the fundamental rights of trans people, regardless of the fact that no further legislation had yet been passed.[92] The Federal Court of Justice made this recognition subject to several criteria,[93] and a 1980s

[87] *Corbett* v. *Corbett* [1970] 2 All ER 33 [106].

[88] TGI La Seine, 18 jan. 1965, JCP G, II, no. 14421; CA Paris, 18 jan. 1974, D., 1974, p. 198.

[89] Ten decisions of Cass civ. 1e, 16 déc. 1975, Bull civ. I, no. 374, p. 312 to Cass. civ., 5 fév. 1991 – no. 89-18.017.

[90] OLG Frankfurt, 8 Dec. 1965, 6W56/65; OLG Frankfurt, 14 Feb. 1969, 6W311/68; LG Berlin, 31 March 1969.

[91] BGH, 21 Sept. 1971, IV ZB 61/70, p. 10.

[92] BVerfGE 49, 286, 11 Oct. 1978, Arts. 55–60.

[93] BGH, 14.03.1979 – IV ZB 156/78, Arts. 6 and 6a.

Act created a legal framework applicable to sex change.[94] While gender stereotyping was not reflected in the 1980 Act, the 1979 decision required 'an overall appraisal of the personality', suggesting a perfectly stereotypical control over sex reassignment applications by judges (based on 'external physical constitution and nature'; 'his appearing as a man in the sexual sphere'; 'his entire behaviour').[95]

Gender stereotypes were legally required and were thus used by trans people to convince judges that they were facing a man or a woman. They also invoked 'absurd results that are harmful to social order, such as possessing obviously inaccurate identification documents',[96] as well as the violation of their right to private life,[97] as in the 1992 application against France before the European Court of Human Rights (ECtHR).[98] But the judges not only made the redefinition of legal sex subject to physical change, they also required that everything that could be changed should be changed. The French Court of Cassation thus necessitated 'medical and surgical treatment, carried out for therapeutic purposes', and furthermore that the person adopted the general appearance of the claimed sex 'to which their social behaviour corresponds'.[99] Therefore, civil status remained an instrument for enforcing a normative meaning of sex assignment in all aspects of life even as the possibility of changing one's sex over the course of one's life was acknowledged.

The different legal statuses conditioning rights, gendered dress code, differentiated social and professional activities, may no longer be legally required for all after birth, yet are explicitly reaffirmed in their normative dimension by doctors as a norm for intersex rearing, and by judges in relation to the conditions governing sex change for trans people. Judges have taken note of the fact that the applicants played 'soccer',[100] or

[94] Gesetz über die Änderung der Vornamen und die Feststellung der Geschlechtszugehörigkeit in besonderen Fällen (TSG), 10-09-1980, Bundesgesetzblatt.

[95] BGH, 14.03.1979 – IV ZB 156/78, Art. 6d, p. 11. In Western Australia, the Gender Reassignment Act 2000, Part 3, section 15, 1bii, required that the person 'adopt[] the lifestyle and has the gender characteristics of a person of the gender to which the person has been reassigned'.

[96] ECtHR, *Case of van Oosterwijck* v. *Belgique*, App. No. 7654/76 (6 November 1980), 13.

[97] ECtHR, *Case of Rees* v. *UK*, App. No. 9532/81 (10 October 1986), 34; ECtHR, *Case of Cossey* v. *UK*, App. No. 10843/84 (27 September 1990), 4.

[98] ECtHR, *Case of B* v. *France*, App. No. 13343/87 (25 March 1992), 59 and 63.

[99] Cass, ass. plén., 11 déc. 1992, JCP, II, 1993, 21991, p. 46.

[100] CA Poitiers, 15 déc. 2004, no. 03/01138.

performed several 'essentially male jobs, such as welder or warehouse worker',[101] while femaleness should be demonstrated by being a nurse,[102] but not a maintenance worker, which 'is not specifically feminine'.[103] In some cases, the legal sex change was accepted because she 'behave[d] like a particularly refined housewife [... so that], there is no evidence that public order would be disturbed by the consecration of the appellant's feminine status'.[104] Stereotypes relating to appearance are routinely present in judicial decisions.[105] The trans person's claim to obtain a legal sex change was only accepted to the extent that they performed sexual expectations of the sex that they claimed. The social order would not be disturbed if the segregated social fate that originally justified the establishment of sex at birth was reaffirmed.

3. The Transformation of Gender Categories under Pressure of Individual Rights[106]

This definition of a 'sexed subject' – binary, de-politicized, hetero-determined – now seems to be questioned under pressure of the constitutional and human rights of intersex, trans and non-binary people, which is discussed in this section.[107] Any such evolution admittedly does not follow a straight line. Developments mushroom differently in multiple jurisdictions, often under pressure from advocates and activists. A joint analysis might involve the risk of oversimplification. Furthermore, it may even contribute to a globalized, and de-contextualized, potentially even detrimental, queer discourse. Not least, the discourse of rights, especially when it is accompanied by a specific definition of the right-holder, may itself be

[101] CA Aix en Provence, 9 nov. 2001, no. 00/20236.
[102] In Germany, BverfGE 49, 286, Art. 50.
[103] CA Aix-en-Provence, 28 nov. 2007, no. 07/14524. This is an obstacle to a first name change.
[104] CA Agen, 24 juin 1987, no. 1987-044463.
[105] CA Paris, 22 oct. 1987, no. 1987-026727; CA Colmar, 15 mai 1991, no. 1991-044799, etc.
[106] This section is authored by Stefano Osella. See also S. Osella, 'Degendering the Civil Status? A Public Law Problem' (2020) 18 *International Journal of Constitutional Law* 471–475.
[107] Legislative change is also transforming the 'sexed subject'. Yet, mostly due to space concerns, the current section primarily focuses on the constitutional and human rights levels.

the source of normalization and suppression – rather than protection and empowerment – of difference.[108] Yet, despite these complexities, these developments broaden our legal horizons. They offer theoretical alternatives to the traditional understanding of the 'sexed' subject and challenge what seem to be the main assumptions upon which the 'sexed' subject has rested. As such, as will be argued, they demonstrate that an entirely new way to think of 'sexed subjects' in the law becomes possible. This transformation seems be happening in four directions. To begin with, the protection of intersex physical integrity has shown that a plurality of bodies is – so to speak – legally possible, and has problematized any naturalistic discourse which grounds the legal binary in a supposed 'biological' reality. Second, the right to gender self-determination has empowered people to seek recognition of their gender identity without having to conform to pre-established and intelligible standards. Third, the right to non-binary recognition has opened the possibility to imagine a law where the male–female dyad is overcome. Finally, the constitutional neutrality of sex registration' in the personal status is calling into question the very existence of a 'sexed subject in the civil status. The result is obviously a Copernican transformation of the possibilities of existence of 'sexed' subjectivities.

One last caveat: The following discussion does not aim to provide a list of *all* the evolutions that are taking place. Rather, it selects cases to demonstrate how a new 'sexed subject' is becoming legally thinkable. They have been selected – mostly at the constitutional and human rights level – because they show a plurality of new ways to understand the transformation of such a subject. In so doing, particular attention has also been paid to ensure geographical diversity.

A. Intersex Rights

The halt of culturally motivated involuntary treatments on intersex infants, also called intersex genital mutilations (IGMs) to highlight their

[108] See Osella, 'Reinforcing the Binary'; Repo, 'Governing Juridical Sex'; T. Dreyfus, 'The "Half-Invention" of Gender Identity in International Human Rights Law: From Cedaw to the Yogyakarta Principles' (2012) 37 *Australian Feminist Law Journal* 33–50. At a more theoretical level, see B. Golder, *Foucault and the Politics of Rights* (Stanford, CA: Stanford University Press 2015), 89–113; W. Brown, 'Suffering Rights as Paradoxes' (2000) 7 *Constellations* 208–229.

devastating effects,[109] has been at the core of intersex demands since the dawn of intersex activism. To this purpose, Bo Laurent (aka Cheryl Chase) founded the Intersex Society of North America (ISNA) in the mid-1990s.[110] Since then, intersex activism has acquired a global dimension and keeps pursuing the physical integrity of intersex people.[111]

Approaching intersex physical integrity from a queer perspective requires a certain degree of attention. This demand differs from, yet is arguably connected to, the addition of a non-binary legal identity. The former is widely present in intersex movements, albeit manifesting in varying strategies and approaches.[112] Non-binary recognition is more divisive. Some intersex advocates hold that identity recognition and physical integrity are inseparable. Without the rejection of binary normativity, the eradication of IGMs also seems unattainable to them.[113] Yet others prefer to keep these demands separate.[114] They argue that not doing so may expose intersex advocacy to what can be seen as politically controversial alliances with queer movements. This argumentation may furthermore miss the point that involuntary treatments are a problem of medical practice, rather than a general societal form of discrimination. Finally, intersex demands, it has been argued, might be appropriated by LGBTQ+ movements.[115]

At the same time, the contrast with involuntary medical treatments can undeniably complicate the representation of 'sex' in the law. Safeguarding the integrity of intersex bodies challenges the existence of a sexual binary. It questions the pathologizing understanding of bodies that fall outside the categories of maleness and femaleness, and, as such, politicizes any

[109] M. Bauer, D. Truffer and D. Corocetti, 'Intersex Human Rights' (2020) 24 *International Journal of Human Rights* 724–749; M. Jones, 'Intersex Genital Mutilations – A Western Version of FGM' (2017) 25 *International Journal of Children's Rights* 396–411.

[110] Chase, 'Hermaphrodites with Attitude'.

[111] M. Carpenter, 'The Human Rights of Intersex People: Addressing Harmful Practices and Rhetoric of Change' (2016) 24 *Reproductive Health Matters* 74–84.

[112] M. Sudai, 'Revisiting the Limits of Professional Autonomy: The Intersex Rights Movement's Path to De-Medicalization' (2018) 41 *Harvard Women's Law Journal* 1–54.

[113] See the 2013 Malta declaration; 2014 Statement of Riga; 2017 Vienna Statement; the Yogyakarta Principles+10, all available at https://oiieurope.org/malta-declaration/.

[114] Zwischengeschlecht.org/StopIGM.org (Compiled by V. Guillot), NGO Report to the 7th Periodic Report of France on the Convention Against Torture, 28 March 2016, http://intersex.shadowreport.org/public/2016-CAT-France-NGO-Zwischengeschlecht-Intersex-IGM.pdf, 32–37.

[115] Bauer, Truffer and Crocetti, 'Intersex Human Rights', at 741.

discourse which grounds legal sex categories in a supposedly biological core. The protection of intersex characteristics in practice underlines the cultural and political dimension of the 'sexual' binary in the law and furthermore problematizes the hetero-cisnormative assumptions that are aimed to legitimize intersex treatments.[116]

A particularly telling example is the jurisprudence of the Colombian Constitutional Court. Since 1995, this court has produced a uniquely abundant case law on intersex children's physical integrity.[117] Despite falling short of a complete moratorium,[118] the Colombian court has devised a form of reinforced – 'qualified, informed, and persistent' – consent for such treatment on children. The explicit aim is to discourage them. This case law not only represents a human rights achievement, but evidently also contributes to redefining the 'sexed subject'. In the SU-337/99 landmark decision, the court referred to the binary as a cultural construction.[119] It underscored that intersex treatments are motivated by the normative understanding of the body, as well as the bias and hostility against diversity. Finally, the court recognized that intersex is an opportunity to learn, to question assumptions and to open new horizons, and is and should not be shameful or carry a stigma.[120]

Similarly, the High Court of Madurai, citing the World Health Organization (WHO), condemned the treatments that aim to 'make [children] conform to gendered physical norms', thereby arguably acknowledging the cultural assumptions behind the binary.[121] When granting gender recognition to non-binary people, the Constitutional Court of Austria also clarified that intersex characteristics are no

[116] M. Cabral, 'Pensar la Intersexualidad, Hoy', in D. Maffia (ed.), *Sexualidades Migrantes. Género y Transgénero* (Buenos Aires: Feminaria Editora, 2003); Domurat-Dreger, *Hermaphrodites*, 184; A. Domurat-Dreger, 'Ambiguous Sex or Ambivalent Medicine' (1998) 28 *Hastings Centre Report* 24–35 at 31.

[117] R. Rubio-Marín and S. Osella, 'Between Rights and Pragmatism: Intersex Rights before the Colombian Constitutional Court', in J. Scherpe, A. Dutta and T. Helms (eds.), *The Legal Status of Intersex Persons* (Cambridge: Intersentia, 2018).

[118] An exception is sexual reassignment at birth, which has been completely banned in the decision Corte Constitucional, Sala Séptima de Revision, Octubre 23, 1995, Sentencia T-477/95, www.corteconstitucional.gov.co/relatoria/1995/t-477-95.htm.

[119] Corte Constitucional, 12 Mayo 1999, Sentencia SU-377/99, para. II.36, www.corteconstitucional.gov.co/relatoria/1999/SU337-99.htm.

[120] Rubio-Marín and Osella, 'Between Rights and Pragmatism', 337.

[121] *Arunkumar* v. *Inspector General of Registration*, WP(MD) No. 4125 of 2019 and WMP (MD) No. 3220 of 2019, 22 April 2019, [18] and [21].

pathology. The court ruled that intersex treatments could only be performed on the strictest medical indications. It explicitly excluded social or parental anxiety as justification for them.[122] In so doing, the court acknowledged that parental panic and social anxiety caused by intersexuality has weighed heavily in decisions to perform operations on children.[123] Not only courts are restricting such treatments, legislation in Germany,[124] Portugal,[125] Malta[126] and Uruguay[127] represents examples of how the protection of physical characteristics is increasingly, yet evidently insufficiently, gathering momentum. In other countries, such as Spain, protection of intersex integrity is presently being debated.[128] Likewise, numerous international, supranational and human rights bodies have spoken up against intersex treatments,[129] including the Committee of the Rights of the Child,[130] the Committee against Torture,[131] the Parliamentary Assembly of the Council of Europe,[132] the EU Parliament[133] and the Inter-American Commission of Human Rights.[134]

The prohibition of IGMs sanctions the legitimacy of non-normative bodies and their belonging in the legal system. As a result, a binary

[122] VGH, G77/2018-9, 15 Juni 2018, Art. 16.

[123] Karkazis, *Fixing Sex*, 89; D. J. Hester, 'Intersex(es) and Informed Consent: How Physicians' Rhetoric Constrains Choice' (2004) 25 *Theoretical Medicine and Bioethics* 21–49.

[124] Gesetz zum Schutz von Kindern mit Varianten der Geschlechtsentwicklung, 25 March 2021.

[125] Lei 38/2018, Art. 5

[126] The Gender Identity, Gender Expression and Sex Characteristics Act 2015, Act No. XI of 2015 (Malta), https://meae.gov.mt/en/Public_Consultations/MSDC/Pages/Consultations/GIGESC.aspx.

[127] Ley no. 19580, de 22 diciembre 2017, de violencia hacia las mujeres basada en genero.

[128] Ley LGBTI. [129] Bauer, Truffer and Crocetti, 'Intersex Human Rights', at 727.

[130] UN Doc, 'Concluding Observations on the Combined Second to Fourth Periodic Reports of Switzerland', crc/c/che/co/2-4, 2015.

[131] UN Doc, 'Concluding Observations on the Seventh Periodic Report of Switzerland', CAT/C/CHE/CO/7. 2015.

[132] Parliamentary Assembly of the Council of Europe Resolution 2191 on promoting the human rights of and eliminating discrimination against intersex people (2017).

[133] European Parliament Resolution of 14 February 2019 on the rights of intersex people, 2018/2878(RSP).

[134] Inter-American Commission on Human Rights, 'Violencia contra Personas Lesbianas, Gays, Bisexuales, Trans e Intersex en América', 12 November 2015, OAS/Ser.L/V/II. rev.1, www.oas.org/en/iachr/reports/pdfs/violencelgbtipersons.pdf, para. 182; European Parliament Resolution of 14 February 2019 on the rights of intersex people, www.europarl.europa.eu/doceo/document/TA-8-2019-0128_EN.html.

understanding of the 'sexed subject' seems more untenable. These developments suggest that the 'sexed subject' may be diverse in its very corporeality: It can open the way to a myriad of different bodies.

B. The Right to Gender Self-Determination

The right to gender self-determination arguably represents a seismic shift in the definition of the 'sexed subject'. Since the 1970s, national and supranational courts – among which, notably, the ECtHR[135] – have enunciated a constitutional and human right to 'establish details of [one's own legal] identity', including 'sex' status.[136] On the one hand, this case law has undeniably changed the notion of legal sex. No longer meant to reflect what was and is perceived as an objective fact, legal sex rather began to mirror individual identity as well. On the other hand, gender recognition is often characterized by the establishment of specific requirements (for example, medical treatments, behavioural standards or family status), to be checked by an external authority (such as an administrative or judicial body).[137] This combination of preconditions and controls is typically intended to keep gender diversity under control, especially in consideration of the many public interests and fundamental rights that still rely on legal sex categories. Yet not only has such a procedure triggered a barrage of human-rights-based complaints. The imposition (or legitimation in the case of supranational courts) of preconditions on trans people defines a 'transsexual' subject that is acceptable in the eyes of the law, and the rejection of other gender identities. Hence, this right has enabled normalizing and biopolitical mechanisms.[138]

[135] For an exhaustive discussion, see D. Gonzalez-Salzberg, *Sexuality and Transsexuality under the European Convention on Human Rights: A Queer Reading of Human Rights Law* (Portland, OR: Hart Publishing, 2019).

[136] ECtHR, Grand Chamber, *Christine Goodwin* v. *United Kingdom*, App No. 28597/1995 (11 July 2002), 92; ECtHR, Grand Chamber, *I.* v. *United Kingdom*, App No. 25680/1994 (11 July 2002); ECtHR, *Van Kuck* v. *Germany*, App No. 35968/97 (12 September 2003). See also Osella, 'Reinforcing the Binary'; J. Scherpe (ed.), *The Legal Status of Transsexual and Transgender Persons* (Cambridge: Intersentia, 2015).

[137] Scherpe, *The Legal Status of Transsexual and Transgender Persons.*

[138] Osella, 'Reinforcing the Binary'; Repo, 'Governing Juridical Sex'.

Requirements for gender recognition, especially the sterilization and single-status requirements, have increasingly been the target of legal actions, and often successfully so.[139] Since the mid-1990s, following the contestation of such requirements, gender self-determination – emphatically the 'gold standard' of gender recognition – has become a central demand by trans advocates.[140] As clarified in Principle 31 of the 2017 Yogyakarta Principles +10, everyone shall have a right 'to change gendered information' contained in identity documents. States are called on to '[recognize and affirm] each person's self-defined gender identity' and to ban 'eligibility criteria, such as medical or psychological interventions, a psycho-medical diagnosis, minimum or maximum age, economic status, health, marital or parental status, or any other third-party opinion'. The individual, it is advocated, must be the ultimate authority over their own identity. Since 2012, when Argentina became the first country to legislate it,[141] gender self-determination has been taking hold at the legislative[142] and constitutional level.[143] The Constitutional Court of Colombia, in particular, has developed a doctrine that entrenches gender self-determination in principles such as

[139] On the sterilization requirement, see BVerfGE, Beschluss des Ersten Senats, 11 January 2011, 1 BvR 3295/07, Rn. 1-82, www.bverfg.de/e/rs20110111_1bvr329507.html (Germany); Court of Cassation, 25 July 2015, no. 15138 (Italy); Constitutional Court, 221/2015 (Italy); ECtHR, Grand Chamber, A.P., Garçon, Nicot v. France, App. Nos. 79885/12, 52471/13 and 52596/13 (6 April 2017). At other times, however, the sterilization surgeries were continued: Hong Kong Tse Henry Edward v. Commissioner of Registration [2019] HKCFI 295. See M. Wan, 'Queer Temporalities and Transgender Rights: A Hong Kong Case-Study' (2021) 30 *Social & Legal Studies* 563–580.

[140] Legal scholar Peter Dunne used this, I believe, fortunate expression in a hearing before the House of Commons, on 13 October 2015. See Women and Equalities Committee, *Transgender Equality* (HC 2015-2016, 390) [40], https://publications.parliament.uk/pa/cm201516/cmselect/cmwomeq/390/390.pdf.

[141] Law No. 26.743, 24 May 2012.

[142] Law 182, 11 June 2014 (Denmark); The Gender Identity, Gender Expression and Sex Characteristics Act 2015 (Malta); Gender Recognition Act 2015 (Act No. 25/2015) (Ireland); Gender Recognition Act, 1 June 2016 (Norway); Law 25 June 2017 (Belgium); Law No. 21120, 15 November 2018 (Chile); Law 38, 7 August 2018 (Portugal); Law 19.684, 25 October 2018 (Uruguay); Gender Autonomy Act, 1 July 2019 (Iceland).

[143] Cour Constitutionnelle (CC) [Constitutional Court], Decision No. 99/2019 (19 June 2019) (Belgium); Corte Constitucional [CC][Constitutional Court], Sala Primera de Revisión, 13 Febrero 2015, Sentencia T-063/15, www.corteconstitucional.gov.co/RELATORIA/2015/T-063-15.htm (Colombia).

gender equality, free development of personality, and the right to legal personality. The presence of requirements on recognition has been deemed by this court a disproportionate interference with such rights.[144] In other countries, reform of the right to gender recognition has been discussed.[145] Although limited to soft law, gender self-determination also seems to be cautiously making an appearance in international human rights law.[146] This is the case, for instance, for the Parliamentary Assembly of the Council of Europe,[147] the 2019 Resolution of the European Parliament, and the 2017 Opinion of the Inter-American Court of Human Rights.[148]

Gender self-determination is logically related to the recognition of fluid – that is, non-permanent – gender identities. To be the ultimate authority over one's own identity at least in principle means the possibility to change one's status as much and as often as is needed. Yet multiple recognitions are virtually always restricted. In some instances, including before human rights bodies such as the ECtHR, the limitation of gender recognition to (irreversibly changed) post-operative transsexual people has been seen as a guarantee of the certainty of legal relations relying on gender.[149] Perhaps surprisingly, gender fluidity is also restricted when gender self-determination is the standard. External controls can be established, as under Argentinian law, where judicial supervision is required for subsequent changes.[150] Alternatively, minimum time lapses between the

[144] Stefano Osella and Ruth Rubio-Marin, 'The Right to Gender Recognition before the Colombian Constitutional Court: A Queer and Travesti Theory Analysis' (2021) 40(5) *Bulletin of Latin American Research* 650–664.

[145] See, for instance, the debate in the United Kingdom on the reform of the Gender Recognition Act 2004, and in Spain on the Ley Trans.

[146] See P. Canoot and M. Decoster, 'The Abolition of Sex/Gender Registration in the Age of Gender Self-Determination: An Interdisciplinary, Queer, Feminist and Human Rights Analysis' (2020) 1 *International Journal of Gender, Sexuality and Law* 26–55.

[147] Parliamentary Assembly of the Council of Europe Resolution 2048(2015) on Discrimination against Transgender People in Europe (22 April 2015), para. 6.2.

[148] Identidad de género, e igualdad y no discriminación a parejas del mismo sexo, Advisory Opinion OC-24/17, Inter-Am. Ct. HR (Nov. 2017, 24), www.corteidh.or.cr/docs/opiniones/seriea_24_eng.pdf.

[149] See, the Italian Court of Cassation, 20 July 2015, n. 15138, or *Christine Goodwin* and *I.* See E. Grabham, 'Governing Permanence: Trans Subjects, Time, and the Gender Recognition Act' (2010) 19 *Social and Legal Studies* 107–126.

[150] Ley No. 26.743, 24 May 2012, Art. 8.

first and subsequent recognitions can be set.[151] Recognition may also be limited in number.[152]

One conspicuous exception is represented by Belgium. In its Decision 99/2019, the Belgian Constitutional Court enunciated a constitutional right to multiple subsequent changes, with the express purpose to extend recognition to gender-fluid people. The 2017 Belgian Law limited gender self-determination to first-time applicants, only subject to a (loose) control role by the public attorney. Second-time applications were however subject to the jurisdiction of family courts: a reinforced mechanism ostensibly aimed to constrain identity fraud. The Constitutional Court ruled that, albeit motivated by a legitimate objective, this restriction represented a disproportionate interference with the right to self-determination (Article 22 of the Belgian Constitution) and equality (Articles 10 and 11 of the Belgian Constitution) of gender-fluid people. The court found that the routine controls established in the law for first-time applicants would suffice to avoid fraud.[153]

The right to gender self-determination, especially in its fluid dimension, has a considerable transformative potential for the 'sexed subject'. When granted, the 'ultimate say' over the individual's sex status is bestowed on the individual person. Third authorities are no longer called on to 'certify' the fulfilment of specific requirements. In the words of the Colombian Constitutional Court, gender self-determination allows individuals to escape 'heteronormative extremes'. Arguably, the person is bestowed with the possibility to redefine their gender in an innovative and subversive way.[154] Thus, gender self-determination in the sense of allowing the person to reimagine their identity along individualized axes, may enable

[151] For example, five (Uruguay, Law 19684) or ten years (Colombia, Decreto 1227 of 2015). Yet, the Colombian Constitutional Court has recently ruled that the time limitation on subsequent gender recognitions violates the rights to free development of personality (Art. 16 CP), to legal personality (Art. 14 CP), as well as the general principle of dignity (Art. 1 CP). See CC, Sala Sexta de Revisión, 4 Febrero 2022, Sentencia T-033/22, https://www.corteconstitucional.gov.co/Relatoria/2022/T-033-22.htm (Colombia).

[152] Colombian law, for instance, restricts the possible changes to two: Decreto 1227 of 2015, Art. 2.2.6.12.4.6.

[153] Cour Constitutionnelle, Decision No. 99/2019, [B.8.8]. See P. Cannoot, 'The Limits to Gender Self-Determination in a Stereotyped Legal System: Lessons from the Belgian Gender Recognition Act', in E. Brems, P. Cannoot and T. Moonen (eds.), *Protecting Trans Rights in the Age of Gender Self-Determination* (Cambridge: Intersentia, 2020).

[154] Osella and Rubio-Marín, 'The Right to Gender Self-Determination before the Colombian Constitutional Court'.

a defiance of gender standards, legibility and intelligibility.[155] It allows trans people to reimagine their gender performance for themselves as they see fit. In fact, a single 'masculine' or 'feminine' 'sexed subject' is substituted by a plurality. At a deeper level, however, gender self-determination, taking power from the medico-legal complex that determines individual identities, challenges gender as 'the apparatus by which the production and normalization of masculine and feminine take place along with the interstitial forms of hormonal, chromosomal, psychic, and performative that gender assumes'.[156] Gender self-determination can contribute to the – at least partial – disestablishment of the creation of *the* 'sexed subject' recognized by the legal system. It challenges gender as a mechanism of meaning-making.

Admittedly, situations may still occur in which a 'sexed subject' is defined even if legal sex is 'decertified', as in the case of gender self-determination. In the plurality of legal orders that we inhabit, gendered personhood may still be defined through a multiplicity of legal discourses pertaining to the most diverse bodies and institutions.[157] Yet when gender self-determination is allowed, the 'sexed subject' is undeniably deferred to the individual, the ultimate definer of their own identity, at least for state law purposes, leaving the essential role to uphold and protect diversity to the state.

C. Non-Binary Recognition

The addition of a legal category of non-binary identity represents a further change in the definition of the 'sexed subject'.[158] From a strictly binary understanding, it shifts to a more inclusive dimension. The demand of non-binary recognition features pre-eminently in trans and at least in part of intersex advocacy. The Yogyakarta Principles +10 once again offer a telling example. Principle 31 calls on lawmakers to 'make available a

[155] C. Rizki, 'Latin/x American Trans Studies: Toward a Travesti-Trans Analytic' (2019) 6 *TSQ Transgender Studies Quarterly* 145–155; M. Wayar, *Travesti: Una Teoria lo Suficientemente Buena* (Buenos Aires: Editorial Muchas Nueces, 2018).

[156] J. Butler, *Undoing Gender* (New York and London: Routledge, 2004), 42.

[157] D. Cooper and F. Renz, 'If the State Decertified Gender, What Might Happen to Its Meaning and Value?' (2016) 43 *Journal of Law and Society* 483–505.

[158] See Stefano Osella, 'When Comparative Law Walks the Path of Anthropology', presented at Law and Anthropology Workshop, Max Planck Institute for Social Anthropology, December 2021.

multiplicity of gender marker options'.[159] The insistence on going beyond the strictures of the male–female dyad has been present in a plurality of contexts. Non-binary activism can be found in many jurisdictions, albeit with considerable differences from context to context.[160]

A first approach to non-binary recognition can be found in some judicial developments that took place in South-East Asia. These decisions are not only limited to identity recognition. Rather, they aim to curb discrimination and ensure equality in a plurality of aspects. In 2007, the Nepalese Supreme Court recognized for a plurality of gender-diverse people the right to be legally registered in the 'third sex'. This recognition was particularly significant in ensuring access to social rights and obtaining a degree of institutional and social acceptance.[161] As of 2009, the Pakistani Supreme Court passed a series of decisions aimed to grant legal recognition to non-binary people, protecting them from discrimination in a plurality of settings.[162] In 2014, the Indian Supreme Court was faced with a claim, in the form of public interest litigation, intended to protect the rights of trans and non-binary people. Non-binary recognition was envisioned as part of a larger set of remedies to the conditions of discrimination and deprivation that trans and non-binary– especially *hijra* – people face, also as a result of colonial oppression. The court ruled that autonomy and dignity (deriving from the due process clause, Art. 21), equality (Arts. 14, 15 and 16) and freedom of expression (Art. 19) ensure recognition in their gender for non-binary people.[163] 'Contradictory tendencies' run through the Indian judgment.[164] A push towards self-determination can be observed. Yet the non-binary 'subject' is defined with specific – not only gender, but more generally social – characteristics, that are, as Rao suggests, 'rooted in

[159] Principle 31. [160] See Baars, 'Queer Cases Unmake Gendered Law'.

[161] *Sunil Babu Pant and Others* v. *Government of Nepal and Others* (2008)1 Writ No. 917 2064 BS (2007 AD) 2NJALJ 261. See also M. F. Moscati and H. Phuyal, 'The Third Gender Case Decision of the Supreme Court of Nepal on the Rights of Lesbian, Gay, Bisexual, Transsexual and Intersex People' (2009) 4 *Journal of Comparative Law* 291–297.

[162] Supreme Court of Pakistan, 12 December 2009, *Khaki* v. *Rawalpindi*. See V. Hamzic, *Sexual and Gender Diversity in the Muslim World: History, Law, and Vernacular Knowledge* (London: I. B. Tauris, 2016); S. Khan, 'What Is in a Name? Khwaja Sara, Hijra and Eunuchs in Pakistan' (2016) 23 *Indian Journal of Gender Studies* 218–242; S. Khan, 'Khwaja Sara, Hijra, and the Struggle for Rights in Pakistan' (2017) 51 *Modern Asian Studies* 1283–1310.

[163] *National Legal Service Authority* v. *Union of India*, WP (Civil) No. 604 of 2013.

[164] A. Dutta, 'Contradictory Tendencies: The Supreme Court's NALSA Judgement on Transgender Recognition and Rights' (2014) 5 *Journal of Indian Law and Society* 225–236.

tradition'.[165] Although the protected subject is also non-binary, this identity seems to be defined and not self-determined.

Non-binary recognition can also be more explicitly connected to a physical dimension. This is the case of the Constitutional Court of Germany.[166] In October 2017, the Federal Constitutional Court of Germany (FCC) examined the claim for a 'third option' in the civil status for a person with a non-binary gender identity and a 'variation of sex development'. It ruled that the lack of such an option for people with the characteristics of the applicant violated the general right to personality,[167] in conjunction with the rights to human dignity[168] and equality.[169] This decision, which can be traced back to intersex activism,[170] redefined the 'sexed subject', opening the way to non-binary identities. The courts did not explicitly exclude endosex people – that is, people whose anatomy conforms to the male–female standard – from the scope of the new right. Yet, despite this possibility of an evolutive interpretation,[171] the 'sexed subject' of these decisions seems narrowly constructed to be defined as a non-binary identifying intersex person.

A different form of non-binary recognition was granted by the Constitutional Court of Belgium. Prompted by three LGBTQI+ associations, the court granted a third option purely based on self-determination.[172] The

[165] R. Rao, *Out of Time: The Queer Politics of Postcoloniality* (Oxford: Oxford University Press, 2020), 180.

[166] BVerfGE, 10 October 10 2017, 1 BvR 2019/16. The Austrian Constitutional Court ruled similarly in: Verfassungsgerichtshof [VfGH] (Constitutional Court), 19 June 2018, G-77/2018, www.vfgh.gv.at/medien/Personenstandsgesetz_-_intersexuelle_Personen.php (Austria). A right to register a person beyond the binary has been recognized in Australia, in the case of Norrie-May Welby (High Court of Australia, 2 April 2014, Case S273/2013, *NSW Registrar of Births, Deaths and Marriages* v. *Norrie*), yet with a less substantiated gender reasoning.

[167] Art. 2(1). [168] Art. 1(1). [169] Art. 3(3) GG.

[170] See, on Germany, A. Von Wahl, 'From Object to Subject: Intersex Activism and the Rise and Fall of the Gender Binary in Germany' (2021) 28(3) *Social Politics* 755–777. Both decisions were preceded by reports of, respectively, the Austrian and German ethical councils on the treatment of intersex people.

[171] For a discussion on the evolutive interpretation in the German case, see P. Dunne and J. Mulder, 'Beyond the Binary: Towards a Third Sex Category in Germany?' (2018) 19 *German Law Journal* 627–647.

[172] Loi réformant des régimes relatifs aux personnes transgenres en ce qui concerne la mention d'une modification de l'enregistrement du sexe dans les actes de l'état civil et ses effets du 25 juin 2017, www.ejustice.just.fgov.be/cgi_loi/change_lg.pl?language=fr&la=F&cn=2017062503&table_name=loi.

2017 law on gender recognition limited gender self-determination to the binary. The court ruled that it disproportionately interfered with the rights of non-binary people. Indeed, gender self-determination requires that 'the deeply felt gender identity, be that binary or non-binary', is equally respected in the law.[173] The court also ruled that the special importance of equality between men and women that may indeed still refer to a binary (Art. 10.3 and 11-bis), 'does not entail that the Belgian constitutional order is founded on the binary' and 'does not hinder measures aimed to fight against the difference of treatment based on non-binary gender identity'.[174] The law preventing non-binary people from being recognized, the court found, violated the principle of equality[175] in combination with self-determination.[176] In contrast to the other courts, grounding non-binary recognition in self-determination, the decision of the Belgian Constitutional Court does not define a non-binary sexed subject.

All non-binary recognition reshapes the sexed subject. First, the traditional binary understanding thereof is replaced by a more complex and inclusive one. Second, non-binary recognition forces the lawmaker to reflect on the binary structure of the law and to question the political dimension of binary categories. Yet, despite its obvious innovative potential, the recognition of a third gender per se may replicate beyond the binary a mechanism of identity definitions that ultimately establishes standards for 'the sexed subject'. As Butler argued, gender is the 'apparatus by which the production and normalization of masculine and feminine take place'. Hence:

> [T]o assume that gender always and exclusively means the matrix of the 'masculine' and 'feminine' is precisely to miss the critical point that the production of that coherent binary is contingent, that it comes at a cost, and that those permutations of gender which do not fit the binary are as much a part of gender as its most normative instance. [Gender may be] a mechanism by which notions of masculine and feminine are produced and naturalized'.[177]

When non-binary identity is detached from gender self-determination, as it is in all jurisdictions discussed except for Belgium, a – certainly new and complex – non-binary 'sexed subject' is defined. While empowering some,

[173] Cour Constitutionnelle, 99/2019, [B.6.5].
[174] Cour Constitutionnelle, 99/2019, [B.6.6].
[175] Arts. 10 and 11 Belgian Constitution.
[176] Art. 22 Belgian Constitution.
[177] Butler, *Undoing Gender*, 42.

such a definition entails a restriction of the pool of beneficiaries of non-binary recognition. Conversely, the recognition of a non-binary identity as an expression of gender self-determination lays the groundwork for individual self-determinations. Conditions are set for a plurality of non-binary subjecthoods to flourish, challenging the mechanisms of external attribution of one's status.

D. Contestation of Categories per se

Recently, the possibility to be 'legally sexless' is becoming more concrete, taking either an individualized form, in which individual persons are allowed not to 'tick the box', or a more generalized contestation of categorization. Other than those mentioned earlier, this evolution questions the very presence of the 'sexed subject'. Although probably less vocally advocated for than the right to gender recognition and the halt of IGMs, the elimination of 'sex' categories is gaining momentum too.[178] Significantly, Principle 31 of the Yogyakarta Principles +10 calls on states to 'end the registration of the sex and gender of the person in identity documents such as birth certificates, identification cards, passports and drivers' licences, and as part of their legal personality', only allowing it for legitimate purposes.

One example of the 'individualized' sexless status is Decision T-450A/13 of the Colombian Constitutional Court. In this judgment, the court specified that intersex children have a right to be registered in civil registries by leaving the gender marker blank, so that they may access all public services they need, in order to avoid health discrimination.[179] Similarly, in *Norrie*,[180] the High Court of Australia granted the right to a non-binary trans person to be legally 'non-specific'. The court held that the applicant's record should leave the 'sex' unspecified as registration must reflect reality faithfully.[181] Such examples do not however represent an overall

[178] Fogg Davis, *Beyond Trans.*

[179] Corte Constitucional [CC] [Constitutional Court], Sala Segunda de Revision, Julio 16, 2013, Sentencia T-450A/13, www.corteconstitucional.gov.co/relatoria/2013/t-450a-13.htm.

[180] *New South Wales Registrar of Births, Deaths, and Marriages* v. *Norrie* ([2014] HCA 11).

[181] R. Wallbank, 'Australia', in J. Scherpe (ed.), *The Legal Status of Transsexual and Transgender Persons* (Cambridge: Intersentia, 2015), 247–248.

contestation of gender categories. They are instead exceptions motivated by specific conditions of the applicants' bodies. In fact, as intersex activists as well as legal scholars have argued, this kind of registration may in fact reinforce the binary by highlighting the exceptions to the rule.[182]

A different situation occurs when courts proclaim a constitutional neutrality over the presence of 'sex' categories in the civil status altogether. The legislator can legitimately eliminate them in such cases. In the 2017 case on the 'third option', the German FCC held that the Basic Law does not require sex/gender to be part of the civil status.[183] Accordingly, the legislator would have the option to add categories, or alternatively eliminate them, to accommodate non-binary intersex people. Similar conclusions were reached by the Austrian Constitutional Court in 2018,[184] and by the Belgian one in 2019.[185] Should this possibility be picked up by parliaments, we would see a considerable curb on the presence, or even disappearance, of the 'sexed subject', at least as a general criterion of individual categorization for state law purposes.[186] Obviously, a 'sexless' civil status is not a 'sexless law'. Removing 'sex' as a general criterion of classification does not prevent individuals from being gendered again through the law. Yet removing this general criterion of classification means that the legal status of the individual will no longer formally include 'sex'. The practical and symbolical significance of this change can hardly be overestimated.

This elimination of the 'sexed subject' from the civil status evidently comes with its own set of challenges. In particular, it raises complex questions relating to the pursuit of constitutionally legitimate objectives, especially those aimed at reversing past gender discrimination. Scholars have discussed what legitimate purposes gender registration may serve, as well as whether such interests can be achieved through means other than registration.[187]

182 T. Helms, 'The 2013 German Law: Analysis and Criticism', in J. Scherpe, A. Dutta and T. Helms (eds.), *The Legal Status of Intersex Persons* (Cambridge: Intersentia, 2018), 372.

183 BVerfGE, 10 October 2017, 1 BvR 2019/16, Rn. 50.

184 Verfassungsgerichtshof [VfGH] (Constitutional Court), 19 June 2018, G-77/2018, 6.2.

185 Cour Constitutionnelle (CC) [Constitutional Court], Decision No. 99/2019, 19 June 2019, www.const-court.be/public/f/2019/2019-099f.pdf (Belg.), B.7.3.

186 See Cooper and Renz, 'If the State Decertified Gender'. But also C. Hutton, 'Legal Sex, Self-Classification and Gender Self-Determination' (2018) 11 *Law and Humanities* 64–81.

187 Fogg Davis, *Beyond Trans*; G. Mayeda, 'Who Do You Think You Are? When Should the Law Let You Be Who You Want to Be?', in L. Shrage (ed.), *'You've Changed' Sex*

4. Conclusion

In this chapter, we have discussed how the 'sexed subject' has been defined and reconstructed in the law. In Section 2, the 'straitjacketing' of 'unruly' bodies and identities is detailed. It all begins at birth, with everyone being assigned to one of the two sexes established by the gender order. By instituting sexed subjects, men and women, multiple hierarchies (of sexes, of sexualities, of bodies) are created. Intersex bodies are rejected, as they do not fit the binary construction of the law. They are seen as ambiguous bodies, a threat to the binary legal and social order that presupposes only two sexes, and organizes the world according to their different domains. Intersex people and the medico-legal treatment that is imposed on them, show how legal categorization – such as in the civil status – is about enforcing roles and representation, at the cost of imposing mutilations to uphold them. Similarly, the treatment of trans identity has illustrated how the imposition of medico-behavioural preconditions on gender recognition had the same purpose. In both cases, the legal systems maintain the binary by keeping diversity outside its protection rather than within. Law manifests itself as a part of the regulatory gender apparatus. It imposes its norms on identity, bodies and behaviour on all. Law can become a tool for the suppression of diversity and for the homogenization of human traits, with evident biopolitical implications.

At the same time, as discussed by Osella in Section 3, the law can also be a vehicle for the transformation of the 'sexed subject'. Through the law, and specifically constitutional and human rights, individuals are slowly achieving power over their own identities. As noted, this is a slow transformative process, which is now dawning and far from established. Yet it is enough to challenge, and open the way to new conceptualizations of, the legal 'sexed subject'. From anatomically normative, binary, externally defined and permanent status, the subject is encountering more possibilities to become individualized, diverse and fluid. New temporalities, ways

Reassignment and Personal Identity (Oxford: Oxford University Press 2009); D. Borrillo, 'Le sexe et le Droit: De la Logique Binaire des Genres et la Matrice Hétérosexuelle de la Loi' (2011) *Jurisprudence – Revue Critique* 263–274; P. Guez, 'Faut-il Supprimer la Mention du Sexe de la Personne à l'État Civil?' (2015) *Revue des Droits de l'Homme*, http://journals.openedition.org/revdh/1660; Osella, 'Degendering the Civil Status?'; L. Shrage, 'Does the Government Need to Know Your Sex?' (2012) 20 *Journal of Political Philosophy* 225–247.

of living one's bodies and representations are now present in the law. First, the protection of physical intersex characteristics is transforming the anatomical dimension of the sexed subject, making it more diverse and distant from the binary. Second, thanks to gender self-determination, the 'sexed subject' now seems to be free to depart from normative notions of masculinity and femininity, and to embrace re-imaginative, individualized and more empowering forms of gender manifestations. At a deeper level, the right to gender self-determination is questioning the role of the state to act as a mechanism of meaning-making, and transferring the authority over identity to the individual. The recognition of non-binary identities is challenging the binary understanding of the legal 'sexed subject', opening to 'third genders' which are often 'third options', even if not self-determined in their entirety. Although the development is still in its early stages, human rights protection has begun to transform the temporality of gender with an initial protection of gender-fluid identities. Consequently, this has caused constitutional courts to question whether 'sex' should be part of the civil status at all. Finally, the very permanence of the 'sexed subject' – even as transformed along such lines – seems to be called into question.

The changes in the rationales and methods for attributing and managing individual identity that are discussed in this chapter seem to signal further paths of research. Some questions in particular come to mind. First, if heteronormativity is so central in the definition of the binary, what are the implications of the changes regarding marriage, procreation and filiation on the need to regulate gender identities? Second, and importantly, more research is needed to create understanding on how characteristics other than sexuality have influenced the creation of the 'sexed subject' in the law. Further questions that could be explored include the following ones. In what way is 'sex categorization' affected by the transformation of the sexed subject? What part of this categorizing system remains intact if many of the rationales upon which it was built come to be questioned – with special, although not exclusive, reference to the preservation of the heterosexual matrix in the law? What are the reasons to preserve these categories? And if so, under what name should they continue? Does it make sense to keep speaking of 'sex' categories at all? And what are the challenges occasioned by this 'new' 'sexed' subject? Unfortunately, this chapter does not allow the space to carry the investigation forward.

However, suffice it to say that all these questions cannot be answered without heeding the fundamental rights of gender-diverse people – especially from an intersectional perspective – and the profound injustice and violence to which they have been subjected under the 'current' system of categorization.

2 The Foetal Subject

Law, Gender and Embodiment

Michael Thomson

1. Introduction

Reference to embodiment is increasingly visible in legal scholarship, where it is assigned a number of meanings. At times it is employed descriptively to mean the fleshiness of the human condition, indistinguishable from reference to the body or corporeality. Elsewhere, it is used to signify something more than this fleshiness: in part, a challenge to the mind/body split that has haunted legal thought and practice. Finally, for a growing number of legal scholars, it refers to the experience of our corporeality at the intersection of discourses and institutions. While a theoretically richer account of our lives as 'bio-social'[1] beings is impacting on legal scholarship, what embodiment might mean with regard to the specific discourses and institutions of law and legal scholarship is only just beginning to be explored.[2] In response, this chapter sets out to clarify and develop a clear understanding of *legal embodiment*; that is, the particular place of law in processes and practices of embodiment. In doing so, it identifies the body as an important site where law and gender entwine in processes that construct legal subjects.

I would like to thank Chris Dietz, Beth Goldblatt, Isabel Karpin, Mitchell Travis and the volume editors for their insightful and constructive comments on earlier drafts of this chapter. I would also like to thank Ray Carr for his research assistance.

[1] E. Grabham, 'Bodily Integrity and the Surgical Management of Intersex' (2012) 18 *Body & Society* 1–26 at 3.

[2] See, for example, M. Thomson, 'A Tale of Two Bodies: The Male Body and Feminist Legal Theory', in M. Fineman (ed.), *Transcending the Boundaries of Law: Generations of Feminism and Legal Theory* (Oxford: Routledge, 2010), 143–156; M. Fox and M. Thomson, 'Bodily Integrity, Embodiment, and the Regulation of Parental Choice' (2017) 44 *Journal of Law & Society* 501–531; C. Dietz, 'Governing Legal Embodiment: On the Limits of Self-Declaration' (2018) 26 *Feminist Legal Studies* 185–204; M. Travis, 'The Vulnerability of Heterosexuality: Consent, Gender Deception and Embodiment' (2019) 28 *Social & Legal Studies* 303–326.

To fully articulate how we might understand legal embodiment, this chapter addresses changing legal understandings of the foetus – shifting jurisprudential 'fetal imaginings'[3] – and how this shapes the embodied reproductive body. This case study allows an exploration of the particularity of legal discourses and practices, and the need to centre gender in any analytical model focused on the body. Indeed, it starts from the premise that scientific, legal and other discourses that address the body are only intelligible in the context of historically specific understandings of gender.[4] As with the other contributions to this book, gender is positioned as a normative order that produces sex differences and their regulation. Thus, the focus is how, through the body, law and gender co-produce complex legal subjects, hierarchies and identities.[5]

My consideration of the foetal subject begins with the 'foetal heartbeat' bills that have become increasingly visible in the battle over abortion care in the United States. These proposals aim to outlaw abortion care once rhythmic electrical activity is medically detectable in the foetus. This takes place at around six weeks, a point at which many women do not know they are pregnant. This most recent attack on abortion care provides a site where we can examine the role of legal and scientific discourses in embodiment. To fully understand these socio-political processes, the contemporary legal propositions are placed alongside a socio-legal history of *quickening*. Quickening refers to the moment at which the pregnant woman first experiences foetal movement. Historically, it was taken to happen at around fourteen weeks. In the medieval period in Europe, the phenomenon of quickening became overlaid by ecclesiastical doctrine when it was identified with ensoulment: the point at which the soul entered the foetal body. During the nineteenth century in the United Kingdom, the United States, Canada and Australia, an emerging medical profession mobilized foetal identity as part of their professionalization projects.[6] Challenging church authority, and staking moral and epistemic

[3] S. Dubow, *Ourselves Unborn: A History of the Fetus in Modern America* (Oxford: Oxford University Press, 2011), 6.

[4] Thomson, 'A Tale of Two Bodies'.

[5] See the Introduction to this volume.

[6] For the United Kingdom, see A. McLaren, *Reproductive Rituals: The Perception of Fertility in Britain from the Sixteenth Century to the Nineteenth Century* (London: Methuen, 1984); J. Keown, *Abortion, Doctors, and the Law* (Cambridge: Cambridge University Press, 1988); M. Thomson, *Reproducing Narrative: Gender, Reproduction and Law* (Dartmouth: Dartmouth Publishing, 1998); M. Thomson, 'Abortion Law and Professional Boundaries'

claims, elite practitioners campaigned against abortion and the legal recognition of quickening, arguing that the foetus had moral status from conception. Competing discourses in the context of the emergence of professional society came to define foetal identity, moral value, and women's reproductive choices and experience. Contemporary legislation focusing on newly detectable electrical activity that indicates the earliest stages of cardiac development is the natural consequence of these early competing discourses that sought to secure epistemic authority by defining foetal identity. As Sara Dubow notes, 'Although multiple and competing fetuses have always coexisted, particular historical circumstances have generated and valorized different stories about the fetus.'[7]

The early disciplinary 'turf wars' that played out over who may define the ethical and legal status of foetal life demonstrate the dynamics of embodiment, both in its broad bio-social meaning and in the specific context of law. Law plays a key role in the construction of bodies. While much work on embodiment has focused on the life sciences, it is important to acknowledge and explore the role of other discourses – including law – in these processes, as 'bodies are produced through networks that fold and cut across science and other fields'.[8] Yet law is not an isolated discipline or practice. Rather, and as these discourses illustrate, law is a domain within which truth claims compete for legitimacy and authority – a process where different disciplinary discourses 'fold and cut across' each other.[9] Law also provides the space within which its own authority is challenged by other domains of knowledge (for example, medicine).[10] In terms of legal embodiment, truth claims that are adopted have enduring effects, as once particular understandings are embedded in law they become sticky:

(2013) 22 *Social & Legal Studies* 191–210. For the United States, see J. Mohr, *Abortion in America: The Origins and Evolution of National Policy, 1800–1900* (New York: Oxford University Press, 1978); K. Luker, *Abortion and the Politics of Motherhood* (Berkeley: University of California Press, 1985); R. Siegel, 'Reasoning from the Body: A Historical Perspective on Abortion Regulation and Questions of Equal Protection' (1992) 44 *Stanford Law Review* 261–381.

7 Dubow, *Ourselves Unborn*, 19.

8 C. Roberts, '"A Matter of Embodied Fact": Sex Hormones and the History of Bodies' (2012) 3 *Feminist Theory* 7–26.

9 Ibid.

10 See Thomson, 'Abortion Law and Professional Boundaries'; S. McGuinness and M. Thomson, 'Medicine and Abortion Law: Complicating the Reforming Professions' (2015) 23 *Medical Law Review* 177–199 at 177; S. McGuinness and M. Thomson, 'Conscience, Abortion, and Jurisdiction' (2020) 40 *Oxford Journal of Legal Studies* 819–845 at 819.

privileged, reified and difficult to dislodge. Thus, they play an important role in shaping women's embodied experience of pregnancy and reproductive choices. This exploration of the formation of a modern foetal identity provides the resources to help formulate a rich account of legal embodiment. The aim is to equip us with an analytical lens through which to understand how law and gender, entwined with other disciplinary discourses – most notably the biomedical sciences – shape bodies, embodiment and legal subjects. Starting from the proposition that we experience our embodiment at the intersection of institutional discourses and practices that are specific to time and place, it is proposed that legal embodiment is understood as the role of law in these processes, acknowledging the specificity of law as both a practice and a domain.

The argument is developed in three parts. The chapter starts with the development of approaches to embodiment in feminist scholarship and legal studies. It then considers the foetal subject and starts by addressing 'foetal heartbeat' laws. It locates these within a history of quickening, foregrounding the different disciplinary discourses and institutional interests and practices that compete and become entwined in the processes of defining foetal value, epistemic authority and women's reproductive choices. The medics' ultimate epistemological conquest profoundly shaped gender as the new foetal identity written into law marginalized women's experiences, knowledge and interests. Employing a historical perspective highlights the contingent nature of scientific claims; that is, their historical, social and cultural specificity. This is key to the understanding of legal embodiment developed in this chapter. This approach also acknowledges the importance of history in ethico-legal enquiry,[11] where it can counter the 'abstraction and a-contextuality' of law and the mainstream bioethics that often structures the contours of such work.[12] In the final section, I return to 'foetal heartbeat' legislation to further explore its embodied affects. I do this by addressing the wider context of 'speech and display' provisions and the materiality of rhetoric. Such work on rhetoric can add

[11] M. Thomson, 'Bioethics and Vulnerability: Recasting the Objects of Ethical Concern' (2018) 67 *Emory Law Journal* 1207–1233; McGuinness and Thomson, 'Medicine and Abortion Law'; McGuinness and Thomson, 'Conscience, Abortion, and Jurisdiction'. See also D. Wilson, 'What Can History Do for Bioethics' (2013) 27 *Bioethics* 215–223 at 215.

[12] J. Harrington, 'Time and Space in Medical Law: Building on Valverde's Chronotopes of Law' (2015) 23 *Feminist Legal Studies* 361–367 at 362; Wilson, 'What Can History Do for Bioethics'; McGuinness and Thomson, 'Conscience, Abortion, and Jurisdiction'.

to our understanding of legal embodiment. Conversely, embodiment theory can enrich our understanding of what it means to claim that rhetoric has material consequences.

2. Embodiment

A. The Body and Embodiment in Feminist Theory

While the political and social consequences of differential male and female embodiment provided an important focus for first- and second-wave feminists, the body of their analysis was 'natural' and pre-discursive. Post-structuralist and postmodern feminists, by contrast, have frequently focused on the discursive construction of the body. These scholars have examined the disciplining and production of women's bodies, via gender-normative ideals and (self-)surveillance, in particular through health, bio-medicine, exercise, dieting and fashion.[13] This scholarship points to the ways that biomedical or health regimes and popular culture produce the bodies they seek to regulate.[14] Judith Butler, in particular, challenges the notion that one could ever have access to a pre-discursive biological body. Rather, she argues that descriptions or images of the biological/anatomical body are inherently productive, playing a role in performatively materializing specific (sexed) bodies.[15] These post-structuralist accounts all speak to the importance of social structures, institutions and power relations in the experience of gendered embodiment and a need to deconstruct or reimagine gender norms. The biological functioning of the body itself, however, does not typically play a role in this work. Rather, as Margrit Shildrick states, 'Corporeality is just another construct, and sexual difference is no more stable than gender difference.'[16]

Feminist phenomenologists have focused on the lived body, describing the ways that patriarchal social structures shape lived bodily experiences

[13] See, for example, S. Bordo, *Unbearable Weight: Feminism, Western Culture, and the Body* (Berkeley: University of California Press, 2004); S. L. Bartky, *Femininity and Domination: Studies in the Phenomenology of Oppression* (New York: Routledge, 2015).

[14] See, for example, M. Shildrick, *Leaky Bodies and Boundaries: Feminism, Postmodernism and (Bio)Ethics* (London: Psychology Press, 1997).

[15] J. Butler, *Bodies That Matter: On the Discursive Limits of 'Sex'* (London: Psychology Press, 1993).

[16] Shildrick, *Leaky Bodies and Boundaries*, 175.

of women, while also valorizing the critical potential of descriptions of women's embodiment.[17] Moira Gatens, for example, directs attention to *bodily imaginaries* as they connect to embodiment, a relationship that is central to the concept of legal embodiment articulated in this chapter. Gatens stresses that it is bodily imaginaries – including those generated in legal discourse and practice – that structures lived experience. An imaginary body, Gatens argues, is 'socially and historically specific in that it is constructed by: a shared language; the shared psychical significance and privileging of various zones of the body (for example, the mouth, the anus, the genitals); and common institutional practices and discourses (for example, medical, juridical and educational) which act on and through the body'.[18] These socially and historically contingent imaginary bodies interrelate with material bodily differences, so that the body itself confirms these expectations of difference expressed in the social order.[19] For Elizabeth Grosz, as for Gatens, sexual bodily differences are constitutive of existence and social relations.[20] Material bodies, nonetheless, cannot be separated from their discursive and social context. Grosz emphasizes the interconnections between the biological (physiological) body, subjectivity and social structures. Experience of the body is neither given completely in itself nor reducible to the social; rather, embodiment requires completion in interaction with the psyche and the world. The 'openness' of the body allows it to respond to the 'social meanings attributed to the body in its concrete historical, social, and cultural particularity'.[21] The account of legal embodiment developed here addresses the role of legal discourse in its particularity. This is meant both in the sense of what is particular to law and legal systems, as well as recognizing the specificity of the changing discourses that play out in legal domains. In *Volatile Bodies*, Grosz stresses that we must be attentive to the ways in which biological sexual difference both precedes and interacts with the social: how women and men are both

[17] See, for example, I. M. Young, *On Female Body Experience: 'Throwing Like a Girl' and Other Essays* (New York: Oxford University Press, 2005), 10.

[18] M. Gatens, *Imaginary Bodies: Ethics, Power and Corporeality* (London: Routledge, 2013), 12. See also G. Weiss, *Body Images: Embodiment as Intercorporeality* (New York: Routledge, 2013).

[19] Gatens, *Imaginary Bodies*, 10.

[20] E. A. Grosz, *Volatile Bodies: Toward a Corporeal Feminism* (St Leonards: Allen & Unwin, 1994).

[21] Ibid., 27.

differently constituted (have different physiological/biological potentialities) and are constituted differently (for example, positioned differently in relation to bodily imaginaries and social structures, and subject to different processes of bodily disciplining).[22] Changing biomedical and legal claims regarding the foetus illustrates this process and the importance of law and legal embodiment within it.

While Grosz and other feminists have focused on the phenomenology of the *lived* body, Donna Haraway has long pointed to the ways that bodies and body parts (cells, embryos, organs and so forth) are socially and materially constructed iteratively within practices of science and technology, which are themselves thoroughly socially and historically inflected yet determinedly material.[23] As Sarah Franklin writes, Haraway demonstrates how it is not possible for 'scientific understandings to escape the interpretive devices, taxonomic conventions or situated and historically specific understandings of how we know anything at all'.[24] Feminist science studies scholars, anthropologists, sociologists and socio-legal scholars have taken up the mantle of analysing the specificities of how (female) bodies and body parts are produced by particular contemporary or historical cultures and scientific practices. As Margrit Shildrick explains:

> The Renaissance anatomists ... who saw the female reproductive organs as homologous to male genitalia, were neither unobservant nor simply bad scientists. The 'truth' they expressed was the truth of their age. This relationship between cultural values and constructions of the body, as part of what Foucault would call the power/knowledge regime, is a symbiotic one.[25]

We continue to see this as body parts have become increasingly isolated, detachable and distributed. Today's Renaissance anatomists might well be those working in the postgenomic field of environmental or social epigenetics. Here, gender is fundamentally shaping the nature and design of laboratory experiments. These experiments then confirm these gendered

[22] Ibid.

[23] D. J. Haraway, *Simians, Cyborgs, and Women: The Reinvention of Nature* (New York: Routledge, 1991).

[24] S. Franklin, 'The Cyborg Embryo: Our Path to Transbiology' (2006) 23 *Theory Culture Society* 167–187 at 178.

[25] Shildrick, *Leaky Bodies and Boundaries*, 15.

assumptions and become embedded in the scientific claims regarding epigenetic processes and responsibilities that emerge.[26] This extends to the (epi)genetic level the processes whereby bodily differences are always determined in the pre-existing context of gender and, in turn, are used to justify gendered inequalities.[27]

B. Embodiment Theory in Law

It has been argued that socio-legal scholars turned to embodiment in an attempt to recuperate 'the body' in legal studies, where it has often played second fiddle to 'the mind' as the object of concern. Ruth Fletcher argues that engagement with the concept 'emerged from a desire to avoid mind/ body dichotomies and to capture the interactive process by which mind and body respond to each other in producing knowledge'.[28] Those legal scholars who were at the forefront of explorations in embodiment theory sought to make sense of this new analytical frame, map nascent socio-legal work, and explore the implications for future legal scholarship.[29] For these scholars, embodiment directs us to attend to how regulation genders the body but also enables us to value the body as the means by which we move through and experience the material world.[30] In this vein, Marie Fox and Therese Murphy have argued that engaging embodiment as an analytical frame mandates 'a broader focus on lived experience and the question of how we inhabit and experience the world through our bodies'.[31] They also highlight the need to engage with the specific power and reach of law, arguing that 'embodiment directs attention to which

[26] S. Lewis and M. Thomson, 'Social Bodies and Social Justice' (2019) 15 *International Journal of Law in Context* 344–361.

[27] As Elizabeth Grosz writes, 'Women's corporeal specificity is used to explain and justify the different (read: unequal) social positions and cognitive abilities of the two sexes. By implication, women's bodies are presumed to be incapable of men's achievements, being weaker, more prone to (hormonal) irregularities, intrusions, and unpredictabilities.' Grosz, *Volatile Bodies*.

[28] R. Fletcher, 'Embodied Practices' (2009) 17 *Feminist Legal Studies* 315–318 at 316–317.

[29] R. Fletcher, M. Fox and J. McCandless, 'Legal Embodiment: Analysing the Body of Healthcare Law' (2008) 16 *Medical Law Review* 321–345 at 335.

[30] Ibid., 321.

[31] M. Fox and T. Murphy, 'The Body, Bodies and Embodiment: Feminist Legal Engagement with Health', in M. Davies and V. E. Munro (eds.), *The Ashgate Research Companion to Feminist Legal Theory* (London: Routledge 2013), 249–268 at 260.

bodies, and which embodied choices, law values and validates ... [I]t requires us to think through the corporeal consequences of legal decision making'.[32]

A number of the themes that can be discerned in this early work have been explored in work I conducted with Marie Fox to develop the concept of embodied integrity.[33] This intervention aims to explain why bodily integrity is increasingly relied upon and to clarify what we really seek to protect when we invoke this fundamental right.[34] In doing so, it provides a robust theoretical conception of this value. The concept of embodied integrity is underpinned by the bio-social body and an understanding that interventions on the body are biographical; that is, they contain the potential to shape future life. Such bodily changes include non-consensual interventions (such as sterilization and genital cutting performed on male and female minors and those born with intersex variations), work done on the adult body as part of the reflexive project of self-identity (for example, cosmetic and modification procedures) or the exercise of reproductive choice.[35] Thus, the body is conceived 'not as an *object* but as an *event*',[36] with bodily integrity a continual process rather than a static state.[37]

The starting point for this work was an exploration of how legal engagement with traditional notions of bodily integrity have been gendered.[38] Thus, while female genital cutting is frequently identified as an infringement of bodily integrity and a human rights abuse, male genital cutting is identified as a parental and religious freedom and invoking bodily integrity is highly controversial.[39] While the history and meaning

[32] Ibid.

[33] M. Fox and M. Thomson, 'Bodily Integrity, Embodiment, and the Regulation of Parental Choice' (2017) 44 *Journal of Law and Society* 501–531; M. Fox, M. Thomson and J. Warburton, 'Non-Therapeutic Male Genital Cutting and Harm: Law, Policy, and Evidence from UK Hospitals' (2019) 33 *Bioethics* 467–474; M. Fox, M. Thomson and J. Warburton 'Embodied Integrity, Shaping Surgeries, and the Profoundly Disabled Child', in C. Dietz, M. Travis and M. Thomson (eds.), *A Jurisprudence of the Body* (Cham: Palgrave, 2020).

[34] Fox and Thomson, 'Bodily Integrity, Embodiment, and the Regulation of Parental Choice'.

[35] A. Giddens, *Modernity and Self Identity* (Cambridge: Polity Press, 1991).

[36] S. Budgeon, 'Identity as an Embodied Event' (2003) 9 *Body & Society* 35–55 at 36.

[37] D. Cornell, *The Imaginary Domain: Abortion, Pornography and Sexual Harassment* (New York: Routledge 1995).

[38] Fox and Thomson, 'Bodily Integrity, Embodiment, and the Regulation of Parental Choice'.

[39] Bodily integrity was recognized in the controversial case in Cologne in 2012: Landgericht Koln (Cologne District Court), Judgment on 7 May [2012] No. 151 Ns 169/11. For discussions of this case and the response of the German government, see G. B. Levey, 'Thinking

of different genital cutting practices is complex and must be acknowledged, it is clear that in responding to genital cutting, law and gender reinforce one another narrating and constituting very different legal subjects. This takes place notwithstanding the fact that in many instances the procedures are equally invasive and involve the loss of analogous tissues.[40] Thus, law in the United Kingdom prohibits all cutting of female genitals whether the individual is a child or adult. In this, adult women are denied the ability to exercise their autonomy over genital cutting in a way that is seen in few other areas. At the same time, no jurisdiction currently outlaws the cutting of male genitals, which – conversely – is a failure to protect male children in a way seen with no other non-therapeutic intervention of this order.[41] Here we see familiar gender tropes intertwining with law, and indeed frequently bolstered by biomedical knowledge claims. Thus, women need higher levels of surveillance and protection, and are – at times – deemed incapable of decision-making regarding their own bodies. We see this elsewhere in the contexts of sex and reproduction, including abortion care, as discussed below. Men's bodies, in contrast, are safe, bounded, invulnerable.[42] Pain is a marginal concern and may, in fact, be constitutive of a robust masculinity.[43] Men exercise dominion over their bodies; replaying a tenacious and gendered mind/body split. Thus, law and gender scaffold each other, and result in different responses to risk, embodied choices and legal subjects. This chimes with Grosz's assertion that women and men are both *differently constituted* (physiological and biological) and *constituted differently* (positioned differently in relation to social structures and processes of bodily disciplining).[44]

about Infant Male Circumcision after the Cologne Court Decision' (2013) 3 *Global Discourse* 326–331; S. R. Munzer, 'Secularization, Anti-Minority Sentiment, and Cultural Norms in the German Circumcision Controversy' (2015) 37 *University of Pennsylvania Journal of International Law* 503–582.

40 Fox and Thomson, 'Bodily Integrity, Embodiment, and the Regulation of Parental Choice'; B. Earp, J. Hendry and M. Thomson, 'Reason and Paradox in Medical and Family Law: Shaping Children's Bodies' (2017) 25 *Medical Law Review* 604–627.

41 Some may contend that ear piercing or otoplasty (ear pinning) are analogous and lawful but this would fail to account for the functional and erogenous nature of the tissue removed in male genital cutting and the risks involved.

42 N. Naffine, 'The Body Bag', in N. Naffine and R. Owens (eds.), *Sexing the Subject of Law* (London: Law Book Company, 1997); M. Thomson, *Endowed: Regulating the Male Sexed Body* (London: Routledge, 2007).

43 Naffine, 'The Body Bag'; Thomson, *Endowed.*

44 Grosz, *Volatile Bodies.*

Work that has sought to track and develop the emerging work on embodiment in legal studies is important. It maps where we have been and the implications of embodiment theory for legal studies. Yet it is questionable the degree to which this work has detailed a specifically *legal* embodiment or reflect the dynamic and affective nature of embodiment detailed by Gatens, or captured by Rosemary Garland-Thomson when she describes embodiment as the 'dynamic encounter between flesh and the world'.[45] However, two more recent interventions in the development of legal thinking around embodiment provide a stronger focus on the institutional and affective dimensions of embodiment. Both attend to questions of the relationship between law, gender and the body.

In his response to a contemporary re-emergence of law's concern with 'deception as to gender', Mitch Travis defines embodiment as 'the material experience of the body and its relationships with both discourse and institutions'.[46] Travis underscores the importance of attending to institutions, arguing that they 'not only shape the material experience of the subject but also structure the possibilities, potential and emergence of our corporeal selves ... [I]nstitutions contribute to, create and construct our embodiment and restrict the ways in which bodies and identities can be understood'.[47]

Drawing on his work on intersex and non-normative embodiment,[48] Travis explores the ways in which 'law, medicine, culture and society' determine our bodies and embodied experiences. This is particularly apparent with those whose corporeality 'fall[s] outside of traditional sex or gender categories as it highlights the difficulties in decoupling material experiences from their legal and medical contexts'.[49] Reference to medicine is important and Travis's focus on 'institutions' means we do not privilege law over other domains. This is particularly important when we acknowledge the role of medicine and the biomedical sciences in the

[45] R. Garland-Thomson, 'Misfits: A Feminist Materialist Disability Concept' (2011) 26 *Hypatia* 591–609.

[46] Travis, 'The Vulnerability of Heterosexuality'. [47] Ibid., 323.

[48] F. Garland and M. Travis, 'Legislating Intersex Equality: Building the Resilience of Intersex People through Law' (2018) 38 *Legal Studies* 587–606; M. Travis, 'Accommodating Intersexuality in European Union Anti-Discrimination Law' (2015) 21 *European Law Journal* 180–199; M. Travis, 'Non-Normative Bodies, Rationality, and Legal Personhood' (2014) 22 *Medical Law Review* 526–547.

[49] Travis, 'The Vulnerability of Heterosexuality', 306.

processes of embodiment. As Margaret Lock and Vinh-Kim Nguyen assert, biological facts 'are technophenomena that constitute only a partial view of reality',[50] yet they shape 'how the self is made "real"'.[51] Thus, assemblages of biomedical, medico-legal and other discourses provide for the emergence of particular bodies and identities.

While Travis encourages us to focus on the role of institutions in processes of embodiment, Chris Dietz narrows this to law without losing sight of the importance of this wider framing. Dietz's consideration of embodiment starts by acknowledging that this focus has moved us 'beyond the question of how bodies are produced by discourse, to consider affective aspects of regulation'.[52] He articulates legal embodiment in the following terms: 'If embodiment is understood as the moment when ontology (what I am) meets epistemology (how I identify and am identified), [legal embodiment] addresses the specifically institutional effects of such processes.'[53] As he continues, when institutional regulations coalesce, they have a significant impact on the practices of embodiment, and, echoing Garland-Thomson's 'dynamic encounter',[54] this process is iterative. So, for Dietz, legal embodiment is an 'ongoing process which produces normative bodies and behaviours, and shapes the conditions and possibilities for embodied resistance'.[55] This chimes with Budgeon's argument that the body is not a representational object but rather an event, emerging 'within the context of a multiplicity of practices and regimes'.[56]

The acknowledgement in embodiment theory of the importance of institutions must address the specificity of law, in the same way that attention has been directed towards biomedical discourses.[57] While feminist and other critical literatures have long recognized the limits of law,[58] it nevertheless has particular authority and power. It defines the legitimate and illegitimate and has the power to authorize other institutions, conferring authority and jurisdiction.[59] This requires that we pay particular attention

[50] M. Lock and V. Nguyen, *An Anthropology of Biomedicine* (Hoboken, NJ: John Wiley & Sons, 2018), 109.
[51] Ibid., 284. [52] Dietz, 'Governing Legal Embodiment', 87. [53] Ibid., 186. [54] Ibid.
[55] Ibid., 186–187. [56] Budgeon, 'Identity as an Embodied Event', 52.
[57] Lock and Nguyen, *An Anthropology of Biomedicine.*
[58] See, for example, C. Smart, *Feminism and the Power of Law* (New York: Routledge, 1989).
[59] McGuinness and Thomson, 'Conscience, Abortion, and Jurisdiction'.

to the discourses that are played out in the legal domain, as competing truth claims are directly tied to claims to power.

The more recent contributions to legal literature on embodiment direct us to consider institutional and affective dimensions. They move us 'beyond the discursive realm to address how governing processes saturate bodies with meaning' and its affect.[60] In building upon this, I bring this institutional focus together with attention to the historical, social and cultural specificity and contingency of knowledge claims. I propose that *legal embodiment* be understood as the role that legal discourses and practices play, when we experience our embodiment at the intersection of discourses and institutional practices that are specific to time and place. I join the growing calls for methods from history, anthropology, science and technology studies, and critical rhetorical studies to have a more prominent place in health law,[61] where the body is too often left uncontested and unchallenged 'in the "natural" realm of biology'.[62] Understanding and challenging the socio-political foundations of embodiment requires that the 'natural' realm be subject to critical scrutiny, particularly in addressing how gender becomes naturalized within biological and biomedical discourses which then become embedded in law. As Sarah Franklin notes in response to Donna Haraway's early work on embryology, and foreshadowing the section that follows, 'we cannot even look at the embryo – objectively, scientifically, in the laboratory, under a microscope – without seeing it through the lens of our own, pre-fabricated, culturally inherited, ubiquitous, constitutive, real and inescapable frames of reference'.[63]

As feminist science and technology scholars and others have demonstrated time and again, these 'inescapable frames of reference' include gender. Acknowledging the foetus as a site where gender as a normative order is enacted, I turn next to the foetal subject, emphasizing the shifting and contested claims made within the legal domain and the implications of

[60] Dietz, 'Governing Legal Embodiment', 194.

[61] Fox and Murphy, 'The Body, Bodies and Embodiment'; J. Edwards and M. Thomson, 'Provincialising the Clitoris', in M. Jacob and A. Kirkland (eds.), *Research Handbook on Socio-Legal Studies, Medicine and Health* (Cheltenham: Edward Elgar, 2020).

[62] Dietz, 'Governing Legal Embodiment', 198–199, citations omitted.

[63] S. Franklin, 'The Cyborg Embryo: Our Path to Transbiology' (2006) 23 *Theory Culture Society* 167–187 at 178.

these. While feminist legal scholars have done much to interrogate and map the foetuses of the legal imagination,[64] the focus here, rather, are the discursive processes that enable law to imagine and enact the foetus in different ways.

3. The Foetal Subject

A. 'Foetal Heartbeat' Laws

At the time this chapter was begun, the focus of US abortion politics was Georgia. In May 2019 Governor Brian Kemp signed into law one of the most restrictive abortion provisions in the United States. Georgia House Bill 481, the Living Infants Fairness and Equality (LIFE) Act, prohibited the termination of a pregnancy once a 'foetal heartbeat' was medically detectable, taken to be six weeks from conception.[65] Although Georgia was the fourth state that year to introduce such legislation – after Kentucky, Mississippi and Ohio – it attracted greater media attention. While 'foetal heartbeat' laws have recently attracted heightened attention, they first emerged in 2011 when Ohio House Bill 125 was introduced but failed to pass.[66] At the time of Kemp's signing, at least sixteen states were

[64] See, for example, I. Karpin, 'The Uncanny Embryos: Legal Limits to the Human and Reproduction without Women' (2006) 28 *Sydney Law Review* 599–623; I Karpin, 'Taking Care of the Health of the Preconceived Embryos or Constructing Legal Harm', in J. Nisker, F. Baylis, I. Karpin, C. McLeod and R. Mykitiuk (eds.), *The 'Healthy' Embryo: Social, Biomedical, Legal and Philosophical Perspectives* (Cambridge: Cambridge University Press, 2010); I. Karpin, 'The Legal and Relational Identity of the "Not-Yet" Generation' (2012) 4 *Law, Innovation and Technology* 122–143; S. McGuinness, 'The Construction of the Embryo and Implications for Law', in M. Quigley, S. Chan and J. Harris (eds.), *Stem Cells: New Frontiers in Science and Ethics* (Singapore: World Scientific Publishing Co., 2015); M. Fox and S. McGuinness, 'The Politics of Muddling Through: Categorising Embryos', in C. Stanton, A.-M. Farrell, S. Devanney and A. Mullock (eds.), *Pioneering Healthcare Law: Essays in Honour of the Work of Margaret Brazier* (New York: Routledge, 2016).

[65] For a detailed discussion of the Bill and its political and legal context, see B. A. Sizemore, 'Under Kemp's Eye: Analyzing the Constitutionality of the Heartbeat Restriction in Georgia's LIFE Act and Its Potential Impact on Abortion Law' (2019) 71 *Mercer Law Review* 417–442.

[66] A similar provision, House Bill 248 was introduced in 2013, but failed on the House floor in December 2014. Ohio's third attempt was successful in 2019.

considering similar restrictions on abortion care.[67] The Georgia bill was due to come into effect on 1 January 2020. It was temporarily blocked by a federal judge on 1 October 2019, and declared unconstitutional on 13 July 2020.[68] By this date, almost 100 'foetal heartbeat' laws had been introduced to legislatures in twenty-five states.[69]

By the time this collection was moving towards production, Texas and its 'foetal heartbeat' law – Senate Bill 8 – was the focus. Similar in many regards, Texas SB 8 offered the novel addition that rather than authorize state officials to enforce the Act, it 'deputizes ordinary citizens as bounty hunters'.[70] Under this scheme, citizens can recover damages of $10,000 plus legal costs by suing anyone who provides an abortion in contravention of the Act, 'aids or abets' such a termination, or intends to do so. Both the Georgia and Texas legislation were introduced notwithstanding that all other 'foetal heartbeat' legislation has been deemed unconstitutional. These rulings recognize that proscribing abortion care before the third trimester is in direct contravention of the constitutional protections provided by *Roe* v. *Wade*[71] and *Planned Parenthood* v. *Casey*.[72] Specifically, in *Roe*, the Supreme Court recognized viability as the earliest point at which a state's interest in foetal life may permit an absolute prohibition on the performance of an abortion.[73] In *Casey* in 1992, the court upheld Roe, restating that a state may not prohibit a woman 'from making the ultimate decision to terminate her pregnancy before viability'.[74] Nevertheless, the court asserted that states have a legitimate interest before viability in protecting the health of the woman and the life of the foetus, and this may justify regulations that do not place an undue burden on a woman's ability to obtain abortion care.[75] An 'undue burden' exists if the purpose or

[67] D. P. Evans and S. Narasimhan, 'A Narrative Analysis of Anti-Abortion Testimony and Legislative Debate Relating to Georgia's Fetal "Heartbeat" Abortion Ban' (2020) 28 *Sexual and Reproductive Health Matters* 1–17 at 2.

[68] 'US Judge Blocks Georgia Abortion Ban', *The Guardian*, 14 July 2020, www.theguardian.com/us-news/2020/jul/13/us-judge-blocks-georgia-abortion-ban.

[69] Evans and Narasimhan, 'A Narrative Analysis of Anti-Abortion Testimony'.

[70] *United States* v. *Texas* 595 US (2021), at 2.

[71] *Roe* v. *Wade* 410 US 113 (1973).

[72] *Planned Parenthood* v. *Casey* 505 US 833 (1992).

[73] The court indicated that viability 'is usually placed at about seven months (28 weeks) but may occur earlier, even at 24 weeks'. *Roe* v. *Wade* at 160.

[74] *Planned Parenthood* v. *Casey* at 879.

[75] The right of states identified in *Casey* to regulate to protect the health of the woman and the foetus before viability has resulted in a significant number of Targeted Regulation of Abortion Providers (TRAP) laws. These seek to indirectly limit access to abortion through

effect of a regulation is 'to place a substantial obstacle in the path of a woman seeking an abortion before the fetus attains viability'.[76] Before viability, 'the state's interests are not strong enough to support a prohibition of abortion'.[77] This has been upheld in a number of decisions since *Casey*,[78] including in response to 'foetal heartbeat' legislation. In *EMW Women's Surgical Center* v. *Beshear*, for example, the federal district court held the Kentucky 'foetal heartbeat' law unconstitutional, noting that the Supreme Court in *Casey* 'stated in no uncertain terms that regardless of whether exceptions are made for particular circumstances, a State may not prohibit any woman from making the ultimate decision to terminate her pregnancy before viability'.[79]

The proliferation of such legislative interventions has been motivated in part by the hope that one will lead to a Supreme Court reconsideration of *Roe* and *Casey*. The writing of deliberately unconstitutional bills accelerated in response to the appointment of Justices Brett Kavanaugh and Amy Coney Barrett to the Supreme Court. Georgia Governor Kemp at a signing ceremony at the State Capitol stated that his administration was preparing for a court fight: 'Our job is to do what is right, not what is easy. We are called to be strong and courageous, and we will not back down.'[80]

regulation. They have resulted in the closure of clinics across the United States. In 2019, six states had only one clinic offering abortion care. W. Arey, 'Web Roundup: Abortion Bans, Heartbeat Bills and the Future of Roe v Wade', *Somatosphere*, 28 June 2019, http://somatosphere.net/2019/web-roundup-abortion-bans-heartbeat-bills-and-the-future-of-roe-v-wade.html/

[76] *Planned Parenthood* v. *Casey* at 925. [77] Ibid.

[78] 'Beginning in 2013, the US Courts of Appeals for the Eighth and Ninth Circuits have respectively invalidated state laws in Arizona, Arkansas, Idaho, and North Dakota prohibiting the performance of an abortion once a fetus has reached a gestational age younger than 24 weeks. In their decisions, the two appellate courts have cited the *Casey* plurality's determination that a state may not prohibit a woman from having an abortion before a fetus attains viability'. J. O. Shimabukuro, 'Reviewing Recently Enacted State Abortion Laws and Resulting Litigation', Congressional Research Service: Legal Sidebar, 6 September 2019, p. 2. Thus, in *McCormack* v. *Herzog* the Ninth Circuit struck down Idaho's Pain-Capable Unborn Child Protection Act, which prohibited terminations after a gestational age of twenty weeks. The statute applied regardless of viability: '[T]he broader effect of the statute is a categorical ban on all actions between twenty weeks gestational age and viability. This is contrary to the Court's central holding in *Casey* that a woman has the right to "choose to have an abortion before viability and to obtain it without undue interference from the State".'

[79] *EMW Women's Surgical Center* v. *Beshear* 920 F.3d 421 (6th Cir. 2019).

[80] P. Mazzei and A. Binder, 'Georgia Governor Signs "Fetal Heartbeat" Abortion Law', *The New York Times*, 7 May 2019.

Similarly, Alabama introduced a bill that would ban abortion outright. House Bill 314, approved by the State House of Representatives, provided no exemption for rape or incest and a doctor providing such health care would in most instances face up to ninety-nine years in prison. State Representative Rich Wingo, a supporter of the bill, stated: 'House Bill 314 goes directly after Roe. We're trying to keep the bill as clean and direct so there's not any ambiguity.'[81]

Texas SB 8 is similarly written to drive a challenge to a Supreme Court that has become more critical of *Roe* v. *Wade*. This is seen not only in its 'near categorical ban' on abortion care after six weeks, but also its attempt to restrict constitutional and procedural defences by moving enforcement from state officials to private citizens. On 1 September 2021 – the day SB 8 took effect – and in response to an action led by the Center for Reproductive Rights, the Supreme Court refused to enjoin the Act, citing 'complex and novel' procedural questions about whether it had authority to do so.[82] On 22 October, and following a challenge by the Department of Justice, it agreed to hear the case on 1 November 2021 – a significantly expedited timeframe – but again refused to block the application of the legislation until the case was heard.[83] As Justice Sotomayor noted in dissenting from the decision to refuse such action in the face of a 'patently unconstitutional' provision:

> There is no dispute that under this court's precedents, women have a constitutional right to seek abortion care prior to viability ... S.B.8 was created to frustrate that right by raising seemingly novel procedural issues, and it has had precisely that effect. Under such unique circumstances, the equities plainly favour administrative relief while this Court sorts out these issues.[84]

The impact has been 'catastrophic'. As Sotomayor noted in her dissent, 'the State (empowered by this Court's inaction) has so thoroughly chilled the exercise of the right recognised in *Roe* as to nearly suspend it within its borders and strain access to it in other States'.[85] The Supreme Court will hear both cases together. A challenge to legislation in Mississippi that bans abortion after fifteen weeks is also scheduled to be heard in December.[86]

[81] Ibid.

[82] *Whole Woman's Health* v. *Jackson* 594 US (2021). See also https://reproductiverights.org/case/texas-abortion-ban-whole-womans-health-jackson/.

[83] *United States* v. *Texas* (2021). [84] Ibid., 7. [85] Ibid., 6.

[86] *Dobbs* v. *Jackson Women's Health Organization* (2020) 19-1392.

Many expect the Supreme Court to overturn or restrict *Roe* v. *Wade*. It is believed that this would lead to restrictive legislation in more than half of states. Overturning *Roe* would see 'trigger' legislation in twelve states come into effect, banning abortion outright.[87] These developments would have a devastating effect on reproductive rights and justice in the United States, with effects felt further afield. While this is an extraordinarily important moment for abortion law and women's rights in the United States, the focus here is on the embodied effects of these legislative discourses. These effects will be felt regardless of the ultimate deliberations of the Supreme Court. With the legislative interventions framed around 'foetal heartbeat', there is a clear aim to disrupt thinking around foetal viability and personhood. While this is directed at restricting legal access to essential health care, it should also be understood in the context of an entangling of biological matter with discourses and institutional practices that generate embodied subjects. To better understand this and what is at stake, I turn now to the early origins of our modern foetal identity.

B. A Socio-Legal History of Quickening

In her discussion of the 'foetal heartbeat' laws, Lois Shepherd argues that they will have an impact because they are 'cloaked in the language of science and medicine, replete with references to esteemed professional organizations and widely accepted laws'.[88] Shepherd is correct to highlight the potential force and impact of this co-mingling of scientific claims, legal propositions and professional authority – a constellation now explored with an earlier mixing of human reproductive material and biomedical claims. This section details the emergence of medical knowledge claims regarding the beginning of life, providing a socio-legal history of the life and death of quickening. The wider social history of quickening is long and contested.[89] The focus here is limited to law, specifically how medicine came to define foetal identity in law 'through

[87] https://maps.reproductiverights.org/what-if-roe-fell

[88] L. Shepherd, 'Fetal Heartbeat Bill Gets the Science and the Law Wrong' *Jurist*, 21 March 2019.

[89] For an account of this longer history, see M. S. Scott, 'Quickening in the Common Law: The Legal Precedent *Roe* Attempted and Failed to Use' (1996) 1 *Michigan Law & Policy Review* 199–268.

the intersection of technique and ideology'.[90] This was motivated, in part, by the desire of elite members of the profession to secure control over the domain of health by expelling competing health providers. Through this, biomedicine came to define the social and legal truth of foetal life. This has shaped public discourse, women's reproductive choices, embodied experiences and gender.

The origins of the quickening doctrine sit with Aristotle, who claimed that life began when sperm was nourished by the woman's uterine blood. Early life – compared to a wakening seed – was supported by a vegetative soul. This was replaced by a 'sensitive' soul that allowed animal life to begin, and finally the 'rational' soul: 'the life-principle that enables matter to become a man in actuality'.[91] For Aristotle, quickening happened for male foetuses at around forty days, but not until eighty days for females. The entry of the rational soul animated the foetus, resulting in movement or quickening. While evident in Catholic teaching since at least the third century, quickening was confirmed as Catholic dogma in 1312, with the Council of Vienne adopting St Thomas Aquinas' endorsement of Aristotle's theory.[92] While Aquinas accepted the theory of 'delayed hominization',[93] he claimed that ensoulment happened for both sexes at around forty days. Thus, for ecclesiastical doctrine and law, woman's first experience of foetal movement denoted the entry of the soul.[94] As such, quickening can be understood as an overlay by natural philosophy and then ecclesiastical doctrine of what had previously structured women's experience of pregnancy; an earlier claim to truth. Aquinas' position was adopted by European common law courts and subsequently exported to colonial jurisdictions, such as the United States and Australia,[95] by British colonial law. Few records exist of prosecutions,[96] with the crime regarded as a matter for the ecclesiastical courts because of its association with magic

90 Dubow, *Ourselves Unborn.*

91 N. M. Ford, *When Did I Begin? Conception of the Human Individual in History, Philosophy and Science* (Cambridge: Cambridge University Press, 1988), 35.

92 Dubow, *Ourselves Unborn.* 93 Ibid.

94 This was widely taken to happen at fourteen weeks after conception.

95 L. Featherstone, 'Becoming a Baby? The Foetus in Late Nineteenth-Century Australia' (2008) 23 *Australian Feminist Studies* 451–465 at 451.

96 There is, however, reliance on the quickening doctrine in tort cases where pregnant women brought actions against people who assaulted them, causing the loss of the foetus. Spivak argues that it is these cases that have led to some erroneous statements regarding the status of abortion in law in the medieval and early modern periods. See C. Spivak, 'To "Bring

and sorcery.[97] Nevertheless, Aristotle's theory remained largely unchallenged for nearly 2,000 years.[98]

Historical accounts of the changing social and legal status of abortion are, of course, political interventions. While there are rare claims that abortion has always been a significant concern of the criminal law,[99] the prevailing view is that before the beginning of the nineteenth century abortion was a crime – a common-law misdemeanour – only if it took place after quickening.[100] Such accounts wrestle with both the complexity of thought[101] and legal systems[102] in the medieval and early modern periods to conclude that the quickening doctrine was 'long embedded in the common law'.[103] Thus, writing in the thirteenth century – the point at which laws concerning pregnancy and childbirth became more prevalent[104] – Henry de Bracton stated that in English common law: 'If there

Down the Flowers": The Cultural Context of Abortion Law in Early Modern England' (2007) 14 *William and Mary Journal of Women and the Law* 107–151.

97 D.S. Davies, 'The Law of Abortion and Necessity' (1938) 2 *Modern Law Review* 126–138 at 132; B. Dickens, *Abortion and the Law* (Bristol: MacGibbon and Kee, 1966).

98 C. Cameron and R. Williamson, 'In the World of Dolly, When Does a Human Embryo Acquire Respect?' (2005) 31 *Journal of Medical Ethics* 215–220 at 215.

99 See, for example, J. W. Dellapenna, *Dispelling the Myths of Abortion History* (Durham, NC: Carolina Academic Press, 2006). Joseph Dellapenna's book challenges the historical account of abortion in American law that is articulated by Justice Blackmun in *Roe v. Wade* (1973). Dellapenna's account is robustly challenged by Spivak, 'To "Bring Down the Flowers"'.

100 'The quickening doctrine itself appears to have entered the British common law tradition by way of the tangled disputes of medieval theologians over whether or not an impregnated ovum possessed a soul. The upshot was that . . . women in 1800 were legally free to attempt to terminate a condition that might turn out to have been a pregnancy until the existence of that pregnancy was incontrovertibly confirmed by the perception of fetal movement.' Mohr, *Abortion in America*, 4. For an account of the later historical period, see R. Solinger, *The Abortionist: A Woman against the Law* (Berkeley: University of California Press, 1994).

101 For an account of differing attitudes to abortion during the medieval periods see L. Harris, 'Old Ideas for a New Debate: Medieval and Modern Attitudes to Abortion' (2017) 53 *Medieval Feminist Forum: A Journal of Gender and Sexuality* 131–149; Spivak, 'To "Bring Down the Flowers"'.

102 As Spivak writes, 'Part of the reason for this very real confusion is that medieval and early modern England did not have a single unified legal system, though one was evolving: law was still partly related to local custom and could vary from place to place; multiple court systems were in play; ecclesiastical law and common law had contested and at times overlapping jurisdictions.' Ibid., at 109-110.

103 P. Gajdusek, 'Quickening Doctrine' (2003) 5 *Common Law Review* 23–25.

104 Fiona Harris-Stoertz argues that such laws became more prevalent in the twelfth and thirteenth centuries, representing the '"thin end of the opening wedge" of male control of

is anyone who strikes a pregnant woman or gives her a poison which produces an abortion, if the foetus be already formed or animated, and especially if animated, he commits homicide.'[105]

By the end of the eighteenth century, elite regular physicians came to oppose the legal position on abortion. In this, the first legislative responses to abortion at the beginning of the nineteenth century have been tied to the campaign launched by the university-educated ('regular') physicians as part of their processes of professionalization.[106] As Lynn Morgan argues, 'embryos do not take their meanings from immanent qualities. Embryos do not themselves pose conundrums or create disputes; rather, social controversies provide the interpretive lenses through which embryos are imbued with meaning'.[107] Central to the physician's campaign was a claim to scientific knowledge regarding embryonic and foetal life that was not shared by competing practitioners: the midwives, herbalists, apothecaries and so forth. Thus, opposition was a tool for professional advancement, a rare (perhaps singular[108]) means for the regular physicians to seek to legally distinguish themselves from their competitors.

In the eighteenth century, physicians, surgeons and apothecaries worked in the guild structure. The guilds were responsible for teaching, and exerted some control over conduct and practice. While they set parameters for the practice of their members, they could not prescribe other models of health care. As such, the regular physicians worked in competition with folk, lay and other practitioners. As Peterson writes: 'Quacks, "empirics", and drug peddlers' practised freely and outside of possible legal sanctions, 'while a physician in London could be disciplined by his college for preparing and

pregnancy and childbirth and helped pave the way for the greater loss of female hegemony in later centuries'. F. Harris-Stoertz, 'Pregnancy and Childbirth in Twelfth- and Thirteenth-Century French and English Law' (2012) 21 *Journal of the History of Sexuality* 263–281.

105 H. de Bracton, *On the Laws and Customs of England*, trans. S. E. Thorne, 4 vols. (Cambridge, MA: Belknap Press, 1968), vol. II.

106 Thomson, *Reproducing Narrative*.

107 L. Morgan, 'Embryo Tales', in S. Franklin and M. Lock (eds.), *Rethinking Life and Death: Toward an Anthropology of the Biosciences* (Santa Fe, CA: School of American Research Press, 2003), 262.

108 Mohr argues that the physicians' inability to effectively treat the ills of the day left them with few other ways of distinguishing themselves from competing providers. Mohr, *Abortion in America*.

selling a prescription to his patient'.[109] As Peterson concludes, the provision of medicine in the eighteenth and early nineteenth century was 'near chaos'.[110] The method by which the regular physicians addressed this chaos, harnessing the issue of abortion to gradually criminalize the activities of their competitors and gain occupational closure is well documented.[111] As Reva Siegel writes of the US history: 'Men interested in establishing their professional authority ... encouraged other men to assert their political authority over women's role in reproduction by criminalizing the means of controlling birth, each acting to preserve life in the social order as they knew it.'[112]

In this process, campaigning elites 'presented the protection of unborn life as a means to various social goals as much as an end in its own right'.[113] A similar history is evident in the United Kingdom, where physicians, in their campaign to criminalize abortion and abortionists, 'corporealized the preoccupations of civic governance and their own parochial professional concerns'.[114] This saw the female body become the 'repository for social concerns, contemporary anxieties, and the professional aspirations of medicine'.[115] As Angus McLaren observes, while our collective memory attributes changes in abortion law to religious sentiment, scientific insights and developing regard for children, 'significant, also, were the pragmatic concerns and professional interests of lawyers and doctors seeking to implement laws that would best serve their needs'.[116]

Following successful lobbying by elite regular physicians in the United Kingdom, Lord Ellenborough's Act 1803 provided for a statutory crime of abortion for the first time. However, this Act inscribed the quickening doctrine into statute. Before quickening, abortion was punishable by a fine, corporal punishment, imprisonment or transportation for up to fourteen years. Aborting a quickened foetus was punishable by death. Lord Ellenborough's Act had an influence beyond English law with the first US anti-abortion statute based on the 1803 legislation.[117] In response to statutory entrenchment of the ecclesiastical doctrine, the years that

[109] M. J. Peterson, *The Medical Profession in Mid-Victorian* (Berkeley: University of California Press, 1978), 5.
[110] Ibid. [111] See references in fn. 6. [112] Siegel, 'Reasoning from the Body', 318.
[113] Ibid., 315. [114] Thomson, *Reproducing Narrative*, 10. [115] Ibid.
[116] McLaren, *Reproductive Rituals*, 144. [117] Gajdusek, 'Quickening Doctrine', 24.

followed saw growing medical opposition to quickening as a site of disciplinary or jurisdictional conflict. This opposition relied on alternative claims that (morally significant) life began at conception, not quickening. Again, we should not think that embryos and foetuses existed, pre-formed with meaning, awaiting to be discovered and mobilized. As the anthropologist Lynn Morgan writes, foetuses only exist in the context of a constellation of relations 'that includes those who bought them into social being'.[118] In this, foetuses are material and social products that the emerging field of embryology gave a particular meaning and value. The early embryologists took what had previously been unremarkable human waste, and in changing its meaning and value, created their own professional identity:

By producing visible evidence of the embryo's contours and dimensions, the embryologists set the stage for major epistemological and ideological shifts. They claimed human gestational development as a biomedical enterprise, the embryo itself as a neutral biological product, embryo collecting as a valuable, legal and ethically justifiable enterprise, and themselves as experts in a new professional speciality.[119]

The physicians harnessed this new meaning to their own professionalization project. Significantly, while the physicians reacted against ecclesiastical encroachment on what was now perceived as within the medical domain, they also opposed a model of foetal life that allowed the pregnant woman to usurp medical expertise.[120] Quickening allowed the pregnant woman to define when life became morally and legally relevant. As such, it was a site of struggle over who knew the truth of pregnancy – woman, church or medicine – and this struggle (for jurisdiction or authority) took place in the realm of law. Medicine's success saw women's knowledge and experience marginalized. This process continued with the development of embryology as a discipline,[121] and the emergence of technologies that

[118] L. M. Morgan, *Icons of Life: A Cultural History of Human Embryos* (Berkeley: University of California Press, 2009), 16.

[119] Morgan, 'Embryo Tales', 263.

[120] McLaren, *Reproductive Rituals*, 139.

[121] See Lynn Morgan's observation on the work of the early embryologists and the emergence of human embryology as a discipline: 'They created a new vocabulary that alienated embryological "specimens" from their origins in women's lives. They cast alternative forms of pregnancy knowledge – such as that produced by women and midwives – as insignificant, superstitious, or wrong . . . The work they did resulted in the consolidation of embryological knowledge, as well as the embryos themselves, within a powerful and

visualize the foetus,[122] as well as those that assist reproduction in increasingly complex configurations.[123]

These early claims to know the truth of foetal identity, usurping experiential and ecclesiastical knowledge claims, were part of medicine's successful project to assert dominion over life. Morgan claims that there is a reciprocal relationship between foetuses as socially constituted entities and 'the societies that produce them that affects and changes both sides'.[124] The elite regular physician's 'bio-theological' discourse created a 'new political identity for the foetus'[125] that has shaped how we continue to discuss, understand and experience the foetus. As such, it created the conditions of possibility for the 'foetal heartbeat' laws and the wider 'pro-life is pro-science' political strategy. In other words, this professionalization strategy had immediate effects on women's (legal) reproductive choices but also a longer and perhaps more profound effect on processes of embodiment, as science succeeded in its right to define the meaning and value of reproduction and life itself. The new foetal identity entrenched particular understandings of female reproductive function and gender in law, and through processes of legal embodiment impacted all female subjects.

The Offences Against the Person Act 1837 removed the ecclesiastical distinction marking the legal death of quickening, although it remained part of Catholic dogma until 1869.[126] In the United States, while states had previously adopted a 'cautious, ambiguous, or defensive attitude to abortion',[127] the medical profession saw some success in changing state laws in the first half of the nineteenth century. This intensified after the formation of the American Medical Association in 1847. By the end of the century, there were anti-abortion statutes in every state.[128] As Gajdusek writes, these laws address a range of disparate concerns, including market competition and challenges to traditional gender roles:

tenacious biomedical context.' 'Embryo Tales', 268. Further: '[T]he embryologists granted themselves the prerogative of animating the embryos and deciding what they had to say.' Ibid.

122 See, for example, B. Katz Rothman, *The Tentative Pregnancy: Prenatal Diagnosis and the Future of Motherhood* (New York: Viking, 1986).

123 Isabel Karpin argues that the female body has disappeared in both the IVF clinic and the regulation that governs the activities of such clinics, see Karpin, 'The Uncanny Embryos'.

124 Morgan, 'Embryo Tales', 16.

125 Dubow, *Ourselves Unborn*, 20.

126 Ibid., 19.

127 Mohr, *Abortion in America*, 224.

128 Gajdusek, 'Quickening Doctrine'.

The new laws were a triumph for physicians now fully invested with scientific authority. Midwives and 'irregular' doctors were excluded as legitimate abortion practitioners, and the women-centred 'quickening' doctrine was abandoned. The new laws were sharply moralistic. For example, they deepened the stigma attached to abortion by associating it with 'obscenity'. In addition the laws reflected a triumph for sexual conservatism and medical doctors' determination to block middle-class women from employing abortion as a tool for resisting traditional roles and facilitating new ones.[129]

The same was seen in European jurisdictions, with courts beginning to follow this new biological truth. Barbara Duden notes how nineteenth-century German court records capture the tension between old ways of knowing and the new biological framework. Before this point, 'the situation had been reversed; since antiquity only a woman's statement that she had quickened had provided the physician with a solid indication to predict an impending birth after due time'.[130] Duden interprets the 'epistemological, psychological, and social' demise of quickening as imbricated in the cultural moves whereby women's interior bodies become part of public discourse in medical, legal and administrative realms, while at the same time the 'female exterior' – her place in the world – becomes scientifically proscribed to the private realm:

> On the one hand, it is the newly discovered naturalness of domesticity, motherhood, domestic work, familial sociability, the need for protection, and marital dependency that places women in the 'private realm' in law, education, and ethics. On the other, science uncovers and professionals mediate her womb as a public space. Her flesh becomes the public stage whose proceedings are of immediate interest to the state and the body politic, to public hygiene and the church and also to the husband.[131]

The scientific 'fact' of the presence of life from the point of conception therefore gained its facticity by its mobilization and instrumental insertion into medical and legal networks.[132] John Keown argues that anti-abortion provisions from Lord Ellenborough's Act until 1861 were influenced by the

[129] Ibid., 25.

[130] B. Duden, 'Quick with Child: An Experience That Has Lost Its Status' (1992) 14 *Technology in Society* 335–344 at 341.

[131] Duden, 'Quick with Child', 335–336.

[132] B. Latour, *Science in Action: How to Follow Scientists and Engineers through Society* (Cambridge, MA: Harvard University Press, 1987).

elite regular practitioners who 'relentlessly urged the need for suppression by the law of a practice that threatened fetal and maternal welfare but also the interests of their profession'.[133] As Latour argues, a proposition – here a scientific claim regarding foetal life – is not simply a claim or a statement. It involves articulating a body into a new set of arrangements or relations.[134] In this context, the scientific proposition articulates the pregnant body into a different set of (related) medical and legal relations. At the same time, a particular foetal identity and female reproductive body and subject emerge. These complex and shifting discourses overlay the material body, making it intelligible and determining how it is lived. As Grosz writes:

> By 'body' I understand a concrete, material, animate organization of flesh and organs, nerves, skeletal structure, which are given a unity, cohesiveness, and form through the psychical and social inscription of the body's surface. The body is, so to speak, organically, biologically 'incomplete'; it is indeterminate, amorphous, a series of uncoordinated potentialities that require social triggering, ordering, and long-term 'administration'.[135]

Barbara Duden similarly observes that 'science and technology filter and shape what we sense and experience'.[136] She goes on more fully and autobiographically to state:

> Women of my generation now look at their insides with medical optics that create scientific facts. The remnant of quickening is at best a feeble reminder of what a woman once knew. During the 1980s it thus became increasingly impossible to distinguish between separate spheres of the private and the public. Today not only the authorities ... but also the woman herself, discovers her child – not through quickening, but by recognizing it as a public fact.[137]

This section has focused on the legal life and death of quickening. This provides a means of exploring how we might best understand and articulate the dynamic nature of legal embodiment. It foregrounds the historically and culturally specific nature of the disciplinary discourses and institutional claims that are played out in the legal domain, and therefore the contingency of the 'imaginary anatomies' in relation to which

[133] Keown, *Abortion, Doctors, and the Law*, 49. [134] Ibid.

[135] E. Grosz, *Space, Time and Perversion: Essays on the Politics of Bodies* (New York: Routledge, 2018), 104.

[136] Duden, 'Quick with Child', 335. [137] Ibid., 343.

embodiment is crafted and experienced.[138] While the focus has been the legislative 'life course' of the quickening doctrine, it is worth acknowledging the ongoing and developing life of the foetus in legal, regulatory and professional discourses. In the decades that saw in the twentieth century, 'embryology became a modern science, obstetrics became a profession, . . . birth control became a movement, eugenics became a cause, and prenatal care became a policy'.[139] Each of these saw a shifting and contested understanding of foetal identity, with 'scientific racism, the regulatory state, and professionalization'[140] themes that shaped and emerged within these various 'fetal meanings'[141] and which in turn mediated women's experience of pregnancy and embodiment.

In terms of the medical profession, having effectively campaigned to extend the criminal prohibition of abortion in the nineteenth century, the beginning of the twentieth century saw medical elites campaign to extend their lawful jurisdiction into the terrain previously occupied by their competitors.[142] *R.* v. *Bourne* [1938] marked the conclusion of a successful campaign to see the criminal law entrench exceptions to the statutory prohibition on abortion, but only when the appropriateness of a termination was determined, and was subsequently performed, by a medic.[143] The only limit placed on medical discretion was the 'golden rule' – the requirement to seek a second opinion from another doctor.[144] As such, medicine had secured the right to define the legality and ethics of abortion, extending its domain into territory it had previously cleared of competing providers. With *Bourne*, the common law extension and protection of medical discretion provided the conditions for the reforms to come nearly three decades later with the Abortion Act 1967.[145]

The closing decades of the twentieth century saw embryo and foetal identity continue to be shaped by the shifting interplay of law, science and the work of professional ethicists. With the work of the philosopher Mary

138 C. Waldby, 'Destruction: Boundary Erotics and Refigurations of the Heterosexual Male Body', in E. Grosz and E. Probyn (eds.), *Sexy Bodies and the Strange Carnalities of Feminism* (London: Routledge, 1995), 268.

139 Dubow, *Ourselves Unborn*, 7. 140 Ibid., 36. 141 Ibid., 184.

142 Thomson, *Reproducing Narrative*; Thomson, 'Abortion Law and Professional Boundaries'.

143 [1938] 3 All ER 61. For a discussion of the case, see Thomson, 'Abortion Law and Professional Boundaries'; McGuinness and Thomson, 'Conscience, Abortion, and Jurisdiction'.

144 Thomson, 'Abortion Law and Professional Boundaries', 204–205. 145 Ibid.

Warnock and the enactment of the Human Fertilisation and Embryology Act 1990, the primitive streak emerged as a 'biological *and* ontological landmark' supposedly settling 'philosophical questions of when a human individual could be said to begin'.[146] As with earlier claims, significance and meaning has been talked into being, and these entities remain the product of the 'dynamic engagement between scientific theories, moral frameworks such as utilitarianism, and ... rhetoric'.[147] Moving into our 'embryo-strewn world of the 21st century',[148] Marie Fox has argued in the context of admixed embryos that understandings of embryos and foetuses remain fluid and contingent and a means through which science and other disciplines continue to enact the human.[149]

These are the historic and contemporary contexts within which 'foetal heartbeat' laws are located. This mandates that we do not simply debate 'good' and 'bad' science. Rather, we must attend to the social and political nature of scientific knowledge claims ('good' and 'bad') that come to shape embodied subjects. This is central to the understanding and definition of legal embodiment promoted here. In Section 4, I return to the 'foetal heartbeat' legislation. I further explore the embodied effects of this legislation, acknowledging the gendered impacts of this entwining of scientific and legal discourses. To do this, I address the wider context of increasing 'speech and display' provisions in the United States,[150] and how addressing these in the context of rhetoric and its materiality might advance further our understanding of legal embodiment.

4. Science, Law and Material Rhetoric

On the introduction of 'foetal heartbeat' legislation in Ohio, Attorney General Dave Yost welcomed the opportunity to defend his state's law

[146] Wilson, 'What Can History Do for Bioethics', 221.

[147] Ibid. See also D. Wilson, *The Birth of British Bioethics* (Manchester: Manchester University Press, 2014).

[148] S. Franklin, 'The Cyborg Embryo: Our Path to Transbiology' (2006) 23 *Theory, Culture & Society* 167–187 at 168.

[149] M. Fox, 'What Is Special about the Human Body?' (2015) 7 *Law, Innovation and Technology* 206–230.

[150] For a general discussion of the development of these provisions see, J. A. Robertson, 'Abortion and Technology: Sonograms, Fetal Pain, Viability, and Early Prenatal Diagnosis' (2011) 14 *University of Pennsylvania Journal of Constitutional Law* 327–390; M. Kreutzfeld, 'Avert Your Eyes: The Ethical and Constitutional Injustice of Pre-Abortion Mandatory Ultrasound Laws' (2017) 21 *Journal of Gender, Race and Justice* 201–237.

and challenge *Roe* v. *Wade*: 'In the last 46 years, the practice of medicine has changed ... Science has changed. Even the point of viability has changed. Only the law has lagged behind.'[151] This 'pro-life is pro-science' political strategy has its origins in the early debates around quickening. While it is important to challenge the legitimacy of the science that is mobilized to support such legislative moves, two points need to be made. First, this cannot be done at the expense of problematizing the understanding of science that underpins both sides in the debates. While many contest the validity of the science, both sides generally rely on a model of science as objective truth, rarely considering that facts – whether generated by Shildrick's Renaissance anatomists or today's epigeneticists – are not severable from the context of their fabrication.[152] This broader context is essential to understanding embodiment as a socio-political practice and how law, science and gender interrelate in processes of embodiment. Second, engaging with science can be read as supporting the biomedical lens through which we regulate, view and experience reproduction. This potentially reinscribes the epistemic violence done by early campaigning physicians and the emerging embryologists. Thus, while it is necessary to challenge the misuse of science, it is also essential to work to uncouple reproduction from a monopolistic scientific gaze.[153]

Model legislation refers to 'fetal cardiac activity' as a marker of 'an unborn human individual'.[154] The sponsor and supporters of Georgia HB 481 asserted that detection of a 'heartbeat' was a 'legally significant and medically sound' indicator of life, 'pregnancy viability' and personhood. These assertions were repeatedly described as 'common sense'[155] and warrant further consideration. In clinical practice, the detection of cardiac activity is used as a marker of the health of the pregnancy and to reassure the pregnant woman and any partner that the pregnancy is developing. However, the legislation uses this as a point of moral and potentially legal significance, deliberately drawing on and obscuring existing understandings of viability. Legislative findings quote the American College of Obstetricians and Gynecologists 2015 guidelines that identify ultrasound as 'the preferred modality to verify the presence of a viable intrauterine

[151] S. Jaffe, 'Legal Battles over Abortion Heat Up in the USA' (2019) 393 *The Lancet* 1923–1924 at 1924.

[152] Latour, *Science in Action.*

[153] I am grateful to Isabel Karpin for emphasizing this point.

[154] See, for example, the model legislation provided at www.f2a.org/

[155] Evans and Narasimhan, 'A Narrative Analysis of Anti-Abortion Testimony', 4.

gestation'.[156] These guidelines refer to pregnancy loss and miscarriage and are concerned with a viable pregnancy rather than a pregnancy that is viable outside the uterus, the accepted meaning within abortion jurisprudence and wider public discourse.[157] It is important to highlight the co-option or appropriation of viability in this way. It is possible, after all, that this strategy may contribute to the unsettling and eventual recalibration of how viability is understood. This would obviously have a significant impact on abortion politics and care. Evans and Narasimhan note that such appropriation was a key tactic used by Georgia HB 481 advocates:

> [A]nti-abortion legislators and community members oversimplified complex concepts and directly appropriated language relating to viability, defining death, and child development. They reduced complicated scientific processes, medical experiences and decisions into extremely simple terms. Use of 'heartbeat' was deliberate evoking popular knowledge, for example, hearing fetal heart tones using a Doppler ultrasound; advances in sonography were also used to advocate for increased ability to see and hear the presence of 'life' during pregnancy.[158]

In focusing on the present misuse of science, there is a danger that it leaves the question of viability as a legally and morally significant 'marker' unproblematized. Focusing on the appropriation of viability does nothing to draw attention to the culturally and historically contingent and arbitrary nature of viability itself. As with quickening, viability provides an example of how the meaning and significance of bodies and their processes emerge within professional and institutional contexts.[159] Further, the use of 'viability' is a strategy that works in concert with reference to 'heartbeat', with the immediate and visceral responses that this word triggers. As Representative Ed Setzler, sponsor of Georgia HB 481 asserted: 'Protecting life in the womb with a human heartbeat is what science, law, and human conscience would suggest.'[160] As Whitney Arey writes: 'the language is very intentional; it uses the heart beat as a universal "sign of life" to draw on and ultimately establish a shared legal understanding of what it means to be "alive".'[161]

[156] Shepherd, 'Fetal Heartbeat Bill Gets the Science and the Law Wrong'. [157] Ibid.

[158] Evans and Narasimhan, 'A Narrative Analysis of Anti-Abortion Testimony', 4.

[159] For an example in a related context, see S. Hennette-Vauchez, 'Words Count: How Interest in Stem Cells Made the Embryo Available: A Look at the French Law of Bioethics' (2009) 17 *Medical Law Review* 52–75.

[160] Shepherd, 'Fetal Heartbeat Bill Gets the Science and the Law Wrong'.

[161] Arey, 'Web Roundup'.

Notwithstanding the caveats noted, it is, nonetheless, important to state that at six weeks the foetus is 3–4 millimetres long. It is beginning to form very immature neurological and cardiovascular systems. At this point there is no recognizable heart or cardiac system. What new technology is able to detect is a group of cells with electrical activity. This activity starts with the development of the foetal pole, the first sign of a developing embryo.[162] So, rather than a 'heartbeat' we might instead understand it as 'a little flutter in the area that will become the future heart' and, indeed, a range of other organs.[163] The 'foetal heartbeat' underpinning these interventions is no more than rhythmic electrical impulses 'helping to encourage the development of an organised vasculature and circulatory system – a prerequisite for future viability but not sufficient alone'.[164] In response to the appropriation and distortion of language, some refer to 'foetal cardiac activity' or 'foetal pole cardiac activity'. Others sidestep the misrepresentation of science, and indeed the medicalization of the abortion debate, referring instead to 'six-week abortion bans'.

Since the early embryologists, technology has been instrumental in the politics of foetal identity and it is technological developments that have enabled the 'foetal heartbeat' to join 'the growing use of sonogram technology as an anti-abortion weapon'.[165] As Sarah Horvath from the American College of Obstetricians and Gynecologists states: 'What's really happening at that point is that our ultrasound technology [is now] able to detect activity in a rudimentary group of cells.'[166] Here we have a very familiar mixing of (medical) technology with moral and legal claims. Feminist scholars have long considered the impact of technologies that visualize the foetus.[167] This has ranged from anatomical drawings of foetal

[162] Ibid.

[163] Dr Saima Aftab, Fetal Care Center, Nicklaus Children's Hospital, Miami in R. Rettner, 'Is a "Fetal Heartbeat" Really a Heartbeat at 6 Weeks', *Live Science*, 17 May 2019.

[164] A. Rogers, '"Heartbeat" Bills Get the Science of Fetal Heartbeats All Wrong', *WIRED*, 14 May 2019.

[165] Robertson, 'Abortion and Technology', 332.

[166] As Horvath continues: 'I do think there's a deliberate conflation of terms going on in legislation in order to try to co-opt the science, or at least the scientific language. These bans are really just arbitrarily chosen points in time in a pregnancy that are strictly there because they want a complete ban on abortion care.' Rogers, '"Heartbeat" Bills'.

[167] As Featherstone writes: 'Feminist historians, theorists, ethicists and sociologists have long suggested that the foetus is not a universal, "natural", biological figure. Historically, it had to be "discovered", and, most importantly, have meaning rendered to this discovery. Technology has marked a key shift here: if the foetus could once only be felt and

development circulating at the beginning of the nineteenth century,[168] through Lennart Nilsson's famous *Life* photographs of the seemingly free-floating foetus – 'Drama of Life Before Birth' – in 1965,[169] to contemporary sonograms.[170] This criticism details the erasure of the woman and the decontextualizing of pregnancy and its consequences.[171] Communications scholar Amanda Edgar has extended this analysis in her consideration of 'foetal heartbeat' technologies. While she addresses 'speech and display' laws, her analysis of this sonic act is applicable across its different deployments.[172] Edgar compellingly argues that the phenomenon can be understood as rhetoric. She draws on the work of Michael McGee and others who explore the materiality of rhetoric; the way it acts like a force, pushing against us like 'air and water'.[173] Such attention to material rhetoric can support the renewed interest in critical rhetorical analysis in socio-legal studies.[174]

imagined, now the foetus has been intensely scrutinised through visual and audio media. Such "visions" were, of course, mediated, even distorted, through the lens of culture, but were nonetheless naturalised and seemingly made coherent'. Featherstone, 'Becoming a Baby?', at 459.

168 B. Duben, 'The Fetus on the "Farther Shore": Towards a History of the Unborn', in L. M. Morgan and M. W. Michaels (eds.), *Fetal Subjects, Feminist Positions* (Philadelphia: University of Pennsylvania Press, 1999).

169 R. P. Petchesky, 'Fetal Images: The Power of Visual Culture in the Politics of Reproduction' (1987) 13 *Feminist Studies* 263–292; C. A. Stabile, 'Shooting the Mother: Fetal Photography and the Politics of Disappearance' (1992) 28 *Camera Obscura* 178–205.

170 L. M. Mitchell, *Baby's First Picture: Ultrasound and the Politics of Fetal Subjects* (Toronto: University of Toronto Press, 2016); J. Roberts, *The Visualised Foetus: A Cultural and Political Analysis of Ultrasound Imagery* (London: Routledge, 2016).

171 Karpin, 'The Uncanny Embryos'.

172 It is also important to acknowledge that moves to restrict access to abortion care is far from an exclusively US or Anglo-American preoccupation. A recent ruling by Poland's constitutional tribunal and subsequent high-profile public protests demonstrate this. They also illustrate the different ways in which discourses regarding foetal identity may be mobilized and should be subject to an analysis for their embodied affect. On the Polish ruling, see: 'Poland Rules Abortion Due to Foetal Defects Unconstitutional', *The Guardian*, 22 October 2020, www.theguardian.com/world/2020/oct/22/poland-rules-abortion-due-to-foetal-defects-unconstitutional

173 M. C. McGee, 'A Materialist's Conception of Rhetoric', in R. E. McKerrow (ed.), *Explorations in Rhetoric: Studies in Honor of Douglas Ehninger* (Glenview, IL: Scott, Foresman, 1982), 26.

174 See J. Harrington, L. Series and A. Ruck-Keene, 'Law and Rhetoric: Critical Possibilities' (2019) 46 *Journal of Law and Society* 302–327; J. Harrington, *Towards a Rhetoric of Medical Law* (London: Routledge, Glasshouse, 2017).

Edgar draws attention to North Carolina's Woman's Right to Know Act, which required women seeking abortion care to undergo a sonogram, 'foetal heartbeat' auscultation, and listen to a state-mandated statement by the physician who would perform the procedure. The statute provided that the statement must include: 'a medical description of the dimensions of the embryo or fetus, the presence of cardiac activity, and the presence of external members and internal organs'.[175] The statement was to be rendered in the physician's 'own voice'. A number of federal courts have found that such provisions violate the First Amendment because they 'compel ideological speech'.[176] Edgar argues that:

> The speech is designed not to stand on its own, but instead to work in tandem with sonogram imagery and heartbeat sounds. The physician's narration is layered over the sounds of the Doppler heartbeat reading and sonically produced fetal imagery. As the rhetoric of the state is forced from the physician's mouth, it leaks into the fetal and maternal sounds, all of which are saturated with the state's ideological meaning.[177]

For Edgar, the sonic 'fetal heartbeat', sonogram and mandated speech, act as material rhetoric with 'real consequences for bodies and environments'.[178] She explains the materiality of rhetoric by turning to law. As she writes, abortion law rhetoric materially impacts on the bodies of women, 'who must either carry fetuses to term or obtain illegal, often dangerous abortions'.[179] Returning to the political mobilization of the 'foetal heartbeat', Edgar argues that coupled with the other aspects of 'speech and display' provisions, sonic abortion rhetorics 'push against women's bodies, working not only to restrict those bodies from some medical treatments but also to limit the ways those bodies are understood in popular culture'.[180] Edgar's analysis is provocative and persuasive.[181] Yet the degree to which this material rhetoric 'pushes against' women's bodies can be extended. While she identifies the impact on popular culture,

[175] *Stuart* v. *Loomis* MDNC 1:11-CV-804 (2014), para. 2.

[176] Kreutzfeld, 'Avert Your Eyes', 203.

[177] A. N. Edgar, 'The Rhetoric of Auscultation: Corporeal Sounds, Mediated Bodies, and Abortion Rights' (2017) 103 *Quarterly Journal of Speech* 350–371 at 360.

[178] Ibid., 351. [179] Ibid. [180] Ibid.

[181] In this context, it is interesting to note John Robertson's reference of sonograms as 'an anti-abortion cudgel'. Robertson, 'Abortion and Technology', 346.

this is indivisible from women's embodied experiences of reproduction, which are formulated in response to 'imaginary anatomies' in circulation.[182] That is to say, we experience our embodiment in relation to the bodies imagined and projected within culture – whether that is scientific, legal or popular – in a particular time and place.[183]

The interplay of technology, biomedical discourse, law and popular culture is important. Changing foetal identities are generated at the intersection of these overlapping fields. As Lisa Featherstone writes, 'changing conceptualisations of the foetus are not only dependent on technologies but rather on complex social, cultural, political and economic interactions, grounded in distinct times and places'.[184] Yet we must recognize that biomedicine and its technologies have a particular weight. While they are partial and incomplete, they shape 'how the self is made "real"'.[185] The heightened impact of biomedical discourse comes with added responsibility. The mobilization of the 'foetal heartbeat' has achieved purchase in popular, political and academic realms.[186] This is no doubt due to the rich significance this purposefully draws upon. As such, it is incumbent on all, but particularly those in biomedical fields, to exercise care. It is regrettable, therefore, that influential and globally read journals such as the *British Medical Journal* use 'foetal heartbeat' uncritically when reporting on these legislative interventions. In so doing, they risk validating the erroneous and deliberately misleading claims that provide the political power behind these campaigns.[187] While Barbara Duden is correct to remind us that 'words forge meaning',[188] we should also note that they forge lived experience and political possibility.

[182] Waldby, 'Destruction'. [183] Thomson, 'A Tale of Two Bodies'.

[184] Featherstone, 'Becoming a Baby?', 451.

[185] Lock and Nguyen, *An Anthropology of Biomedicine*, 284.

[186] For an example of academic pro-'foetal heartbeat' commentary, see D. F. Forte, 'Life, Heartbeat, Birth: A Medical Basis for Reform' (2013) 74 *Ohio State Law Journal* 121–148.

[187] See, for example: O. Dyer, 'Georgia Limits Abortion to Six Weeks and Eyes Supreme Court', *BMJ*, 2 April 2019; O. Dyer, 'The US State of Georgia's Majority Republican Legislature Has Passed a Bill Outlawing Abortions once a Fetal Heartbeat Can Be Detected', *BMJ*, 2 April 2019; A. R. A Aiken, 'Erosion of Women's Reproductive Rights in the United States', *BMJ*, 5 July 2019; A. R. A. Aiken, 'In March 2019, Mississippi Enacted Legislation That Would Prohibit Abortion once a Fetal Heartbeat Can Be Detected', *BMJ*, 5 July 2019.

[188] Duden, 'Quick with Child', 338.

5. Conclusions

In responding to the developing 'foetal heartbeat' legislation, legal academic Mary Ziegler observed: 'Over the past few decades, the abortion wars have become as much a fight about science and medicine as they are about the law and the Constitution.'[189] This is a common and incomplete understanding of the development of abortion law and politics. Since the early nineteenth century, elite medical professionals have been instrumental in the development of abortion law and therefore the social and political contestation that has followed. This has continued.[190] Early campaigning physicians harnessed claims regarding embryonic and foetal life to assert their intellectual and ethical superiority over competing providers and therefore secure legal privileges. As Lynn Morgan writes, embryos get 'recruited as evidence' and 'discursively produced within particular social dramas'.[191] The physicians' instrumental mobilization of abortion saw the female body corporealize the social and political anxieties of the day, including those that centred on women's place in society.[192] Early recruitment of the foetus and abortion law in the regular physicians' professionalization project has had an enduring impact on how pregnancy and abortion care is understood and experienced. As Jenni Millbank observes, discourses of foetal life 'cast a long shadow over procreative practices' and women's embodied experiences.[193]

In exploring shifting jurisprudential 'fetal imaginings',[194] this chapter has stressed how knowledge claims are contingent and shaped by the specific milieu within which they emerge. An important aspect of the milieu is gender, which structures the context within which bodies, and the technologies that make them intelligible in particular ways, are imagined and created. Bodies and subjects are also always shaped by political economy; here the emergence of a highly gendered and stratified

[189] Shepherd, 'Fetal Heartbeat Bill Gets the Science and the Law Wrong'.

[190] This was the case throughout the nineteenth and twentieth century, see Keown, *Abortion, Doctors, and the Law*; Thomson, *Reproducing Narrative*; Thomson, 'Abortion Law and Professional Boundaries'; McGuinness and Thomson, 'Medicine and Abortion Law'; McGuinness and Thomson, 'Conscience, Abortion, and Jurisdiction'.

[191] Morgan, 'Embryo Tales', 263.

[192] Siegel, 'Reasoning from the Body'; Thomson, *Reproducing Narrative.*

[193] J. Millbank, 'Exploring the Ineffable in Women's Experiences of Relationality with Their Stored IVF Embryos' (2017) 23 *Body & Society* 95–120.

[194] Dubow, *Ourselves Unborn*, 6.

professional society. As Kane Race states, 'markets, facts and subjects are mutually constitutive, processual and emergent'.[195] These elements articulated here as scientific claims regarding embryonic and foetal life were necessary for the development of a medically dominated market for health. These claims were also necessary for a medicalized female subject who would become a significant and enduring focus for that expertise and market.

Shifting medical claims regarding the embryo and foetus changed the meaning and significance of quickening. This impacted not only statutory provisions but also women's experience of reproduction and embodiment. Quickening moved from 'that experience of movement or animation which was the woman's first and primary perception of foetal motility, to simply one and even a somewhat less important event along a scientifically mediated continuum'.[196] Medical claims shifted the circulating imaginary bodies (foetal and pregnant) in relation to which women's embodiment and lived experience is structured. Thus, legal and biomedical discourses entwined with one another, shaping gender and embodiment, and constructing a particular relationship between women and the state. As already noted, knowledge claims become sticky when they enter legal discourse and practice, and these claims have continued to shape lived experience and the regulation of reproduction. This point is worth stressing as Texas SB8 is considered by the Supreme Court. It is likely that much will focus on the unprecedented legislative scheme designed to prevent judicial scrutiny,[197] and the standing of *Roe* v. *Wade*. This will leave the newly figured six-week foetus with its 'heartbeat' – an imaginary anatomy – circulating in public discourse.

Addressing changing legal conceptions of the foetus, the purpose has been to develop a robust account of legal embodiment. This has built on recent socio-legal work that explores the institutional and affective dimensions of embodiment. In this chapter, I have looked at the role of law in constructing bodily imaginaries in relation to which embodiment is formulated and experienced.[198] As Grosz argues, while the body is a material

[195] K. Race, '"Frequent Sipping": Bottled Water, the Will to Health, and the Subject of Hydration' (2012) 18 *Body & Society* 72–98 at 92.
[196] Duden, 'Quick with Child', 335.
[197] www.justice.gov/opa/pr/justice-department-sues-texas-over-senate-bill-8.
[198] Gatens, *Imaginary Bodies*.

and 'animate organization of flesh and organs', it is only made cohesive through social inscription (including in biomedical, legal and popular discourses) and the psychical work in relation to this inscription.[199] The focus on legal embodiment has addressed the interplay of biomedical and legal discourses and how these intertwine with gender to provide an account of foetal and reproductive bodies. This work has sought to denaturalize these bodies and the analysis has stressed the need to interrogate biomedical claims that are made in the legal domain. As Donna Haraway argues, such knowledge claims can be understood as 'frozen moments' of the 'fluid social interactions constituting them, but they should also be viewed as instruments that enforce meanings'.[200] In both regards, gender should be understood as a normative order that provides a pervasive and inescapable context within which science asks its questions, designs its research and interprets its results. This also allows us to understand how – through the body – law, gender and the discourses of science together constitute legal subjects, hierarchies and identities.

[199] Grosz, *Space, Time and Perversion*, 104.

[200] D. J. Haraway, *'A Cyborg Manifesto: Science, Technology, and Socialist-Feminism in the Late Twentieth Century' in Simians, Cyborgs and Women: The Reinvention of Nature* (New York: Routledge, 1991), 164.

3 The Terrorized Subject

A Critique of 'Women', 'Gender Violence' and 'Vulnerability' as Legal Categories

Márcia Nina Bernardes and Sofia Martins

The words 'terror' and 'terrorized' are not new to discussions of gender-based violence. Indeed, these words are often used to describe the lived experience of gender-based violence.[1] Likewise, the association between gender violence and other forms of extreme violence, such as torture, has already been established in international law.[2] On the one hand, the recognition of this association allows for greater awareness of the gravity of this particular form of violence. On the other hand, this association has encouraged an overall harshening of punishment and a criminal-law approach to violence. This has been particularly notable in the field of international crime, where there has been a significant increase in the volume of norms criminalizing gender-based violence – many of which have paid special attention to sexual offences, which are now even included in the Rome Statute's Article 7 as one type of crimes against humanity.

Indeed, over the past thirty years, international human rights law, as well as international criminal law and international humanitarian law, have become a major focus of attention for feminists, who have made significant efforts to use them as a means of combating gender-based

[1] R. Copelon, 'Intimate Terror: Understanding Domestic Violence as Torture', in R. Cook (ed.), *Human Rights of Women: National and International Perspectives* (Philadelphia: University of Pennsylvania Press, 1994; S. T. Fried, 'Violence against Women' (2003) 6 Health and Human Rights [88]–[111]; T. Leflouria, 'Under the Sting of the Lash: Gendered Violence, Terror and Resistance in the South's Convicts Camps' (2015) 100 *Journal of African American History* [366]–[384].

[2] See, as examples, UN Committee on the Elimination of Discrimination against Women, General recommendation No. 35 on gender-based violence against women, updating general recommendation No. 19., CEDAW/C/GC/35, [*s. l.*], paras. 15–18, 14 July 2017; UN Committee against Torture, Convention against Torture and Other Cruel, Inhuman or Degrading Treatment or Punishment, CAT/C/GC/2, [*s. l.*], paras. 18, 21–24, 24 January 2008; UN Human Rights Council, Report of the Special Rapporteur on Torture and Other Cruel, Inhuman or Degrading Treatment or Punishment, A/HRC/31/57, [*s. l.*], paras. 5–10, 14, 15, 32, 34–36, 42, 45, 49, 50, 55, 57, 59, 66, 70, 16 March 2021.

violence against women.[3] This strategy arose in response to the widespread impunity and difficulties in the domestic promotion of legal reforms and the borderless nature of violence against women. The hope was that reforms achieved at the international level would begin to trickle down into national legislation, particularly in countries that had been reluctant or unwilling to pass formalized measures to combat gender-based violence.[4] Thus, it was hoped that international law relating to violence against women would (1) provide a model for legal redress through 'norms transfer', (2) promote the spread of new mechanisms and statutes protecting women against gender-based violence, (3) create accountability leading to greater implementation of domestic laws against gender-based violence, and (4) expand protections to women in countries that had not yet implemented such laws.

In this process, several terms emerged as key central categories for the creation of norms and definitions: 'women', 'gender' and 'violence'. The process of creating a standard definition for these essential lexicon items was contested, not only by states but also by feminist activists.[5] In fact, since the first Conference on Women (Mexico 1975) there have been ongoing and important disputes among women's groups about the very vocabulary to be used. These disputes have primarily opposed two branches of modern feminism: consolidated groups that we call here hegemonic feminism (Eurocentric and bourgeois) and subaltern groups, composed of non-white women and the global south.[6] The result is that a

[3] K. Angle, 'From Liberal to Carceral Feminism', in J. Halley et al. (eds.), *Governance Feminism: Notes from the Field* (Minneapolis: University of Minnesota Press, 2019); J. Halley et al., *Governance Feminism: An Introduction* (Minneapolis: University of Minnesota Press, 2018); J. Halley, 'Rape at Rome: Feminist Interventions in the Criminalization of Sex-Related Violence in Positive International Criminal Law (2008) 30 *Michigan Journal of International Law* [3]–[123]; J. L. Ulrich, 'Confronting Gender-Based Violence with International Instruments: Is a Solution to the Pandemic Within Reach?'(2000) 7 *Indiana Journal of Global Legal Studies* [629]–[654].

[4] E. Dowds, *Feminist Engagement with International Criminal Law: Norm Transfer, Complementarity, Rape and Consent*, 1st ed., Series in International Law (Oxford: Hart, 2020), 9. See also M. N. Bernardes, 'Aspectos Transnacionais da Lei Maria da Penha' (2014) 45 *Revista Direito, Estado e Sociedade* 20–40.

[5] V. Oosterveld, 'Constructive Ambiguity and the Meaning of "Gender" for the International Criminal Court' (2004) 16 *International Feminist Journal of Politics* 563–580 at 564.

[6] V. M. Maghodam, 'Transnational Feminist Networks: Collective Action in an Era of Globalization' (2000) 15 *International Sociology* 5–137; C. T. Mohanty, 'Under Western Eyes: Feminist Scholarship and Colonial Discourses' (1984) 12 *Humanism and the University I: The Discourse of Humanism* 333–358; G. C. Spivak, 'Feminismo e

plethora of overlapping, but distinct, definitions of gender-based violence have proliferated at the international level.

Broad definitions of key terms such as 'women', 'gender' and 'violence' allowed international law to evolve.[7] These broad, or unspecific, definitions of the key terms of international gender-based violence law have facilitated consensus and coalition-building around an issue that remains divisive and under-addressed in international and domestic settings. Nonetheless, calculated or strategic forms of definitional ambivalence have led this body of international law to encounter two main problems: that of the successful transfer of these international legal concepts into domestic legal settings, and that of an a priori category of 'woman'. Regarding the first issue, Santos argues that the state's absorption/translation of feminist demands is always selective, moulding the new norms to the state's traditional modus operandi, thus diminishing their impact and innovative strength.[8] The second issue is related to the fact that, as Judith Butler has famously argued,[9] as they advocate for the protection of 'women's rights' as an abstract universal concept, international feminist organizations implicitly promote the existence of an identity – that of the 'woman' who both initiates feminist interests and constitutes the subject for whom political representation is sought. This a priori identity erases how factors such as race, age and class inextricably constitute the way gender and gender violence are experienced by different women.

In this chapter, we address the epistemic and political challenges of crafting the inclusive legal frames the transnational feminist movement has been attempting to institute for the past thirty years. We intend to assess the extent to which both law and feminism can re-entrench social hierarchies or, at best, be simply inoperative in terms of social justice. We argue that domestic norms modelled after international standards

desconstrução, de novo: negociando com o masculinianismo inconfesso', in T. Brennan (ed.), *Para além do falo: Uma crítica a Lacan do ponto de vista da mulher*, trans. A. Xavier (Rio de Janeiro: Record. Rosa dos Ventos, 1997).

7 Oosterveld, 'Constructive Ambiguity', at 564.

8 C. M. Santos, 'Da delegacia da mulher à Lei Maria da Penha: Absorção/tradução de demandas feministas pelo Estado' (2010) 89 *Revista Crítica de Ciências Sociais* 153–170 at 154–155.

9 J. Butler, *Gender Trouble: Feminism and the Subversion of Identity* (New York: Routledge, 1990).

created through transnational feminist activism can create an exclusionary construction of the very subject they intend to represent. This exclusionary construction of the subject fails to include the women who are most vulnerable to this type of violence. Using the example of the Brazilian case law around the Law 1134/2006 against domestic and familial violence, the so-called Maria da Penha Law (MPL), we unearth the ways that laws formed in response to the transnational feminist agenda do not always sufficiently take into account the perspective of subaltern (non-white, transgender, young, old, poor) women when defining who should be considered a victim of domestic violence and what kind of remedies should be granted. In that, this chapter unveils the ways in which the legal construction of the terrorized subject, as captured through the particular lens of legal means to address domestic violence, rests on a specific figure of the gendered subject that is simultaneously exclusionary of some of the most prominent features of the very women that they claim to address – especially in terms of race and class – either because they do not fit into the parameters the law delineates for its 'terrorized subject' or because the justice system does not match their needs.

Indeed, although the subject who is disproportionally exposed to violence is, in the Brazilian case as well as elsewhere, a black woman, laws such as the MPL have failed to provide them with adequate protection against violence. Research data in Brazil show that femicides have risen in the past fifteen years, despite the adoption of the progressive MPL. Since the passing of the Maria da Penha Law, the increase in the rate of violence against women has indeed slowed down, but the numbers of these crimes still rise year after year. While the number of femicides against white women has slightly dropped in this period, those against black women have continued to grow substantially. Between 2006 and 2015, while there has been an overall 2.1 per cent decrease in the number of white women murdered in Brazil, the number of black women murdered has increased by 35 per cent.[10] This data is also incomplete as the murders of trans women are not considered as femicides in Brazil, despite the fact that Brazil is one

[10] Julio Jacob Weiselfisz, *Mapa da Violência 2015: homicídio de mulheres no Brasil*, FLACSO Brasil, 9 November 2015, https://flacso.org.br/2015/11/09/mapa-da-violencia-2015-homicidio-de-mulheres-no-brasil/.

of the countries in which the rate of transphobic violence is highest worldwide.[11]

In using the words 'terror' and 'terrorized subject' to refer to female victims of gender-based violence and what they experience, we are not focusing on the criminal implications of acts considered to be gross violations of the law. Instead, we aim to highlight the coercion, intimidation and intense psychological toll that this type of violence takes on those who experience it. Just as 'terrorism' places the terrorized in a state of extreme and sustained psychological duress,[12] victims of gender-based violence are terrorized by forms of violence that similarly take root in the preservation of traditional submissive roles. Gender-based violence is thus intrinsically political and structural; it is intended to impose, support or strengthen a particular distribution of power in society. This understanding of gender-based violence is useful because it underscores the political and systemic dimensions of the phenomenon while not focusing on who is experiencing or enacting the violence. Rather, it focuses on what is being done and makes visible the surrounding social and political circumstances facilitating this violence.

Without pretending to enter the debates about legal theory and theories of adjudication, or about law itself and its application, we maintain that 'law in action' obeys the imperatives of a liberal, hegemonic and exclusionary order, as is evident in the Brazilian case and many other jurisdictions. The intention here is less to criticize hegemonic feminism's achievements and the rule of law, which are indeed important, but rather to critically analyse their exclusionary effects.[13] By using

[11] IACHR, Avances y desafíos hacia el reconocimiento de los derechos de las personas LGBTI en las Américas', Inter-American Commission on Human Rights, 7 December 2018. OEA/Ser.L/V/II.170 Doc. 184.

[12] I. Primoratz, 'The Morality of Terrorism' (1997) 14 *Journal of Applied Philosophy* 221–233 at 221.

[13] Our critique of the investment of hegemonic feminism in legal reform is, thus, similar to Maria Grahn-Farley's position: 'Post-modern and post-colonial [as well as decolonial] critiques typically direct the reader's attention to the exclusion of women who do not fit general feminist norms . . . describing and talking on behalf of women who are otherwise invisible and unheard within the feminist project. The focus is showing how the feminist project will be challenged and questioned by listening to the voices and learning about the lives of women who do not fit within the general feminist frame.' M. Grahn-Farley, 'The Politics of Inevitability: An Examination of Janet Halley's Critique of the Criminalization of Rape as Torture', in S. Kuovo and Z. Pearson (eds.), *Feminist Perspectives on Contemporary International Law* (Oxford: Hart, 2011), 114–115. It is not a matter of giving

post-structuralist, de-colonial and afro-diasporic approaches, we reveal the epistemic operations that create limits and shortcomings in what the law can achieve. We do not deny that domestic legislation reproducing international feminist priorities has been important in legally establishing certain types of domestic and gender-based violence against women and helping to institute certain mechanisms to curb violence and protect victims.[14] However, the argument we present here is that this law can also fail to protect those who are the victims of the most severe forms of violence.

Section 1 provides a brief overview of the consolidation of the global agenda against gender-based violence in transnational feminism. We maintain that transnational feminism, mostly Western and white, has influenced the domestic agenda of feminism in several countries of the global south, including Brazil, resulting in laws that emphasize access to justice for victims of gender violence, notably through mechanisms that seek to end the aggressors' impunity rather than measures focused on empowering victims, such as housing reforms, better sheltering programmes, professional training and childcare measures. Section 1 also summarizes the standards of protection against gender-based violence that have developed under international human rights law, including in Case 1.2051 (Maria da Penha Maia Fernandes) before the Inter-American Commission of Human Rights, considering MPL as an expression of the feminist agenda in Brazil.

In Sections 2 and 3, we turn to the analysis of Brazilian case law related to domestic violence, specifically how MPL (produced by feminism) construes the terrorized subject. In Section 2, we examine the critique of the foundational conception of the legal subject through the lens of Judith Butler's work. In the context of a feminist law against gender violence, Butler's critique requires the discussion of the very categories of 'woman', 'gender' and 'victim'. On the basis of our case law analysis, our claim in this section is that the terrorized subject law construes is a fragile, dependent, cis woman. As a result, women who do not fit this profile are often not considered 'victims of domestic violence'. In Section 3, drawing on the

up the rule of law – we cannot do without it, in fact – but to critically assess its limits and shortcomings. See also Butler, *Gender Trouble*, 7.

[14] S. A. Carneiro, *Mulheres Negras e Violência Doméstica: Decodificando os números* (São Paulo: Geledes – Instituto da Mulher Negra, 2017), 33.

works of Latin American black feminists and, again, Judith Butler, we assess the discussion of a 'common experience' (of gender violence, for instance) to all women, and how that notion imposes unjustifiable burdens on black women in Brazil. Case law analysed in this section shows that the remedies provided to black women who are victims of violence by the judicial system in Brazil are not adequately protective. Our claim here is that race and class have been the subtexts, or what Butler refers to as 'frames', through which women are constructed as full legal subjects (or not) under the MPL. Accordingly, these frames also determine which remedies are appropriate to guarantee women a liveable life, one that is free from gender-based violence. Entrenched Western legal concepts, such as property, alimony and physical integrity, are put into question to the extent that they seem to be inoperative to these victims. These two sections allow us to review, in Section 4, Butler's conceptions of framing and precarity in the context of gender violence in Brazil and discuss the political implications of the epistemic operations presented in the first sections. We claim in Section 4 that the law itself, as well as those who operate it, is constructed within a frame that is marked by systemic sexism, racism and classism.

1. The Fight against Gender Violence in Transnational Feminism and Its Implications for Domestic Agendas

Although the UN institutional framework for protecting human rights was already relatively consolidated in the 1970s, different UN and Organization of American States (OAS) bodies paid little attention to women's rights. This began to change when the First World Conference on Women was held in Mexico in 1975. One of the results of the conference was the UN's declaration of the 'International Year of Women' and the 'Decade of Women' (1975–1985), along with a set of goals aimed at eradicating discrimination against women. In 1979, CEDAW was signed. The emergence of transnational women's networks is deeply intertwined with the history of the meetings organized by different UN bodies as a part of this initiative. Preparations for the four UN Women Conferences (Mexico 1975, Copenhagen 1980, Nairobi 1985 and Beijing 1995), in addition to the Vienna Conference on Human Rights (1993) and the Cairo Conference on Population and Development (1994), gathered unprecedented numbers of women's groups, thus allowing them to foster connections and work cooperatively.[15]

While this string of landmark conferences made headway into advancing women's issues by bringing together a groundbreaking number of stakeholders and activists, they were unable to create a unified agenda for how to best ensure protection for women around the world. These processes have often proved controversial and tense, with important divisions between women's organizations in the global south, mainly concerned with issues related to development, and those in the north, primarily concerned with issues related to discrimination and equal opportunities.[16]

That this divergence should exist is not surprising. Several post-colonial and de-colonial feminists have long pointed out the limits of establishing cross-border alliances with women from the global north.[17] Mohanty famously argued that one of the major divergences is that northern feminists have tended to consider sexism as a homogenous experience for all women, privileging 'male oppression' and 'sexual difference' as the key

[15] Maghodam also points out that the women's movement really transnationalized only from the 1970s onwards, even though international feminism has existed for more than 100 years and international women's organizations for decades. Maghodam, 'Transnational Feminist Networks', 5.

[16] M. Keck and K. Sikkink, *Activist beyond Borders: Advocacy Networks in International Politics* (Ithaca, NY: Cornell University Press, 1998), 166–172.

[17] Mohanty, 'Under Western Eyes'; R. Kapur, 'The Tragedy of Victimizations Rhetoric: Resurrecting the "Native" Subject in International/Post-Colonial Feminist Legal Politics'(2002) 15 *Harvard Human Rights Law Journal* 1–38; Y. E. Miñoso, 'Etnocentrismo y Colonialidad en los Feminismos Latinoamericanos: complicidades y consolidación de las hegemonías feministas en el espacio transnacional' (2009) 14 *Revista Venezolana de Estudios de la Mujer* 37–54. In her 1986 piece, Chandra Mohanty does not use the expressions 'North' and 'South'. Instead, she talks about the construction of the 'Third-World woman' by 'western hegemonic feminism'. Although 'hegemonic', 'western' or 'northern feminism' are not homogenous currents of thought or action, it has generally contributed to the way that subordinate women are represented hegemonically, with substantial implications in terms of agenda setting. According to her, Western feminists' representation of third-world women as 'sexually constrained, ignorant, uneducated, tradition-bound, domestic, family-oriented, victimized' makes it impossible to reveal the local forms of resistance of these women. According to Mohanty, these representations are formulated from unstated normative referent of Western feminists' self-presentation as educated, modern, having control over their bodies and sexualities: Mohanty, 'Under Western Eyes', at 56. Twenty years later, Mohanty revisited her argument and employed the expressions 'North' and 'South', which, more than a geographical meaning, denote a relation of centre/periphery to power. C. T. Mohanty, '"Under Western Eyes" Revisited: Feminist Solidarity through Anticapitalist Struggles' (2003) 28 *Signs* 499–535.

concepts for understanding women's oppression, while southern feminists have maintained that colonialism, racism and poverty resulted in problems as serious as male oppression (or even more pressing) to women in the south.[18] Women from the global north primarily defend legalistic strategies to confront discrimination and violence against women. In contrast, groups of women connected to grassroots social movements in the global south utilize strategies aimed at preserving the conditions for their autonomy and self-representation. This opposition between hegemonic approaches and social movement approaches[19] was reproduced internally in global south countries – middle-class feminists resorting to the same analytical categories as northern feminists and thus reaching similar political agendas that did not correspond to, and sometimes excluded, the needs or desires of feminists from other socio-economic backgrounds.[20] In this dispute, liberal guidelines have had more space in international organizations and have resulted in policies and legal standards that have influenced domestic policies and legal standards. These policies, on the one hand, constitute important victories; on the other

[18] Mohanty, 'Under Western Eyes'; Mohanty, '"Under Western Eyes" Revisited'. Mohanty pointed out the analytical and epistemic shortcomings in the discursive practice of hegemonic feminism, which had the effect of colonizing conflicts, depriving women of the global south of the ability to represent themselves, and subordinating them to the role of the Other in ways that reinforced and defined the boundaries of the universal subject of modern ideology. Mohanty, 'Under Western Eyes'. This argument questions the capacity of the human rights grammar to support the demands of justice that are especially dear to poor women in the global south, such as economic justice, even though the structural effects of these injustices result in an increase in gender violence. K. Rittich, 'Engendering Development/Marketing Equality' (2003–2004) 67 *Albany Law Review* 575–593; A. C. B. Brandão, 'Governança, Gênero e Cidade: o lugar das mulheres nas políticas urbanas', in E. Araújo and L. Sarmiento (eds.), *Bioética Urbana desde el Sur Global: Territorialidades bioéticas emergentes* (Córdoba: CIECS-CONICET, 2020).

[19] We are following Blakrshnan Rajagopal's distinction between liberal and social movements' approaches to international law and statism. B. Rajagopal, *International Law from Below* (Cambridge: Cambridge University Press, 2003), 255–258.

[20] Mohanty, 'Under Western Eyes', at 52. Indeed, several groups of women from the 'Third World' had an elite profile that brought them closer in viewpoint to the feminists of the global north. According to Espinosa Miñoso, by the 1985 III Feminist Meeting of Latin America and the Caribbean in Brazil, there was already a fracture in the feminist movement. This fracture was between a group of mainly white, bourgeois and liberal women, who were unable to recognize the ethnic and racial multiplicity of female bodies that made up the region, and the women whose lived experience was proof-positive of this very multiplicity. Miñoso, 'Etnocentrismo y Colonialidad en los Feminismos Latinoamericanos'.

hand, they seem to reflect worldviews that are not shared by all women, and that affect them differently.

Despite these controversies, the campaign against violence against women has made it possible to advance the idea that women's rights are human rights. With regard specifically to gender violence, Keck and Sikkink claim that the concept of violence against women, which brings together very different forms of aggression – domestic violence, genital mutilation, death due to dowry, rapes as a war technique, and sexual violence in state custody situations, for example – had to be built by the feminist movement.[21] The fact that many of these assaults occur in the private and family environment constituted an additional challenge in constructing this problem as a violation of international human rights law.[22] It is therefore remarkable that in 1985 the issue of gender violence became a UN priority in the wake of recommendations made by the Nairobi Conference.

By the early 1990s, International Human Rights Law on violence began to proliferate at many levels: the UN, the OAS and the EU.[23] All in all, four standards of protection for women emerged throughout these processes: (i) violence against women is a form of (gender-based) discrimination that contributes to their vulnerability and isolation; (ii) violence against women involves acts, or threats of acts, that inflict physical, mental or sexual suffering; (iii) this form of violence is not limited to acts performed by public agents, and the state must act with due diligence to prevent, investigate and punish the violation committed by private individuals; (iv) the violence need not be intentional; as a consequence, apparently neutral public policies can also amount to violence against women if and when they disproportionately affect women. Specific legal norms such as the Belem do Pará Convention (Art. 2) or the UN Declaration on the

[21] Keck and Sikkink, *Activist beyond Borders*, 172–180.

[22] B. Meyersfeld, *Domestic Violence and International Law* (Oxford: Hart, 2010), 203–205.

[23] See, as examples, General Recommendation 19 of the United Nations Committee for the Elimination of Discrimination against Women (1992), UN Declaration on the Elimination of Violence Against Women (1993), Inter-American Convention to Prevent, Punish and Eradicate Violence Against Women – Belem do Pará Convention (1994), Recommendation Rec (2002) 5 on the Protection of Women against Violence (European Council, 2002), and, recently, the Convention to Combat Violence on Women and Domestic Violence – Istanbul Convention (2011), as well as many reports from different international and regional human rights protection bodies, and judgments from the Inter-American and European Human Rights Courts. Meyersfeld, *Domestic Violence and International Law*, 24–104.

Elimination of Violence Against Women (Art. 2) further establish three types of violence against women depending on whether they are perpetrated by the state, a member of the community, or in domestic settings (cases in which the aggressor and the victim are in an intimate relationship). These standards of protection and categories of violence against women comprise the first major interventions in developing international standards for the protection of women.

Although these conventions and documents list a series of social, cultural and political measures as necessary for the eradication of gender-based violence and thus identify an array of remedies much wider than solely judicial measures, reports and judgments from different UN bodies and regional human rights systems, they have consistently focused exclusively on strictly juridical measures (such as increased due diligence in investigations) at the expense of all others.[24] Indeed, both the European and the Inter-American Courts of Human Rights have developed elaborate standards of due diligence in cases of violence against women. The European Court, in two paradigmatic cases involving domestic violence against women – *Opuz* v. *Turkey*[25] and *Eremia* v. *The Republic of Moldova* (2013)[26] – developed important tests to assess state responsibility, always emphasizing the obligations to investigate and punish aggressors.

The Inter-American Court of Human Rights has proceeded in the same way.[27] The *Cottonfield* v. *Mexico* (2009) example is a case in point: the court examined the kidnapping and murder of several young women in

[24] Without claiming to exhaust this point, the well-known question about the 'justiciability' of social rights, as opposed to the ease with which civil rights are applied judicially, seems to play an important role here. From a critical perspective of liberalism, such as post-colonial and de-colonial ones, this difficulty only manifests the constitutive relationship between the apparatus of the rule of law and capitalism. However, this controversial discussion deserves a more robust and careful examination than this work's limits.

[25] See *Opuz* v. *Turkey* (2009) App. No. 3340/02 [141].

[26] European Court of Human Rights. *Eremia* v. *The Republic of Moldova* (2013) App. No. [3564/11.] [61–65].

[27] Among many others which address gender violence, even if only marginally, we name a few landmark ones: *Case of the Miguel Castro-Castro Prison* v. *Peru*, Judgment of [25 November] 2006; *Case of the 'Las Dos Erres' Massacre* v. *Guatemala*, Judgment of [24 November] 2009; *Case of Fernández Ortega et al.* v. *Mexico*, Judgment of 30 August] 2010; *Case of Rosendo Cantú et al.* v. *Mexico*, Judgment of [15 May] 2011; *Case of Espinoza Gonzáles* v. *Perú*, Judgment of 20 November 2014; *Case of Favela Nova Brasília* v. *Brazil*, Judgment of [16 February] 2017; *Case of Women Victims of Sexual Torture in Atenco* v. *México*, Judgment of [exact date] 2018; *Case of Guzmán Albarracín et al.* v. *Ecuador*, Judgment of [24 June] 2020.

Mexico, using the term 'femicide' for the first time in international human rights case law. In this case, there are critical paragraphs on the importance of prevention of gender violence in a broad sense (including combating a culture of gender stereotypes), but the most widely developed parameters are those related to combating the impunity and inaction of state officials during the investigation and the criminal prosecution of the victims' disappearance and death.[28] In the subsequent case of *V. R. P., V. P. C. et al.* v. *Nicaragua*, the Inter-American Court of Human Rights stated explicitly for the first time that the state could be characterized as a second aggressor of the victim of domestic violence, as institutional violence could qualify as acts of revictimization, according to the parameters established by the Convention of Belém do Pará. The case concerns V. R. P.'s sexual abuse, perpetrated by her father, and irregularities that occurred in the course of the criminal proceedings instituted by Guatemala to investigate the acts. The court analysed the state's obligations of due diligence and the special protection of investigations and criminal proceedings in child abuse cases, referring to the state's duties regarding prosecution and establishing specific rules to avoid revictimization but missed the opportunity to develop meaningful parameters on the state's duty of prevention of gender violence.[29]

As standards and norms progressively consolidated at the international level, they began to transfer down to national levels. The enactment of the Maria da Penha Law in Brazil is one example of a domestic legal system's response to the international elaboration of legal standards for addressing gender-based violence. The MPL does, however, narrow the scope of gender violence to domestic violence and thus excludes forms of violence that are perpetrated against women by the state or by the community.[30] The MPL presents itself as directly connected to international human rights

[28] See *Case of Cotton Field* v. *Mexico*, Judgment of [16 November] 2009 [164].

[29] See *Case of V. R. P., V. P. C. et al.* v. *Nicaragua*, Judgment of [8 March] 2018 [292].

[30] The feminist movement in Brazil, as in many other countries, has pushed for better policies against domestic violence, but has paid little attention to other forms of gender violence, as listed in the UN Declaration on the Elimination of Violence against Women and the Conventions of Belem do Pará, namely, the violence perpetrated by the state and the violence perpetrated by the community. In recent years, the black feminist movement in Brazil and elsewhere has included the discussion on state violence against black women in campaigns such as 'Say her name', 'First Harassment', 'Estupro nunca mais' [Rape never again] and 'Eu empregada doméstica' [I, a housemaid], among others.

law throughout explicit references; it also mentions the case *Maria da Penha Maia Fernandes* v. *Brazil* (IACHR, Case 12.051) before the Inter-American Commission of Human Rights (IACHR), which proved instrumental to the passing of MPL in the country. Maria da Penha is a Brazilian woman who suffered two homicide attempts and became paraplegic. Despite robust evidence against her ex-husband, there had been no judicial decision (either to acquit or convict him) for more than fifteen years. In Report 54/01 on this case, the Inter-American Commission on Human Rights highlighted that the facts characterized a systematic pattern of state negligence on domestic violence. Such violence was deemed to translate and reproduce a discriminatory social order against women, and to restrict their ability to live under equal conditions with men. The importance of the problem of domestic violence, especially against women, is statistically documented. The report affirmed that the Brazilian state bore international responsibility for what Maria da Penha experienced. The IACHR formulated four recommendations, including measures to compensate Maria da Penha, demands for prosecuting and punishing her aggressor, and non-repetition measures. The recommended non-repetition measures are of particular interest, as they included invitations to the state to:

4. Continue and expand the reform process that will put an end to the condoning by the State of domestic violence against women in Brazil and discrimination in the handling thereof. In particular, the Commission recommends:
   a. Measures to train and raise the awareness of officials of the judiciary and specialized police so that they may understand the importance of not condoning domestic violence.
   b. The simplification of criminal judicial proceedings so that the time taken for proceedings can be reduced, without affecting the rights and guarantees related to due process.[31]

The movement from the international sphere to the domestic produced significant changes in the Brazilian legal order. Feminist mobilization to promote discussion about domestic violence against women in Brazil utilized the IACHR recommendations in report 54/01, as well as pressure from the CEDAW committee to comply with these recommendations, to

[31] IACHR, *Maria da Penha Maia Fernandes* v. *Brazil* [61].

push for a special law.[32] Until then, despite some meaningful victories for the feminist movement, Brazilian society lacked awareness of the gravity of the country's domestic violence problem and the need for special policies to address it. Victims, the women's movement and a network of health and legal professionals exposed to the topic had been the only locutors of discussions about domestic violence in Brazil. This scenario changed with the Maria da Penha case, which raised enough support from multiple segments of society to pressure the National Congress to directly address this problem. Initially drafted by a feminist consortium before being sent to Congress, the bill was the subject of several rounds of debates and intense participation by lawyers, judges, psychologists, social workers and other professionals specialized in issues related to domestic violence against women.[33]

Next, we will focus on the discussion of how law constructs the legal subject, examining how MPL has been constructing the terrorized victim of domestic violence. We maintain that, to the extent MPL is a direct result of feminist battles, this examination also provides us with an opportunity to consider how feminism itself participates in the construction of the victim of domestic violence. As mentioned before, in this chapter we are not making the distinction between law itself and the application of law and consider both – law and its application – as manifestations of 'frames' which we will explain in detail in Section D.

2. The Construction of the Victim of Domestic Violence

As theory and praxis, feminism has historically sought to reveal and overcome the ways in which patriarchal cultures have oppressed women for centuries. For several feminist strands, the feminist movements' struggle has been able to 'denounce' institutional practices that subordinate women in their public and private relations. Along these lines,

[32] R. M. R. Lavigne, 'Caso FONAJE', in C. H. Campos (ed.), *Lei Maria da Penha – Comentada em Uma Perspectiva Jur.dico – Feminista* (Rio de Janeiro: Lumen Juris, 2011), 76.

[33] Santos, 'Da delegacia da mulher à Lei Maria da Penha', at 150; Bernardes, 'Aspectos Transnacionais da Lei Maria da Penha', at 126; L. L. Barsted, 'Lei Maria da Penha: uma experiência bem-sucedida de advocacy feminista', in C. H. Campos (ed.), *Lei Maria da Penha – Comentada em Uma Perspectiva Jur.dico – Feminista* (Rio de Janeiro: Lumen Juris, 2011), 30.

feminism 'represents' existing women, who have traditionally had little access to positions of power, and mobilizes law reform so that it becomes a vehicle for protecting women. Consequently, feminists laud laws removing obstacles to equality between men and women and creating special protections for women in areas where they are distinctively vulnerable. The Brazilian Maria da Penha Law, is, without a doubt, one of these achievements and should be celebrated: it brings awareness to the magnitude of the phenomenon of domestic violence in the country; it facilitates some victims's access to judicial remedies that may be important; it also, albeit to a lesser extent, provides general guidelines for prevention of such crimes.[34]

Without diminishing the importance of these social processes that culminate in significant legislative changes, it is vital to investigate the reasons for the shortcomings of most laws against gender-based violence. Part of the problem is that these laws reflect hegemonic views on the subject of law and the rule of law, which are then reproduced by feminists and jurists from the south.[35] With Judith Butler, we argue that the 'subject's foundationalist myth' has a series of problematic implications within the liberal framework with respect to the construction of the legal/terrorized subject who must be protected by the state, and how she should be protected.[36] As we shall see, these implications have both normalizing and exclusionary effects, creating hierarchies and establishing who gets to

[34] M. N. Bernardes, R. de Souza Costa and A. Vidal de Oliveira, *Violência Doméstica, discriminação de gênero e medidas protetivas de urgência*, 1st ed. (Curitiba: Juruá, 2016), 15. Despite its highly participatory approval process, after it was enacted, MPL received many criticisms from conservative sectors on the right – who denied the sexist character of this type of violence and who argued that MPL violated the equal protection clause – and on the left – who, looking mainly at the criminalizing effects of the law on men, accused the statute and the feminist movement of being too repressive. It is important to highlight that the criticism presented in this chapter differs profoundly from these two positions. In particular, we contend that the common refrain that it criminalizes men accused of aggression lacks any consideration for the victims' perspective. We subscribe to Brazilian black feminist critiques that argue that the law's biggest problem is the invisibility of black women who are victims of violence. From the perspective of these women, the criminalization of the aggressor does not seem to solve their problem, but it is also not an a priori problem. A. L. P. Flauzina, 'Lei Maria da Penha: entre os anseios da resistência e as posturas da militância', in A. Flauzina, F. Freitas, H. Vieira and T. Pires (eds.), *Discursos Negros: legislação penal, política criminal e racismo* (Brasília: Brado Negro, 2015); C. Akotirene, *O que é interseccionalidade?* (Belo Horizonte: Editora Letramento, 2018).

[35] Mohanty, 'Under Western Eyes'; Mohanty, '"Under Western Eyes" Revisited'.

[36] Butler, *Gender Trouble.*

live a liveable life. As the research data show, the subject who is most affected by gender violence is left without adequate protection from the state.

Butler reveals a series of systemic operations hidden in feminist discourse in general, and in the laws that protect women in particular. If, on the one hand, feminist discourse, when representing women, increases the visibility of these subjects and their ability to intervene socially and politically, then, on the other hand, there is also a normative function of this language that 'reveals' what is supposed to be true and false in the very category of women.[37] For Butler, in other words, legal systems of power produce the subjects that they later represent. Likewise, arguably, feminism and feminist laws construct the very subjects they later come to represent because their demands are made in the name of a 'woman' that is presented as pre-discursive and, thus, as existing prior to law.

To be sure, Butler relies on a Foucauldian model according to which power is understood as pervasive and constitutive of social relations and subjectification processes. In its microphysics, power instantiates male and female subjectivities in both public and private domains through publicly institutionalized practices and discourses, including the law. As a creative force, power does not simply prohibit, limit, regulate and control. It also forms, defines and reproduces. Power, thus, is not so much an attribute of individual subjects but rather an effect of ongoing strategies and daily micro-practices in social relations that are always tense and dynamic.[38]

It is precisely these processes of subjectification via normative discourses described by Foucault that matter to Butler, and the role played out by law in such processes. Butler argues that the collectively reiterated practice of naming sexual differences has naturalized the distinction between 'men' and 'women', thus creating the fiction of stable gender identities. To be 'called a name' (such as 'woman', for instance), is also to exist, to be recognized. However, the rules of recognition are socially constructed, and to 'be called a name' depends on how well one instantiates those performative rules and acts 'as' a woman.[39] In our case, we are interested in finding out what the rules of recognition of a 'gender violence victim' are and which women fall under this category.

[37] Ibid., 3–7.

[38] M. Foucault, *Discipline and Punish: The Birth of Prison* (London: Penguin, 1991), 27.

[39] Butler, *Gender Trouble*, 198.

For Butler, the association between body, gender and desire is 'performative' rather than 'natural' or 'biological'. The compulsory heterosexual matrix – Butler's analogue to the concept of patriarchy, as a systemic configuration of power – is structured through a binary logic that forges the 'normal man' and the 'normal woman', excluding (and often punishing) all that is not perfectly aligned to these poles. On the one hand, masculine bodies are associated with a male identity that determines virile behaviour and sexual desire for the opposite sex. On the other hand, the female body is correlated to a submissive, fragile identity and also to sexual desire for the opposite sex.[40]

According to Butler, there is no way out of culture, which always imposes a certain intelligibility on our bodies and genders. Concepts such as body, sexual orientation and social role can only acquire a given meaning via the repetition and naturalization of normalizing performative acts within this matrix. They are forged through exclusionary practices which are later invisibilized, once the legal structure they create is established and stabilized. Butler rejects the idea that gender can be understood as the cultural inscription of meaning on a predetermined sex. After all, Butler asks, could there be a sexed body that is not, from the beginning, gendered? Is there any being that becomes gendered at a given point in life? How could this come about?

> [G]ender must also designate the very apparatus of production whereby the sexes themselves are established. As a result, gender is not to culture as sex is to nature; gender is also the discursive/cultural means by which 'sexed nature' or 'a natural sex' is produced and established as 'prediscursive', prior to culture, a politically neutral surface on which culture acts.[41]

One implication of these epistemic and political processes is that 'women' are recognized by law as (fragile, powerless) 'victims' who should be protected from the aggressors that terrorize them. Brazilian case law referring to the application of the Maria da Penha Law illustrates the point that law forges the subject it later claims to represent. The victim of domestic law that appears in the case law is constructed as a fragile, adult cis-woman in a romantic relationship with her aggressor.[42] Both women's

[40] Ibid., 45. [41] Ibid., 10.

[42] M. N. Bernardes and M. I. B. Albuquerque, 'Problemas de gênero da jurisprudência brasileira: desfazendo a lei Maria da Penha' (2019) 55 *Revista Direito, Estado e Sociedade* 231–256.

agency and the systemic dimension of violence are erased in this judicial construction to the extent that, in order to be protected by law, 'fragility' appears as a necessary attribute of the women who demand protection rather than as a social situation in which any woman could find herself.[43]

In 2016, the Maria da Penha Law celebrated its tenth anniversary. But a decade of existence has not resolved the various controversies over the interpretation of its clauses. Art. 5, which defines domestic violence, generated a debate on when violence against women can be interpreted as gender violence. It reads:

> Article 5. For the effect of this Law, domestic and family violence against women is defined as any action or omission based on gender that causes the woman's death, injury, physical, sexual or psychological suffering and moral or patrimonial damage:
>
> I – in the scope of the domestic unit, understood as the permanent space shared by people, with or without family ties, including people sporadically aggregated;
>
> II - in the scope of the family, understood as the community formed by individuals that are or consider themselves related, joined by natural ties, by affinity or by express will;
>
> III – in any intimate relationship of affection, in which the aggressor lives or has lived with the abused woman, regardless of cohabitation.
>
> Sole paragraph. The personal relations listed in this article are independent of sexual orientation.[44]

Domestic violence episodes in Brazil fall under the jurisdiction of specialized courts (*Juizados de Violencia Doméstica e Familiar contra a Mulher*, JVDFM), while the same crimes, if committed in a non-gendered setting, fall under the jurisdiction of common criminal courts and the non-gender-specific criminal code applies. Internal Resolution 253 from November 2011 issued by the Rio de Janeiro State Justice Tribunal (TJRJ, in Portuguese), which serves as a guide to resolve those conflicts that fall under the MPL, stipulates that the jurisdiction of the JVDFM can only be established 'when the criminal behavior is perpetrated due to gender … with the act being committed against a person of the female sex not being

[43] A. Allen, 'Feminist Perspectives on Power', in *Stanford Encyclopedia of Philosophy* (Redwood, CA: Stanford University Press, 2016), https://plato.stanford.edu/entries/feminist-power.

[44] The MPL is available in English at www.institutomariadapenha.org.br/assets/downloads/maria-da-penha-law.pdf.

sufficient'. However, when is violence committed against a woman *because* of her gender? The first fundamental problem, thus, comes from the definition of whether an act is or is not 'based on gender' in order to establish which court has jurisdiction over the case.

Brazilian courts' rationale in a significant number of violence against women cases has centred on the protection of 'fragile women'. A review of TJRJ case law evidences the existence of two broad types of criteria used by the court for characterizing whether gender violence occurred and MPL applies: (a) whether the victim is a woman (this first criterion is interesting in itself, for it seems to contradict Internal Resolution 253 in that it explicitly says the opposite, i.e. that the female sex of the victim is *not* enough to assert the specialized court jurisdiction over a case); and (b) whether the victim is fragile (vulnerable/deprived of assets/dependent).[45]

In relation to the first argument (a), the case law reviewed most frequently used the expressions 'woman' or 'female sex' to configure the jurisdiction of JVDFM; in a limited number of cases, judges have used the expression 'female gender'. However, with the exception of a handful of decisions which refer to the 'biological aspects of the victim' or the 'biological sex of the victim', these expressions are not usually explained: there is no definition of 'woman' or 'female sex'. Under the rationale of these decisions, 'being a woman' essentially appears to be a self-evident condition and one that is sufficient to invoke in order to trigger the application of the protective legislation. In all the conflicts analysed the victims were cis-gender women. Since none of the victims was trans or 'gender fluid', it was not possible from the sample used in this research to ascertain to what extent gender identity affected the use of the categories

[45] Bernardes and Albuquerque, 'Problemas de gênero da jurisprudência brasileira'. Albuquerque and Bernardes conducted research on some conflicting interpretations of crucial terminology for the very definition of domestic violence against women as described in the MPL, analysing 119 Rio de Janeiro State Justice Tribunal rulings, which is the State Court of Appeals, concerning conflict of jurisdiction between the MPL created Special Courts of Domestic and Family Violence against Women and other common criminal courts, created prior to the MPL. To be sure, such 'conflict of jurisdiction' is the procedural resource in Brazilian law to solve disagreements between lower courts when there is a dispute over which one has jurisdiction over a case, depending on the subject matter or geographical issues in question. In the specific conflicts of jurisdiction examined, the TJRJ had to solve 'negative conflicts' that occurred because both specialized and common criminal courts declined the jurisdiction over cases involving incidents of violence against women which had, at least, an *appearance* of domestic violence, according to the legal definition present in MPL.

'sex', 'gender' and 'woman' by the judiciary. To a certain extent, it can be stated that in the cases analysed, when this argument is invoked, the magistrates take both the 'sex' and 'gender' of the victim and the fact that she is a 'woman' as given.[46]

The second type of rationale recurrently used by courts is that of 'the fragile woman'. The centrality of this concept in the MPL case law illuminates the fact that it is not enough for the victim to be of the female sex: the applicability of the MPL and the jurisdiction of the JVDFM are only positively affirmed when it is established that the aggression was also due to the victim's gender, which, in effect, depends on the evidence of her vulnerability, dependency, lack of assets or fragility. It should be noted that the Maria da Penha Law's language does not refer to 'vulnerability' or 'dependency' as a criterion for applying the law; these criteria are a judicial creation from interpretation of the MDP law. Sometimes, this vulnerability criterion is described by the judges: it can be physical, economic, psychological or social. However, they most often say nothing about it; it is just affirmed. Alternatively, in some decisions, judges refrain from referring to the vulnerability of the victim but underline the aggressor's intention of domination/subjugation. The focus is always on the people involved in the episode, who need to be personally recognized as a 'powerful aggressor' and a 'fragile victim'.

A ruling by the TJRJ's seventh criminal chamber involving an episode of violence between two famous actors who were then in a relationship is paramount to explain how the idea of vulnerability is construed by courts. In this case, the defendant allegedly struck the actress in the face and threw her on the ground in a public place because she had bared her breasts in a play in which she was acting. The majority of judges in the appellate chamber accepted the defendant's preliminary exception to declare null his conviction by a lower court specialized in domestic violence cases due to a lack of subject matter jurisdiction. The judges acknowledged that the facts fitted the objective legal description of domestic violence; however, they refused to consider that these facts qualified as such on the grounds

46 Cases involving lesbian women follow the same pattern and, with one exception, were sent to the JVDFM. However, the fact that not one of the cases involved trans women is significant, and begs the question why trans women do not appear (or rarely do so) as victims of domestic violence. Bernardes and Albuquerque, 'Problemas de gênero da jurisprudência brasileira'.

that there was no 'vulnerability' or 'dependency' implied. Violence, in this case, could not be considered to be based on gender. The judges ruled that the defendant's alleged actions, though reproachable, should be tried again as a common assault. The reasoning of the court is worth unpacking:

> *In casu*, before getting into the merits of the case, we are before an imputation of violence of boyfriend against girlfriend, which fits the legal logical concept and allows for the application of Maria da Penha Law.
>
> However, a simple analysis of the personalities of the persons involved in this suit, or the place where the facts occurred – not a domestic one – or even the notoriety of the public figures (both are well-known actors), lead us to the conclusion that the victim ... cannot be considered a dependent or vulnerable women.
>
> It is commonly known that the actress in question had never been oppressed or subjugated in any sense by men (TJRJ 2013).[47]

In other words, the court's reasoning amounts to deciding that female vulnerability to domestic violence cannot be considered a given; instead, it must be verified in each specific situation. Strikingly, the ruling reconstructed the MPL congressional approval process, which indicates that the court understood the concepts behind the enactment of the law, including the international strategies and pressures. The decision even quotes the MPL explanatory memorandum according to which gender oppression is socially constructed and underlines that it would be a mistake to allege any biological justification for gender hierarchy. In other words, it resorts to the distinction between sex (as naturally given) and gender (as culturally constructed), only to then reach the conclusion that a subject's vulnerability and inferiority cannot be automatically inferred from the biological fact that the victim is a woman.[48] Here, as in other TJRJ rulings, the sex/gender distinction in effect weakens women's protection instead of strengthening

[47] For the full decision, see *Request for reconsideration* # 0376432-04.2008.8.19.0001. There are many interesting aspects to this case. One that strikes me is the fact that the defendant not only hit his then girlfriend, he also violently pushed her to the floor when she tried to resist, causing the woman injuries. If the aggression had happened in a domestic setting, it could be tried as domestic violence as well, though with some controversy. Because it happened in a public setting, and there was no affectionate relationship between aggressor and victim, it was tried as common assault.

[48] The court therefore denied the applicability of the Maria da Penha Law and decided for the incidence of gender-neutral Penal Code. See *Request for reconsideration* # 0376432-04.2008.8.19.0001, decided on 1 July 2013.

it. In so doing, the decision is at odds with the initial feminist goal pursued in the very formulation of this distinction.

Additionally, the court's ruling assumes a liberal perspective on power and ignores, or at least does not take sufficiently into account, the disseminated and constitutive character of gender oppression. The decision presumes the notion of 'power' as an 'absolute' attribute of the subject, a resource that they may or may not have.[49] Epistemically, the decision assumes the existence of ontologically free and autonomous subjects, who may 'subsequently' be oppressed by culture. In this sense, the law must guarantee that autonomy is not unjustifiably constrained. Here, as the TJRJ verified that this was not the case, it reached the conclusion that the MPL should not be applied.

Adopting a systemic understanding of power and oppression allows us to unearth the ways in which women are placed in situations of greater vulnerability to domestic violence. Women do not need to be fragile subjects to experience such violence, nor should there be any requirement of an explicit intention to dominate on the part of the perpetrator. In other words, oppression can be construed as a shared gender performance in a domestic conflict. Oppression is an established practice. The actress in question subversively dared to challenge the stereotype of a well-behaved woman and dared to confront her former partner when questioned about her theatrical performance; he felt this entitled him to attack her. Although she does appear to be a powerful woman, as the court rightly observed, she nevertheless suffered and was battered. Indeed, she may well have been attacked precisely because of the fact that she is empowered. This is the deepest meaning of oppression: the fact that some people – empowered or not – will have to navigate through obstacles and social challenges that do not exist for differently positioned individuals in society.

This case was loudly discussed and criticized by lawyers and activists. It was eventually reversed in the Superior Justice Tribunal (STJ, 2014), Brazil's highest court for non-constitutional matters, which established that the application of MPL does not require proof of dependency and vulnerability of women: it clarified that the MPL 'applies to dating, ex-dating, to all intimate relationships of affection, regardless of cohabitation and economic and social class' (STJ, 2014).[50] However, the Brazil

[49] Allen, 'Feminist Perspectives on Power'.
[50] For the full opinion, see Special Appeal # 1.416.580 – RJ (2013/0370910-1).

legal order does not operate on the basis of a *stare decisis* doctrine; and not only is this a minority decision within STJ chambers, the reasoning of the TJRJ decision is also far from isolated.

The aforementioned research involving TJRJ's decisions has revealed the judges' difficulties in differentiating between sex and gender, and the ways in which the case law conveys a clear-cut definition of the profile of a domestic violence victim: a fragile, vulnerable and dependent adult cis-woman.[51] In the next section, we discuss how the construction of domestic violence victims as fragile and dependent may also pose problems to those women who are not generally so perceived due to their race and class. We also discuss how a homogenous conception of 'women' and of 'domestic violence victims' may be detrimental to women who, due to race and class, do not have the same needs as white upper-class women, and who have fewer means to escape a violent environment and wholly exercise their rights and freedoms as full subjects of law.

3. The Problem of Women's 'Common Identity': Questions of Race and Class in the Construction of Victims of Domestic Violence

Butler points out that the 'female gender', which determines what it means to be a woman, has become 'a site of contest, a cause for anxiety' in the feminist and queer movements: 'If one "is" a woman, that is surely not all one is.'[52] Gender is not exhaustive or consistent, because it is always intersected by issues of race, class and sexuality, and the binary structure of sex and gender does not account for all facets of identity.[53] In fact, Butler criticizes several feminist theories for their use of the foundational categories of 'natural sex' and 'real woman'. According to her, 'The insistence upon the coherence and unity of the category of women has

[51] Bernardes and Albuquerque, 'Problemas de gênero da jurisprudência brasileira'.

[52] Butler, *Gender Trouble*, 4.

[53] On intersectionality and domestic violence, see K. Crenshaw, 'Mapping the Margins: Intersectionality, Identity Politics, and Violence against Women of Color' (1991) 43 *Stanford Law Review* [1241]–[1299]. See also A. Harris, 'Race and Essentialism in Feminist Legal Theory' (1990) *Stanford Law Review* 42; P. Collins and S. Bilge, *Intersectionality* (Cambridge: Polity Press, 2016).

effectively refused the multiplicity of cultural, social and political intersections in which concrete array of 'women' are construed.'[54]

Law and policies against gender violence are premised on the assumption of an abstract women that has no race, class or sexuality. When the law is applied, and its (in)effectivity evaluated, discussions of the subject's concrete attributes come to the fore. In fact, the critique of the foundationalist conception of the legal subject and its normalizing/exclusionary effects allows us to discern whose interests and epistemic points of view inform the laws and policies against gender violence. In that sense, we subscribe to black feminism's argument that MPL constructs the victim of domestic violence as a white, middle-class woman and, for this reason, does not work properly to protect black and poor women.[55] According to data available in Brazil, black women's bodies are murdered and terrorized on a much greater scale than white women's bodies. This is an issue the MPL utterly fails to address.[56]

Understanding how black women's bodies have been socially represented unveils the many ways in which current state responses are not truly meant to address them as legal subjects. Pereira shows that the social representation of black women as strong, hard-working women sometimes prevents them from getting help for leaving violent environments. Likewise, their hyper-sexualization may constrain these women in abusive relationships, as a way to prove socially that they are virtuous women.[57] Black women are hardly perceived as 'fragile victims' of patriarchy; it is consequently generally accepted that they endure more intense levels of violence before triggering a state response.[58] While this claim is

[54] Butler, *Gender Trouble*, 46. See also 191 et seq.

[55] Akotirene, *O que é interseccionalidade?*; T. R. Oliveira de Pires, 'Direitos humanos traduzidos em pretuguês', at Seminário Internacional Fazendo Gênero 11 & 13th Women's Worlds Congress (Anais Eletrônicos): Transformações, Conexões e Deslocamentos (Florianópolis, 2017); Flauzina, 'Lei Maria da Penha'.

[56] IBGE, Pesquisa Nacional por Amostra de Domicílio Contínua, 2018, www.ibge.gov.br/estatisticas/sociais/populacao/9171-pesquisa-nacional-por-amostra-de-domicilios-continua-mensal.html?=&t=o-que-e; IPEA, *Atlas da Violencia*, Brasilia, 2019, www.ipea.gov.br/atlasviolencia/download/19/atlas-da-violencia-2019.

[57] B. C. J. Pereira, *Tramas e dramas de gênero e de cor: a violência doméstica contra mulheres negras* (Brasília: Brado Negro, 2016), 134.

[58] Two of the most iconic theorists of black diasporic thought in Latin America, Lélia Gonzalez and Sueli Carneiro, have long argued that the traditional feminist discourse concerning the struggle for the emancipation of black women proved to be inadequate. Black women, warns Lélia Gonzalez, have always worked in 'crops or on the streets, as

empirically hard to substantiate, meaningful research findings support that correlation. For instance, a study conducted with black women victims of domestic violence underlined that racist offences within domestic settings are usually not perceived by the state or by the victims themselves as domestic violence and thus go unreported.[59] Our research reviewing 344 Urgent Protective Measures filed before three lower courts in Rio de Janeiro did not identify a single case in which racist offences operated as basis for domestic violence complaints.[60]

As black feminism has shown, women who are differently situated in social hierarchies have to overcome different obstacles in order to live a violence-free life. Different female bodies face different levels and forms of violence. Many racialized analyses of gender violence criticize public policies and legal choices for adopting mechanisms which are not fit for black, poor gender violence victims. In Brazil, the choice to prioritize judicial proceedings rather than other forms of state action (i.e. administrative solutions to problems related to shelters, housing, childcare, etc.) has proven to be elitist. This choice is further worsened by the fact that the legal remedies tend to be of a criminal nature, focusing on holding the aggressor accountable. In Brazil, case law has conditioned the application of MPL provisions focusing on the victim's protection and welfare to the filing of a criminal report. Considering the rates of police brutality against black, poor people and the lack of state services in *favelas* and poor neighbourhoods (except for the many 'war on drugs' police operations),

salespeople or prostitutes' and do not recognize the myth of female fragility in themselves. According to her, the body of the black woman, marked simultaneously by sexism, racism, and also by classism, acquires a specific social intelligibility, which materializes in contemporary Brazil in the figures of the hypersexualized samba dancer (the 'mulata') and the maid. L. Gonzalez, 'Racismo e Sexismo na Cultura Brasileira' (1984) *Revista Ciências Sociais Hoje* [223]–[244] at 224. Sueli Carneiro's statement is illuminating: 'we [black women] are part of a contingent of women, probably in the majority, who ... did not understand anything when feminists said that women should take to the streets and work!' S. Carneiro, 'Enegrecer o feminismo: a situação da mulher negra na América Latina a partir da perspectiva de gênero', in Ashoka Empreendimentos Sociais (ed.), *Racismos Contemporaneous* (Rio de Janeiro: Takano Editora, 2003), 12. See also Oliveira de Pires, 'Direitos humanos traduzidos em pretuguês'.

59 Pereira, *Tramas e dramas de gênero e de cor*, 74.

60 Bernardes, de Souza Costa and Vidal de Oliveira, *Violência Doméstica, discriminação de gênero e medidas protetivas de urgência.*

these choices, among other problems, make black women very hesitant to seek state help.[61]

When black women decide to pursue remedies in the judicial system, notwithstanding the problems mentioned, they are faced with additional obstacles that are not usually faced by the 'normal', white, middle-class, domestic violence victim. We read these as 'framing' problems related to which facts count as legally relevant as opposed to those aspects that are left out but would however be pivotal in order to tackle the violent situation.

Case law analyses show that the material and economic aspects of the violence black women endure are consistently left out of legal system consideration. This point is established by our research on 'urgent protective measure' proceedings in which the victims are black women.[62] The MPL establishes an extensive list of 'temporary restraining orders' (Arts. 18 to 24). While MPL does include provisions aiming at addressing issues related to the victim's material needs, these are highly ineffective.

Material allegations by women victims are routinely ignored by the police and the courts, as illustrated by the case of M. M., who suffered years of domestic violence before finally divorcing her husband. After the divorce, M.'s husband broke into her house and stole her fridge and stove. M. decided to go to the police because she worked on a minimum wage and was not able to buy new appliances. Remarkably, the police and the prosecutor's office characterized M.'s husband's conduct as 'arbitrary exercise of self-help' (Brazilian criminal code Art. 354). The definition of this crime requires a previous legitimate debt to be collected from the victim – a fact assumed by the police and prosecution and not even described on the record, let alone proven in court. The temporary restraining orders granted by the court forbade contact with the victim (MPL Arts. 22, III, 'a' and 'b'). However, the court ignored the one relief measure

[61] Flauzina, 'Lei Maria da Penha', 129.

[62] M. N. Bernardes and M. I. B. Albuquerque, 'Violências Interseccionais silenciadas em Medidas Protetivas de Urgência' (2016) 7 *Revista Direito e Praxis* 1–26. In this research, Bernardes and Albuquerque reviewed 187 Protective Measures issued by three domestic violence courts in the Rio de Janeiro state in favour of black women, aiming to identify the ways in which the judicial system does or does not acknowledge intersectional forms of violence.

that could truly have been of help to M.: 'restitution of property unduly subtracted from the victim by the aggressor', established in MPL Art. 24.[63]

This pattern of ignorance of substantial facts is also found in other cases, such as the one filed by C., a woman who was battered by her partner on the street after an argument over her request for child support to their daughter. C. decided to go the police and file a complaint. She indicated that she did not feel safe returning home after the incident. Her factual description was recorded in the police report as a 'complaint against minor bodily injury' (Brazilian Criminal Code Art. 129). The court granted a temporary restraining order (MPL Art. 22, III, a). However, the court never referred to the provisions of the MPL that would have allowed restricting his access to their daughter and establishing provisional alimony (MPL Art. 22, IV and V). The court also ignored MPL Art. 23, II, which states the right of 'return of the victim and her dependents to the respective domicile, after the aggressor's eviction'. Before filing the complaint, C. had two pressing problems: economically supporting her daughter and dealing with an abusive partner. After the complaint, she had several additional ones: finding a place to stay, creating a way for him to visit their daughter without compromising the one protective measure she was granted, or hiding their daughter from him, in case she feared for the child's safety.[64]

In these cases, the vulnerability of the victims was increased by the absence of an effective support network and financial resources that would have enabled them to leave their violent environment. The victims' impoverishment made them more susceptible to attacks as they were deprived of escape options due to the precarious structure of their households, the difficulty of access to the few shelters available, the lack of resources to pay for hotels or rent, and to the burden on their family members (generally poor and living under precarious conditions themselves) to host them. Significantly, petitions to remove the defendants from home were denied even when prohibitions to contact or to approach the victim were granted, regardless of the sheer contradiction in terms as, in the case of cohabitation, the granting of one without the other is ineffective, if not impossible. In general, the measure of removal from home is considered

[63] Ibid., at 731. [64] Ibid., at 715.

extremely burdensome to the defendant, especially when the home is owned by both or just by the aggressor.[65]

To be sure, these can be considered as cases primarily involving property rights, as well as the rights to physical or emotional integrity, and the right to life. But these legal translations do not capture the level of precariousness that these women, as well as their aggressors, endure, making the formal mechanisms of the law inaccessible or ineffective to them. Likewise, the typical remedy associated with the violation of these rights does not significantly help these victims. For example, the increasing informality in the labour market affects the black/poor population more profoundly than the white/middle class and makes judicially ordered alimony somewhat illusory as often the aggressor has no proved income. Likewise, the frequent absence of formal property titles on the houses in which victims and their aggressors live makes it difficult to proceed with legal mechanisms of asset distribution that are typical in divorce proceedings.[66] Moreover, even when the property is duly distributed, women overburdened with childcare and lower salaries in the job market are unable to buy other real estate and the money obtained from the distribution is quickly exhausted on rent payments.[67]

What underlies these findings is the fact that MPL, and the rule of law in general, is forged to attend to the needs of women who are victims of domestic violence *and also* have social and economic capital to leave a violent environment. This is the terrorized legal subject whom the MPL (as well as most domestic violence laws worldwide) was designed to safeguard. To protect this subject, all that is necessary is to keep the aggressor at bay and decide on patrimonial matters (such as alimony and property distribution after divorce). Black women who are victims of domestic violence, however, also need access to the material conditions that will allow them

[65] Ibid., at 716.

[66] Marilia Montenegro's work based on empirical research in the city of Recife also highlights the impact of social class in the use of judicial bodies and points out that because access to family law courts is made difficult for the lower classes due to high costs, the need for a lawyer, insufficient or non-existent public defenders, formal and slow processes, poor women direct to JVDF their typical problems related to the end of relationships, such as dividing assets, determining the cost of children's needs, etc. M. Montenegro, *Lei Maria da Penha: uma análise criminológico-crítica* (Rio de Janeiro: Revan, 2015), 171–172.

[67] P. R. Marinho, *Ocupações performativas: moradia, direito e corpos em aliança, thesis* (Rio de Janeiro: Pontifícia Universidade Católica do Rio de Janeiro, 2021), 30.

to leave the violent environment. These, however, are not adequately provided by law.

Black diasporic thought has denounced time and time again the intrinsic relation between rule of law, property and race which started in colonial times.[68] Likewise, one of the universally shared assumptions of de-colonial thinkers is that of the connection between coloniality, capitalism and racism.[69] According to this argument, whiteness has legitimized the violent access to property through legally mediated operations. The same capitalist-liberal framework from which the idea of rule of law and individual property stems also naturalized the brutalization of savage, non-European, bodies.[70] As a privileged aspect of personhood, whiteness has become an attribute of legal personhood via colonial, racist processes of domination.[71]

The last two sections have illuminated the ways in which Brazilian case law on domestic violence tends to require that women be vulnerable in order to be victims. To be comprehended as vulnerable, in turn, depends largely on the characterization of the victim as an adult, cis, woman, in a romantic relationship (current or past) with her aggressor. Arguably, therefore, women who most significantly benefit from the law tend to be white, middle-class women who have resources (or access to a support network) to help them secure a way out of the context of violence, and for whom the restriction on the aggressor's access to them is sufficient as an emergency protective measure. Without denying the importance of this

[68] C. L. Harris, 'Whiteness as Property' (1993) 106 *Harvard Law Review* [1710]–[1791]; A. L. Roberto and C. Ribeiro, *Racismo Estrutural e Aquisição da Propriedade* (São Paulo; Editora Contracorrente, 2020).

[69] F. C. Gutiérrez, A Quijano and F. C. Weffort, *Nuevos temas, nuevos contenidos? Las ciencias sociales de América Latina y el Caribe ante el nuevo siglo* (Caracas: UNESCO, 1989), 46; A. Quijano, 'Colonialidad del poder y clasificación social' (2000) 6 *Journal of World-Systems Research* 342–386 at 360.

[70] M. Lugones, 'Rumo a um feminismo descolonial' (2014) 22 *Estudos Feministas* 935–952 at 936.

[71] On this topic, Cheryl Harris' assertion is illuminating: 'Whiteness . . . is simultaneously an aspect of self-identity and of personhood, and its relation to the law of property is complex. Whiteness has functioned as self-identity in the domain of the intrinsic, personal and psychological; as reputation in the interstices between internal and external identity; and as property in the extrinsic, public and legal realms. According whiteness actual legal status converted an aspect of identity into an external object of property, moving whiteness from a privileged identity to a vested interest.' Harris, 'Whiteness as Property', at 1725.

law in terms of advancing women's rights, how can we make sense of these jurisprudential constructions? Can it be the case that the MPL itself is progressive and democratic but the case law it generates is not? Are the state officials in charge of domestic violence cases (police officers, prosecutors, judges) responsible for the law's ineffectiveness for many women? This would be an overly simplistic interpretation, and therefore an erroneous one, that would fail to capture the ways in which power operates epistemically and politically.

4. The Framing of Domestic Violence and the Politically Induced Precarity of Some Women

According to Butler, vulnerability is a hallmark of our human existence. We are physically vulnerable to an exteriority composed of other bodies and institutions that can make us live, or let us die.[72] Being a body, she says, is necessarily being exposed to a continuous social process of being crafted through discourse, work and desire. The beings that 'persist and flourish' achieve this due to an extensive social network of continuous support from childhood through adulthood: if we live, it is because we did not die, and this is inexorably due to the social infrastructure that has supported us.[73]

We are not, however, all vulnerable in the same way. For Butler, 'The more or less existential conception of "precariousness" is thus linked with a more specifically political notion of "precarity"'.[74] The precariousness of bodies can be politically induced by unequal distribution of access to the social infrastructure of shelter, food, work and health, which supports life and turns it into a liveable life, one that is protected from injury and in relation to which death is followed by grief. Precarity, in a political sense, thus refers to 'that politically induced condition of maximized vulnerability and exposure for populations exposed to arbitrary state violence, to street or domestic violence, or other forms not enacted by states but for

[72] Foucault, *Discipline and Punish*.

[73] J. Butler, *Precarious Life* (London: Verso, 2004), 22; J. Butler, *Frames of War* (London: Verso, 2009), 14; J. Butler, *Notes toward a Performative Theory of Assembly* (Cambridge, MA: Harvard University Press, 2015), 99.

[74] Butler, *Frames of War*, 3.

which the judicial instruments of states fail to provide sufficient protection or redress'.[75]

Which living beings are recognized as beings whose lives matter, and which are not? This framing occurs through a series of epistemic operations that naturalize an unequal distribution of access to this infrastructure, selecting those who are able to be recognized as subjects. These frames, these epistemic operations, provide us with the intelligibility scheme which lends us the terms necessary to recognize life.[76] They establish the fields of recognizability – that is, the general conditions, historically articulated, that produce the concrete norms of recognition of the subjects of rights in each context, and thus are prior to the recognition itself. These conditions 'prepare or shape a subject for recognition'.[77]

The framing of liveable lives are, as Butler says, 'politically saturated', and are 'themselves operations of power'.[78] Like the framing in a photograph, you may draw attention to something specific you want to highlight. What is chosen to be framed in photography, as in life in general, is the result of hegemonic norms of recognizability; and the chosen frame simultaneously reproduces and naturalizes these norms in social life. Even when the framing shows something that ought to generate criticism, it is in relation to the hegemonic norms that it does so.[79]

So, if we think of gender violence as a frame, who would be framed in this photo? When is 'violence' recognized as such? Which facts are framed as legally relevant? Who has a gendered exposure to violence that is recognized as such? In the analysis of the case law provided, we suggest that the power dynamics structured around racism, sexism and classism provide the intelligibility schemes that allow us to answer these questions. They are the frames which allow the naturalization of black women's 'maximized vulnerability and exposure' to domestic violence. They also provide the general and historical conditions that create the norms of recognition for potential victims: vulnerable, white, middle class, ciswomen.

It is undeniable, however, that the MPL also applies to black women who have suffered gender violence. In fact, in many jurisdictions, it applies

[75] Butler, *Notes toward a Performative Theory of Assembly*, 33.

[76] M. I. B. Albuquerque, *De quantos caminhos se faz um direito? Mobilidade e gênero nos quadros da cidade* (Rio de Janeiro: Gramma, 2020), 129.

[77] Butler, *Frames of War*, 5. [78] Ibid., 1. [79] Ibid., 78–84.

mainly to cases of violence against black women, if only because white women tend to seek remedies for the same problems in family courts.[80] Therefore, the relevant inquiry is the extent to which these women are actually protected by the law. To what extent do they matter within the scheme of intelligibility of living lives? The fact that black women can be included in legal proceedings and are commonly declared victims of domestic violence is not enough to affirm that the state, in fact, protects them as subjects of law. As Albuquerque writes, 'There is no clear limit [in relation to who is inside or who is outside the frame] mainly because the frame is not for bodies, but for conditions of comprehension.'[81] Certainly, whoever is outside the 'photo' does not cease to exist, but their existence is not apprehended by the structures of power as a full subject of rights: 'it is living, but not a life'.[82] 'Inside' and 'outside' are constitutive of the very possibility of framing.[83]

But some opportunities invite us to put the frames in question[84] – to 'frame the frame'.[85]When these things happen, one is confronted with different views on what is framed, potentially bringing it to crisis:

> [W]hen a frame breaks with itself that taken-for-granted reality is called into question, exposing the orchestrating designs of the authority who sought to control the frame. ... As a consequence, the frames that, in effect, decide which lives will be recognizable as lives and which will not, must circulate in order to establish their hegemony. This circulation brings out or, rather, is the iterable structure of the frame. As frames break from themselves in order to install themselves, other possibilities for apprehension emerge.[86]

Some judicial decisions on domestic violence, which are extreme in terms of faulty apprehension of black women as subjects of rights, may (or may not) create the same effects. In one way, they reiterate the hegemonic norms of recognizability of domestic violence victims; in another, they offer an opportunity to bring this frame into question. For instance, the case of M. previously described, whose ex-husband broke into her house and stole her fridge and stove, invites us to this exercise.

[80] Montenegro, *Lei Maria da Penha.*
[81] Albuquerque, *De quantos caminhos se faz um direito?*, 131.
[82] Butler, *Frames of War*, 8.
[83] Albuquerque, *De quantos caminhos se faz um direito?*, 130.
[84] Butler, *Notes toward a Performative Theory of Assembly*, 21.
[85] Butler, *Frames of War*, 8. [86] Ibid. 12.

Both the legal framing of the facts ('arbitrary exercise of one's rights') and the protective measures issued (prohibition to approach and to contact), as well as the silence about Art. 23, I (obligation to return stolen goods), when brought into focus, create an incongruent picture of what transpired. It is undeniable that the legal response to the facts in this case is unsuccessful in terms of providing effective protection to the victim. She is not recognized as a full subject of rights.

However, critical review of case law opens the opportunity to criticize how Western law in general frames the subject of rights. When the operations of power which create the field of recognizable subjects are revealed, the limits to this frame are exposed. If we do not understand how sexist, racist and class societies operate, it will not be enough to indicate those who are systematically excluded from recognition by these structures. The task is to bring the entire frame into crisis, creating opportunities for new forms of power operations, which create more egalitarian and democratic frames.

5. Concluding Remarks

In this chapter, we use Brazilian case law on domestic violence as a case study to examine the implications of international norms on gender violence resulting from transnational feminist activism. The results of this activism, on the one hand, are significant achievements. On the other hand, however, they can be seen as focusing on the reproduction of forms of violence against subjects whose bodies are already subordinated by the power structures that underlie both feminism and the rule of law – namely racism and classism. We subscribe to analyses that call attention to the internal divergences of transnational feminism and maintain that its major victories in the fight against gender violence since the 1980s manifest a hegemonic worldview of feminism that does not confront or undo these power structures. These achievements in international law have influenced domestic legislation fighting gender-based violence, and how this legislation has been interpreted in various countries, as is evidenced by the example of the MPL in Brazil. Based on the analysis of the MPL case law, we maintain that the terrorized subject is a political and epistemic construction of the rule of law that the law itself later claims to represent. This subject, the victim of domestic violence, is construed as a fragile and vulnerable cis-woman, who needs to be urgently removed from her aggressor for protection. This profile, however, does not apply perfectly to all female bodies, either because they are not perceived as fragile, or because the mere removal of the aggressor through the usual legal resources will not provide sufficient protection. These women are racially marked and have historically been deprived of a support network that allows the material conditions to escape the situation of violence. In other words, these black and low-income women do not have the material resources that the standard legal subject is supposed to have. We maintain that this is not an isolated problem of the MPL and nor does it result only from judges who lack a sense of social justice, rather it results from implicit rules of recognition of the victim of violence from social intelligibility schemes or frames, which are determined by racism and classism.

These epistemological and political considerations indisputably pose different challenges for the design and implementation of more egalitarian public policies. If, still with Butler, there are no paths for the production of subjectivity outside power relations, any attempt to build frames immune to relationships of power, in reality, serves to further naturalize the epistemic operations of normalization and exclusion, increasing the exposure of those 'outside' to politically induced precarity. However, the social processes of construction of the conditions of recognizability, which gradually and repeatedly affirm the norms of subject recognition, are not homogeneous, stable or infallible. Each time they are reiterated, through the law's application, an opportunity is provided to reveal their operations and generate new standards. In terms of protection for women terrified by gender violence, each of these terms – 'women', 'violence' and 'gender', as well as 'victim' – need to be brought to crises so that the frames of intelligibility that give them meaning, as well as their political effects in terms of induced precarity (or protection from it) may be revealed. In the case of black women, criticizing these terms will reveal, among other things, how the state deals with the material conditions underlying domestic violence.

4 The Sexual Subject

Recasting the Sexual Citizen

Melissa Murray

How do we construct sexual citizenship? Put differently, how do we as a society identify those whose sexual conduct and identities as sexual beings are consistent with our notions of citizenship and the public good? Often, identifying the ideal sexual citizen means identifying the traits associated with sex and sexuality that we deem useful, beneficial and productive – the kinds of sexual conduct we value, reward and encourage. But, as is often the case when constructing ideals, our understanding of that which is normatively desirable and desired is often informed by its foil – that which is decidedly undesirable. In this regard, the construction of a normative ideal of sexual citizenship has been tethered to the production of the sexual outlaw – those individuals who live their lives outside of the bounds that constrain citizenship. But it is not just that the law's construction of the ideal sexual subject depends on the construction of its foil (the sexual outlaw); law also constructs sexual citizenship in ways that are deeply gendered and raced.

1. Constructing the Sexual Citizen

Historically, in the Anglo-American legal tradition, a large part of construction of sexual citizenship relied on the interplay of marriage and the criminal law. Indeed, the task of casting the ideal sexual citizen was organized along two distinct rubrics: marriage and crime. On one side of the ledger was marriage, the normative ideal for adult intimate life. The procedures for executing a valid marriage in the United States speak to marriage's role in constructing sexual citizenship. Procedurally, in all jurisdictions in the United States, lawful marriage requires compliance with the state's licensing apparatus.[1] Through licensing, the couple confirms to each other, and the overseeing state, their consent to the union and their capacity – in terms of mental and physical fitness and age – to enter into marriage.[2] In addition to satisfying these procedural requirements, applicants for a marriage licence must further comply with any substantive restrictions as to who may and may not marry. For example, all American jurisdictions prohibit marriages between more than two persons, between consanguineous relations, and between parties where one (or both) of the participants is below the jurisdiction's age of consent.[3] Historically, this litany of substantive restrictions was even more robust. Until 1967, some US jurisdictions prohibited interracial marriages;[4] and until quite recently, most US jurisdictions universally prohibited marriages between persons of the same gender.[5]

Despite variation in law across the United States, the procedural and substantive restrictions on marriage are surprisingly consistent and uniform – and indeed, that is the point. Through these restrictions, law clearly establishes those relationships that are eligible for state recognition; but equally important, together, these restrictions also purposefully articulated an ideal of marriage and intimate life. Until the twentieth century, these rules and restrictions made clear that marriage was an intra-racial, monogamous, exogamous and heterosexual union between consenting adults. And while the modern-day legal understanding of marriage in the United States has evolved to include interracial and same-sex unions, marriage continues to be understood in all American jurisdictions as a monogamous and exogamous enterprise undertaken by consenting adults.

In this regard, through the legal regulation of entry into marriage, law lays out the normative parameters for intimate life by articulating what marriage is and should be. In so doing, it marks marriage as the normative ideal of intimate life. Moreover, it constructs a boundary that separates sexual behaviour deemed worthy and legitimate (marriage) from that which is unworthy and illegitimate (behaviour ineligible for, or inimical

[1] M. Murray, 'Strange Bedfellows: Criminal Law, Family Law, and the Legal Construction of Intimate Life' (2009) 94 *Iowa Law Review* 1253–1314 at 1264–1265.

[2] Ibid., at 1264. [3] Ibid., at 1264 and n. 43, identifying example statutes.

[4] Ibid., at 1265. See *Loving* v. *Virginia*, 388 US 1 (1967), holding state bans on interracial marriage unconstitutional.

[5] Murray, 'Strange Bedfellows', at 1265. See *Obergefell* v. *Hodges*, 135 S. Ct. 2584 (2015), holding state bans on same-sex marriage unconstitutional.

to, marriage). In this regard, the boundary that divided marriage from non-marriage was not simply about distinguishing sexuality deemed worthy and legitimate from that which was not; it also simultaneously defined the type of sex and sexuality that would be subject to law's protections, and that which would be unprotected, and instead subject to law's punishment.

However, even as law prescribes marriage as the normative ideal for intimate life, historically it has been hobbled in trying to police these boundaries. How to ensure that sexual conduct is limited to marriage? How to ensure that married couples do not flout these procedural and substantive restrictions when entering into marriage? How to ensure that their sexual conduct as married persons remains socially productive – that is, monogamous and reproductive? To be sure, there have been precious few civil mechanisms for maintaining marriage's position as the normative ideal for intimate life. Certainly, annulment provided one legal channel for maintaining marriage's normative priority, but its reach was limited. If individuals flouted the procedural or substantive restrictions on marriage, their union could be deemed null *ab initio* (in the case of most substantive restrictions) or voidable (in the case of the procedural restrictions).[6] But the prospect of annulment often was an inadequate deterrent to substantive and procedural deviations from marital norms. After all, if procedural and substantive formalities had not been observed, rather than annul the union, couples could simply mask the truth of their legal status and continue to live as though validly married.

In circumstances involving sustained marital misconduct, divorce, rather than annulment, might serve as a means of sanctioning an errant spouse, but historically, divorce was unevenly available, required litigation and often entailed serious social consequences, even for the 'innocent' spouse.[7] Amatory torts, such as the torts of seduction and intentional interference with the marital relationship,[8] might confer a legal sanction

[6] See D. K. Weisberg, *Modern Family Law*, 7th ed. (New York: Wolters Kluwer, 2020), 179–180: 'Substantive defects (same-sex, bigamous, and incestuous unions) render the marriage void.'

[7] For a description of the difficulties of obtaining a divorce before the rise of no-fault regimes, see L. M. Friedman, 'A Dead Language: Divorce Law and Practice Before No-Fault' (2000) 86 *Virginia Law Review* 1497–1536 at 1501–1510.

[8] For a discussion on the tort of seduction, see M. Murray, 'Marriage as Punishment' (2012) 112 *Columbian Law Review* 1–65 at 12–16; see generally Corbett, for a discussion of the tort of intentional interference with the marital relationship. W. R. Corbett, 'A Somewhat Modest Proposal to Prevent Adultery and Save Families: Two Old Torts Looking for a New Career' (2001) 33 *Arizona State Law Journal* 985–1055.

on an errant spouse, but the deterrent effects were weak, particularly if the wrongful actor was wealthy. The punishment – money damages – could be easily disbursed and the wrongful conduct resumed.

But perhaps the most critical impediment to law's ability to police marriages and ensure compliance with its normative vision of marriage through civil means was the rhetoric of family privacy, which traditionally marked the interior of family life as impervious to state intrusion and regulation.[9] Although marriage law could regulate entry into and exit from marriage, it was unable to regulate an intact marriage or intimate arrangements that existed outside marriage. It could prohibit consanguineous relatives from marrying, but it could not prohibit them from having sex or an intimate relationship with one another outside marriage. It could insist that marriage and marital sex should be procreative, but it could not actually prevent married couples from taking steps to avoid pregnancy and reproduction.

If the law of marriage was limited to policing at the gates of marriage and only gestured vaguely to what existed outside marriage, how then did it enforce the normative ideal of marriage as the archetype of intimate life and protect it from the corrosive influences of external forces? As I explain, the civil means available – procedural and substantive restrictions on marriage, annulment, divorce and amatory action – were inadequate to police the normative ideal of marriage. Instead, the law of marriage relied on criminal law to assist in defining what marriage is and is not, and to police marriage's normative boundaries.[10] More importantly, while law constructed marriage as the normative ideal, it only referenced that which is outside of marriage by the vaguest implication. That is, though family law and these other civil interventions could mark what is 'good', they were far less forceful in marking what is 'bad'. For this reason, criminal law's intervention was doubly important. Not only did criminal law reinforce marriage's position as the normative ideal for intimate life by preventing that which is normatively bad from corrupting and contaminating marriage, it also explicitly marked what is bad *as bad*.

[9] This principle is exemplified by *McGuire* v. *McGuire*, 59 N.W.2d paras. 336, 337 (Neb. 1953). There, the court refused to compel a husband to support his wife in the manner she desired on the grounds that '[p]ublic policy' dictated that '[t]he living standards of a family are a matter of concern to the household, and not for the courts to determine'. Ibid., para. 342.

[10] Murray, 'Strange Bedfellows', at 1266.

Criminal law accomplishes all of this in a number of ways. In most, if not all, jurisdictions, family law's substantive restrictions on entry to marriage are reinforced by criminal bars on the same conduct. For example, not only was interracial marriage once prohibited as a civil matter, it was also subject to criminal penalties.[11] Indeed, interracial sex itself was criminalized as miscegenation,[12] simultaneously underscoring the understanding of marriage as intra-racial and the notion of sex as deeply constitutive of marriage itself. Likewise, while marriage between consanguineous relatives is prohibited as a civil matter, sex (again, an essential incident of marriage) between such relatives is criminalized as incest.[13]

At every turn, criminal law's prohibitions reinforce marriage law's substantive restrictions. The procedural and substantive restrictions on

[11] See, e.g., *Jackson* v. *State*, 72 So. 2d para. 114 (Ala. Ct. App. 1954), cert. denied, 72 So. 2d para. 116 (Ala. 1954), cert. denied, 348 US 888 (1954), sentencing an African-American woman to five years in prison for marrying a white man.

[12] The Supreme Court upheld an Alabama anti-miscegenation law in 1883, *Pace* v. *Alabama*, 106 US 583, 585 (1883), before declaring a Florida anti-miscegenation statute unconstitutional in 1964. *McLaughlin* v. *Florida*, 379 US 184, 196 (1964). For an argumentation stating that natural law prohibits miscegenation, see also R. Desty, *A Compendium of American Criminal Law* (San Francisco, CA: Sumner Whitney & Co., 1882), 59a. For an outline of the adoption of traditional nuptial prohibitions, see M. Grossberg, *Governing the Hearth: Law and the Family in Nineteenth-Century America* (Chapel Hill: University of North Carolina Press, 1985), 105–108. For a definition of miscegenation, see T. W. Hughes, *A Treatise on Criminal Law and Procedure* (Indianapolis, IN: Bobbs-Merrill, 1919), 802. For an examination the effect of marriages within prohibited degrees of relationship, see E. W. Spencer, *A Treatise on the Law of Domestic Relations and the Status and Capacity of Natural Persons as Generally Administered in the United States* (New York: Banks Law Publishing Company, 1911), 57. For a description of miscegenation, see F. Wharton, *A Treatise in Criminal Law*, 9th ed., 2 vols. (Philadelphia, PA: Kay and Brother, 1885), vol. 2, p. 1754.

[13] For a description of the crime of incest, see J. P. Bishop, *Commentaries on the Criminal Law*, 2 vols. (Boston, MA: Little, Brown and Company, 1858), vol. 2, 15. Noting the criminalization of incest, see L. M. Friedman, *Crime and Punishment in American History* (New York: Basic Books, 1993), p. 128. For a description of the crime of incest in New York, see F. Wharton, *A Treatise on the Criminal Law of the United States*, 4th ed. (Philadelphia, PA: Kay and Brother, 1857), 2621. For a discussion on the criminalization of incest in the United States, see C. McNiece Metteer, 'Some "Incest" Is Harmless Incest: Determining the Fundamental Right to Marry of Adults Related by Affinity without Resorting to State Incest Statutes' (2000) 10 *Kansas Journal of Law & Public Policy* 262 at 273–274.

marriage say what marriage is, and criminal law underscores this normative understanding by criminalizing behaviour, and actors, ineligible for or inimical to marriage. In this way, there is a structural symmetry between criminal law and marriage law. They work together, cooperatively defining what marriage is and what it is not.

But this is not the full extent of criminal law's role in helping family law regulate marriage and intimate life. Until the late twentieth century, the criminal law in most jurisdictions prohibited fornication[14] – consensual sex outside marriage – thereby highlighting marriage's role as the licensed locus for sexual activity.[15] Further, the historic availability of marriage as a defence to fornication effectively channelled the offensive conduct and actors into marriage where 'lust was transformed into virtue'.[16]

Beyond simply identifying marriage as the appropriate site for sex, criminal law also assisted in elaborating the normative content of married life. Consider fornication's analogue, rape. At common law, rape was the unlawful carnal knowledge of a woman, not the defendant's wife, forcibly and without her consent.[17] This common law definition thrice underscored

[14] See, e.g., *Doe* v. *Duling*, 782 F.2d paras. 1202, 1204 (4th Cir. 1986), discussing Virginia's fornication law, enacted in 1819. For a discussion of the long history of the criminalization of fornication, see Bishop, *Commentaries on the Criminal Law*, 46. For a discussion of colonial social norms regarding out-of-wedlock sex, see J. D'Emilio and E. B. Freedman, *Intimate Matters: A History of Sexuality in America* (Chicago, IL: University of Chicago Press, 1988), 18. For a discussion of marriage's place as the approved site for sexual activity, see Friedman, *Crime and Punishment in American History*, 127. For a discussion on fornication, see F. Wharton, *A Treatise on the Criminal Law of the United States*, 5th ed., 2 vols. (Philadelphia, PA: Kay and Brother, 1861), vol. 2, 2667. Case acknowledges that marriage licenses sexual activity, but notes that, presently, unwanted marital sex is restricted by the criminal law. M. A. Case, 'Marriage Licenses' (2003) 89 *Minnesota Law Review* 1758–1779 at 1769.

[15] D'Emilio and Freedman note that prohibitions on sex were not intended to 'squelch sexual expression, but rather to channel it into what they considered to be its proper setting . . . marriage'. D'Emilio and Freedman, *Intimate Matters*, 16; Friedman, *Crime and Punishment in American History*, 127: 'By law, only married people were entitled to any kind of sex life at all'; A. R. Dubler, 'Immoral Purposes: Marriage and the Genus of Illicit Sex' (2006) 115 *Yale Law Journal* 756–813 at 777: 'Marriage . . . was the core legal site for licit sex'.

[16] Dubler, 'Immoral Purposes', at 763. For a description of the channelling function of family law by emphasizing how 'law may shape behavior in complex ways through its affirmation or condemnation of various types of conduct', see also M. C. Regan, Jr, *Family Law and the Pursuit of Intimacy* (New York: NYU Press, 1993), 136.

[17] Blackstone defines rape as 'the carnal knowledge of a woman forcibly and against her will'. W. Blackstone, *Commentaries on the Laws of England*, 4 vols. (Oxford: Clarendon Press, 1770), vol. 4, *210. Under common law, a husband could not be found guilty of raping his wife. See *State* v. *Huffman*, 87 SE.2d paras. 541, 555 (Va. 1955). 'At common law . . . the

the role that marriage played in distinguishing between lawful (marital) sex and criminal sex. As an initial matter, the common law definition referred to this form of criminal sex as both 'unlawful' and non-consensual. In this regard, it made clear that what distinguished rape – unlawful sex – from lawful sex was the fact of legal status: marriage. Sex within marriage was per se lawful, as spouses were 'in laws' to one another.[18] Likewise, the emphasis on consent further distinguished rape – non-consensual sex – from marriage, which, by law, was a legal status that required the consent of both parties.[19] On this account, sex that occurred in marriage was presumptively consensual simply because it proceeded from the parties' lawful status as man and wife.[20] Finally, the imagined rape victim was a woman who was not the defendant's *wife*, making clear that sex that occurred within the confines of marriage was distinct and distinguishable from sex that occurred in an 'unlawful' status – that is, outside marriage. As a number of commentators have explained, the common law understanding that consent to marriage included consent to all sexual activity within marriage underwrote the historic prohibition on

crime of rape is carnal knowledge, forcibly and against her will, of a female person, not his wife, by a male person who is capable of performing such act'; *State* v. *Golden*, 430 A.2d paras. 433, 435 (RI 1981), defining common law rape as the 'act of sexual intercourse committed by a man with a woman not his wife and without her consent'; J. Chitty, *A Practical Treatise on the Criminal Law*, 4 vols. (Philadelphia, PA: Edward Earle, 1816), vol. 3, 811: 'A man cannot, indeed, be himself guilty of a rape on his own wife'; W. L. Clark and W. L. Marshall, *A Treatise on the Law of Crimes*, 2 vols. (St. Paul, MN: Keefe-Davidson Law Book Co., 1900), vol. 1, 422: '[A] man cannot be guilty of this offense [rape] by having carnal knowledge of his wife, and it can make no difference that he does so by force and against her will.'

18 See, e.g., W. L. Clark, Jr, *Hand-Book of Criminal Law* (St. Paul, MN: West Publishing Co., 1894), 190. 'It is lawful for a husband to have carnal knowledge of his wife, and the fact that he uses force does not make him guilty of rape.'

19 See n. 2 and accompanying text.

20 See, e.g., *State* v. *Haines*, 25 So. 372, 372 (La. 1899). 'The husband of a woman cannot himself be guilty of an actual rape upon his wife, on account of the matrimonial consent which she has given, and which she cannot retract'; *Frazier* v. *State*, 86 SW paras. 754, 755 (Tex. 1905), stating that 'all the authorities hold that a man cannot himself be guilty of actual rape upon his wife' and that 'one of the main reasons being the matrimonial consent which she gives when she assumes the marriage relation, and which the law will not permit her to retract in order to charge her husband with the offense of rape'; M. Hale, *The History of the Pleas of the Crown*, 1st US ed., 2 vols. (Philadelphia, PA: R. H. Small Publisher, 1847), vol. 1, 628: '[T]he husband cannot be guilty of a rape committed by himself upon his lawful wife, for by their mutual matrimonial consent and contract the wife hath given up herself in this kind unto her husband, which she cannot retract.'

recognizing and prosecuting marital rape.[21] In these ways, the criminal law defining rape and fornication not only made clear that marriage was the lawful locus for sex; it also underscored that sex within marriage was desirable and expected, such that wives were presumed to consent each and every time their husbands sought or demanded sex.

And just as the rhetoric of family privacy assisted in defining the scope of marriage law's interventions, it also helped to elaborate criminal law's role in defining the normative understanding of marriage. Historically, the norm of marital privacy did not simply limit civil regulation on intact marriages, it also counselled against criminal regulation and intervention into intact marriages. Consider the examples of marital rape and domestic violence. Traditionally, spousal violence was exempted from state intervention and criminal prosecution.[22] In the case of domestic violence, state intervention was considered unwarranted because, at common law, husbands retained the prerogative to physically chastise errant wives.[23] In the case of marital rape, criminal prosecution was deemed unsuitable because consent to marriage included consent to conjugal sex.[24]

In discussing these omissions from criminal regulation, most scholars have focused on privacy's role in secluding the family from state

[21] For a discussion of Sir Matthew Hale's consent theory, see J. E. Hasday, 'Contest and Consent: A Legal History of Marital Rape' (2000) 88 *California Law Review* 1373–1506 at 1398–1400. On the origins of the marital rape exemption, see R. M. Ryan, 'The Sex Right: A Legal History of the Marital Rape Exemption' (1995) 20 *Law & Social Inquiry* 941–1001 at 944–947.

[22] Minow noted that '[f]or husbands and wives, it was the boundary of the home' that placed intimate violence 'beyond the reach of the law'. M. Minow, 'Between Intimates and between Nations: Can Law Stop the Violence?'(2000) 50 *Case Western Reserve Law Review* 851–868 at 852. Siegel noted that in the nineteenth century, it became 'commonplace' to depict the home and family as 'fundamentally distinct from other spheres of social life'. R. B. Siegel, '"The Rule of Love": Wife Beating as Prerogative and Privacy' (1996) 105 *Yale Law Journal* 2117–2208 at 2147.

[23] See Blackstone, *Commentaries*, vol. 1, 444: 'The husband also ... might give his wife moderate correction. For, as he is to answer for her misbehaviour, the law thought it reasonable to intrust him with this power of restraining her, by domestic chastisement, in the same moderation that a man is allowed to correct his servants or children'. For a discussion of the husbandly privilege of marital chastisement, see R. E. Dobash and R. Dobash, *Violence against Wives: A Case against the Patriarchy* (New York: Free Press, 1979), 48–74.

[24] See nn. 20–21 and accompanying text.

intervention.[25] However, law's construction of the marital family as a private entity unsuitable for legal intervention is only one aspect of this dynamic. In refusing to intervene in these situations, criminal law further elaborated the normative content of marriage. By refusing to characterize spousal violence as assault and unwanted conjugal sex as rape, criminal law underscored that marriage was a status relationship with attendant obligations and prerogatives that could not be redefined or renegotiated by the parties. It was a space where husbands had a right to 'correct' wives and where conjugal sex was expected and welcomed.

The criminal law went beyond simply reinforcing marriage's place as the licensed site of sexual activity. It also helped to elaborate the normative contours of marriage and marital sex, while also reinforcing the gender roles forged in marriage. For example, sodomy and other forms of same-sex sexual activity historically were criminalized.[26] In this way, criminal law underscored marriage's heterosexual character – and in so doing, solidified marriage's place as a crucible for the production of gender roles.[27] And to the extent that sodomy and other same-sex activity could not result in pregnancy, criminal prohibitions on these forms of sex further emphasized the procreative potential – and expectations – of marriage. Likewise, criminal prohibitions on abortion and contraception, even by married couples, further clarified the procreative nature of marriage.[28] And

[25] Fineman noted that dependency is privatized within the family unit. M. L. A. Fineman, 'Masking Dependency: The Political Role of Family Rhetoric' (1995) 81 *Virginia Law Review* 2181–2215 at 2187. For a description of legal regulation of the family as 'a system that privatizes dependence, placing responsibility for caretaking on the family rather than the state', see J. S. Hendricks, 'Essentially a Mother' (2007) 13 *William & Mary Journal of Race, Gender, and Social Justice* 429–482 at 464. Rosenbury observes that states have 'recognized families as a means to privatize dependency, particularly the dependency of children on their parents and the financial and emotional dependencies thought to arise when individuals share a household'. L. A. Rosenbury, 'Friends with Benefits?' (2007) 106 *Michigan Law Review* 189–242 at 193.

[26] On the history of anti-sodomy laws, see generally W. N. Eskridge, Jr, *Dishonorable Passions: Sodomy Laws in America 1861–2003* (New York: Viking Penguin Group, 2008.

[27] Of course, criminal sodomy prohibitions as an explicit condemnation of same-sex intimacy are a product of the late twentieth century. See Brief for Professors of History George Chauncey et al. as Amici Curiae Supporting Petitioners, *Lawrence* v. *Texas*, 539 US 558 (2003), at *2–3, *7, indicating that anti-sodomy laws were not directed at same-sex couples until the 1970s.

[28] For a discussion on the history of criminal prohibitions on abortion and contraception, see Grossberg, *Governing the Hearth*, 159–178.

to the extent that heterosexual marriage was intended to be a procreative enterprise that yielded children, criminal laws that prohibited non-procreative sex acts fuelled the cultivation of reproductive sex roles in marriage. With criminal law's assistance, marriage was not simply cast as a procreative enterprise; it was one in which the woman's 'paramount destiny and mission' was 'to fulfill the noble and benign offices of wife and mother'.[29]

The legal treatment of seduction is also instructive on this point. In the mid-nineteenth century, in an effort to stanch the spread of prostitution, many US jurisdictions began criminalizing seduction.[30] In most jurisdictions, the elements of the crime were: (1) an illicit connection (sexual intercourse); (2) with a young woman of previously chaste character (in fact or by reputation); and (3) under a promise to marry.[31] As one jurisdiction's high court explained, the crime was intended 'to prevent the obtaining of the female's consent to sexual intercourse' by 'the arts of designing and unprincipled men, in whom she may repose trust and confidence, and to whose solicitations she may yield, believing that their promises of marriage are made in good faith, and will be fulfilled'.[32]

Importantly, the requirement that the 'illicit connection' occur in conjunction with a promise to marry not only distinguished seduction from other categories of criminal sex, it also laid bare the nature of the victim's injury. 'The evil which led to the enactment of [the seduction statute] was not that females were seduced ... but that after the ends of the seducer were accomplished his victim was abandoned to her disgrace.'[33] Recognizing that the defendant's promise to marry was the gravamen of the offence, most jurisdictions allowed the defendant to avoid prosecution and punishment by marrying the victim.[34]

Although marriage could serve as a defence to seduction, the law was clear – the defendant was not getting off easy. Marriage was not a convenient way to avoid the seduction prosecution – it was a mitigated

[29] *Bradwell* v. *Illinois*, 83 US 130, 141 (1872) (Bradley J, concurring).

[30] Murray describes the push by moral reformers to criminalize seduction. Murray, 'Marriage as Punishment', at 8–18.

[31] Ibid., at 18–19 and n. 88.

[32] *Callahan* v. *State*, 63 Ind. Apras. 198, 204 (1878), citing 2 Ind. Rev. Stat. 431 para. 15 (Edwin A. Davis ed., 1876).

[33] *State* v. *Otis*, 34 NE paras. 954, 955 (Ind. 1893).

[34] For a collection of statutes, see Murray, 'Marriage as Punishment', at 21, n. 99.

penalty that relieved the defendant of a criminal conviction and imprisonment so that he might undertake spousal obligations to support his wife and family. On this account, marriage did not absolve his initial crime; it merely transferred responsibility for disciplining the defendant from the penitentiary to the marital family[35] – from the domain of criminal to the law of marriage. Once married and subject to marriage's duties and obligations, the defendant was transformed from a deviant into a husband responsible for providing for his wife and family. Like criminal sanctions, marriage required consistent hard work and the imposition of certain behavioural norms that were understood to provide discipline and structure, diverting the defendant from any latent deviant tendencies and allowing him to rejoin society as a productive (sexual) citizen.

The obligations and responsibilities of marriage also proved disciplinary and redemptive for the victim, whose own moral character was compromised by seduction and its 'illicit connection'. The consistent labour and work associated with wifely domesticity diverted the victim from less worthy pursuits and reformed her errant ways.[36] Like the defendant, marriage's discipline allowed her to be reformed and to rejoin society under the mantle of respectability and stability associated with matronhood.

Accordingly, marriage's role in the administration of criminal seduction statutes supported the criminal law's interest in punishment and reform, and in so doing, underscored marriage's role as a means of sexual regulation and discipline. Though marriage might appear an unusual sanction to modern readers, for nineteenth- and twentieth-century legal actors it was

[35] Some jurisdictions instead made marriage akin to probation. Texas, for example, criminalized seduction and provided that a subsequent marriage would suspend the defendant's prosecution. See *Waldon* v. *State*, 98 SW paras. 848–849 (Tex. Crim. App. 1906). If the defendant lived with his wife for two years thereafter, the prosecution would be dismissed entirely. Ibid. However, if the defendant deserted his wife within two years, or otherwise failed to uphold his husbandly obligations, the prosecution would be revived and marriage would provide no defence. Ibid. In some jurisdictions, the law required some assurance that the defendant would uphold the responsibilities of a husband. Georgia, for example, allowed a seducer to avoid prosecution by marriage only if he posted bond for his wife's support. *Duke* v. *Brown*, 38 SE paras. 764, 765 (Ga. 1901). If he could not post bond, the seducer's prosecution would not be dismissed until he had cohabited with, and supported, his wife for five years. Ibid.

[36] Ristroph and Murray noted that 'women were disciplined by their caregiving obligations and their financial dependence on their husbands'. A. Ristroph and M. Murray, 'Disestablishing the Family' (2010) 119 *Yale Law Journal* 1236–1279 at 1258.

understood to be a potent means of punishment, discipline and redress. For both parties, the obligations of marriage imposed deprivations of liberty and freedom, as much as it offered the possibility of love and commitment. And importantly, it did so for life. In this way, the vision of marriage promoted by criminal seduction statutes was not a misty-eyed, storybook ideal of companionate marriage. Instead, marriage was a more nuanced and complicated institution that came with positive attributes as well as an onerous set of sociolegal obligations.

In this regard, both marriage and crime were, as a historical matter, the principal means by which law constructed and enforced its understanding of sexual citizenship. Marriage law prescribed an ideal of productive sexuality – marriage and marital sex that resulted in a family unit sustained by disciplined and self-regulating spouses. Criminal law reinforced this vision by proscribing conduct deemed inconsistent with this normative vision of appropriate and productive sex and sexuality. And, in the case of seduction and rape, marriage's role as a defence to certain sexual offences further underscored the normative content of marriage and its role as an independent means of policing and enforcing particular sexual norms and mores.

Under this binary scheme, classifying sex and sexuality – and distinguishing between 'good' and 'bad' sexual citizens was relatively straightforward. The relevant determination was whether the parties were bound by a state-recognized marriage. If the parties were validly married, their sexual conduct was presumptively lawful, even if violent and coercive. If, on the other hand, the parties were not validly married, their sexual interactions were de facto illicit and criminal. Significantly, in certain cases, the fact of criminal sex and sexuality could be 'cured' by entering into marriage. And when this occurred, the fact of the marriage was not an indication that punishment or discipline for errant sexuality had not been imposed, but rather that it *had* – through a different, though no less potent means of sexual regulation and discipline.

Evidence of the role that marriage law and criminal law have played in regulating and structuring the legal regulation of sex and sexuality dot our legal landscape. Consider *Griswold* v. *Connecticut*, which invalidated a Connecticut statute prohibiting the use of contraception, even by married couples.[37] Before *Griswold* was decided, married couples' use of contraception was a criminal act – one justified by the state's interest in deterring promiscuity and other forms of sexual immorality.[38] *Griswold*, however, not only invalidated the Connecticut ban but also recast contraceptive use as something that was moral and appropriate when conducted within marriage.[39] Put differently, the court's decision relocated the use of contraception by married couples from criminal law's regulatory domain to the domain of marriage.[40]

Likewise, in *Loving* v. *Virginia*, the court's decision striking down Virginia's laws prohibiting miscegenation and interracial marriage[41] transformed Richard and Mildred Loving from outlaws to in-laws.[42] Prior to the court's historic decision, the state considered the Lovings' conduct – miscegenation and interracial marriage – a crime because it deviated from the 'natural' order of racial homogamy.[43] But in one fell swoop, the *Loving* court relocated miscegenation from criminal law's domain to the regulatory purview of marriage. In doing so, it made clear that this conduct was neither criminal nor immoral but entirely appropriate for recognition as a lawful marriage.[44]

[37] *Griswold* v. *Connecticut*, 381 US 479, 480 (1965).

[38] Pomfret quoted Connecticut's special prosecutor arguing before Supreme Court that purpose of ban on contraceptive devices was '[t]o reduce the chances of immorality ... [and] [t]o act as a deterrent to sexual intercourse outside marriage'. J. D. Pomfret, 'Marital Status Becomes an Issue in High Court Birth-Control Case', *New York Times*, 31 March 1965, p. 41.

[39] For a description of how Griswold characterized contraceptive bans as 'criminalization of intimate conduct ... [which is] repugnant to the very notion of marriage itself', see Murray, 'Strange Bedfellows', at 1294.

[40] For an explanation of Griswold's decriminalization of contraceptive use by married persons was grounded in idea of 'marriage as a space removed from criminal law', see ibid.

[41] *Loving* v. *Virginia*, 388 US 1, 12 (1967), holding Virginia's statutes violated 'freedom to marry' on equal protection and due process grounds.

[42] See K. M. Franke, 'Longing for Loving' (2008) 76 *Fordham Law Review* 2685–2708 at 2687: 'On June 11, 1967, the Lovings were criminals in ... Virginia, but on June 12, 1967 (the day the Supreme Court issued the decision in their favor), they were not. On June 11, 1967, the Lovings were not legally married ... but on June 12, 1967, they were.'

[43] Indeed, in applying the law against the Lovings, the Virginia trial judge noted that the 'fact that he separated the races show[ed]' that miscegenation offended the sensibilities of 'Almighty God' himself. *Loving*, para. 3, quoting Virginia trial court's opinion.

[44] Murray, 'Strange Bedfellows', at 1296: 'In one fell swoop, the Court transported interracial marriage from the zone of criminality ... [to] the confines of family law ... [M]arrying outside of one's race ... was legitimized.'

Together, *Loving* and *Griswold* not only illustrate the operation of the marriage–crime binary but also suggest the totality of this model of sexual regulation. Under this binary structure, sex could either be marital (legitimate and moral) or criminal (illegitimate and immoral). And critically, in defining sex as either marital or criminal, the binary structure sharply defined the nature of gendered sex roles. On this account, state regulation confined acceptable female sexuality to wifehood. For a woman, the prospect of sex outside marriage risked her being cast as a sexual libertine (fornication or prostitution) or as an unwilling victim (rape). For a man, the binary structure meant that sex outside marriage rendered him a criminal in most circumstances, although the practical consequences of criminal sex depended entirely on whether such private conduct ever came to light. And, outside of rape and sexual assault, many jurisdictions were willing turn a blind eye to men's out-of-marriage sexual indiscretions, provided the conduct did not become habitual or otherwise raise problems. Predictably, husbandhood remained the most exalted expression of male sexuality, but it too came at a cost – a lifelong obligation to provide physical protection and economic support to a wife and family. Regardless of whether one was cast as a wife or harlot, husband or libertine, the binary structure ensured that whether criminal or marital, sex was subject to some form of state governance and was defined by the state's account of its normative worth.[45]

If *Loving* and *Griswold* reflect this binary arrangement, then they are also evidence of its last gasps. Over the last fifty years, there have been important changes that suggest the unravelling of this binary regulatory model.[46] Today, most Americans engage in – or have engaged in – some

[45] In the context of *Loving*, Franke noted that the shift from criminal regulation to civil regulation through marriage means sex remains 'under the direct control of government and governance'. Franke, 'Longing for Loving', at 2687; Murray, 'Strange Bedfellows', at 1296: '[T]he binary tradition ... makes clear that legal regulation of sex is the default position. Because intimate acts and choices are categorized as either marital or criminal, they always are subject to either family law or criminal law. In the binary tradition, sex always is subject to law's governance.'

[46] The loosening of social mores regarding out-of-wedlock sexuality can be seen in a variety of contexts. D'Emilio and Freedman noted that 'sex became an integral part of the public domain' in the 1960s. D'Emilio and Freedman, *Intimate Matters*, 300. For a discussion on these changes, see Friedman, *Crime and Punishment in American History*, 342–350. Legal developments echoed this cultural shift. In 1962, the American Law Institute (ALI) promulgated a Model Penal Code (MPC) that decriminalized adult consensual sex acts, including sodomy. Model Penal Code and Commentaries, para. 213.2 cmt. 2 (Am. Law

kind of sexual conduct outside marriage.[47] Moreover, most do not fear the threat of criminal prosecution when they engage in private, consensual sexual conduct with another adult.[48] There appears to be some space for sex that is neither criminal nor marital and as such is outside the state's regulatory ambit. On this account, our understanding of what it means to be a good sexual citizen may continue to be framed by the marriage–crime binary, but it no longer *depends* upon it. One need not be married to be understood as a good sexual citizen, and one need not be considered a bad sexual citizen (or indeed, a sexual criminal) simply because one has had sex outside marriage.

This shifting regulatory landscape is the result of three key developments: (1) the liberalization of laws criminalizing private, consensual adult sex;[49] (2) the emerging sensibility that the state should not use the criminal law to express moral judgements about private, consensual, sexual

Inst., Official Draft 1980), including text as adopted in 1962, discussing exclusion of private, consensual, homosexual activity from criminalization. For a discussion on the 1955 tentative draft of MPC, which recommended decriminalizing sodomy, see also W. N. Eskridge, Jr, 'No Promo Homo: The Sedimentation of Antigay Discourse and the Channeling Effect of Judicial Review' (2000) 75 *NYU Law Review* 1327–1411 at 1341–1342. Over the next two decades, twenty-two states also decriminalized sodomy. Apasu-Gbotsu et al. list twenty-two states that 'decriminalize[d] private, consensual homosexual acts' in the 1970s. Y. Apasu-Gbotsu et al., 'Survey on the Constitutional Right to Privacy in the Context of Homosexual Activity' (1986) 40 *University of Miami Law Review* 521–657 at 526–527, 526 n. 28. Hassel details 'loosening of sexual mores' in law and culture from the 1960s to the 1980s. D. Hassel, 'The Use of Criminal Sodomy Laws in Civil Litigation' (2001) 79 *Texas Law Review* 813–848 at 819–820.

47 L. B. Finer, 'Trends in Premarital Sex in the United States, 1954–2003' (2007) 122 *Public Health Reports* 73–78: 'Data from the 2002 survey indicate that by age 20, 77 per cent of respondents had had sex, 75 per cent had had premarital sex, and 12 per cent had married.'

48 Dubler notes that individuals 'can engage in noncommodified acts of consensual, nonmarital sex in their homes without fearing that they might run afoul of the criminal law'. See A. R. Dubler, 'From McLaughlin v. Florida to Lawrence v. Texas: Sexual Freedom and the Road to Marriage' (2006) 106 *Columbian Law Review* 1165–1187 at 1187.

49 For a more detailed discussion of this liberalization effort, see M. Murray, 'Griswold's Criminal Law' (2015) 47 *Connecticut Law Review* 1045–1073 at 1049–1054. On criminal law liberalization efforts of the 1950s and 1960s, see also P. Brest et al., *Processes of Constitutional Decision-Making: Cases and Materials*, 6th ed. (New York: Wolters Kluwer, 2015), 1630.

behaviour;[50] and (3) the emergence – and expansion – of constitutional protection for private, consensual adult sex, whether marital or not.[51]

Lawrence v. *Texas*[52] exemplifies – and indeed is the culmination of – all these impulses and the changed regulatory landscape they underwrite. In invalidating Texas's criminal ban on same-sex sodomy,[53] *Lawrence* fundamentally disrupted the marriage–crime binary that has traditionally structured the legal regulation of sex and sexuality.[54] Although *Lawrence* decriminalized same-sex sodomy, it made clear that the conduct (and those engaged in it) were not eligible for marriage.[55] In stark contrast to *Griswold* and *Loving*, where formerly criminal sexual conduct was recast as legitimate marital conduct,[56] *Lawrence* restructured the marriage–crime binary to interpose a space between these two sites of regulation for sex that was neither marital nor criminal.[57] Lodged between marriage and crime, the two traditional sites of legal governance, this

[50] Murray identifies voices calling for 'limits on the state's authority to criminalize private, consensual conduct' in the 1940s and 1950s. Murray, 'Griswold's Criminal Law', at 1049–1054.

[51] Murray, 'Strange Bedfellows', at 1299–1301. For an observation that Lawrence 'explicitly limits the state's ability to punish nonmarital sex, and in so doing recognizes new rights to sexuality outside marriage', see Franke, 'Longing for Loving', at 2686.

[52] *Lawrence* v. *Texas*, 539 US 558 (2003).

[53] See ibid., para. 578: 'The Texas statute furthers no legitimate state interest which can justify its intrusion into the personal and private life of the individual.'

[54] Murray suggests that, in Lawrence, 'the traditional marriage–crime binary is disrupted in favor of a continuum where marriage and crime remained fixed as outer extremes framing an interstitial space where intimate acts and choices are neither valorized as marital behavior nor vilified as criminal behavior'. Murray, 'Strange Bedfellows', at 1256; see also Murray, 'Marriage as Punishment', at 54: 'In decriminalizing same-sex sodomy while also reserving the question of same-sex marriage, Lawrence challenged the marriage–crime binary that traditionally has been used to regulate sex and sexuality.'

[55] *Lawrence*, para. 578, noting that the 'present case … does not involve whether the government must give formal recognition to any relationship that homosexual persons seek to enter'.

[56] For an analysis of *Griswold* and *Loving* within the marriage–crime binary, see nn. 36–43 and accompanying text.

[57] See Murray, 'Strange Bedfellows', at 1300: '[I]n Lawrence, John Geddes Lawrence and Tyron Garner are transformed from criminals ineligible for marriage to non-criminals who continue to be ineligible for marriage.' Ever attentive to claims that the decriminalization of sodomy would lead inexorably to the legal recognition of same-sex marriage, the court took great care to specify that its decision in Lawrence did not constitute such recognition. See n. 54.

interstitial space was distinct in that it existed outside the state's regulatory presence.[58]

By its terms, *Lawrence* offers constitutional protections for the kinds of sexual conduct that might exist in the interstitial space between marriage and crime – non-marital, non-criminal sex. As importantly, the decision imposes limits on the state's authority to regulate sex in order to achieve conformity with majoritarian sexual values. As the court acknowledged, criminal regulation of same-sex sodomy historically had been the product of majoritarian sexual mores that sought to discredit and punish homosexuality.[59] Nevertheless, the court made clear that, going forward, the desire to enforce majoritarian sexual mores could not furnish the basis for discrediting and punishing private, consensual, adult sexual conduct.[60] As the court explained, 'The issue is whether the majority may use the power of the State to enforce these views on the whole society through operation of the criminal law. "Our obligation is to define the liberty of all, not to mandate our own moral code".'[61]

The *Lawrence* court's discrediting of majoritarian mores that favoured marriage and heterosexuality would seem to disrupt the gender order that marriage produced and maintained. If constitutional protection extended to those in non-marital relationships, the legal distinction between wives and husbands and men and women in non-marital relationships would be less stark. But importantly, even as the *Lawrence* opinion appeared to embrace the prospect of sex that was outside the regulatory domains of criminal law and marriage, its language evinced considerable discomfort at the prospect of sex outside the law. Although Justice Kennedy maintained that the decriminalization of same-sex sodomy did not lead inexorably to

[58] M. Murray, 'Paradigms Lost: How Domestic Partnership Went from Innovation to Injury' (2003) 37 *NYU Review of Law and Social Change* 291–305 at 301: 'Lawrence interposed a space between marriage and crime – the two primary sites through which the state historically has regulated sex and sexuality. This interstitial space is less thickly regulated than the legal categories of marriage and crime that frame it'; Murray, 'Strange Bedfellows', at 1300: 'The continuum that . . . Lawrence puts forth is one that dismantles the marriage–crime binary by creating a space where some acts are not subject to either criminal law's or family law's governance.'

[59] *Lawrence*, para. 571, discussing moral foundations of sodomy prohibitions.

[60] See ibid.: 'For many persons these are not trivial concerns but profound and deep convictions accepted as ethical and moral principles to which they aspire and which thus determine the course of their lives. These considerations do not answer the question before us, however.'

[61] Ibid, quoting *Planned Parenthood of Se. Pa.* v. *Casey*, 505 US 833, 850 (1992).

same-sex marriage, his opinion painted the two male petitioners with the brush of domesticity. Although there was scant evidence for it, the opinion concluded that the two men were engaged in sex within the context of a relationship. And critically, the court understood that conjectured relationship to be one in which 'two adults who, with full and mutual consent' engaged in sex in furtherance of 'a personal bond that was more enduring'. Put differently, though the opinion spoke of protections for non-marital sex, it nonetheless depicted the two men at the heart of the dispute in terms that strongly recalled marriage and the marital couple.

In this regard, *Lawrence*'s protections for non-marital, non-criminal sex are deeply contingent. Constitutional protection for non-marital sex was reserved for those whose relationships were marriage-like – intimate, 'transcendent', private, in the home, monogamous and in service of a relationship. But it was not just that *Lawrence* read non-marital relationships through the lens of marriage. In doing so, the decision, however inadvertently, reified marriage and re-entrenched the gender roles that marriage produced. On this account, even as the court offered limited protections for life outside marriage, obtaining such protection would depend on whether the sex in question was more proximate to, than distant from, marriage. In the same vein, such protection would more likely be available to those whose performance as sexual subjects best approximated to the gender norms and roles articulated in marriage.

2. The Sexual Citizen in a Landscape of Sexual Deregulation

Some have argued that *Lawrence* loosened state control over sex and sexuality, leading to a kind of sexual deregulation. But almost twenty years after *Lawrence* was decided, is it the case that the diminution of criminal law's regulatory presence means that the state no longer punishes or sanctions private, consensual sex outside marriage? Is it the case that the state no longer regulates sex for the purpose of vindicating majoritarian sexual mores and the gender roles that underlie them? The answer, perhaps paradoxically, is no.

Although criminal law was among the most visible means by which the state could punish sex it deemed non-normative, it was not the only means. Through civil and administrative channels such as professional codes of conduct, the state, in its role as a public employer, could penalize the private sexual conduct of public employees. Under this system, police officers, public school teachers and other public employees could face adverse employment consequences (refusals to hire, terminations, reprimands) because of their private sexual conduct.[62]

Meaningfully, this type of civil state regulation of sex and sexuality often occurred in the shadow of extant criminal laws that prohibited the underlying conduct.[63] In many cases, these criminal laws were never enforced; nevertheless, they could have serious collateral civil consequences for those who violated them.[64] For example, in *Andrade* v. *City of Phoenix*, three Phoenix police officers were suspended from their jobs

[62] See, e.g., *Fleisher* v. *City of Signal Hill*, 829 F.2d paras. 1491, 1498–1499 (9th Cir. 1987), upholding discharge of probationary police officer for statutory rape of his fifteen-year-old girlfriend while he was nineteen; *Shawgo* v. *Spradlin*, 701 F.2d paras. 470, 482–483 (5th Cir. 1983), upholding suspension and demotion of two police officers who were cohabiting out of wedlock); *Andrade* v. *City of Phoenix*, 692 F.2d paras. 557, 559–560 (9th Cir. 1982) (per curiam), upholding suspension of police officers for adultery; *Hollenbaugh* v. *Carnegie Free Library*, 436 F. Supp. paras. 1328, 1332 (WD Pa. 1977), reviewing case of two public library employees who had been terminated for living together in 'open adultery', aff'd, 578 F.2d para. 1374 (3rd Cir. 1978).

[63] See, e.g., *Fleisher*, 829 F.2d para. 1498, concluding plaintiff's termination for uncharged commission of statutory rape was proper because '[t]his conduct was illegal, inappropriate in an individual who aspired to become an officer on the Department's police force, and detrimental to the Department as a whole'; *Andrade*, 692 F.2d paras. 559–560, concluding police officers could validly be disciplined for sexual misconduct if their actions fell within state criminal definition of adultery; *Suddarth* v. *Slane*, 539 F. Supp. paras. 612, 617–618 (WD Va. 1982), concluding discharge of police officer for adultery was proper because 'adultery is not protected by the First Amendment' and was criminally proscribed in the jurisdiction; *Wasemann* v. *Roman*, 168 S.E.2d paras. 548, 550 (W. Va. 1969), upholding police officer's discharge based on bastardy because '[v]iolation of the criminal laws of immoral conduct has been held sufficient ground for the removal of police officers'; see also *Cronin* v. *Town of Amesbury*, 895 F. Supp. paras. 375, 384 (D. Mass. 1995), noting 'wide agreement [among lower courts] that [a public employee's] off-duty sexual activities are not protected when they violate a statute'), aff'd, 81 F.3d para. 257 (1st Cir. 1996); *Briggs* v. *N. Muskegon Police Dep't*, 563 F. Supp. paras. 585, 592 (WD Mich. 1983), suggesting violation of sexual morality statute would be sufficient to support police officer's discharge', aff'd, 746 F.2d para. 1475 (6th Cir. 1984).

[64] For an explanation of how unenforced criminal prohibitions on sodomy fuelled discriminatory treatment of LGBT persons in civil contexts, see C. R. Leslie, 'Creating Criminals: The Injuries Inflicted by "Unenforced" Sodomy Laws' (2000) 35 *Harvard Civil Rights–Civil Liberties Law Review* 103–181 at 135–178. These laws could also have other criminal consequences, beyond enforcement. For example, although sodomy was infrequently prosecuted independently, it could be deployed to 'induce guilty pleas in . . . problematic sexual assault cases'. W. J. Stuntz, 'The Uneasy Relationship between Criminal Procedure and Criminal Justice' (1997) 107 *Yale Law Journal* 1–76 at 7.

for 'engaging in sexual relations with women who were not their wives'.[65] Although their extramarital conduct violated existing criminal laws prohibiting adultery,[66] none of the officers were actually criminally prosecuted for their adultery.[67] Nevertheless, the department initiated disciplinary actions against them for violating the department's code of conduct. Two of the officers were administratively charged with 'conduct unbecoming' to a police officer.[68] Critically, what made the conduct unbecoming was not simply that it offended majoritarian sexual values that prioritized marital fidelity and monogamy. Instead, the department's understanding of what was and was not unbecoming was informed by the fact that the underlying conduct was a crime (albeit one that was infrequently enforced). Put differently, the fact that the conduct was criminal made it per se 'unbecoming'. In this way, the criminal prohibition on adultery furnished the predicate for the administrative charge.[69]

Likewise, in *Suddarth* v. *Slane*,[70] a married police officer admitted to having an affair with, and fathering a child by, his married neighbour. Upon learning of the conduct, the police department suspended the officer and charged him with violating various provisions of the departmental code of conduct.[71] As with *Andrade*, the administrative violations were predicated on the fact that the officer's conduct violated extant criminal laws.[72]

To be sure, in *Andrade* and *Suddarth*, the sanctioned police officers were men. On this account, the department's disciplinary actions were at odds with cultural norms that, historically, were more permissive of men's

[65] 692 F.2d para. 558. [66] Ibid., para. 559.

[67] See ibid., noting that the three officers were 'charged' with commission of a crime in administrative disciplinary proceedings.

[68] Ibid., para. 558.

[69] Indeed, one officer was administratively charged with 'commission of a crime and immorality'. The other two officers were administratively charged with 'conduct unbecoming an officer'. Ibid. For one of these officers, 'lewd and lascivious acts' were alleged in addition to adultery as the 'underlying offensive conduct'. Ibid.

[70] 539 F. Supp. para. 612 (WD Va. 1982). [71] Ibid., para. 615.

[72] Ibid., paras. 615–616. The officer in the case was charged with violations of General Order 17, para. 3: engaging in 'criminal, infamous, dishonest, immoral or notoriously disgraceful conduct, or other conduct prejudicial to the Department' and para. 4: violating 'the laws of the United States, the Commonwealth of Virginia, the ordinances of any city, county, or municipality of the Commonwealth of Virginia, or the rules and regulations of the Department'. Ibid.

extramarital activities than those of women.[73] However, the fact that those engaged in the offensive (and illegal) conduct were police officers vested with the public trust helps explain the harsh measures, even at a time when such conduct might otherwise be tolerated among men. Police officers, like other public fiduciaries, were expected to comport themselves to a higher standards than were lay citizens – and, indeed, were expected to refrain from engaging in conduct that was nominally criminal, even if it often was overlooked in a civilian context.

Still, as these cases make clear, the state had two opportunities to mark and sanction the offending conduct. It could prosecute the individual under the criminal law, *and* it could initiate a civil employment action under existing administrative procedures based on the violation of the criminal law. And even if the state chose not to enforce the criminal prohibition, the interaction of these two systems meant that the public employee could nevertheless face the collateral civil consequences of engaging in unlawful, criminal behaviour. Thus, at a time when many objected to the enforcement of laws criminalizing private, consensual sex between adults,[74] the civil and administrative regulatory systems provided a useful alternative to criminal regulation. By resorting to these forms of sexual regulation, the state could continue to communicate its antipathy for the underlying conduct without exposing individuals to the devastating consequences of a criminal conviction or incarceration.[75] In this way,

[73] The law of divorce is instructive on this point. Historically, in American jurisdictions, fault was required to establish grounds for marital dissolution. However, if the faulty spouse was an adulterous wife, as opposed to an adulterous husband, she risked her entitlement to alimony and even child custody. For an explanation that a finding showing that the wife had failed in her 'marital role' would likely relieve the husband of financial obligations to her, and decrease her likelihood of retaining custody of the children, see N. R. Cahn, 'Faithless Wives and Lazy Husbands: Gender Norms in Nineteenth Century Divorce Law' (2002) 2002 *University of Illinois Law Review* 651–698 at 667–668. Chamallas noted that an adulterous wife was likely to lose custody over children after a divorce. M. Chamallas, 'Consent, Equality, and the Legal Control of Sexual Conduct' (1988) 61 *South California Law Review* 777–862 at 785.

[74] These concerns were among those that animated the ALI's reform of sexual offences in the MPC. In 1955, at the inauguration of the MPC project, Judge Learned Hand made clear his views of the state's use of criminal law as a vehicle for enforcing sexual morality. He explained, 'I think [the criminal regulation of sex] is a matter of morals, a matter largely of taste, and it is not a matter that people should be put in prison about'. A. Lewis, 'Morals Issue: Crime or Not?', *New York Times*, 29 November 1964, E10.

[75] This is not to say that the civil penalties could not also have devastating effects. The adverse consequences of civil sexual regulation can have quite pernicious effects on the

the civil system functioned as criminal law's handmaiden – doing much of the regulatory work at criminal law's behest.

In principle, *Lawrence* should have altered this regulatory landscape, muting not just the impact of the criminal law, but also the effects of this shadow system of sexual regulation and the gender norms that undergirded it. By decriminalizing private, consensual, non-marital sexual conduct,[76] *Lawrence* would have eliminated the criminal predicate on which civil and administrative regulation rested. Accordingly, after *Lawrence*, civil and administrative actions of the sort seen in *Andrade* and *Suddarth* arguably would be untenable – or at least more difficult to sustain. If the administrative charges were premised on a violation of criminal law, the fact that the underlying conduct was no longer criminal in nature would mean that there was no longer a predicate for a related civil employment action. Moreover, after *Lawrence*, these kinds of sexual acts ostensibly would be subject to constitutional privacy protections.[77]

individual and their dependants. For example, an employee may lose their job because of an affair. E.g., *Beecham* v. *Henderson Cty*, 442 F.3d paras. 372, 374 (6th Cir. 2005).

[76] See, e.g., Dubler, 'From McLaughlin v. Florida to Lawrence v. Texas', at 1186–1187: 'Lawrence dramatically altered the entire legal landscape of nonmarital sexual intimacy . . . [A]fter Lawrence cross-sex and same-sex adult couples alike can engage in noncommodified acts of consensual, nonmarital sex in their homes without fearing that they might run afoul of the criminal law.' J. K. Strader, 'Lawrence's Criminal Law' (2011) 16 *Berkeley Journal of Criminal Law* 41–111 at 42: '[Lawrence] seemingly invalidated all criminal laws that infringe on private, consensual, noncommercial sexual acts.' J. A. Herold, 'Statute Note, A Breach of Vows but Not Criminal: Does Lawrence v. Texas Invalidate Utah's Statute Criminalizing Adultery?' (2005) 7 *Journal of Law & Family Studies* 253–262 at 261: 'Criminalizing the private sexual conduct, such as adultery, that occurs between two consenting adults is an unconstitutional restriction on the right to privacy [after *Lawrence*].'

[77] Justice Kennedy's majority opinion in *Lawrence* states: 'The case does involve two adults who, with full and mutual consent from each other, engaged in sexual practices common to a homosexual lifestyle. The petitioners are entitled to respect for their private lives . . . Their right to liberty under the Due Process Clause gives them the full right to engage in their conduct without intervention of the government.' *Lawrence* v. *Texas*, 539 US 558, 578 (2003). Although the Lawrence court was speaking to same-sex sodomy, the decision's logic arguably would accommodate other private, consensual sexual conduct between unmarried adults. See also Murray, 'Marriage as Punishment', at 57: 'The constitutional protection afforded in the space between marriage and crime is available to certain types of sex: private consensual sex between two adults . . . [A] wide range of sexual practices . . . might comport with these indicia – everything from ordinary sex between cohabiting adults to sadomasochism ("S&M")' (footnote omitted).

Adults would have some kind of liberty interest in engaging in private, consensual, non-marital sexual activity.[78]

But this has not been the case. Indeed, the facts of *Seegmiller* v. *LaVerkin City*[79] suggest the elusiveness of *Lawrence*'s grant of sexual freedom – especially for women. In *Seegmiller*, Sharon Johnson, a police officer in the midst of a contentious divorce, attended an out-of-town training conference paid for in part by the city.[80] During the conference, but after the training sessions had ended for the day, Johnson had 'a brief affair with an officer from another department who was also attending the conference'.[81]

Based on her estranged husband's allegations of other professional misconduct, the LaVerkin City Council began an investigation into Johnson's activities on and off the job.[82] During the course of the investigation, the council learned of Johnson's affair at the training conference and reprimanded her, invoking a provision in the law enforcement code of ethics requiring an officer to 'keep [her] private life unsullied as an example to all and [to] behave in a manner that does not bring discredit to [the officer] or [the] agency'.[83] According to the reprimand, Johnson had allowed 'her personal life [to] interfere with her duties as an officer by having sexual relations with an officer from [another department] while attending a training session out of town which was paid for in part by LaVerkin City'.[84] The reprimand advised her to 'avoid the appearance of impropriety' and to 'conduct [herself] in the future . . . in a manner that will be consistent with the city policies and the police department policies'.[85] To concretize the city's expectations, the reprimand warned her that future violations of the professional code would result in 'additional discipline up to and including termination'.[86]

Johnson contended that as a result of the reprimand, which was made public, her credibility as an officer was 'seriously undermined', prompting her to resign from her position in the police department.[87] She subsequently filed suit claiming that the city council's investigation and reprimand 'infringed on her fundamental liberty interest in sexual privacy'.[88]

[78] See n. 75, arguing that Lawrence provided some measure of constitutional protection to other forms of sex, including same-sex sodomy, fornication, adultery and non-marital-cohabitation.

[79] 528 F.3d paras. 762, 764-766 (10th Cir. 2008). [80] Ibid., para. 764.

[81] Ibid., para. 765. [82] Ibid. [83] Ibid. [84] Ibid., para. 766. [85] Ibid. [86] Ibid.

[87] Ibid. [88] Ibid., para. 769.

In doing so, she relied heavily on *Lawrence* as establishing constitutional protections for private, consensual adult sex.[89]

Although the Tenth Circuit conceded that '[b]roadly speaking, no one disputes a right to be free from governmental interference in matters of consensual sexual privacy',[90] it nonetheless rejected Johnson's reading of *Lawrence*. Instead, the court interpreted *Lawrence* narrowly, concluding that the decision did not identify a broadly defined fundamental 'right to private sexual activity'.[91] Absent a fundamental right, the city's actions were subject to rational basis review – a standard that, in the court's view, was easily satisfied: 'It is well-settled that a police department may, "in accordance with its well-established duty to keep peace, [place] demands upon the members of the police force . . . which have no counterpart with respect to the public at large".'[92] In terms startlingly reminiscent of cases such as *Andrade* and *Suddarth*, the Tenth Circuit concluded that 'it [is] reasonable for the police department to privately admonish [the officer's] personal conduct consistent with its code of conduct when the department believes it will further internal discipline or the public's respect for its police officers and the department they represent'.[93]

If the outcome in *Seegmiller* turned on the fact of a professional code of conduct, the facts of *Beecham* v. *Henderson County*[94] suggest that other forms of civil and administrative regulation continue to shape and regulate sexual behaviour outside – or inimical to – marriage. *Beecham* confronted the difficulties of running a functioning and productive workplace in the face of an office romance – albeit a messy office love triangle.[95] In October 2002, Steve Milam proposed marriage to June Beecham, with whom he was 'deeply involved in a romantic relationship'.[96] In doing so, Steve seemed to have gotten ahead of himself, for he was still married to Patricia Leigh Milam, who happened to work 'down the hall' from Beecham at the county courthouse.[97] Not surprisingly, this small-town love triangle 'caus[ed] tension in the courthouse in general and in the Circuit Clerk's office', where Beecham served as deputy clerk.[98] Finding

89 See generally *Brief of Appellant, Seegmiller*, 528 F.3d para. 762 (No. 07-4096), 2007 WL 2426131, referencing *Lawrence* repeatedly.
90 *Seegmiller*, 528 F.3d para. 769. 91 Ibid., paras. 770–772.
92 Ibid., para. 772 (alterations in original), quoting *Kelley* v. *Johnson*, 425 US 238, 245 (1976).
93 Ibid. 94 442 F.3d para. 372 (6th Cir. 2005). 95 Ibid., para. 374.
96 Ibid., para. 375 (internal quotation marks omitted), quoting June Beecham.
97 Ibid., para. 378. 98 Ibid., para. 374.

Beecham's relationship with her co-worker's husband to be 'unacceptably disruptive to the workplace', her supervisor dismissed her, prompting Beecham to file a wrongful termination lawsuit claiming violation of her rights under *Lawrence*.[99]

Although the appellate court conceded that the Beecham–Milam relationship was within the scope of constitutional protection, it, like the *Anderson* court, focused on whether the termination imposed a 'direct and substantial influence [sic]' on Beecham's right of intimate association.[100] Analogizing the employer's termination decision to anti-nepotism policies, the *Beecham* court determined that the termination did not pose a 'direct' and 'substantial' interference on Beecham's association rights.[101] That is, her employer's decision did not prevent Beecham from forming or maintaining an intimate relationship. It merely required her to choose between her relationship and her job. Moreover, Beecham's termination did not 'bar her from every form of employment in every sector of society'.[102] Although she was discharged from one position at one courthouse, '[a]ll other employment opportunities [we]re available to her', regardless of her relationship.[103] For these reasons, the *Beecham* court concluded that there was no basis for reviewing Beecham's claims under heightened scrutiny. Applying mere rational basis review, the court upheld Beecham's termination on the ground that the employer's interest in minimizing the workplace disruptions caused by the Beecham–Milam affair was a legitimate governmental interest.[104]

What are we to make of these cases? As an initial matter, the comparison between *Seegmiller* and *Beecham* and *Andrade* and *Suddarth* yield interesting insights about the perpetuation of not only sexual regulation, but the durability of gendered norms about sex and sexuality. In the post-*Lawrence* landscape, where consensual adult sexual activity is no longer criminal, the outcomes in *Seegmiller* and *Beecham* are hard to reconcile. Despite the absence of a criminal predicate, the public employer was nevertheless able to sanction the employee's private sexual activity by

[99] Ibid., paras. 374-376, 378.

[100] Ibid., para. 376 (internal quotation marks omitted), quoting *Anderson* v. *City of LaVergne*, 371 F.3d paras. 879, 882 (6th Cir. 2004)) (misquotation); see also *Anderson*, 371 F.3d para. 882, applying 'direct and substantial interference' test.

[101] *Beecham*, 422 F.3d paras. 376–378. [102] Ibid., para. 376. [103] Ibid.

[104] See ibid., para. 378: 'Plaintiff's claim cannot prevail upon the application of rational-basis review to the employment action taken by her employer.'

adverting broadly to 'the public interest', whether it was the appearance of professionalism or the efficient administration of the local court system. That is, even without the criminal predicate, the state found new avenues for sanctioning non-normative sexual conduct.

And in so doing, the state also credited long-standing gender norms that view errant female sexuality more harshly than that of men. In both *Seegmiller* and *Beecham*, the sanctioned employee was a woman who had gone well beyond the Victorian norm of passive female sexuality. Sharon Johnson was estranged from her husband when she engaged in what might be considered a 'one-night-stand' at a work conference, while June Beecham was the 'other woman' in an unwieldy love triangle. Interestingly, in the age of no-fault divorce and the decriminalization (or desuetude) of adultery, both women were nonetheless penalized for conduct deemed inimical to the marriage bond. Sharon Johnson's conduct likely thwarted any prospect of marital reconciliation, while June Beecham's conduct not only disrupted the atmosphere at the courthouse, but another woman's marriage as well. In this regard, both women were penalized not only for the way their sexual conduct impacted their public workplaces, but likely because their conduct violated gendered expectations.

Because they involve public employees and public institutions, it would be easy to dismiss them as anomalous or context-specific. But regardless of their context, these cases are meaningful. Public employment (outside military service) constitutes almost one-fifth of the American labour field.[105] This means that nearly 20 per cent of working Americans, as well as their dependants, look to the state not only as a sovereign but as an employer who provides income and associated benefits. In this regard, these cases surface a regulatory regime that has the potential to impact a wide swath of the public.

This regulatory regime is one that has for years operated in the shadow of criminal law and marriage, the two dominant modes of sexual

[105] In 2012, federal government and state and local government employed 15 per cent of the US workforce. See Bureau of Labor Statistics, Industry Employment and Output Projections to 2022, tbl.1 (2013), www.bls.gov/opub/mlr/2013/article/industry-employment-and-output-projections-to-2022.htm [http://perma.cc/99GZ-22B7]. Burns cited the 2011 Bureau of Labor Statistics data that government employs 16.49 per cent of the American labour force. C. Burns et al., The State of Diversity in Today's Workforce, Center for American Progress, 2012, www.americanprogress.org/issues/labor/report/2012/07/12/11938/the-state-of-diversity-in-todays-workforce/ [http://perma.cc/UC5U-L8MG].

regulation. And, critically, as marriage law and criminal law have receded as engines of sexual regulation, this alternative regulatory modality has gained new force – in part because of the rise of the administrative state. As the cases discussed suggest, this new mode of sexual regulation relies upon compliance with professional codes of conduct, employment licensing and other forms of regulation that derive from the administrative state and the proliferation of bureaucratic agencies.

To this point, some have argued that 'we are living in a new sex bureaucracy', characterized by 'an elaborate and growing federal bureaucratic structure that', in practice, regulates 'ordinary sex'.[106] This development disturbs them, and with reason. In their telling, the 'bureaucratic turn in sex regulation' has produced results that are not only deeply intrusive, but also undemocratic and violative of individual rights and liberties.[107] As evidence of this 'bureaucratic turn', these critics have pointed to the campaign, begun during the Obama administration, by the US Department of Education (DOE), via its Office for Civil Rights (OCR), to address sexual violence on college campuses.[108] To be sure, this is a powerful example of the bureaucratization of sexual regulation, as the aforementioned cases make clear, it is not the only example. Indeed, administrative agencies at the local, state and federal levels have long been involved in scaffolding the regime of sexual regulation that criminal law and marriage cooperatively constructed. In the face of criminal law's diminished influence, the administrative and bureaucratic aspects of sexual regulation have become more visible and pronounced – at all levels of government.

But the example of the DOE's OCR is a powerful demonstration of not only the breadth and extent of sexual administrative regulation, but its impact on gender norms as well. Exercising its authority under Title IX of the Education Amendments of 1972,[109] as well as more recent statutes

[106] J. Gersen and J. Suk, 'The Sex Bureaucracy' (2016) 104 *California Law Review* 881–948 at 883–884.

[107] Ibid., at 883.

[108] Although the DOE's enforcement of Title IX on college campuses is the authors' primary example, they also see the 'sex bureaucracy' at work in the DOE's regulation of primary and secondary schools, and possibly in the 'extensive rules about sex in the contexts of the military and prison'. Ibid., at 884 n. 7.

[109] Title IX of the Education Amendments of 1972, 20 USC paras. 1681–1688 (2012).

regarding the disclosure of campus crime statistics,[110] the DOE has required colleges and universities 'to take immediate and effective steps to end sexual harassment and sexual violence'.[111] These steps include responding promptly to complaints with a campus-level adjudicative apparatus, reporting allegations of sexual misconduct to the federal government, and taking proactive measures to prevent sexual violence, such as educating community members on the importance and nature of consent.[112] Institutions that fail to comply with the terms of these administrative directives risk losing federal funds.[113]

As a consequence of this regulatory structure, the DOE now dictates what procedures and standards of evidence schools must use to evaluate allegations of sexual misconduct. These procedures and standards do not align with those of the criminal justice process.[114] For example, the prescribed administrative processes do not require the same standards of proof for a determination of guilt, nor do they import the evidentiary standards used in criminal trials. As importantly, however, these new

[110] E.g. Clery Act, 20 USC para. 1092(f) (2012), amended by Campus SaVE Act, 20 USC para. 1092(f) (Supp. II, Vol. 1, 2014), requiring campuses to disclose statistics annually to the Department of Education and empowering the secretary to disseminate this information and coordinate with institutions to identify and recommend 'exemplary' practices.

[111] Office for Civil Rights, US Department of Education, 'Dear Colleague Letter: Sexual Violence', 4 April 2011, www2.ed.gov/about/offices/list/ocr/letters/colleague-201104.pdf.

[112] For a discussion on OCR due process requirements, the evidentiary standard that OCR requires for campus proceedings, the steps OCR mandates to protect complainants, and the affirmative consent policies that colleges and universities have voluntarily adopted, see Gersen and Suk, 'The Sex Bureaucracy', at 897–898, 909. See also M. J. Anderson, 'Campus Sexual Assault Adjudication and Resistance to Reform' (2016) 125 *Yale Law Journal* 1940–2005 at 1973–1975, 1980–1981; Duncan details campus safety statutes and explicating the DOE's guidance to institutions. S. Hanley Duncan, 'The Devil Is in the Details: Will the Campus SaVE Act Provide More or Less Protection to Victims of Campus Assaults?' (2014) 40 *Journal of College and University Law* 443–466 at 447–453. Engle surveys the legal reporting requirements imposed on colleges and universities by federal law, including the Clery Act and the SaVE Act. J. C. Engle, 'Mandatory Reporting of Campus Sexual Assault and Domestic Violence: Moving to a Victim-Centric Protocol that Comports with Federal Law' (2015) 24 *Temple Political & Civil Rights Law Review* 401–421 at 402–408. For a discussion on requirements of prompt responses to complaints, campus employee training and victims' reporting options, see Title IX in Detail, Know Your IX, 4 September 2016, http://knowyourix.org/title-ix/title-ix-in-detail/.

[113] Gersen and Suk, 'The Sex Bureaucracy', at 987–998, 909. On DOE's investigatory and enforcement efforts, see the Chronicle of Higher Education's excellent database, www.chronicle.com/tag/data

[114] Gersen and Suk, 'The Sex Bureaucracy', at 932–946.

procedures and standards prescribe new definitions for determining what kind of sexual conduct is impermissible and, by implication, what kind of conduct is desirable.

As I have argued here, historically, marriage marked the boundary between legal and illegal sex. 'Good sex' occurred in the marital bed; 'bad sex' happened outside of it – a fact underscored by criminal law.[115] Indeed, some laws implied that 'bad sex' was all but impossible within marriage,[116] and some law enforcement practices suggested that marriage could alter, as if by alchemy, the character of prior (criminal) sexual encounters.[117] The legal liberalization of sex that has occurred over the last fifty years further complicates matters. As lawmakers, judges and prosecutors invalidated or ignored criminal prohibitions on non-marital sex, marriage's utility as a boundary marker has diminished.[118]

What then has emerged to fill the vacuum created when marriage and crime no longer work in tandem to define licit and illicit sex? The answer lies in the shadow system of administrative regulation that has emerged as marriage and crime have receded as regulatory forces. As *Seegmiller* and *Beecham* suggested, even under an administrative, rather than criminal, regulatory regime, marriage (and assaults on marriage) could help define the boundary between good and bad sexual conduct. However, the DOE's system of administrative sexual regulation is not defined by marriage, but rather by a classic feature of marriage: consent (or lack thereof). That is, if one party to the sexual conduct at issue does not or cannot consent, the sexual conduct is presumptively impermissible.[119] On this account, in the administrative regime of the DOE, the boundary between good and bad sex

[115] Title IX: Tracking Sexual Assault Investigations, http://projects.chronicle.com/titleix/.

[116] I refer here to the lack of legal protection against forcible sexual encounters within marriage. See Hasday, 'Contest and Consent'; Siegel, 'The Rule of Love'.

[117] Dubler, 'Immoral Purposes', at 776–778; S. Robertson, 'Making Right a Girl's Ruin: Working-Class Legal Cultures and Forced Marriage in New York City, 1890–1950' (2002) 36 *Journal of American Studies* 199–230; S. Robertson, 'Seduction, Sexual Violence, and Marriage in New York City, 1886–1955' (2006) 24 *Law and History Review* 331–373.

[118] Gersen and Suk, 'The Sex Bureaucracy', at 888; see also M. Murray, 'The Space Between: The Cooperative Regulation of Criminal Law and Family Law' (2010) 44 *Family Law Quarterly* 227–254 at 239–240.

[119] Gersen and Suk, 'The Sex Bureaucracy', at 889. On the emergence of consent as a defining feature of the modern landscape of sexual regulation, see also Fischel, identifying '(non) consent as the gravamen adjudicating sexual harm' and asking if 'our nationally privileged sexuality' has shifted from heterosexuality to 'adult consensuality'. J. J. Fischel, *Sex*

(and good and bad sexual citizenship) is not defined by its proximity to or distance from marriage, but rather on whether those engaged in the activity have clearly exhibited consent. But what does it mean for marriage to be 'out' and consent to be 'in' as the principal means of constructing the good sexual citizen? And what does this shift in our understanding of sexual citizenship mean for the perpetuation – or disruption – of gender roles?

Consider, first, how marriage once operated as a boundary-drawing mechanism. When marriage marked the line between lawful and unlawful sex, the relevant determination was whether the parties were bound by a state-recognized marriage. This was not always an easy determination,[120] but once made, all sexual conduct fell into neat and tidy boxes. Generally speaking, if the parties were validly married, their sexual conduct was presumptively lawful, even if violent and coercive.[121] If, on the other hand, the parties were not validly married, their sexual interactions were de facto illicit and criminal.[122] That is, outside the bounds of a state-recognized marriage, they were not in-laws, they were outlaws – and obviously outside the bounds of good sexual citizenship. With marriage as the

and Harm in the Age of Consent (Minneapolis: University of Minnesota Press, 2016), 6–7; S. J. Schulhofer, 'Consent: What It Means and Why It's Time to Require It' (2016) 47 *University of the Pacific Law Review* 665–681 at 665–666: '[T]he unmistakable trend in the recent legislation, jurisprudence, and academic writing is to the effect that, as the FBI definition now puts it, rape is "[sexual] penetration without consent"'. For a discussion of the rise of affirmative consent and the American Law Institute's recent effort to integrate affirmative consent into the Model Penal Code, see J. Shulevitz, 'Regulating Sex', *New York Times*, 27 June 2015, www.nytimes.com/2015/06/28/opinion/sunday/judith-shulevitz-regulating-sex.html.

120 See, e.g., A. Dubler, 'Wifely Behavior: A Legal History of Acting Married' (2000) 100 *Yale Law Journal* 957–1021; K. Abrams, 'Marriage Fraud' (2012) 100 *California Law Review* 1–67; A. Onwuachi-Willig, *According to Our Hearts: Rhinelander v. Rhinelander and the Law of the Multiracial Family* (London: Yale University Press, 2013).

121 *People* v. *Liberta*, 474 N.E.2d paras. 567, 571 (NY 1984), discussing the marital rape exemption.

122 Coughlin observed that sexuality was once considered a 'a force so dangerous that it could not safely be left to self-regulation, but rather should be closely confined, by state law, within marital relationships'. A. M. Coughlin, 'Sex and Guilt' (1998) 84 *Virginia Law Review* 1–46 at 6; D'Emilio and Freedman stated that laws against non-marital sexuality were vigorously enforced in the colonies, carrying 'harsh penalties' for both men and women and punishing '[e]ven behaviors that might lead to sex outside marriage'. D'Emilio and Freedman, *Intimate Matters*, 27–38. See also Perkins and Boyce's tracing of the historical development of the crimes of adultery and fornication. R. M. Perkins and R. N. Boyce, *Criminal Law*, 3rd ed. (St Paul, MN: Foundation Press, 1982), 454–456.

lodestar, sexual regulation was relatively straightforward and efficient – as was the identification of good sexual citizens.

The determination of consent is considerably more difficult than the determination of a valid marriage, which makes the construction of sexual citizenship decidedly more fraught. For many decades now, marriage in the United States has been a public, documented and easily recognized status. Entry into marriage is often celebrated, in front of many witnesses; licences are signed and filed at city hall. By contrast, the giving of consent, especially with regard to sex, often occurs in private and is frequently communicated in terms that are implicit rather than explicit, creating the possibility of conflicting interpretations.

Complicating matters further, unlike a marriage-based system, a consent-based system of sexual regulation requires treating each sexual interaction as a separate transaction for which consent must be secured. Two persons might happily engage in sexual conduct on one occasion, but on another occasion, one or more parties might find that same conduct undesirable. In short, a consent-based regime of sexual regulation leaves the line between licit and illicit sex unstable and perpetually subject to individual negotiation.

For some women's rights advocates and others who have fought for victims of sexual assault, this kind of disaggregation and instability is a good thing, or at least an improvement over the alternative in that it puts the onus on one party to clearly communicate consent, and the other party to clearly discern it – in each and every sexual encounter. In this regard, a consent framework sees women as autonomous individuals, untethered to their sexual pasts and relationships, and any preconceived notions of how female sexuality is exhibited and performed. As Joseph Fischel explains, in the context of rape, a consent framework does not interpret a woman's sexual encounters as a potential 'violation of one man's property (daughter or wife) by another man', but rather focuses on the intentions of 'a rights-bearing person'.[123] On this account, a consent-based regulatory regime is

[123] Fischel, *Sex and Harm*, 10. Relatedly, a consent rubric also shifts the focus from whether one party imposed physical force on the other party (a traditional element of the crime of rape, and one that often worked to the disadvantage of victims) to whether both parties agreed to the sexual encounter. Anderson, 'Campus Sexual Assault Adjudication', at 1951. I have offered just a taste of a large literature on sexual violence and consent. On consent more generally – its nature, its significance – we also note a vast literature in political theory (a literature that we do not attempt to capture here).

one that, in theory, prioritizes all parties to a sexual encounter as autonomous individuals, capable of asserting consent, and capable of understanding whether consent has been given or refused.

Whatever one's view, however, the crucial question is how a consent framework operates in practice. As some critics maintain, the DOE has encouraged institutions to embrace a specific understanding of what counts as consent: affirmative, verbal agreement.[124] Fearing the wrath of the state as regulator, institutions have pushed further, toward not only affirmative agreement but also enthusiasm and excitement in the articulation of consent.[125] The DOE, they note, has also urged specific procedures for identifying non-consensual sexual encounters in the event that one party feels aggrieved. One hallmark of these procedures, critics argue, is that they invite parties to give different meanings to their encounter. Another hallmark is that they make ambiguity entirely consistent with a finding of sexual assault. For those who wish to avoid any allegation of impropriety, the implication is clear: affirmative, enthusiastic consent is the safest path.[126]

[124] Gersen and Suk, 'The Sex Bureaucracy', at 924–931. To be clear, the DOE has never purported to require that colleges and universities adopt affirmative consent policies. It has, however, defined 'sexual violence' to refer to 'physical sexual acts perpetrated against a person's will or where a person is incapable of giving consent due to the victim's use of drugs or alcohol', and it has instructed regulated entities to 'take immediate and effective steps to end sexual harassment and sexual violence'. Office for Civil Rights, US Department of Education, Dear Colleague Letter, 1 (emphasis added), 2. In informal guidance, the DOE has also 'recommended' that institutions provide students with sexual violence training that includes 'the school's definition of consent . . ., including examples'. Office for Civil Rights, US Department of Education, Questions and Answers on Title IX and Sexual Violence, 2014, www2.ed.gov/about/offices/list/ocr/docs/qa-201404-title-ix.pdf. Eager to stay on the right side of the law, institutions have understandably been drawn towards affirmative consent policies. See J. Halley, 'The Move Toward Affirmative Consent', *Signs*, 2015, http://signsjournal.org/currents-affirmative-consent/halley/ (noting the appearance of affirmative consent requirements in campus sexual conduct codes and 'in a parallel campaign for reform of state-based criminal law'). Keenan reports that approximately 1,400 institutions of higher education now use an affirmative consent standard in their sexual assault policies. S. Keenan, 'Affirmative Consent: Are Students Really Asking?', *New York Times*, 28 July 2015, www.nytimes.com/2015/08/02/education/edlife/affirmative-consent-are-students-really-asking.html.

[125] Gersen and Suk, 'The Sex Bureaucracy', at 931. For an explanation of why the University of California adopted an affirmative consent policy six months before state law required it to do so, see J. Napolitano, '"Only Yes Means Yes": An Essay on University Policies Regarding Sexual Violence and Sexual Assault' (2014) 33 *Yale Law & Policy Review* 387–402 at 389–390.

[126] Gersen and Suk, 'The Sex Bureaucracy', at 931–946.

The DOE's preference for affirmative consent is surely the product of a grassroots 'yes means yes' movement, led by a younger generation of activists seeking to transform societal approaches to sex and empower female sexuality. But note how nicely affirmative consent coheres with the practices of modern bureaucracy – and indeed, the 'bureaucratic turn' in sexual regulation. In much the same way that banks, schools, hospitals and other regulated institutions are required to maintain records that authorities might review at a later date, college students are urged to practise sexual record-keeping, so to speak, in the form of securing clear, lucid assurances of affirmative consent from sexual partners and also of registering their own manifestations of enthusiastic consent. These 'records', in turn, make it easier for regulators, adjudicators and enforcers to later determine whether the line between licit and illicit sex has been crossed. There are, of course, enormous differences between the affirmative consent requirements that have emerged from the administrative enforcement of Title IX and the actual record-keeping requirements imposed on other regulated institutions, and this analogy is not intended to imply that affirmative consent standards are anything less than good-faith efforts to prevent sexual assault. Rather, the point is that the model of consent that the DOE has advanced has a decidedly bureaucratic cast, training the subjects of regulation to seek and voice consent in specific, cognizable and ultimately documentable ways.

Setting to one side whether the shift towards consent represents progress in the fight against sexual violence, what does it mean to live in a society where consent – and more specifically, affirmative consent – may be the new marriage? And what might this trend suggest about the broader regime of governance under which we live? These questions are difficult and warrant sustained scholarly attention. The tentative observations are an effort to further this important conversation.

Consent is an essential feature of contract; contract, in turn, is at the heart of classical liberalism.[127] This ideology imagines the good society as one in which sovereign, self-governing individuals pursue their interests – and thereby achieve their just deserts – via private ordering. Meaningfully, the

[127] See, e.g., M. J. Horowitz, *The Transformation of American Law, 1870–1960: The Crisis of Legal Orthodoxy* (Oxford: Oxford University Press, 1992), 33: '[T]he institution of contract ... represented the legal expression of free market principles'. Waldrep refers to contract as 'the legal articulation of classical liberalism'. C. Waldrep, 'Law and Society: Structuring Legal Revolutions, 1870–1920'(2006) 5 *Journal of the Gilded Age and Progressive Era* 309–323 at 316.

state does not play an active role in this privately ordered world; its role is limited to that of a neutral 'night watchman', there to ensure that private agreements are honoured but otherwise receding into the background.[128] A consent-based system of sexual regulation would thus appear to amplify and promote the values that classical liberalism seeks to advance and protect, including individualism, autonomy, liberty and freedom from government paternalism. For many Americans, this would be a good thing, at least in the realm of sex, where the state's regulatory presence and the emphasis on marriage as a marker of good sexual citizenship underscored a particular, state-endorsed, morals-driven vision of sex and sexuality.

But does the move towards consent actually insulate Americans from undue state interference – or the imposition of state-endorsed sexual mores? Arguably, it does not. Under this new regime of sexual regulation, few sexual encounters are presumptively permissible or impermissible; the legitimacy of every encounter hinges on consent. But even (and perhaps especially) in the era of affirmative consent, expressions of consent are subject to interpretation, and thus disagreement – which in turn creates opportunities for the state to intervene and for majoritarian sexual norms to guide interpretation. In the Title IX context, for example, the college and university administrators acting in the DOE's shadow determine whether consent has been secured or whether the boundary has been breached. In this regard, a system that prioritizes individual consent relies on the judgements of individuals to determine when consent has been secured. In this regard, the consent-based regulatory model risks introducing *gendered* judgements about sex and sexuality. Critics of the regime have already noted that the system may pose outsized risks of improper prosecution and discipline to men, and in particular men of colour,[129] who are

[128] In American history, classical liberalism enjoyed its heyday in law and policy during the decades bracketing the turn of the twentieth century. For examples of how deeply this ideology pervaded American life and legal thought, see H. Gillman, *The Constitution Besieged: The Rise and Demise of Lochner Era Police Powers Jurisprudence* (Durham, NC: Duke University Press, 1994); A. D. Stanley, *From Bondage to Contract: Wage Labor, Marriage, and the Market in the Age of Slave Emancipation* (Cambridge: Cambridge University Press, 1998).

[129] Halley raises concerns over disproportionate Title IX enforcement, given a long history ('from Emmet Till to the Central Park Five') of false sexual assault accusations against black men. See J. Halley, 'Trading the Megaphone for the Gavel in Title IX Enforcement' (2015) 128 *Harvard Law Review Forum* 103–117 at 106–108. Bazelon argues that the existing Title IX system denies adequate process for those accused, who are especially

often stereotyped as hypersexual and dangerous. The imposition of individualized judgements as to what constitutes consensual sex may further exacerbate these inequalities by trading on traditional notions of male sexual aggression and female sexual passivity.

In this regard, the consent-based system stands in stark contrast to a status – or marriage-based – regime of sexual regulation. Under such a system, the distinction between good sex and bad sex did not rest on individual judgements of sexual worthiness, but rather on the fact of the existence of a status relationship. And meaningfully, a status-based regime not only limits the imposition of individual judgement, it also limits the opportunities for state intervention and interference. As feminist scholars have long noted, marriage is a public institution with a private valence.[130] Once individuals married, the states' role in their affairs was sharply circumscribed – for better or for worse.[131] Where there was an intact marriage, the state was loath to cross the threshold.[132] Indeed, the state's presence and intervention was only required to acknowledge entry into marriage and mark the dissolution of a marriage. In other words, under a status-based regime, there was a definable threshold beyond which the state could not enter.[133] Where is the threshold in a consent-based regime? It does not exist.

likely to be men of colour. L. Bazelon, 'I'm a Democrat and a Feminist. And I Support Betsy DeVos's Title IX Reforms', *New York Times*, 4 December 2018, www.nytimes.com/2018/12/04/opinion/-title-ix-devos-democrat-feminist.html. Yoffe notes that black men appear to be overrepresented in campus sexual assault cases. E. Yoffe, 'The Question of Race in Campus Sexual-Assault Cases', *The Atlantic*, 11 September 2017, www.theatlantic.com/education/archive/2017/09/the-question-of-race-in-campus-sexual-assault-cases/539361/.

130 See, e.g., Singer, who notes the duality of marriage as a both a 'public institution' and a 'private relationship'. J. B. Singer, 'The Privatization of Family Law' (1992) 1992 *Wisconsin Law Review* 1443–1568 at 1512. Cott documents the many ways in which marriage has served as a 'pillar of the state', despite common perceptions that marriage is a private matter. N. F. Cott, *Public Vows: A History of Marriage and the Nation* (Cambridge, MA: Harvard University Press, 2000)

131 On the 'worse' side of the equation, see E. M. Schneider, 'The Violence of Privacy' (1991) 23 *Connecticut Law Review* 973–1000 at 974: 'Historically, male battering of women was untouched by law, protected as part of the private sphere of family life'.

132 For the sake of our argument, I have painted with broad brushstrokes here. For a more nuanced description of the state's role in regulating the behaviour of married parties, see E. Katz, 'Judicial Patriarchy and Domestic Violence: A Challenge to the Conventional Family Privacy Narrative' (2015) 21 *William & Mary Journal of Women and the Law* 379–433.

133 To be sure, the ideal of family privacy that this theory connotes was more illusory than real. Certain families – those on public assistance, for example – did not enjoy this kind of seclusion from the state. See A. L. Allen, *Uneasy Access: Privacy for Women in a Free Society* (Lanham, MD: Rowman & Littlefield, 1988), 61. Moreover, for some, including

If this argument strikes readers as ironic, it should. The face of consent, particularly affirmative consent, is profoundly libertarian. With that in mind, how can a consent-based regime of sexual regulation be characterized as statist? Indeed, if this seems paradoxical, it should, for it is the very same paradox that scholars have identified in neoliberalism itself.

I invoke the word 'neoliberalism' deliberately, but with some caution, as it has become, in recent years, associated with everything that 'is wrong and horrible'.[134] Used carefully, however, the word still captures better than any other a particular 'political rationality' – one that has deeply marked American governance for at least a generation.[135] To paraphrase David Harvey, neoliberalism is at bottom a theory about how best to advance human wellbeing – a theory based on the idea of 'maximiz[ing]' 'entrepreneurial freedoms' within a framework of 'private property rights, individual liberty, unencumbered markets, and free trade'.[136] It extends a market logic to all realms – that is, not only to the actual buying and selling of goods and labour, but to the education of children, the policing of crime, the provision of public infrastructure, the relief of poverty and, in this case, the regulation of sex.[137]

Indeed, one might discern a neoliberal impulse in the effort to decriminalize consensual adult sex and sexuality. Under the traditional regime in which sex was regulated by marriage and crime, the state's role in defining the boundaries of normative sex and sexuality was thickly pronounced. The effort to get the state of the bedroom emphasized a shift from state-enforced morality to markets. That is, if individuals were engaged in sexual conduct that others found objectionable, rather than calling upon the state to enforce majoritarian sexual norms, objectors could make their own judgements, condemning the behaviour through their individual choices rather than through state regulation.

vulnerable women and children, the fact of family privacy was more problematic than pleasurable, shielding all manner of abuses and impositions from state intervention and enforcement. See Schneider, 'The Violence of Privacy', at 973–974.

134 D. E. Thorsen, 'The Neoliberal Challenge: What Is Neoliberalism?' (2010) 2 *Contemporary Readings in Law & Social Justice* 188–214 at 206.

135 W. Brown, 'American Nightmare: Neoliberalism, Neoconservativism, and De-Democratization' (2006) 34 *Political Theory* 690–714 at 693.

136 D. Harvey, 'Neoliberalism as Creative Destruction' (2007) 610 *Annals of the American Academy of Political and Social Science* 22–44 at 22.

137 See S. Schram et al., 'The Third Level of US Welfare Reform: Governmentality under Neoliberal Paternalism' (2010) 14 *Citizenship Studies* 739–754 at 742; Brown, 'American Nightmare', at 694.

Of course, the deregulatory impulse misjudged the state's omnipresence. As we have seen, even as criminal law receded as a regulatory mode, the state's regulatory impulses were channelled through other means, such as the administrative state. As importantly, even in the shift to the market, the state remains. Put differently, proponents of neoliberal policies often emphasize the importance of a limited role for government – of letting the market do its work. Adherents of neoliberalism rely on the faulty assumption that the market exists apart from the state. Of course, it does not and never has.[138] Indeed, neoliberalism *requires* a state that creates and protects its preferred institutional framework.[139] It also relies on the state to define citizenship, sexual or otherwise, in a particular way – namely, with an emphasis on assuming individual responsibility and pursuing self-sufficiency via 'active engagement with the world of work'.[140] In the United States, at least, entrenching this particular definition of citizenship has required heavy-handed government policies, ranging from complicated schemes of 'workfare' to the expansion of carceral apparatuses. Insofar as it relates to sexual citizenship, it has prioritized families and relationships formed under the auspices of state-recognized marriages. In short, neoliberalism is anti-statist in principle, but deeply statist in practice.[141]

The bureaucratic turn in sexual regulation further illuminates the neoliberal paradox in the realm of sexual regulation. Neoliberalism has so thoroughly pervaded American governance that it has now captured

[138] F. E. Olsen, 'The Family and the Market: A Study of Ideology and Legal Reform' (1983) 96 *Harvard Law Review* 1497–1578; B. E. Harcourt, *The Illusion of Free Markets: Punishment and the Myth of Natural Order* (Cambridge, MA: Harvard University Press, 2011).

[139] Harvey, 'Neoliberalism as Creative Destruction', at 22.

[140] A. Woolford and A. Nelund, 'The Responsibilities of the Poor: Performing Neoliberal Citizenship within the Bureaucratic Field' (2013) 87 *Social Service Review* 292–318 at 293; see also M. T. McCluskey, 'Efficiency and Social Citizenship: Challenging the Neoliberal Attack on the Welfare State' (2003) 78 *Indiana Law Journal* 783–876 at 786: 'In this vision, citizens' primary role is to maximize their private rational self-interest as buyers and sellers in market exchanges.' Brown notes that neoliberalism measures citizens' 'moral autonomy' by 'their capacity for "self-care"'). Brown, 'American Nightmare', at 694.

[141] Centeno and Cohen note that, although neoliberalism valorises limited government, neoliberal reformers have rarely chosen to shrink the size of the state 'in any substantial, absolute sense'. M. A. Centeno and J. N. Cohen, 'The Arc of Neoliberalism' (2012) 38 *Annual Review of Sociology* 317–340 at 325. Wacquant observes that, while the neoliberal state 'embraces laissez-faire at the top, . . . it is anything but laissez-faire at the bottom'. L. Wacquant, 'Crafting the Neoliberal State: Workfare, Prisonfare, and Social Insecurity' (2010) 25 *Sociological Forum* 197–220 at 214.

realms – such as civil rights enforcement – that we tend to associate with a very different political rationality (that of modern or 'New Deal' liberalism). The challenge, going forward, is not only to interrogate the latest instantiation of sexual regulation and the production of sexual citizenship, but also to interrogate the neoliberal order of which it, and indeed most of our efforts to regulate sex and sexuality, is a part.

Part II

Functions

5 The Working Subject

The Collusion of Law and Gender in the Construction of Working Subjects

Joanne Conaghan

1. Introduction: Gender/Sex and Subjectivity

This chapter explores how law and gender come together to co-constitute working subjects and with what conceptual, normative and distributive effects. The notion of subjectivity deployed here is both ontological and epistemological. It is ontological in the sense of being concerned with aspects of being – with who or what the subject is; and it is epistemological in that it is engaged with questions of knowledge – with how knowledge of and by the subject is produced and validated. Thus understood, subjectivity offers a space of enquiry into questions about the formation, shape and consequences of consciousness and the production, validation and effects of knowledge.

Enlightenment thought traditionally posits the subject as a pre-social abstraction. Subjects align with reason and operations of the mind, while objects map onto materiality, including, but not confined to, human bodies. Consciousness thus derives from internal mental operations which, applied to an objectively constituted world, produce knowledge. This broadly Cartesian model contrasts with notions of subjectivity as discursively construed, the outcome of social, symbolic and linguistic practices which shape collective understanding to produce historically situated, socially embedded subjects.[1] It is this latter understanding that underpins the present analysis – an understanding which recognizes that subjects come into being as the effects of networks of social relations and practices that structure experience to confer meaning and value and institute normative regimes.

This is not to reduce subjects to the status of pure social artefacts. Subjectivities emanate from the social but their sphere of operation is

[1] For a useful overview of these contrasting models of subjectivity, see S. Hekman, *Gender and Knowledge* (Boston, MA: North Eastern University Press, 1990), 62–73.

'ineluctably material'.[2] Subjects live, breathe, excrete and expire in an undeniably physical world, albeit that social arrangements influence how subjects apprehend and navigate their physical environment and provide frames of reference for the interpretation and management of materially engendered experiences and effects. Materiality is always more than its social representation(s). The material world manifests an 'excess, force, vitality, relationality, or difference . . . render[ing] matter active, self-creative, productive, unpredictable'.[3] These agentic qualities compel a theorization of subjects not wholly contained by discourse, not least because material considerations – including but not limited to sentient needs, desires and emotions – place limits on the extent to which, in any given social order, human subjects may be exploited or coerced. Subjects then are neither wholly determined, as some theories of social construction would have us conclude, nor fully autonomous, as liberal individualist models often assume. Understood in this way, subjectivity aids our apprehension of the dynamic interplay of material and representational processes in consciousness formation and knowledge generation, from which 'real' subjects, living 'real' lives emerge.[4]

How does gender feature in processes of subjectification and what do we mean by 'gender' for these purposes? The terms 'gender' and sex are often distinguished through the alignment of gender with social construction and sex with materiality and embodiment. In so far as subjectivity is socially constructed, this would seem to direct our attention to gender rather than sex – which would assume the status of biologically given. To take this position, however, is precisely to neglect the coalescence of materiality and representation in processes of subjectivity formation. Bodies are not *tabulae rasae* upon whose surfaces meaning is simply inscribed: Cells, hormones, genes and genitalia have active, self-propelling properties. At the same time, the grounding and significance of corporeal operations in schemes of sexual differentiation inevitably depend on discursive and meaning-making

[2] D. Coole and S. Frost, *New Materialisms* (Durham, NC: Duke University Press, 2010), 1.

[3] Ibid., 9.

[4] That something is socially constructed does not render it any less 'real'. As Haslanger argues, the very idea that reality is something which exists 'independent of us' is itself a social construct, a conflation of what is real with what is 'natural'. S. Haslanger, *Resisting Reality: Social Construction and Social Critique* (New York: Oxford University Press, 2012), 204. Acknowledging the socially constructed dimensions of reality helps us to recognize how 'real' phenomena 'depend, *in ordinary ways*, on us, particularly on our attitudes and our interactions'. Ibid., 214, and generally ch. 6.

practices. Just as concrete corporeal variations are called upon to undergird ideologies of race and even class,[5] variations in anatomical form and genetic make-up are mobilized to support sex difference and its social ordering. The result is to problematize any simplistic understanding of sex and gender as occupying opposite ends of the matter/meaning spectrum and to call for an approach to subjectivity which recognizes the *integration* of gender and sex in processes of identity formation. For this reason, biologist Anne Fausto-Sterling rejects analytical approaches which dichotomize sex and gender and utilizes the term 'gender/sex', understood as 'a softly assembled dynamic system that comes into being . . . and is maintained through one-on-one interactions with others and *via cultural enforcement of gender/sex*'.[6] Her approach perfectly captures the entanglement of sex and gender in material and representational processes and, while gender continues to be deployed as the primary category here, it should be understood to encompass the integrated approach advocated by Fausto-Sterling.

How then is gender/sex as a dynamic system of identity formation 'culturally enforced'? Judith Butler's theory of gender performativity offers a useful framework for understanding the processes through which gender comes to be experienced as a natural, internally coherent dimension of selfhood.[7] Within Butler's analytical frame, gender is reconceived, not as a characteristic which inheres in individuals, but as an *effect* of performative practices in turn compelled by social norms.[8] A strength of Butler's theory is that it carries no commitment to the idea that subjectivities are wholly discursively determined: In so far as subject positions are effected by performance, they can be disrupted through performative modes of resistance. A weakness perhaps is that her theory does not adequately account for the norm-creating impetuses that prompt performative practices.[9]

[5] The corporeal dimensions of class exploitation are less visible than in relation to gender and race, but operate nonetheless: consider, for example, how the mind/body schematic is called upon to account for income inequalities, the 'brute' strength of the labourer being deemed to have less market value than the intellectual acuity of the lawyer/financier.

[6] A. Fausto-Sterling, 'Gender/Sex, Sexual Orientation, and Identity Are in the Body: How Did They Get There?' (2019) 56 *Journal of Sex Research* 529–555 at 532 (emphasis added).

[7] J. Butler, *Gender Trouble* (New York: Routledge, 1990).

[8] Ibid. Butler explains 'sex' as the materialization of gender normativity in sexed bodies. In other words, sex and gender are posited as interdependent and similarly subject to processes of social/cultural construction. J. Butler, *Bodies That Matter* (New York: Routledge, 1993).

[9] K. Weeks, *Constituting Feminist Subjects* (Ithaca, NY: Cornell University Press, 1998), 124–134.

Because Butler locates norm creation within the general realm of signification – in which linguistic and discursive practices confer meaning and value – her theory offers little insight into how or why normative regimes assume a particular shape and form.[10] Why, for example, do sex and race repeatedly materialize as hierarchical social relations? Why is labour invariably a site for the performance of exploitative practices? Performance alone does not readily account for the historical specificities of inequality regimes. Nor does it advance analysis of how distinct domains of action, meaning and signification – the economic, cultural, political and so on – take form and interrelate. It is necessary therefore to supplement Butler's theory of performativity with social theory – that is, perspectives attentive to the development of social practices, the shaping of social relations, and the emergence of structural and systemic[11] potencies in social orderings. Federici observes:

> Performance is a useful concept but its range of applications is a limited one . . . It overlooks that gender is the result of a long process of disciplining and that it is maintained not simply through the imposition of 'norms', but through the organization of work, the division of labor, the setting up of differentiated labor markets, and the organization of the family, sexuality and domestic work.[12]

In exploring how subjects become gendered, then, we need to look beyond the realm of signification (though this remains important) to probe the connections between signification and social ordering, including, as we shall see, the signifying practices which support the social organization of work and the gender division of labour.

2. Work as a Key Site of Subjectivity Formation

As a structured social environment characterized by varying levels of stratification, hierarchization and coercion, work is a promising site for

[10] S. Federici, *Beyond the Periphery of the Skin: Rethinking, Remaking and Reclaiming the Body in Contemporary Capitalism* (Oakland, CA: Kairos, 2019), 46–47.

[11] Acknowledging the structural features of social orderings tell us little about the scope or force of structural operations or the opportunities to disrupt or undermine their effects. These are empirical questions requiring contextual investigation of specific social orderings.

[12] Federici, *Beyond the Periphery of the Skin*, 46.

investigating how subjectivities are formed and operationalized. Marx serves as a useful starting point for theorizing the significance of work/labour in shaping consciousness and knowledge production. His historical materialism offers an account of human development and cooperation rooted in the practicalities of everyday life and basic human needs, specifically the reproduction and sustenance of the species. Marx explains how the 'life-process', understood as 'real individuals, their activities and the material conditions in which they live',[13] engenders forms of social cooperation, including the organization of labour and the development of technologies of production and reproduction. These social arrangements come to underpin how lives are lived and experienced, how ideas are fashioned and disseminated, and how power is acquired and exercised. Marx goes on to argue that the social relations which develop from and support the mode of production he identifies as capitalist are structured around a distinct form of labour exploitation. However, one does not need fully to commit to this position to concur with Marx's key insight, namely that labour, and the social relations to which it gives rise, are central, not only to sustaining human life but to making it meaningful. Indeed, these themes resonate in other philosophers' work. In *The Human Condition*, Hannah Arendt foregrounds work and labour as fundamental aspects of the *vita activa*, those forms of activity which, she argues, set the conditions for human existence.[14] Adopting a very different theoretical framework to Marx, Arendt's analysis affirms the centrality of work/labour as a site of enquiry into questions of being and consciousness as she advances an account of historical development in which work/labour practices fundamentally shape conceptions of value and human purpose.

Iterations of the existential and ethical aspects of work may also be found in political and legal commitments to a 'right to work'.[15] To conceive of work as a right or entitlement is to attribute to it social and ethical value. Work is 'a crucial good', Mantouvalou tells us, not just because, for most people, it is a necessary means of meeting material needs, but also

[13] E. Kamenka, *The Portable Karl Marx* (Harmondsworth: Penguin, 1983), 163.

[14] H. Arendt, *The Human Condition* (Chicago, IL: University of Chicago Press, 1998).

[15] See e.g. Universal Declaration of Human Rights, Art. 23. The ethical imperative to work also contributes to constructions of worklessness as an immoral state, a trope frequently deployed to promote neoliberal labour activation and welfare policies. A. Paz-Fuchs, 'The Right to Work and the Duty to Work', in V. Mantouvalou (ed.), *The Right to Work: Legal and Philosophical Perspectives* (Oxford: Hart, 2015).

because, at least ideally, it is creative, sociable and dignity-enhancing.[16] This attribution of ethical value to work sits uneasily alongside the practical reality of work as a common and pervasive site of exploitation. The causes and consequences of labour exploitation are of course contested: Although Marx views exploitation as an inherent feature of the wage–labour relationship, in liberal philosophical terms, waged labour constitutes a voluntary exchange between two formally equal parties legally captured in the contract of employment. Even within such a liberal framing, however, the *risk* of exploitation is generally acknowledged to be real and substantial, with most modern labour law regimes evolving around a perceived need to mediate conflicts of interest between employers and workers, and to redress inequalities of bargaining power to ensure a fair bargain is struck.[17] Other aspects of the employment relation also activate a need for regulatory protection. The ongoing, often indefinite duration of the employment relationship produces uncertainty and incompleteness around what the parties have agreed, requiring, as a matter of practical necessity, Collins argues, the vesting of discretionary power in a controlling party.[18] The resulting legal relation yields an asymmetry of power in which one party, the employee, is placed in a formally subordinate position to another, the employer[19] – necessitating a regulatory mechanism to check against possible abuses.

Work then is coercive not just in the sense that workers are obliged to engage in it to meet their material needs, but also because the configuration of work as a social activity and legal form incorporates a degree of subordination. This strengthens the case for attending closely to work when probing the interlinkages between social arrangements and social subjects. Foregrounding work as a space of enquiry into subjectivity formation helps to highlight human vulnerability and co-dependence

[16] V. Mantouvalou, *The Right to Work: Legal and Philosophical Perspectives* (Oxford: Hart, 2015), 1.

[17] H. Collins, K. Ewing and A. McColgan, *Labour Law*, 2nd ed. (Cambridge: Cambridge University Press, 2019), 5–6.

[18] H. Collins, 'Is the Contract of Employment Illiberal?' in H. Collins, G. Lester and V. Mantouvalou (eds.), *Philosophical Foundations of Labour Law* (Oxford: Oxford University Press, 2018).

[19] In *Ready Mixed Concrete* v. *Minister of Pensions & National Insurance* [1968] 2 QB 497, MacKenna J identifies subordination as a key component of the contract of employment: '[The servant] agrees, expressly or impliedly, that in the performance of that service he will be subject to the other's control in a sufficient degree to make that other master'.

and the corresponding risks (and opportunities) these present for exploitation and coercion.

3. Gender and the Social Organization of Work

A. Industrialization and the Gender Division of Labour

The starting point to understanding how law contributes to the construction of gendered working subjects is the distinction between paid and unpaid labour, and the function this distinction performs in defining labour law as a regulatory field. The 'labour' of labour law is presumed to be remunerated, distinct from unremunerated labour performed, for example, by women in the family home.[20] This intuitive sense that labour law corresponds with paid work – which still, for the most part, governs legal, policy and academic engagements with the field – is bolstered by a perception, materially and culturally engrained, that work and family occupy distinct social realms. Within this social imaginary, work, understood as labour which commands a wage, aligns with production and relations of exchange, while family, understood as a biologically underpinned social unit, corresponds with reproduction[21] and relations of intimacy and affect. This sharp spatial segmentation of everyday experience is naturalized in wider social arrangements – in temporal demarcations ('the working day'), attributions of value (care work as 'low-skilled') and hierarchically imbued social roles ('breadwinners' and 'dependants') – which find expression, inter alia, in gender norms and expectations.

[20] J. Conaghan, 'Gender and the Labour of Law', in H. Collins, G. Lester and V. Mantouvalou (eds.), *Philosophical Foundations of Labour Law* (Oxford: Oxford University Press, 2018).

[21] The term 'reproduction' is commonly deployed to denote the biological reproduction of the species. However, within feminist scholarship a broader conception of the term is being utilized, captured in the concept of 'social reproduction', and understood to encompass the institutions, processes and practices necessary to reproduce social life as it is lived and experienced in a particular time and place. The concept applies to childbearing and childrearing but extends well beyond these activities to bring into view a broader range of caregiving practices. It can also include the cultivation of communities and other social institutions that support social order and well-being. For further elaboration of the concept of social reproduction and its deployment in labour law, see J. Fudge, 'Feminist Reflections on the Scope of Labour Law: Domestic Work, Social Reproduction and Jurisdiction' (2014) 22 *Feminist Legal Studies* 1–22, at 7–8.

There is nothing 'natural', however, about the social and spatial distancing of work and family. This landscape of labouring practices is historically and materially rooted in the transition from feudalism to capitalism which witnessed the displacement of the family/household as the core economic unit,[22] and the social disconnection of work from family life.[23] Before the transition to a predominantly wage-based, market-centred economy, households – which generally comprised a broader range of people than those directly tied by blood or marriage[24] – engaged in both production (making clothes, food, objects for use) and reproduction (care and sustenance of household members). 'Home' and 'work' were not typically conceived as separate spheres serving separate functions, and while the bulk of responsibility for reproductive labour fell upon women – medieval life was no idyll of gender equality[25] – such work was acknowledged to make a key contribution to the functioning of the household as an economic unit.[26]

In the shift from feudalism to capitalism,[27] this old way of life broke down. There were many features to this economic and social transition, but of particular significance for our purposes was the reconfiguration of labouring practices to meet the emergent needs of industrial production.

[22] B. Hill, *Women, Work and Sexual Politics in Eighteenth Century England* (London: Routledge, 1989).

[23] L. Taylor, 'Marriage, Work and the Construction of the Family in Nineteenth Century English Law and Legal Thought', Unpublished SJD thesis (Faculty of Law, University of Toronto, 2019).

[24] A. Lawrence, *Women in England 1500–1760* (London: Phoenix, 1994), 8–9.

[25] There is a longstanding debate among feminist historians as to whether the transition from feudalism to capitalism enhanced or diminished women's status, the weight of historical evidence suggesting that in both contexts, women's work was undervalued. See e.g. J. M. Bennett, 'Medieval Women, Modern Women: Across the Great Divide', in D. Aers (ed.), *Culture and History 1350–1600: Essays on English Communities, Identities and Writing* (Hemel Hempstead: Harvester Wheatsheaf, 1992); M. Berg, 'What Difference Did Women's Work Make to the Industrial Revolution?' (1993) 35 *History Workshop* 22–44; A. Vickery, 'Golden Age to Separate Spheres? A Review of the Categories and Chronology of English Women's History' (1993) 36 *Historical Journal* 383–414.

[26] Hill, *Women, Work and Sexual Politics*, ch. 3.

[27] In England broadly dating from the fourteenth through to the seventeenth centuries. See generally M. A. Zmolek, *Rethinking the Industrial Revolution: Five Centuries of Transition from Agrarian to Industrial Capitalism in England* (Leiden: Brill, 2013); S. Federici, *Caliban and the Witch: Women, the Body and Primitive Accumulation* (New York: Autonomedia, 2004); C. Middleton, 'Patriarchal Exploitation and the Rise of English Capitalism', in E. Gamarnikow, D. Morgan, J. Purvis and D. Taylorson (eds.), *Gender, Class and Work* (London: Gower, 1983), 1.

The expansion of production-for-exchange (as opposed to production-for-use) led to the movement of much productive work out of the household and into the mills and factories. At the same time, reproductive work – feeding, caring for and reproducing labour – continued to be performed by women in the 'home', a space from which production was steadily expunged.

One should not overstate the extent or uniformity of these changes, which took place over a long period and were contextually mediated. For some women, social change created new economic opportunities, particularly in early industrialization when both sexes were drawn into manufacturing.[28] Many women – especially single women with no other means of support – had little choice but to work,[29] and throughout industrialization domestic service constituted a primary source of paid employment for working-class women.[30] Patterns of women's paid work also varied across economic sectors. In a recent study of gendered patterns of work in England in the Early Modern period (broadly 1500 to 1700), Whittle and Hailwood detected a sharply gendered division of labour in craft work, a more flexible division in agriculture, while in the commercial sector gender differences were perceived to be far less acute.[31]

These caveats notwithstanding, the reorganization of labouring practices in early capitalism triggered the emergence and solidification of a perception of work and family as separate realms of activity, sensibility and governance. With productive and reproductive labour increasingly spatially distanced, their distinctiveness appeared more pronounced, assuming a tangible visible form which intensified and naturalized the gender division of labour.[32] The spatial reordering of labouring practices in

[28] Berg, 'What Difference Did Women's Work Make'.

[29] Bennett, 'Medieval Women, Modern Women', 157–159.

[30] Lawrence, *Women in England 1500–1760*, 117. The picture in the United States is more complex still as the institution of slavery (and its aftermath) yielded distinct configurations of work and family life for black women and their menfolk. P. Hill Collins, *Black Feminist Thought: Knowledge, Consciousness, and the Politics of Empowerment* (New York: Routledge, 2000), 46–55. These structural, racially mediated divergences in experience did not, as Hill Collins acknowledges, prevent the normative privileging of a (white, middle-class) idealization of the family as a workfree sanctuary.

[31] J. Whittle and M. Hailwood, 'The Gender Division of Labour in Early Modern England' (2020) 73 *Economic History Review* 3–32.

[32] M. Mies, *Patriarchy and Accumulation on a World Scale* (London: Zed Books, 1986), 49–51.

early capitalism thus played a critical role, not only in separating the spheres of 'work' and 'family life', but in instituting a distinct gender-based division of labour to support industrialization.

Time played a role in this process. E. P. Thompson traces the shift in notations of time during industrialization, from 'task-orientation', where time is measured according to the performance of tasks, to 'timed work', where tasks become subject to the discipline of clock time.[33] According to Thompson, this transition from task-based to timed work was a vital step in the process of economic transition, instituting a temporal regime which allowed employers to secure labour regularly and for prescribed periods. Significantly, because 'work' was temporally demarcated to exclude the simultaneous pursuit of other 'life' activities, the hitherto easy intermingling of productive and reproductive labour became incompatible with the new work-time discipline.

Thompson stops short of making a direct link between the transition from task orientation to timed work and the constitution of a new gender order under capitalism, but it is easily gleaned from his account: For workers to engage exclusively in timed work, arrangements had to be in place to ensure that other essential activities, including reproductive work, continued to be performed. The emergent solution – in which men participated in production on a timed basis while women continued to carry out the bulk of reproductive work – delivered a supply of workers who, by virtue of being unencumbered by care responsibilities, could commit their time almost exclusively to their employers' needs. In this way, women's unpaid labour served as a crucial enabling feature of the transition from task orientation to timed work during the early period of industrialization.

B. Gendered Patterns of Paid Work Participation

The gendered consequences of social and legal arrangements predicated on the conceptual, normative and distributive dichotomization of production and reproduction have been well rehearsed by feminist scholars.[34] They effected the structural engineering of women's economic dependence on

[33] E. P. Thompson, 'Time, Work-Discipline and Industrial Capitalism', in E. P. Thompson (ed.), *Customs in Common* (Penguin: Harmondsworth, 1991).

[34] For a comprehensive analysis and overview of this scholarship as it pertains to labour law, see J. Fudge, 'From Women and Labour to Putting Gender and Law to Work', in M. Davies

men, expressed in a normative family model comprising a male breadwinner/female caregiver.[35] This model was subsequently incorporated into the regulatory frameworks of Western industrialized economies, supporting the social organization of work and the governance of welfare and family life.[36] The outcome of this purpose-built 'gender contract',[37] was not just severely to circumscribe women's *access* to paid work but to shape fundamentally the terms of women's engagement with paid work opportunities. To accommodate family responsibilities, women felt compelled to seek jobs offering curtailed hours and/or temporal flexibility. As a consequence, they clustered in part-time work and in sectors of the labour market which deviated from standard working norms. Entering and exiting employment to the rhythms of reproductive cycles, women's paid work participation was characterized by frequent patterns of interruption, trapping them in short-term, insecure posts, which hindered their career progression and prevented them from meeting the eligibility requirements to qualify for many basic employment rights.[38]

These historically pervasive features of women's employment are widely acknowledged, as are their impact on women's access to employment protection rights. Indeed, the gender inegalitarian effects of employment protection provisions have twice been subject to legal challenge in the UK courts: In *R.* v. *Secretary of State ex parte the Equal Opportunities Commission*,[39] the Equal Opportunities Commission (EOC), at that time the body charged with responsibility for tackling sex discrimination, successfully challenged the minimum hours threshold governing access to employment protection on the grounds that the adverse impact of the provision on women workers violated Article 141 TEC. A similar challenge

and V. Munro (eds.), *The Ashgate Research Companion to Feminist Legal Theory* (Farnham: Ashgate, 2013).

[35] J. Lewis, 'The Decline of the Male Breadwinner Model: The Implications for Work and Care' (2001) 8(2) *Social Politics* 152–170.

[36] N. Fraser, 'After the Family Wage: A Postindustrial Thought Experiment', in N. Fraser (ed.), *Justice Interruptus: Critical Reflections on the 'Postsocialist' Condition* (New York: Routledge, 1997).

[37] J. Fudge, 'A New Gender Contract? Work/Life Balance and Working-Time Flexibility', in J. Conaghan and K. Rittich (eds.), *Labour Law, Work and Family: Critical and Comparative Perspectives* (Oxford: Oxford University Press, 2005).

[38] For a useful overview of patterns of women's workforce participation in nineteenth- and twentieth-century Britain, see S. Fredman, *Women and the Law* (Oxford: Clarendon Press, 1997), ch. 3.

[39] [1995] 1 AC 1.

to continuity of employment requirements in *R.* v. *Secretary of State ex parte Seymour-Smith No. 2*[40] failed, the House of Lords eventually holding that while the two-year qualifying period for access to unfair dismissal did adversely impact on women workers, the provision was justified because it furthered a government policy to promote employment recruitment.[41] After the EOC challenge, the UK government enacted legislation removing the minimum hours requirement. Stringent continuity of employment requirements, however, continue to determine access to many UK employment rights.

In recent years, the male breadwinner/female caregiver model has increasingly given way to the rise of dual-earner families.[42] In the last half-century, the extent of women's participation in paid work has risen exponentially, currently falling not far short of men's.[43] And in the last decade, the proportion of women engaged in full-time work has grown to hitherto unprecedented levels.[44] What is striking, however, is that, notwithstanding these changes, the UK labour market continues to exhibit deeply gendered workforce patterns. For example, although women's employment participation rate is currently at 72.4 per cent (compared to men at 80.6 per cent)[45] and approximately 60 per cent of women workers now work full-time, women are still far more likely than men to work part-time and continue to make up the vast majority of part-time workers.[46]

40 [2000] UKHL 12.

41 This was notwithstanding prior consideration of the case in the European Court of Justice (ECJ) suggesting the burden of justification could not be met by 'mere generalizations concerning the capacity of a specific measure to encourage recruitment' (Case C-167/97, *R* v. *Secretary of State for Employment ex parte Seymour Smith & Perez* [1999] ECR I-00623).

42 Lewis, 'The Decline of the Male Breadwinner Model'; Fudge, 'A New Gender Contract?'

43 B. F. Devine and N. Foley, 'Women and the Economy', House of Commons Briefing Paper No. CBP06838, 4 March 2020, 4.

44 Ibid., 4–5.

45 Within certain ethnic communities, the female employment participation rate is considerably lower. For example, in the Bangladeshi and Pakistani communities, men's employment participation rate is 75 per cent while women's is only 39 per cent (Department of Work and Pensions, 2020).

46 In the United Kingdom in 2019, 40 per cent of women in employment were working part-time compared to 13 per cent of men (Devine and Foley, 'Women and the Economy', 4); about 74 per cent of part-time workers are women. Women's Budget Group, 'Crises Collide: Women and Covid-19', UK Policy Briefing, 9 April 2020, https://wbg.org.uk/wp-content/uploads/2020/04/FINAL.pdf.

Equally striking is the kind of paid work many women perform: Women remain heavily concentrated in service-based industries such as retail and hospitality,[47] and predominate in the health, social care and education sectors.[48] The clustering of women in occupations which resemble the unpaid labour they traditionally perform in the home evidences the tenacious grip of gendered conceptions of work, even in the domain of paid work. Moreover, this gendered division of labour manifests materially in deeply entrenched gender-based inequalities which shape and determine patterns of work and reward: It is not just the type of work that women do but the conditions under which they do it. Women comprise the majority of low-paid earners, the majority of those living in poverty, and women populate the world of insecure, precarious and exploitative work.[49] The deleterious impact on women workers of state responses to Covid-19 is but the latest illustration of the fragility of women's employment position in the context of labour market slumps and volatilities.[50]

Situating the gendered aspects of contemporary employment patterns within the broader socio-historical context of a gender division of labour – itself in the process of adapting to the challenges of global economic and political restructuring – allows us to view the systemic embedding of gender precarity within the social organization of work, with gender divisions manifesting both at the micro and macro level, in the everyday experiences of precarious work and in the complex matrix of social relations and practices which shape and underpin these everyday experiences and render them intelligible.

[47] Institute of Fiscal Studies, 'Sector Shutdowns during the Coronavirus: Which Workers Are Most Exposed?', IFS Briefing Note BN 278, 6 April 2020.

[48] In the health and social work sector 79 per cent of jobs and in education 70 per cent of jobs are held by women (Devine and Foley, 'Women and the Economy', 6).

[49] Women's Budget Group, 'Crises Collide'. The 'feminization of employment' is a frequently used term to denote either the growth or marketization of 'women's work (e.g. domestic and care work) and/or the extension to workers generally of the precarious working conditions historically associated with women's paid employment. Both understandings exemplify the symbiotic operation of gender and work to forge new forms of commodification and opportunities for exploitation.

[50] J. Conaghan, 'Covid-19 and Inequalities at Work: A Gender Lens', *Futures of Work: Issue* 13, 7 July 2020, https://futuresofwork.co.uk/2020/05/07/covid-19-and-inequalities-at-work-a-gender-lens/.

4. Labour Law and Gender Subjectivities

We have seen that subjectification – the process by which subjects come into being – occurs at the point where social arrangements and individual consciousness converge in the emergence of subject positions which materialize in the form of internally coherent, choosing selves. How, though, does law contribute to these processes which simultaneously enable and obfuscate the operation of gender in labouring practices? While gendered patterns of paid work participation have long been acknowledged by lawmakers to present problems of inequality and social justice, the predominant legal response has been, and continues to be, to corral such concerns within an anti-discrimination framework. Yet decades of experience across multiple jurisdictions reveals that gender-based disadvantage cannot be erased by anti-discrimination measures alone. Indeed, the claim-making structure in antidiscrimination law, requiring the crafting of a case around the contours of comparison, often serves to normalize existing working arrangements by positing their priority in measurements of sameness and difference. A similar logic is at work in appeals to extend labour law protections to 'non-standard' or 'atypical' workers,[51] in so far as they presume a 'standard' or 'typical' worker with whom labour law is, or ought to be, most closely concerned.

Moreover, although historically, and to a considerable extent contemporaneously, such designations of standard and non-standard work correspond closely with gendered patterns of participation in paid work, gender is rarely a formal or explicit feature of debate around the scope of labour law protections. Indeed, outside the narrow confines of equality regulation, gender is barely a category of relevance in the conceptual architecture of labour law at all. Notwithstanding its empirical significance

[51] Legal initiatives to extend employment rights to non-standard/atypical workers vary from jurisdiction to jurisdiction but are increasingly prompted by supranational policy concerns to promote labour market flexibility. E.g. the EU, in addition to the extensive anti-discrimination law framework which member states are obliged to adopt, has enacted a number of provisions to bolster 'flexible' working arrangements, including directives conferring (limited) protections on part-time (Directive 96/34) and fixed-term (Directive 99/70) workers and, most recently, the Work/Life Balance Directive 2019/1158 (inter alia, extending the right to request flexible work). See E. Caracciolo di Torella, 'An Emerging Right to Care in the EU: A "New Start" to Support Work–Life Balance for Parents and Carers', 18 *ERA Forum* 187–198.

in the social configuration of labouring practices, gender is not apprehended as a constituting feature of labour law as a normative order.

How can this be, given the gendered topography of work arrangements? And what are the consequences of positioning law outside the processes by which such arrangements come into being? To understand why gender is legally invisible requires attention to the constitution in conventional legal thought of the legal and the social as distinct realms of operation and effect. While few would deny that law and society are connected, within the legal imaginary they tend to be set apart, enabling law to self-present as an autonomous repository of norms. As a discursive practice, and notwithstanding that it is a thoroughly social creation, law tends to proceed as if the boundaries between the legal and social are clear and delineable.[52]

This discursively constructed demarcation between the legal and the social has certain consequences for how gender is mobilized and conceptualized in law. Specifically, it positions gender as a *social* rather than legal category, a product of social arrangements not legal forms. Because gender is conceived as extraneous to law, law may comfortably acquit itself of responsibility for gender-unequal outcomes. The conceptual frame is one in which gendered social patterns (such as those which characterize working arrangements) find expression in legal norms and operations, but as social facts not legal creations.

However, if we adopt a conceptual frame which positions law within rather than without the iterative processes contributing to the construction of the social fabric, another picture of the relation between law and gender emerges. In this alternative conception, law does not simply act upon an already gendered social world; it is already imbricated in processes by which gender roles and relations come into being and garner normative potency. Law *genders*: In conjunction with other forms of discourse, law constrains and enables gendered identities and behaviours, fashioning and refashioning distinct gendered subjectivities. To assert that law genders is, in Butler's terms, to acknowledge the performative effects of law as an authoritative source of norms, values and meanings, influencing the adoption, abjuration, evaluation and reification of gendered ways of being and knowing. We see this played out repeatedly in legal operations and

[52] J. Conaghan, *Law and Gender* (Oxford: Clarendon Press, 2013).

practices – in the construction of heteronormatively privileged conceptions of parenthood in family law and in the reification of gendered stereotypes of sexual behaviour in criminal law. Labour law, too, is a gendering practice, contributing to the institutionalization and naturalization of a historically specific gender division of labour founded in the 'disarticulation' of work and family life and the privileging of productive over reproductive labour.[53] Let's take a look at how these gendering processes play out in legal norms and discourses governing work.

A. The Construction of Work as a Distinct and Bounded Space of Activity, Meaning and Value

I have already alluded to the way in which the concepts of space and time contribute both to the delineation of work as a distinct sphere of activity and to the incorporation of gender norms and relations within its internal order. Indeed, it is precisely because gender is imported into working arrangements via the medium of these seemingly 'natural', pre-discursive categories, that we struggle to see it, let alone track its operations. Consequently, the conceptual and normative significance of gender as a feature of work regulation remains largely hidden, as do the (gendered) power relations therein.

Take, for example, the idea that work is carried out in a dedicated space – a 'workplace' – which has long been at the heart of labour regulation and is particularly associated with the norms and practices of collective worker organization, around which much of modern labour law has developed.[54] The historical concentration of large numbers of workers in manufacturing

[53] Luke Taylor has recently produced a detailed study of the developments in English law which contributed to the disarticulation of work and family life and the privileging of productive over reproductive labour in the long nineteenth century. Encompassing not just labour law but also family and social welfare regulation, his analysis sheds valuable light on the ideas and influence which shaped the emergence of a framework of legal norms, converging in a formal narrative of social ordering which still holds sway today, even as the economic conditions which prompted its articulation are undergoing fundamental alteration. Taylor, *Marriage, Work and the Construction of the Family*.

[54] K. Klare, 'The Horizons of Transformative Labour and Employment Law', in J. Conaghan, R. M. Fischl and K. Klare (eds.), *Labour Law in an Era of Globalization: Transformative Practices and Possibilities* (Oxford: Oxford University Press, 2004); H. Arthurs, 'Labour Law after Labour', in G. Davidov and B. Langille (eds.), *The Idea of Labour Law* (Oxford: Oxford University Press, 2004).

outlets ('factories') inevitably influenced the development of trade unionism as an institutionalized expression of worker identity. However, a consequence of this is that workers outside the manufacturing model, and particularly those who work in small, disparate locations (for example in retail, services and the care sector), have often struggled to access and utilize the full benefits of labour collectivism.[55] Home- and piece-working arrangements also sit uneasily alongside a collective organizational framework predicated on the physical concentration of workers in large numbers. Indeed, historically, unions have resisted homeworking precisely because the predominance of women in such arrangements has enabled employers to pay low wages.[56]

The gendered consequences of a regulatory framework (encompassing legal norms and collective bargaining arrangements) in which work is spatially delineated are plain to see: Workers who align most closely with the regulatory model premised on a workplace are historically male and workers least likely to enjoy regulatory protections are historically – and still predominantly – female. More significant, however, is the design of labour law as an academic and policy field around a model of workplace organization which is both historically contingent and selective in its reach and effects. The effects are evident even in areas of law specifically concerned with tackling work-based inequalities. British equal pay law is a case in point, funnelling claims into a narrow, workplace-centred framework by confining pay comparisons to workers 'employed in the same establishment' or 'establishments where common terms apply'.[57] These technical limitations, which broadly mirror the shape and substance of their EU law derivation, make it difficult to claim equal pay where all or most of those who work in an establishment are of the same sex and/or come within the scope of a common pay scheme.[58] This failure to disrupt

[55] Fredman, *Women and the Law*, 137.

[56] D. Simonton, *A History of European Women's Work 1700 to the Present* (London: Routledge, 1998), 155. The historically gendered character of homeworking across Europe, particularly in the garment trade and other 'sweated' industries, was of course another consequence of the shift to industrialization. See generally ibid., 148–155.

[57] Equality Act 2010, s. 79 (3)(b)); s. 79(4)(b) &(4)(c).

[58] The 'common terms' requirement has generated lots of case law, particular in public sector employment. See e.g. *British Coal Corporation* v. *Smith* [1996] ICR 515 (HL); and *North* v. *Dumfries and Galloway Council* [2013] UKSC 45 (SC). In *Asda Stores* v. *Brierley* [2021] UKSC10, which is among the first mass equal pay claims to be taken by private sector

gendered patterns of occupational segregation fatally undermines the capacity of equal pay law to tackle gender-based pay disparities.

Not only does British law limit equal pay claims to the same establishment, or different establishments where common terms apply; it also requires that comparators work for the same or an associated employer.[59] The result is to preclude comparisons between those who work 'in the same establishment' but, by virtue, for example, of contracting-out arrangements, do not formally share the same employer.[60] Thus, for one legal purpose, the workplace/establishment is conceived as a physical space, and for another, it is legal, constituted by the particular contractual arrangements which govern individual employment. In other words, competing conceptions of 'space' are harnessed to legal techniques to limit the reach of equal pay protection.

Lydia Hayes argues that the whole framework of equal pay law hinges on the operational effects of collective bargaining arrangements forged around the traditional workplace model.[61] She highlights, inter alia, the centrality of job evaluation schemes to the activation of claims,[62] the insistence on real, not hypothetical, comparators, and the slim opportunity provided by the 'common terms' exception to cut across forms of sex segregation which already enjoy the imprimatur of collective agreement. Most significantly, her analysis reaffirms that the tightly circumscribed limits on the range and measure(s) of legal comparison not only leave gendered pay arrangements largely intact but fasten such arrangements to

employees, the UK Supreme Court affirmed the broad approach to interpreting 'common terms and conditions' adopted in *BCC* v. *Smith* and *North*.

[59] EA 2010, ss. 79(3)(a) & (4)(a).

[60] On the scope/interpretation of the 'same employer' requirement, see in particular Case C-320/000, *Lawrence* v. *Regent Office Care Limited* [2002] ECR I-7325; Case C-256/01, *Allonby* v. *Accrington and Rossendale College* [2004] ECR I-873.

[61] L. Hayes, '"Women's Voice" and Equal Pay', in A. Bogg and T. Novitz (eds.), *Voices at Work: Continuity and Change in the Common Law World* (Oxford: Oxford University Press, 2014).

[62] Ibid. The Equal Pay Act 1970, as originally enacted, confined claims to comparisons based on 'like work' or 'work rated as equivalent' under an existing job evaluation study. This lodged the latter route squarely within the context of collectively agreed pay structures. It was only after the European Commission successfully challenged the UK government for failing fully to comply with the requirements of the Equal Pay Directive (75/117) that an additional provision permitting comparisons based on 'work of equal value' was added (Case C-61/81, *Commission of the European Communities* v. *United Kingdom* [1982] ECR 2601 at 288).

employer strategies to limit their equal pay obligations.[63] By incorporating gendered aspects of work into the legal regulatory regime, equal pay law provides a framework for pay determinations which *entrenches* sex segregation at work by placing many such arrangements beyond the practical scope of legal challenge.[64] In this way, legal norms designed around the organization of work and the configuration of spaces of work promote gendered ways of working, structuring work relations within a regulatory frame in which gender operates invisibly to produce work-based subjectivities differentially positioned with regard to accessing and effecting formal legal entitlements.

In recent years, and particularly with the decline in manufacturing and advances in information and communications technology generating an enhanced capacity in many sectors to work 'offsite', traditional spatial conceptions of work have come under challenge. At the turn of the century, Karl Klare noted 'the trend in business organization . . . away from huge, centralized and vertically integrated entities towards decentralized networks of smaller, more flexible, specialist units',[65] and reflected on the implications of this trend for workplace-centred notions of work and workers. The decline of traditional workplaces and the rise, for example, of technology-enabled homeworking arrangements inevitably unsettles previously taken-for-granted spatial delineations of work, eroding the work/life boundary and presenting new possibilities for reconceiving work in ways which might disrupt the normative order governing work and advance more gender-egalitarian working arrangements. At the same time, the gendered detrimental effects of the recent exponential shift to homeworking occasioned by state and employer responses to the threat of Covid-19 suggest that the dissolution of a spatial separation between home and work will not by itself deliver gender justice and may indeed generate new inequality challenges.[66]

B. The Legal Construction of Precarious Working Subjects

As the preceding analysis shows, it is not difficult to detect a correlation between the terms on which women access and engage in paid work and

[63] Hayes, '"Women's Voice" and Equal Pay'. [64] Ibid., 38.

[65] Klare, 'The Horizons of Transformative Labour and Employment Law', 17.

[66] See e.g. IFS evidencing the uneven distribution of the ability to engage in remote working during the Covid-19 pandemic across race, class and gender lines. Institute of Fiscal Studies, 'Sector Shutdowns during the Coronavirus'.

the demarcation of social life into work and family realms. What is perhaps more difficult to discern is the role played by law in transforming these gendered social arrangements into concrete, gender-based disadvantage. Mantouvalou's conception of exploitation as 'the abuse of a person's vulnerability that is created or exacerbated by law'[67] usefully expresses how law becomes implicated in enabling exploitative labour practices, as well-intentioned laws – such as those governing equal pay, working time or minimum wage protection – create structural vulnerabilities, in the form of gaps and loopholes in legal protection, conferring upon employers a bargaining advantage in their dealings with legally excluded workers.[68] By setting the (unequal) conditions within which contractual bargains are struck, law enables certain forms of work-based exploitation.

The experience and treatment of domestic workers – that is, workers whose paid labour supports their employer's household – offers some insight into the process by which law contributes to the construction of exploitable working subjects. In the United Kingdom, as in many other jurisdictions, domestic workers are subject to significant exclusions from working time[69] and minimum wage laws.[70] Indeed, in a range of legal contexts, such workers are treated as prima facie outside the scope of employment protection.[71] Lacking basic legal rights, domestic workers are all too easy to exploit. Many, particularly those who 'live-in', are from overseas, entering the United Kingdom on an overseas domestic worker visa sponsored by their employer.[72] Their migrant status not only limits

[67] V. Mantouvalou, 'The Right to Non-Exploitative Work', in V. Mantouvalou (ed.), *The Right to Work: Legal and Philosophical Perspectives* (Oxford: Hart, 2015), 49.

[68] V. Mantouvalou, 'Legal Construction of Structures of Exploitation', in H. Collins, G. Lester and V. Mantouvalou (eds.), *Philosophical Foundations of Labour Law* (Oxford: Oxford University Press , 2018).

[69] Working Time Regulations 1998, Reg. 19, excluding workers 'employed as a domestic servant in a private household'. The Working Time Directive 93/104, which precipitated the enactment of these regulations, contains no definition of 'worker' and therefore does not specifically exclude domestic workers, but the Framework Health and Safety Directive, from which it derives its legal base, defines a worker as 'any person employed by an employer, including trainees and apprentices but excluding domestic servants' (Council Dir. 89/391/EEC Art. 3(a)).

[70] National Minimum Wage Regulations 2015, Reg. 57.

[71] E. Albin, 'From Domestic Servant to Domestic Worker', in J. Fudge, S. McCrystal and K. Sankaran (eds.), *Challenging the Legal Boundaries of Work Regulation* (Oxford: Hart, 2012).

[72] For details of the overseas domestic visa regime and its deleterious impact on migrant domestic workers, see Kalayaan, 'Dignity not Destitution: The Impact of Differential Rights of Work for Migrant Domestic Workers Referred to the National Referral Mechanism',

their access to public and legal benefits but reinforces their dependence on their employer, upon whom their entitlement to remain in the country remains closely tied.[73]

Ideas of space operate here to vest and validate exclusionary legal norms. Because it straddles the home/work boundary, domestic work poses an anomaly for labour law; and because such work is 'anomalous', the exclusion from, or limited access of domestic workers to, standard legal protections seems to accord with common sense.[74] Notions of space also surface in the geo-politics of global labour mobility, fostering the flow of migrant labour into work which, by virtue of its association with domesticity, is perceived as low-skilled and is therefore poorly rewarded. Mantouvalou contends that the bleak plight of many overseas domestic workers exemplifies the collusion of law with structures of sexism and racism to create the conditions for work-based exploitation.[75] Indeed, one could go further: Law does not simply work *with* sexism and racism to produce exploitable working subjects; law itself is a sexist and racist structure. Law creates, orders and validates networks of social relations that contribute to processes of gendering and racialization, just as extra-legal processes of gendering and racialization contribute to the conceptualization and reification of legal categories.[76] In the context of migrant domestic work, law relies on hierarchies of gender and race to render the category intelligible and validate the distributive outcomes it produces, the coalescence of gender norms and racial tropes helping to account for (and to some extent excuse) the resulting ill-treatment and abuse.[77]

October 2019, www.kalayaan.org.uk/wp-content/uploads/2019/10/Kalayaan_report_October2019.pdf.

[73] Ibid.

[74] The adoption by the International Labour Organization (ILO) in 2011 of a Domestic Work Convention (Convention No. 189 concerning decent work for domestic workers) directly challenges this common-sense perception by 'plac[ing] the regulation of domestic work squarely into the domain of labour law'. Fudge, 'Feminist Reflections on the Scope of Labour Law', at 11.

[75] Mantouvalou, 'Legal Construction of Structures of Exploitation', 197.

[76] On the role of legal categories in processes of racialization, see N. El-Enany, *(B)ordering Britain: Law, Race and Empire* (Manchester: Manchester University Press, 2020).

[77] The nature and extent of the exploitation of migrant domestic workers has been visibly exposed in some recent UK Supreme Court cases. In *Hounga* v. *Allen*, [2014] ICR 847, a migrant domestic worker successfully challenged the barring of a claim for discriminatory treatment on grounds of the illegality of the employment arrangement. By contrast, in *Onu* v. *Akwiwu*, [2016] IRLR 719, the discrimination claim was rejected on grounds that

The content and effects of the 'family worker' exemption in UK minimum wage legislation exemplify the constitutive role of gender in the construction and operationalization of legal norms. Whether or not 'work done by a worker in relation to an employer's family household' qualifies for minimum wage protection turns on whether the worker 'resides in the *family home*' and 'is not a member of that *family, but is treated as such*'.[78] The concept of family is pivotal here in defining and defending the exclusion, but what exactly does it mean? 'Family' is nowhere defined in the legislation and we are left to glean its meaning from its usage in the text, wherein family is aligned with 'home', and the 'treatment' of 'family members' indicates a set of relations qualitatively distinct from those governing workplaces. The regulations also state that in assessing whether a domestic worker is treated as a family member, consideration should be given to 'the provision of living accommodation and meals and the sharing of tasks and leisure activities',[79] suggesting that the intermingling of labour (tasks) and family (leisure) life helps to place domestic work outside the scope of legal protection. This is further reinforced by a requirement that the work in question is 'done by a worker in relation to an employer's family household'.[80] It is not *any* work performed within the confines of the family home that is exempt from minimum wage protection but *domestic* work, those tasks and activities, such as cooking, cleaning, laundry and childcare, which contribute to the reproduction of the family on a daily and generational basis. But *why* should this kind of work be exempt from minimum wage protection? What assumptions about its quality and distinctiveness operate to justify its exclusion from the scope of work as a general regulatory category?[81]

ill-treatment because of migrant status did not constitute discrimination on grounds of race. The facts of both cases highlight the vulnerability of such workers to the risk of serious ill-treatment and abuse.

78 NMWR 2015, Reg. 57(1) and (3) (emphasis added).

79 Reg. 57(3)(b). These provisions present genuine difficulties for courts required to assess whether a domestic worker is treated as a family member, see *Nambalat* v. *Taher & Anor; Udin* v. *Pasha & Ors* [2012] EWCA Civ. 1249.

80 Reg. 57(1).

81 Conceptions of time also operate to consign domestic work to the margins of labour law. The task-oriented nature of reproductive work sheds interesting light on the difficulties domestic and care workers meet conforming to models of employment governed by clock-time. Live-ins, for example, are exempt from working time regulation, in part because their residential status makes the demarcation of a clear boundary between work and life difficult to draw, but also because our expectations of such work are task not time

Suppose we were to substitute the notion of the family/home in the minimum wage legislation with a pre-industrial conception of family/household – a veritable hub of labour activity and the economic cornerstone of medieval life. The text, premise and underlying rationale of NMW Reg 57 would then make little sense. All members of the medieval household were expected to work and all, regardless of blood or lineage, were 'treated as family' (understood to encompass not just relations of affect but certain commercial ties such as apprenticeships). Such a household was also the site for a lot of the kind of work which is nowadays performed outside the home for a wage – for example, weaving yarn into cloth or making things to be put to household use.[82] This historically prior conception of family highlights the specificity of our modern understanding of family as a private, intimate space, free from the demands of work and from which relations not bound by ties of blood and affect have been largely excluded. This modern understanding is, as we have seen, historically contingent upon the reconfiguration of labouring practices triggered by industrial capitalism, yielding a gendered division of labour grounded in the spatial and social distancing of work and family life. Only against the backdrop of this gender-enabled social and spatial separation does the exceptionality of domestic work, even when it commands a wage, make sense. The dilemma of the domestic worker is exposed as social and legal creation while the deeply troubling consequences of this regulatory framing are all too real.

C. Gender and the Legal Mapping of Work Relations

There is a further twist to this tale of legal exceptionalism, one which historicizes domestic work within the development of labour law and tracks its connection to the legal crafting of the modern employment relation. The legal origins of the employment relation lie in the old common law framework governing master and servant. According to Blackstone, master and servant constituted 'one of the three great relations

governed. J. Conaghan, 'Time to Dream: Flexibility, Families and the Regulation of Working Time', in J. Fudge and R. Owens (eds.), *Precarious Work, Women and the New Economy* (Oxford: Hart-Bloomsbury, 2006).

[82] Lawrence, *Women in England 1500–1760*, 8–10.

of private life', the others being husband and wife, and parent and child.[83] Blackstone subdivided the master–servant category into four 'species of servant', comprising domestic servants, apprentices, labourers and 'superior servants . . . such as stewards, factors, and bailiffs'.[84] Each of these was subject to distinct regulatory requirements setting the conditions of service and framework of obligations. Domestic service, then, was a formally significant category in pre-industrial employment law.

The intensification of industrialization brought a shift away from Blackstone's multi-pronged classificatory scheme towards a unitary juridical model of the waged-labour contract. Master–servant law provided the legal archetype for the 'contract of service', ensnaring waged labourers in a web of statutory and common law obligations which employers could enforce both civilly and criminally.[85] Although by the close of the twentieth century, the contract of service had been redesignated as 'the contract of employment', many vestiges of the old master–servant relation remained. And while understood as a generalized expression of the legal work relation, the contract of employment corresponded most closely with the working arrangements of full-time, long-term workers in a direct and stable relationship with a single employer. Thus, the legal form encouraged the regulatory normalization of working arrangements deaf to the practicalities of domesticity, consigning most women workers to the margins of paid employment to serve as a reserve of flexible labour upon whom employers could call as market demands dictated.

In the context of these wider developments, domestic service, which once occupied a prominent place in the legal classification of work relations, was steadily expunged from the regulatory context.[86] The

[83] W. Blackstone, *Commentaries of the Law of England*, 4 vols. (Oxford: Clarendon Press, 1765–1769), vol. 1, ch. XIV.

[84] With regard to slavery, Blackstone declares: '[it] does not, nay cannot, subsist in England . . . whereby an absolute and unlimited power is given to the master over the life and fortune of the slave. And indeed, it is repugnant to reason and the principles of natural law, that such a state should subsist anywhere'. Ibid., vol. 1, ch. XIV, Pt. I). In fact, at the time he was writing (1765), the Atlantic slave trade was thriving. It was not formally abolished in England until the Slave Trade Act 1807 and although Lord Mansfield in *Somersett's Case* (1772) 98 ER 49 refused to recognize the state of slavery 'on English soil', the practice continued throughout the British Empire until the Slavery Abolition Act 1833.

[85] S. Deakin and F. Wilkinson, *The Law of the Labour Market: Industrialization, Employment and Legal Evolution* (Oxford: Clarendon Press, 2005), 61–67.

[86] Albin, 'From Domestic Servant to Domestic Worker'.

incremental side-lining of domestic service as a form of employment coincided with the evolution of modern labour law and the entrenchment of master and servant law in firmly industrial terrain. The nineteenth-century mobilization of master and servant laws to discipline workers in manufacturing and related industries led to the enactment of successive Acts, instituting industrial order and effecting the transmigration of a set of service relations, forged under feudalism and refined in the early stages of capitalist development, to mass manufacturing.[87] As a growing site of labour conflict and political concern, factories assumed paradigmatic status as the space in which work relations were constituted and expressed, hastening the eclipse of domestic service from the developing field of labour regulation, notwithstanding that, for women in particular, domestic work continued to be an important source of paid employment well into the twentieth century.[88]

In 1875, the Employers and Workmen Act (which repealed the previous Master and Servants Acts) expressly excluded domestic servants from the evolving category of 'workman',[89] a conception which thenceforth underpinned much of the legislative engagement with work regulation, including the Workmen's Compensation Acts of the early twentieth century.[90] And while the legislative regime of employment protection introduced in the United Kingdom in the late twentieth century did, at least formally, encompass domestic workers, by this time domestic service had transformed from full-time, predominantly residential employment to part-time, casual work[91] – presenting new problems for domestic workers as many were unable to meet the criteria for access to the new employment rights.[92] Furthermore, limited formal exclusions peppered the regulatory

[87] Deakin and Wilkinson, *The Law of the Labour Market*, 67–71.

[88] According to Todd, one in three women in paid employment in Britain worked as servants in 1901, and one in four during the inter-war years. S. Todd, 'Domestic Service and Class Relations in Britain, 1900–1950' (2009) 203 *Past and Present* 181–204 at 183–184. Moreover, Albin cites figures from the 1911 census to show that domestic service was the occupation with the largest number of worker (1,302,438) in turn-of-the-twentieth-century Britain. Albin, 'From Domestic Servant to Domestic Worker', 233.

[89] Employers and Workmen Act 1875, s. 10 ('The expression "workman" does not include a domestic or menial servant').

[90] Albin, 'From Domestic Servant to Domestic Worker', . 237.

[91] 'The Second World War marked the end of residential domestic service as a major employer, but not the end of domestic work'. Todd, 'Domestic Service and Class Relations in Britain', 187.

[92] For further details, see Section 3.B.

framework.[93] Most significantly, because private households were regarded as an inappropriate space for public regulation, domestic servants were – and still are – largely excluded from health and safety laws.[94]

Thus, the regulatory regime which evolved around employment protection helped further to embed a normative ideal of full-time, long-term, care-unencumbered work expressed in modern labour law, developing a dichotomous framing of work relations around employment, on the one hand, and self-employment on the other. The contract of service/employment became the primary legal expression of the work relation, while the 'contract for services' (also known as the 'independent contractor' model) was used to designate a diverse range of work relations falling outside standard norms of employment, all of which were legally conceived as forms of self-employment. The employment/self-employment distinction was then incorporated into the legislative framework of employment protection and utilized to limit access to legal entitlements, including rights to redundancy pay, protection from dismissal, and even maternity rights.[95]

[93] See e.g. Employment Protection Act 1996, s. 61 limiting the right to redundancy pay where the domestic worker falls within a set of specified family relations with the employer.

[94] Health and Safety at Work Act 1974, s. 51 (exclusion of application to domestic employment).

[95] Adams argues that the concept of 'employee' adopted and embedded in the late-twentieth-century employment protection regime was intended to include casual work arrangements. Citing parliamentary debate around the enactment of the Contracts of Employment Act 1963 (which, inter alia, introduced a statutory right to notice of termination of employment), Adams maintains that 'employment' was posited as the default legal model for wage labour which employers could dispute only by presenting evidence that the working arrangement did not carry any mutual expectation of ongoing relations. Z. Adams, 'Labour Law and the Labour Market: Employment Status Reconsidered' (2019) 135 *Law Quarterly Review* 611–634.

Adams' characterization of employment protection as inclusive is consistent with Kahn-Freund's designation of such legislation as setting 'minimum standards' (O. Kahn-Freund, *Labour and the Law*, 2nd ed. (London: Steven & Sons, 1977), 26), constituting 'a floor on which all could stand' (ibid., 43). However, the nature of the restrictions which accompanied the emerging regulatory frame – the right to notice introduced by the 1963 Act, for example, did not cover employees working less than twenty-one hours a week – sits ill with a professed commitment to inclusivity. At the very least, it suggests that legislators and commentators alike underestimated the extent to which the employment norms being imported into the new regulatory framework reflected and reinforced deeply gendered patterns of employment. Indeed, a concern with the gendered consequences of the regulatory regime did not really emerge until the 1980s. See e.g. P. Kahn, 'Unequal Opportunities: Women, Employment and the Law', in S. Edwards (ed.), *Gender, Sex and Law* (Beckenham: Croom Helm, 1985), 79.

As Fredman and Fudge point out, this bifurcated model of work relations maps all too neatly onto gendered configurations of paid work, the contract of employment easily capturing the patterns of full-time, secure and often unionized employment traditionally typifying men's work but struggling to encompass the part-time, interrupted, casual and specifically sectoral features of women's paid employment.[96] The result, Fredman and Fudge contend, is a 'fundamental mismatch between the binary divide that is inscribed in law and many women's experiences'.[97] Few would deny the existence of an empirical correlation between the prevailing legal taxonomy of work relations and gendered patterns of work. The challenge is how to account for it. That markedly gendered patterns of precarious and/or exploitative work occasion neither great surprise nor real concern already attests to the simultaneous investment and invisibility of gender in working arrangements. The construction of social life around a series of binaries – work/family, public/private, state/market, individualism/altruism – supports a mapping of work as a terrain in which sex/gender differences manifest in social arrangements too materially embedded and culturally engrained to be called into serious question.

Understanding law as part of the process through which social practices develop, social relations form and social structures emerge and embed themselves in the fabric of social lives allows us to challenge any conception of patterns of inequality as exterior to legal regulatory frameworks. It is the political *and* legal inscription of a specific norm of employment, predicated on the male breadwinner/female caregiver family model, which has given rise to the problems confronted by those whose paid work patterns are shaped by a practical need to perform unpaid family-based labour. Until we confront the dependence of labour law, conceptually and normatively, formally and substantively, on a conception of work as a

[96] S. Fredman and J. Fudge, 'The Contract of Employment and Gendered Work', in M. Freedland, A. Bogg, D. Cabrelli, H. Collins, N. Kountouris, A. C. L Davies, S. Deakin and J. Prassl (eds.), *The Contract of Employment* (Oxford: Oxford University Press, 2016).

[97] Ibid., 240. In a recent comparative analysis of legal conceptualizations of employment, Davidov, Freedland and Kountouris conclude that 'the tests and indicia used to identify "employees" are quite similar around the world, and the trend appears to be towards greater convergence'. G. Davidov, M. Freedland and N. Kountouris, 'The Subjects of Labor Law: "Employees" and Other Workers', in M. Finkin and G. Mundlak (eds.), *Research Handbook on Comparative Labor Law* (Northampton, MA: Edward Elgar, 2015), 129. The gender exclusionary effects of labour law classifications are therefore likely to be cross-jurisdictional.

space into which the practical demands of family life do not normally or ideally intrude, legal solutions to gender inequality are unlikely to yield great results.

Anti-discrimination law has gone some way towards exposing and/or dislodging the gender-normative underpinning of working arrangements with the concept of indirect discrimination offering a legal means of challenging work-based policies and practices which, by virtue of their inattention to domestic and/or care responsibilities, impact differentially on men and women workers.[98] Moreover, the political and legal mainstreaming of 'family-friendly' policies, most notably in the introduction of a right for carers to request flexible work,[99] evidences belated state efforts to prompt the restructuring of working practices in ways that accommodate the continued rise in women's paid work participation.[100] At the same time, the political and legal conceptualization of the problem posed by women's employment in terms of a need to 'reconcile' work and family (as, for example, remains the dominant framing in an EU law and policy context) bolsters a perception that production and reproduction are separate spheres of activity and affect. Mediating work and family conflict becomes a subjective dimension of the identity and experience of most women workers, underpinned by the contours and content of a legal discursive frame which continues to naturalize women's unpaid caregiving and situates such work outside the scope of labour regulation.

It is this which enables us to understand labour law's continued reliance on the legal bifurcation of work relations even when it comes to family-friendly interventions. The statutory right to request flexible work, for

[98] E.g. in *Edwards* v. *London Underground (No. 2)* [1998] IRLR 364 (CA) a female London Underground train driver successfully established that a proposed shift system, with which she could not comply for reasons of childcare, constituted indirect sex discrimination.

[99] ERA 1996, s. 80F; Flexible Working Regulations 2014, SI 2014 No. 1398. The creation of a right to request flexible work (in 2003) represents a legal and policy effort to change the culture of work in relation to the accommodation of family responsibilities. For an assessment of these provisions in the context of the broader package of family-friendly measures operating in UK law, see G. James, 'Family-Friendly Employment Laws (Re) Assessed: The Potential of Care Ethics' (2016) 45 *Industrial Law Journal* 477–502.

[100] On the emergence of a family-friendly agenda in British law and politics, see N. Busby and G. James, *A History of Regulating Working Families: Strains, Stereotypes, Strategies and Solutions* (London: Hart Bloomsbury, 2020), 48–51. On the development EU law and policy, see E. Caracciolo di Torella and A. Masselot, *Reconciling Family Life in EU Law and Policy* (London: Palgrave MacMillan, 2010); Caracciolo di Torella, 'An Emerging Right to Care in the EU'.

example, is limited in UK law to those who work under a contract of employment. As a consequence, the impact of such initiatives has largely been confined to workers employed under standard working arrangements, further entrenching the divide between protected and precarious work. This is notwithstanding that, in recent years, as the continued demand for flexible labour reshapes working patterns and practices, the binary classification has struggled to capture the growing variety and complexity of working arrangements.[101] Since the late 1990s, and in part to counter the use by employers of non-standard employment to avoid legal protections, a new generation of laws encompassing, inter alia, working time and wage protection, has made use of the term 'worker',[102] a wider legal concept which attempts to straddle the traditional employee/independent contractor distinction by bringing into the scope of protection those who, while formally engaged as 'independent contractors' are, for all practical purposes, economically dependent upon those who contract their services.[103] These might include casual workers hired to meet the demands of seasonal or market fluctuations,[104] temporary workers covering short-term gaps, particularly those hired via an agency[105] and, increasingly, 'zero hours' workers and/or those who provide a service through a digital platform.[106]

The success of the worker category in breaking the grip of an increasingly unfit-for-purpose binary classification of work arrangements is open to debate. One of the difficulties is that the judicial approach to interpreting 'worker' – particularly the application of the 'limb b criterion'[107] – is

[101] Adams, 'Labour Law and the Labour Market'.

[102] 'Worker' is defined in the Employment Rights Act 1996, s. 230(3):

> In this Act 'worker' . . . means an individual who has entered into or works under (or, where the employment has ceased, worked under) –
>
> (a) a contract of employment, or
>
> (b) any other contract, whether express or implied and (if it is express) whether oral or in writing, whereby the individual undertakes to do or perform personally any work or services for another party to the contract whose status is not by virtue of the contract that of a client or customer of any profession or business undertaking carried on by the individual.

[103] The worker concept, albeit slightly differently defined, also underpinned the anti-discrimination framework introduced in the 1970s.

[104] See e.g. *O'Kelly* v. *Trusthouse Forte* [1984] QB 90 (CA) (hotel workers).

[105] *James* v. *Greenwich LBC* [2008] IRLR 302 (care worker).

[106] *Uber* v. *Aslam* [2021] UKSC 5 (Uber drivers).

[107] See n. 103.

still developing and hovers between merely adapting the traditional stance deployed to determine employee status, and crafting a distinct, purposive approach to worker status.[108] There is a real risk that the worker concept will echo rather than eclipse employment status, with the legal topography of work continuing, more or less, to stay within its well-established lines and contours.

The gendered impact of this marginal remapping thus appears limited. Although the worker category, and particularly by virtue of its inclusion in minimum wage legislation, has conferred some benefits on the lowest paid workers, a significant proportion of whom are women, it has barely scratched the surface of a gendered division of labour as an institutional feature of a working world, undergirded by a social and legal framework in which work and family continue to be posited in opposition. For this reason, the use of legal techniques to minimize employer obligations to workers engaged in reproductive labour, even on a paid basis, continues,[109] with the prevalence of casual and exploitative arrangements reflecting and reinforcing the devaluation and low status of traditional women's work. Moreover, the resonance between formal legal categories and gendered working norms limits the capacity of law to tackle these problems.

5. Conclusion: Whose Law, Whose Subjects? Reconstituting the Subjects of Labour Law

One of the consequences of the Covid-19 pandemic has been to expose the annexing of policy initiatives, introduced to support workers in the context of unanticipated economic disruption, to legal norms and schemas in which gendered patterns of paid work are already deeply embedded.

[108] A. Bogg, 'Employment Status in the Social Democratic Constitution: Law and Politics', in A. Bogg, J. Rowbottom and A. Young (eds.), *The Constitution of Social Democracy: Essays in Honour of Keith Ewing* (London: Bloomsbury, 2020). In *Uber* v. *Aslam*, L. Leggatt (paras. 71–89) affirms that a purposive approach should be taken to the construction and interpretation of 'worker' for purposes of ERA 1996, s. 230(3).

[109] *Nowak* v. *Chandler Bar Group Ltd* UKET 3200538/2019, in which a dancer in a strip club successfully established worker status, serves as a rare example of the extension of worker status to a new, hitherto legally unrecognized, form of reproductive labour. See K. Cruz, 'Dancers Are Workers: Nowak v Chandler Bars Group Ltd and the History of Dancer Organising in London', 30 April 2020, uklabourlawblog.com.

An overwhelming volume of data confirms a correlation between gender, race and class inequalities and the distribution of risks and impacts resulting from Covid-19.[110] Such impacts are particularly stark in the United Kingdom, but the gender-regressive effects of Covid-19 are increasingly being recognized at a global level.[111] Other inequality indicators such as age and disability also feature in the distribution of job losses, as well as in differential capacities to engage in homeworking or to access statutory schemes supplementing income losses.[112] Indeed, what the Covid-19 crisis has revealed, all too visibly and viscerally, is how deeply and widely multiple, intersecting inequalities are rooted in the contemporary world of work.

In Britain, after a decade of austerity and several generations of neoliberal government operating on the premise that distributional matters are best resolved through market operations, the widening inequality gap is a reality to which, as a society, we have become reluctantly accustomed. However, this once again begs a question that frequently preoccupies labour lawyers – namely, what, and more importantly *who*, is labour law for? What responsibility does labour law bear for the persistence and pervasiveness of gender and other patterned inequalities at work? Within a discursive frame traditionally grounded in a singular notion of work and worker, it has been difficult to see, let alone articulate in terms which are legally intelligible, the systematicity of worker disparities as they manifest in apparently spontaneous market operations. Less visible still is the precise set of historical circumstances which precipitated the development of labour law as a field of regulation and scholarship, fashioning labour law's key norms and concepts around certain unchallenged premises about the social organization of work and the autonomous nature of market transactions. The legal concept of the contract of employment is particularly complicit here, representing structured social relations mediated by inequalities of power and resources in individuated, juridified form.

Reflecting on the idea of labour law in 2010, Harry Arthurs observes: 'Whatever its substantive content, we can be sure that labour law is about

[110] Institute of Fiscal Studies, 'Sector Shutdowns during the Coronavirus'.

[111] McKinsey Global Institute, 'Covid-19 and Gender Equality: Countering the Regressive Effects', 22 September 2020.

[112] A. Adams-Prassl, T. Boneva, M. Golin and C. Rauh, 'Inequality in the Impact of the Coronavirus Shock: Evidence from Real Time Surveys' (2020) 189 *Journal of Public Economics Article* 104245.

"labour", that it operates in the context of "employment", that it is designed to protect "workers".'[113] The present analysis simultaneously affirms and challenges Arthurs' characterization of labour law's fundamentals. It does so by further unpacking the socially and historically contingent character of the concepts Arthurs foregrounds – the concepts of labour, employment and workers. It has been argued that the content of each of these key terms, as they are mobilized in labour law discourse, derives from a gendered work imaginary that is legally instituted in the categories, doctrines and schematic conventions that constitute the field. Labour law has been crafted around a very particular manifestation of the gendered division of labour which emerged with industrialization and, as a consequence, labour law excludes, marginalizes and devalues much of the kind of work women perform while adversely affecting the conditions in which they perform it. The 'fundamental mismatch' that Fredman and Fudge highlight is not just an empirical accident – it is a structured, engineered, legally determined outcome.[114]

In a recent, highly original study of the operation of labour regulation in the social care sector, Lydia Hayes explores the interaction of law with the lives and experiences of homecare workers.[115] Deploying an ethnographical approach, Hayes discloses how legal norms help to produce distinct subjectivities derived from experiences of exploitation, abjection, precarity and human connection. Hayes' analysis enables us to view the operation and effects of law from the standpoint of women who carry out work of high social value for low economic reward, presenting a series of 'experiential truths'[116] which cast critical light on working life in a largely unprotected sector of the workforce. Hayes' analysis starkly highlights the visceral realities of law's failure to protect the most vulnerable workers, exposing law's collusion in the denigration of socially reproductive work and workers.[117] 'Law at work', Hayes claims, 'marginalises homecare workers' economic interests, facilitates stereotyping and upholds a social hierarchy in which their silencing in social policy debates appears justified.'[118]

[113] Arthurs, 'Labour Law after Labour', 18.
[114] Fredman and Fudge, 'The Contract of Employment and Gendered Work'.
[115] L. Hayes, *Stories of Care: A Labour of Law* (London: Palgrave, 2017).
[116] Ibid., 24.
[117] Hayes coined the term 'institutionalised humiliation' to capture the process of abjectification to which law contributes. Ibid., 4–5.
[118] Ibid., 27.

Hayes' notion of law in *Stories of Care* extends beyond the bald rules and principles which make up the corpus of labour law as a set of norms to encompass manifestations of law in concrete material settings and from the experience and viewpoints of living, breathing human beings. This wider conceptualization helps to show how the denial of legal protection, and the reliance of law and policy on normative structures which are imbued with gender and class, express and endorse a stance on homecare work as of little value in the overall scheme of work as a mode of being. Within the conceptual, normative and distributive spaces law helps to fashion and maintain, distinct subjectivities are forged, ways of being and knowing which are lived and experienced by ordinary people – fleshy, material, agentic. Hayes brings these subjects to life in her analysis while simultaneously grounding them in the matrix of norms, processes and relations which engender their being as working subjects.

Hayes' analysis shows that legal categories have ontological/epistemological as well as regulatory and distributive effects. Her approach resonates with the concern of this chapter, which has been to examine work as a key site of processes of gendered subjectification, processes in which law is deeply implicated. Law participates directly in the processes through which social relations are formed and social practices instituted, producing structured configurations of power and privilege which take root in everyday lives and experiences. Because we are trained to view law as a bounded space, an autonomous realm of self-governance which gives, at best, limited quarter to 'non-legal' considerations of a social, moral or political nature, we struggle to readjust our lens to a more expansive idea of law, an idea of 'law unlimited',[119] as Davies puts it, law as mobile, multi-sited, material, plural and relational.

The starting point, then, to addressing the role of labour law in the production and perpetuation of work-based inequalities is to embrace a conception of law which extends beyond formal norms and principles and relocates the legal firmly within the frame of social forms and operations. In this broader context, social reproduction – the activities, practices, relations, institutions and processes which go into the reproduction of social life – serves as a vital critical lens through which to view and expose not only the myopic vision of current labour law but the direction of travel

[119] M. Davies, *Law Unlimited* (London: Routledge, 2018), 1.

that a re-envisaged labour law might take. A key virtue of social reproduction as an organizing frame is that it places at its core a broad and inclusive conception of work and plots out a terrain which rides roughshod over the fences and boundaries within which the discipline of labour law has historically been confined. An additional virtue is that social reproduction helps to cast valuable light not only on gender inequality but on inequalities much more broadly, history all too plainly revealing how the forms of social cooperation which develop to sustain human life draw upon a variety of social divisions, harnessing notions of race, class and colonization as well as gender to the organization of labouring practices. In fact, it might plausibly be argued that the primary challenge facing many Western societies currently is a crisis of social reproduction, a breaking down of the arrangements supporting the reproduction of social life. There are many reasons for this breakdown – Covid-19, austerity, public sector shrinkage, poverty growth, to name but a few. However, the problem of social reproduction is made visible only when a gender lens is applied to work, and to the role and significance of gendered working subjects in the context of broader economic and political trends.

6 The Reproductive Subject

The Reproductive Subject and the Embodied State of International Human Rights Law

Joanna N. Erdman

This chapter engages the reproductive subject of international human rights law, a subject who conceives, gestates and births, or seeks to avoid them. Reproduction is a fascinating site for the critical study of gender and law because it necessitates grappling with bodies.[1]

The fascination stems from a seeming impasse. Gender theory has abandoned bodies, while reproductive rights refuse to give them up. In human rights law, reproduction is generally conceptualized as a series of events in female sexed bodies, and so embodied, women are essentialized as its reproductive subject. Gender does not disturb this convention but protects women from any social disadvantage or inequality in reproduction. For example, the *Convention on Elimination of All Forms of Discrimination Against Women* (CEDAW), declares that 'the role of women in procreation should not be a basis for discrimination'.[2] In reproductive rights, the sex binary stands while the gender hierarchy falls, keeping sex and gender distinct, and so, too, biological and social reproduction. Gender theory, on the other hand, challenges the idea of sex and reproduction outside the social world, and thus any inherent difference between men and women or 'women' itself as a category.[3] For some, gender therefore challenges the reproductive rights of women. For when sex is collapsed into gender, the biological into the social, women are without their bodies

[1] E. Annandale and J. Clark, 'What Is Gender? Feminist Theory and the Sociology of Human Reproduction' (1996) 18 *Sociology of Health & Illness* 17–44.

[2] Convention on the Elimination of All Forms of Discrimination against Women (CEDAW), preamble.

[3] L. Birke, *Feminism and the Biological Body* (Edinburgh: Edinburgh University Press, 1999); D. Riley, *'Am I That Name?' Feminism and the Category of 'Women' in History* (Minneapolis: University of Minnesota Press, 1989).

and the special protection of the law. The reproductive subject becomes no body at all.[4]

Yet there are real human bodies in human rights law, bodies in which sperm travel, eggs fertilize, embryos implant, foetuses are grown and eventually birthed. People do things with their bodies. People act and are acted upon through their bodies. There must therefore be some way out of the bind between the bio-reductionism of sex and the social construction of gender. Somewhere in the middle must lie the body.[5]

In answer to the challenge, this chapter uses body theory to explore how gender and law construct the reproductive subject of the nation-state in international human rights law in ways that break with its conventions, specifically the sexed category of 'women' as the reproductive subject of law, and the subject–state relation of gender as hierarchy that it sustains. The chapter first introduces these conventions by describing the historical relationship of sex and gender in reproductive rights, and specifically how human rights law calls for the gender hierarchy of reproduction to be dismantled, but not the sex binary which reflects an embodied and thus inherent state. This refusal to relinquish the sexed body of reproduction is impossible and imprudent for the law to maintain. The sex binary is no less a social construction than any gender hierarchy premised upon it. Moreover, the construct of gender as hierarchy that the sex binary maintains entrenches a subject–state relation in human rights law of victim-protector that obscures more complex expressions of gender and reproduction in nation-building and state formation. These breaks of convention are the focus of the chapter's three case studies on human rights in abortion, childbirth and assisted reproduction. These studies explore the ways in which gender and law are creating anew the reproductive body as a site of diverse subjectivity; that is, as a site of expression and experience, social resistance and relations, and ideological inscription.

1. Gender and Reproductive Rights in International Law

Gender arrived late to international human rights law, and long after women to whom UN treaties assigned reproduction when they mentioned

[4] S. Bordo, 'Postmodern Bodies', in *Unbearable Weight: Feminism, Western Culture, and the Body* (Berkeley: University of California Press, 1993).

[5] P. Rothfield, 'Subjectivity and the Language of the Body' (1986) 75 *Arena* 157–165 at 165.

the subject at all. In these treaties, reproductive rights are textually tied to the bodies of women, bodies that gestate, birth and lactate. Under the International Covenant on Economic, Social and Cultural Rights, for example, the right to family life accords 'special protection ... to mothers during a reasonable period before and after childbirth'.[6] Under CEDAW, women's right to be free from discrimination in the field of health care includes a specific provision on 'appropriate services in connection with pregnancy, confinement and the post-natal period'.[7] These provisions are artefacts of early feminist activism to recognize women as subjects of law, entitled to maternity protection in their own right rather than as the dependants of men.[8] Through their bodies, women acquired rights in reproduction as a measure of equality with men, and in this way, women became the reproductive subject of international human rights law.[9]

In the 1990s, when the term 'gender' was introduced into international human rights law, it was often read as a synonym for 'women', specifically in their socially constructed differences from men.[10] International law thus accommodated gender theory by separating sex from gender, reflecting an already existing practice in the law to separate biological from social reproduction, and maternity from motherhood. Gender posed little challenge to the sex of reproduction. Rather '[g]ender is simply ... bodily sex ... in the mirror of representation – no questions asked, none needed'.[11]

6 International Covenant on Social, Economic and Cultural Rights (CESCR), Art. 10.

7 CEDAW, Art. 12(2).

8 See D. Otto, 'International Human Rights Law: Towards Rethinking Sex/Gender Dualism and Asymmetry', in M. Davies and V. Munro (eds.), *Ashgate Research Companion to Feminist Legal Theory* (London: Routledge, 2013); D. Otto, 'Lost in Translation: Re-scripting the Sexed Subjects of International Human Rights Law', in A. Orford (ed.), *International Law and Its Others* (Cambridge: Cambridge University Press, 2006).

9 CESCR, General Comment No. 22 (E/C.12/GC/22) (2016), para. 25.

10 A. Miller, 'Fighting over the Figure of Gender' (2011) 31 *Pace Law Review* 837–872. See e.g. CEDAW, General Recommendation No. 28 (CEDAW/C/GC/28) (2010), para. 5: 'The term "sex" refers to biological differences between men and women, while "gender" refers to socially constructed identities, attributes and roles for women and men and society's social and cultural meaning for these biological differences resulting in hierarchical relationships between women and men and in the distribution of power and rights favouring men and disadvantaging women.' CEDAW distinguishes between biological and socio-economic factors that differ for women in comparison with men. CEDAW, General Recommendation No. 24 (A/54/38/Rev. 1) (1999), para. 12.

11 S. Stryker, '(De)subjugated Knowledges: An Introduction to Transgender Studies', in S. Stryker and S. Whittle (eds.), *The Transgender Studies Reader* (New York: Routledge, 2006). See also J. Repo, *The Biopolitics of Gender* (Oxford: Oxford University Press, 2015).

With sex as the real thing and gender its social reflection, international human rights law came to assume that only gender can dominate and oppress, but biological sex cannot.[12] Gender turns sexed bodies – specifically a reproductive body, a woman's body – into a subordinated state, and as such, any social disadvantage that women suffer in their sexed bodies needs no further explanation as gender inequality.[13] The gender hierarchy in reproduction was to be dismantled, but not the sex binary – an embodied state.[14]

Reproductive rights in international law thus begin with the sexed body, a woman's body, and have refused to relinquish this body to gender theory. Yet it is a convention that is impossible, and imprudent for the law to maintain.

It is impossible because gender theory in international law continues to push on the sex binary and the category of 'women' as reproductive subject. With sexual dimorphism having been debated since antiquity, the sex of reproduction proves no less a social construction than any gender hierarchy premised upon it.[15] Reproductive anatomical difference emerged only in the seventeenth century when ovaries, uterus and fallopian tubes were first represented as independent organs with specific functions.[16] Prior to the eighteenth century, there was no term equivalent to 'reproduction' in which insemination, conception, pregnancy and birth

[12] See CEDAW, Art. 5: 'States Parties shall take all appropriate measures: (a) To modify the social and cultural patterns of conduct of men and women, with a view to achieving the elimination of prejudices and customary and all other practices which are based on the idea of the inferiority or the superiority of either of the sexes or on stereotyped roles for men and women.'

[13] CESCR, General Comment No. 20 (E/C.12/GC/20) (2009), para. 20: 'Since the adoption of the Covenant, the notion of the prohibited ground "sex" has evolved considerably to cover not only physiological characteristics but also the social construction of gender stereotypes, prejudices and expected roles.'

[14] See T. Loenen, 'Rethinking Sex Equality as a Human Right' (1994) 12 *Netherlands Quarterly of Human Rights* 253–270; D. Rosenblum, 'Unsex CEDAW, or What's Wrong with Women's Rights' (2011) 20 *Columbia Journal of Gender and Law* 98–194; B. E. Hernandez-Truyol, 'Unsex CEDAW? No! Super-Sex It!' (2011) 20 *Columbia Journal of Gender and Law* 195–223.

[15] T. Laquer, *Making Sex: Body and Gender from the Greeks to Freud* (Cambridge, MA: Harvard University Press, 1990); G. Herdt (ed.), *Third Sex, Third Gender: Beyond Sexual Dimorphism in Culture and History* (New York: Zone Books, 1993).

[16] E. V. Spelman, 'Women as Body: Ancient and Contemporary Views' (1982) 8 *Feminist Studies* 109–131.

were all subsumed.[17] In the latter twentieth century, the study of hormones, genes and cellular reproduction provoked a further epistemic shift by revealing sex as indefinitely complex.[18]

Sex is an amalgam of genitals, organs, chromosomes, gonads, hormones and secondary characteristics within bodies, with no absolute distinction among them but variations along a continuum more densely populated at its outer edges.[19] The sexual labelling of bodies is thus a social act.[20] Moreover, that men, intersex and gender-diverse people become pregnant and give birth further defy the reproductive body as women's alone, even if this presumption cruelly denies their existence.[21] Many women too live in the shadow of this essential womanhood, with bodies that do not reproduce by reason of birth or age, or by acts of violent suppression.[22] Yet the sex binary of reproductive rights disappears them all. Their bodies unimaginable within it.[23] Gender diversity, however, has arrived in international human rights law. Adopted in 2007, the Yogyakarta Principles acknowledged gender identity and expression outside a binary,[24] and with the fundamental violence of this construct now acknowledged, human rights law today speaks of 'all genders', and of gender itself as diverse

[17] A. Muri, 'Imagining Reproduction: The Politics of Reproduction, Technology and the Woman Machine' (2009) 31 *Journal of Medical Humanities* 53–67.

[18] V. Rosario, 'Quantum Sex: Intersex and the Molecular Deconstruction of Sex' (2009) 12 *GLQ: A Journal of Lesbian and Gay Studies* 267–284.

[19] J. Epstein, 'Either/Or – Neither/Both: Sexual Ambiguity and the Ideology of Gender' (1990) 7 *Genders* 99–142.

[20] A. Fausto-Sterling, *Sexing the Body: Gender Politics and the Construction of Sexuality* (New York: Basic Books, 2000).

[21] L. Karaian, 'Pregnant Men: Repronormativity, Critical Trans Theory and the Re(conceive)ing of Sex and Pregnancy in Law' (2013) 22 *Social and Legal Studies* 211–230; C. Strangio, 'Can Reproductive Trans Bodies Exist?' (2016) 19 *CUNY Law Review* 223–245; M. Toze, 'The Risky Womb and the Unthinkability of the Pregnant Man: Addressing Trans Masculine Hysterectomy' (2018) 28 *Feminism & Psychology* 194–211.

[22] S. Colen, '"Like a Mother to Them": Stratified Reproduction and West Indian Childcare Workers and Employers in New York', in F. Ginsburg and R. Rapp (eds.), *Conceiving the New World Order: The Global Politics of Reproduction* (Berkeley: University of California Press, 1995).

[23] W. O'Brien, 'Can International Human Rights Law Accommodate Bodily Diversity?' (2015) 15 *Human Rights Law Review* 1–20; S. Duffy, 'Contested Subjects of Human Rights: Trans and Gender-Variant Subjects of International Human Rights Law' (2021) 84 *Modern Law Review* 1041–1065.

[24] Yogyakarta Principles on the Application of International Human Rights Law in Relation to Sexual Orientation and Gender Identity (2007). See D. Otto, 'Queering Gender [Identity] in International Law' (2015) 33 *Nordic Journal of Human Rights* 299–318.

and fluid, unmoored from sexed bodies.[25] Gender diversity has made it impossible to keep the reproductive body as women's alone, or reproductive subjectivity itself as gender-stable.

In the end, it also imprudent for human rights law to ground reproductive subjectivity in a lynchpin of historical oppression: the sex binary and the fixed categories of men and women that follow. This convention leaves intact a bodily artefact to rebuild gender hierarchies because many hetero-patriarchal orders also rest on the truth of the sex binary.[26] The very gender hierarchies that the law seeks to dismantle, in other words, survive by the sex binary, which keeps real the categories of women and men and, more so, makes comparison between them the only measure of gender equality. All facts in every context are read through this singular and Western notion of gender as hierarchy, where one class, men, dominates another class, women.[27] Yet this universal abstraction of gender obscures more complex expressions of gender in daily life and across social context, and in the structures and relations of power within economic and political systems.[28]

Moreover, the reduction of gender to a class-based hierarchy between women and men entrenches a particular and concerning form of state power.[29] Specifically women's bodily vulnerability in reproduction

[25] Report of the Independent Expert on protection against violence and discrimination based on sexual orientation and gender identity (A/HRC/47/27) (2021), para. 3. Committee on the Rights of Persons with Disabilities, General Comment No. 5 (CRPD/C/GC/5) (2017), para. 23.

[26] Report of the UN Working Group on Discrimination against Women and Girls (A/HRC/38/46) (2018). D. E. Buss, 'Robes, Relics and Rights: The Vatican and the Beijing Conference on Women' (1998) 7 *Social and Legal Studies* 339–363; M. A. Case, 'Trans Formations in the Vatican's War on "Gender Ideology"' (2019) 44 *Signs* 639–664.

[27] CEDAW, General Recommendation No. 25 (CEDAW/C/GC/25) (2004), n. 2: 'Despite variations across cultures and over time, gender relations throughout the world entail asymmetry of power between men and women as a pervasive trait ... the unequal structure of power that underlies the relationship between the sexes.' C. Mudgway, 'Can International Human Rights Law Smash the Patriarchy? A Review of "Patriarchy" According to United Nations Treaty Bodies and Special Procedures' (2021) 29 *Feminist Legal Studies* 67–105. See also S. Walby, 'Theorising Patriarchy' (1989) 23 *Sociology* 213–234.

[28] O. Oyewumi, *The Invention of Women: Making an African Sense of Western Gender Discourses* (Minneapolis: University of Minnesota Press, 1997); M. Lugones, 'Heterosexualism and the Colonial/Modern Gender System' (2007) 22 *Hypatia* 186–209; M. Lugones, 'Toward a Decolonial Feminism' (2010) 25 *Hypatia* 742–759; R. Connell, *Gender: In World Perspective*, 4th ed. (Cambridge: Polity Press, 2020).

[29] D. L. Rhode, 'Feminism and the State' (1994) 107 *Harvard Law Review* 1181–1208.

justifies measures of state action and protection.[30] In other words, human rights law calls on state power to 'alleviate, the inherent disadvantage that women experience [in reproduction]'.[31] Reproductive rights empower the nation-state as a neutral but purposeful actor to dismantle the gender hierarchy.[32] Yet nationalism and state formation themselves depend on powerful constructions of gender.[33] From the eighteenth century, the modern state has used women's reproductive labour – biological, cultural and symbolic – for its own reproduction: women as 'mothers of the nation'.[34] Reproductive subjectivity has thus long been a part of ideologies of national (re)birth and central to state-formation, which have differently encouraged, discouraged and forced women, often based on race and ethnicity, to procreate.[35] Human rights law, however, tends to read reproductive rights in individualist terms, and its convention to invite rather than interrogate state power obscures these biopolitics of gender and reproduction in nation-making and state-formation, and thus the reproductive subject as a political subject.

How can reproductive rights in international law engage these multiple levels of gender analysis from the microbiological to the macropolitical?[36]

[30] See critique of construct in the jurisprudence on violence against women. A. M. Miller, 'Sexuality, Violence against Women, and Human Rights: Women Make Demands and Ladies Get Protection' (2004) 7 *Health and Human Rights* 16–47.

[31] CESCR, General Comment No. 22 (E/C.12/GC/22) (2016), para. 27.

[32] CEDAW, General Recommendation No. 28 (CEDAW/C/GC/28) (2010), para. 9: 'The obligation to protect requires that States parties protect women from discrimination by private actors and take steps directly aimed at eliminating . . . all other practices that prejudice and perpetuate the notion of inferiority or superiority of either of the sexes, and of stereotyped roles for men and women . . . The obligation to fulfil requires that States parties take a wide variety of steps to ensure that women and men enjoy equal rights . . . That fulfil the specific needs of women . . . [towards] quality with men.' See H. J. Kim-Puri, 'Conceptualizing Gender–Sexuality–State–Nation: An Introduction' (2005) 19 *Gender and Society* 137–159.

[33] N. Yuval-Davis and F. Anthias (eds.), *Woman–Nation–State* (London: Palgrave Macmillan, 1989); V. S. Peterson, 'Sexing Political Identities/Nationalism as Heterosexism' (1999) 11 *International Feminist Journal of Politics* 34–65; S. Walby, 'Gender, Nations and States in a Global Era' (2000) 6 *Nations and Nationalism* 523–540.

[34] N. Yuval-Davis, 'Women and the Biological Reproduction of "the Nation"' (1996) 19 *Women's Studies* 17–24.

[35] A. M. Alonso, 'The Politics of Space, Time and Substance: State Formation, Nationalism, and Ethnicity' (1994) 23 *Annual Review of Anthropology* 379–405; S. Lettow, 'Population, Race and Gender: On the Genealogy of the Modern Politics of Reproduction' (2015) 16 *Distinktion: Journal of Social Theory* 267–282.

[36] F. Ginsburg and R. Rapp, 'The Politics of Reproduction' (1991) 20 *Annual Review of Anthropology* 311–343; R. Almeling, 'Reproduction' (2015) 41 *Annual Review of Sociology* 423–442.

At present, the reproductive subject of human rights law does little more than hold space for women in a sexed body. Yet turning this body into mere social discourse for gender theory denies that reproduction has not shed its human form and human rights law is unlikely to lose its subjects either.[37] Bodies matter deeply to reproductive rights, and thus this chapter seeks to engage deeply with them.

Through a diversity of body theory, the chapter explores different constructions of the reproductive subject in international human rights law that avoid the impasse between sex essentialism and gender construction, and, indeed, binaries altogether. By allowing for an analysis at once individual and social, material and abstract, gender and law construct the body as a site of diverse subjectivity.[38] From a phenomenological view, the body is analysed as lived by the subject. From a performative view, the body is analysed as identity and expression. From a postmodern view, the body is analysed as a cultural script or discursive object. Body theory, in other words, trades the impossible and imprudent 'woman's body' of human rights law for 'specific bodies that by their physical reality hold space as sites of expression and experience, and as sites of inscription and intervention'.[39] Body theory thus reveals breaks in the conventions of human rights law; that is, the sexed category of 'women' as the reproductive subject of law, and the subject–state relation of gender as hierarchy that it sustains.

These breaks of convention are the focus of this chapter as studied through select human rights communications on abortion, childbirth and assisted reproduction. Communications are human rights claims brought by individuals against states parties before UN bodies, which then issue views on the merits of the claims with remedy. Communications thus represent a kind of jurisprudence in international human rights law.[40]

[37] N. Snaza, 'Biopolitics without Bodies: Feminism and the Feeling of Life' (2020) 46 *Feminist Studies* 178–203.

[38] E. Grosz, 'Notes towards a Corporeal Feminism' (1987) 5 *Australian Feminist Studies* 1–16; M. Gatens, *Imaginary Bodies: Ethics, Power and Corporeality* (New York: Routledge, 1996).

[39] K. Canning, 'The Body as Method? Reflections on the Place of the Body in Gender History' (1999) 11 *Gender & History* 499–513.

[40] Human Rights Committee, General Comment No. 33 (CCPR/C/GC/33) (2009), para. 11: 'While the function of the Human Rights Committee in considering individual communications is not, as such, that of a judicial body, the views issued . . . exhibit some important characteristics of a judicial decision. They are arrived at in a judicial spirit, including the impartiality and independence of Committee members, the considered interpretation of the language of the Covenant, and the determinative character of the decisions.'

By convention their reasoning is short, but rather than any deficiency, this feature invites an analysis of the entirety of the communication: controversies of reason, but also noted facts and unwritten contexts. The chapter also focuses on communications because by form, an individual claiming against a state, they manifest the idea of bodies before and under law, a jurisprudence of reproductive subjectivity. The chapter thus analyses the communications less for what they say about an issue (abortion, childbirth, sterilization or assisted reproduction) than for what they say about how gender and law make meaning of the bodily work of reproduction.

2. Subjects of Law: Abortion and the Sex Binary

The reproductive subjects of human rights law are embodied, but in an essentialist way – that is, of the female sex and thus of women alone. This convention need not hold. Bodies – and the bodies of women – would still matter in law, even if freed from the sex binary and made biosocial. In other words, gender need not threaten the reproductive rights of women. This is the controversial idea in *Mellet* v. *Ireland* and *Whelan* v. *Ireland*, communications on abortion rights, the quintessential body rights of human rights law.[41]

Amanda Jane Mellet and Siobhán Whelan, both women, received fatal foetal diagnoses during their pregnancies, but were compelled by threat of the criminal law then in effect in the Republic of Ireland to continue their pregnancies or to seek abortions abroad. Both travelled to the United Kingdom for an abortion. Mellet and Whelan claimed that in criminalizing the termination of a non-viable pregnancy, the Irish state had violated their rights to be free from cruel, inhuman or degrading treatment, and to privacy under the International Covenant on Civil and Political Rights. Human rights law has traditionally addressed abortion under the rights to life and health in the protection from unsafe abortion, and under various rights respecting bodily integrity.[42] In these claims, therefore, the

[41] HRC, *Mellet* v. *Ireland*, Communication No. 2324/2013 (2016); HRC, *Whelan* v. *Ireland*, Communication No. 2425/2014 (2017). See commentary by J. N. Erdman, 'The Gender Injustice of Abortion Laws' (2019) 27 *Sexual and Reproductive Health Matters* 4-8.

[42] J. N. Erdman, 'Abortion in International Human Rights Law', in S. Rowlands (ed.), *Abortion Care* (Cambridge: Cambridge University Press, 2014). See HRC, *K. L.* v. *Peru*, Communication No. 1153/2003 (2005); CEDAW, *L. C.* v. *Peru*, Communication No. 22/2009 (2011); HRC, *L. M. R.* v. *Argentina*, Communication No. 1608/2007 (2011).

communications followed convention, and the committee easily viewed the state in violation of these rights.

Yet there was more. The committee also declared that the state had discriminated on the basis of sex.[43] This was ground-breaking. Human rights law has long been reluctant to analyse abortion laws as sex discrimination, or to raise any question of gender equality. Indeed, the committee ran its analysis of the rights to freedom from ill-treatment and privacy without engaging the sex equality guarantee of the covenant, reasoning that nothing further would be added to the analysis.[44] This general reluctance stems partly from the presumed sex-specificity of abortion. Where only women can become pregnant and men do not, there is only a biological difference between them, and no gender inequality. The Irish state defended its law on this argument with the support of dissenting committee members.[45] Other committee members refuted the claim on a well-rehearsed argument of substantive equality.[46] By denying access to 'reproductive medical services that only women need' with 'no equivalent burden on men's access to reproductive health care', criminal abortion laws treat women and men differently, and thus discriminate on the basis of sex.[47] Although these minority committee views arrived at different conclusions, they both hold onto the sex-specificity of abortion, and both root that specificity in biological differences between women and men. These views thus show how the sex binary of reproductive rights keeps real the categories of women and men as a basis to continually rebuild and tear down gender hierarchies.

In its main reasoning, however, the committee broke with this convention and avoided the sex binary. Rather than compare women to men, the committee compared the treatment of Mellet and Whelan under the law to

[43] International Covenant on Civil and Political Rights, Art. 26; HRC, General Comment No. 18 (CCPR/C/21/Rev.1/Add.1) (1989), para. 12.

[44] *Mellet*, para. 7.12; *Whelan*, para. 7.13. See e.g. HRC, General Comment No. 28 (CCPR/C/21/Rev.1/Add.10) (2000), para. 20, applying the right to privacy to women's reproductive functions.

[45] *Mellet*, para. 4.13 and Annex V; *Whelan*, para. 4.13 and Annex V.

[46] *Mellet*, Annex II; *Whelan*, Annex II.

[47] *Mellet*, Annex II, para. 13; *Whelan*, Annex II, para. 13. See CEDAW, General Recommendation No. 24 (A/54/38/Rev.1) (1999); para. 11: 'Measures to eliminate discrimination against women are considered to be inappropriate if a health-care system lacks services to prevent, detect and treat illnesses specific to women'; CEDAW, General Recommendation No. 28 (CEDAW/C/GC/28) (2010), para. 16.

that of women who continued their non-viable pregnancies and declared this inequality of treatment sex-discriminatory.[48] In its analysis, the committee asked: Why is a woman who continues her non-viable pregnancy entitled to receive the full protection of the law, and to care and compassion in the public health care system? Why is a woman who terminates a non-viable pregnancy denied this care, forced outside the system, required to travel abroad, and left with all the social and economic hardships of her effort?

Everyone in the analysis was a woman, and thus pregnancy as a unique sex characteristic of women as compared to men was immaterial to the analysis. Nor did it matter to the analysis that men also become pregnant and that people who are not women have abortions. Rather, the committee focused on the Irish criminal law and how it structured these women's experience of a non-viable pregnancy. Under the law, being pregnant mattered, but what mattered more was how a woman acted towards her pregnancy, her expectations for and what she did with her body. In this respect, the committee characterized the crime of abortion as a gendered crime, embedded with 'a gender-based stereotype according to which the primary role of women is reproductive and maternal'.[49] When faced with a non-viable pregnancy, a woman is expected to let nature run its course, and to give birth and care for the child born. She is expected to be maternal.

In this analysis, gender is something that someone *does*, rather than something someone *is* or something someone *has*.[50] Gender is a set of social norms that shape human experience, including a person's bodily experience of pregnancy.[51] On this theory of gender as performance, the

[48] HRC, General Comment No. 18 (CCPR/C/21/Rev.1/Add.1) (1989), paras. 6–7: 'The Covenant does not define "discrimination" nor indicates what constitutes discrimination, except any "distinction" or "preference" based on ... [sex] ... and which has the purpose or effect of impairing enjoyment of rights/freedoms on an equal footing'.

[49] *Mellet*, para. 7.11; *Whelan*, para. 7.12. See also CEDAW, General Recommendation No. 28 (CEDAW/C/GC/28) (2010), para. 12, defining gender equality as 'the concept that all human beings, regardless of sex, are free to ... make choices without the limitations set by stereotypes, rigid gender roles and prejudices', including those enacted via 'law, and legal and societal structures and institutions'.

[50] J. Butler, *Gender Trouble: Feminism and the Subversion of Identity* (New York: Routledge, 1990).

[51] CESCR, General Comment No. 22 (E/C.12/GC/22) (2016), para. 25: 'Gender-based stereotypes, assumptions and expectations related to ... their [women's] role being solely as

Irish law constructed the female pregnant body into a maternal body and conscripted women into a maternal role by the rewarding or withholding of public care and compassion. In the committee's view, the abortion law discriminated against women not because it socially burdened a uniquely female body, but because it limited bodily identity and expression. By affirming that Mellet and Whelan were free to reject the maternal role of the abortion law, the committee reconstructed reproductive subjectivity into a gender-diverse sexed embodiment.

This articulation of abortion rights as gender diversity is an important advancement in international law, but the committee's views still show a lingering binary in the diversity only to accept or reject the maternal role. On the facts of the communications, however, it is not clear that the authors did reject a maternal role.[52] While abortion is often divorced from motherhood, the separation is not as stark in the lives of people.[53] Mellet sought an abortion to spare her child suffering, and Whelan too felt that she could not continue the pregnancy only to see her baby suffer and die.[54] Mellet and Whelan did not reject a maternal role, but mothered differently by ending their pregnancies rather than by giving birth.[55] The abortion law thus ascribed motherhood to those who rejected it, but the law also denied motherhood to those like Mellet and Whelan who embraced it, albeit in an alternative bodily way.[56]

While the committee did not fully engage Mellett and Whelan as mothers, nor did it wholly ignore their mothering experience. It acknowledged that the Irish health care system abandoned these women as compared to mothers who carried their pregnancies to term and declared

caregivers and mothers, in particular, are obstacles to substantive gender equality ... and need to be modified or eliminated.'

52 A. Rich, *Of Woman Born: Motherhood as Experience and Institution* (New York: Norton, 1976); A. O'Reilly, *Feminist Mothering* (New York: State University of New York Press, 2008).

53 J. E. Hanigsberg, 'Homologizing Pregnancy and Motherhood: A Consideration of Abortion' (1995) 94 *Michigan Law Review* 371–418.

54 *Mellet*, para. 2.3; *Whelan*, para. 2.3.

55 See S. Blaffer Hrdy, *Mother Nature: A History of Mothers, Infants, and Natural Selection* (New York: Pantheon Books, 1999). Both nurture and neglect can be adaptive maternal responses, such that a mother who abandons a child is no less a mother.

56 Elisabeth Grosz describes this notion as 'counterstrategic reinscription'. See E. Grosz, 'Inscriptions and Body Maps: Representations and the Corporeal', in L. McDowell and J. Sharp (eds.), *Space, Gender, Knowledge: Feminist Readings* (New York: John Wiley, 1997).

this state neglect a human rights violation. Moreover, Mellet and Whelan were not the only persons the state abandoned in this way. In the communication, both women are described as having become pregnant with their husbands. Mellet flew to Liverpool with her husband for the abortion, and when they returned together to Ireland, they were denied the counselling offered to couples who suffer a stillbirth.[57] With her husband, Whelan learned that their baby would likely die in utero, or, if carried to term, during labour or soon after birth.[58] Together they decided to end the pregnancy, and together they left their twenty-month-old son with relatives to do so. Whelan's husband arranged for farm relief to say goodbye to his younger son in hospital, and when the couple returned home, together they waited for the courier delivery of their baby's cremated ashes.

Neither husband is an author of the communication, a reproductive subject of the law. Yet if the human right to be cared for by the state derives not from the maternal bodies of these women, but from their acts and burdens of mothering, as the committee reasoned, then this right ought to be enjoyed by all those who mother, and not just women.[59] While these men were not pregnant in an embodied way, they were pregnant with expectation and obligation; they carried the existential burdens of these pregnancies and grieved their loss. They mothered, and as such the abortion law harmed them too.[60] It denied them care and compassion, forced them outside the public health care system, required them to travel abroad, and left them with all the social and economic hardships of these efforts. In other words, the committee's analysis allows not only for gender-diverse women to become the reproductive subjects of law, but also gender-diverse subjects – that is, men too. In this possibility, the communication breaks the sex binary of reproductive rights and the convention of men as the 'second sex' of reproduction, 'less vulnerable to reproductive harm than women'.[61]

[57] *Mellet*, paras. 2.1–2.5. [58] *Whelan*, paras. 2.1–2.7.

[59] E. Jeremiah, 'Motherhood to Mothering and Beyond: Maternity in Recent Feminist Thought' (2006) 8 *Journal of the Association for Research on Mothering* 21–33.

[60] D. Rosenblum, 'Unsex Mothering: Toward a New Culture of Parenting' (2012) 35 *Harvard Journal of Law & Gender* 57–116; D. Rosenblum et al., 'Pregnant Man? A Conversation' (2010) 207 *Yale Journal of Law & Feminism* 207–246 at 208–217.

[61] M. C. Inhorn, T. Tjornhoj-Thomsen, H. Goldberg and M. la Cour Mosegaard (eds.), *Reconceiving the Second Sex: Men, Masculinity, and Reproduction* (New York: Berghahn Books, 2009).

Indeed, the reproductive labours and burdens of diverse family structures and kinship networks all carry expansive visions of motherhood in this way.[62] Yet the conventional separation of sex from gender, human from social reproduction, and maternity from motherhood in human rights law forestalls this kind of analysis. International human rights law tends to resist reproduction as a biosocial phenomenon. Men and society are asked to share in the burdens of motherhood, to care for and to raise children, but maternity, the birthing of children into the world, stays with women alone.[63] By authorship, Mellet and Whelan suffered alone as the subjects of law, their reproductive labour and burdens were recognized as meaningful to them as individuals, but not within their families or the nation-state.[64] The committee analysed maternity as a gender stereotype of the abortion law, but not the abortion law itself as a gender expression. At most, it described the abortion law as 'the profound moral choice of the Irish people', but left untouched the fundamental maternal ideation behind the law – that is, women as mothers of the Irish nation-state.[65] In the communication, maternity remained an embodied state, and never a state ideology.

Nonetheless, in these abortion communications, the body is made biosocial, and multiple forms of binary thinking are challenged: of women and men, of human and social reproduction, of maternity and motherhood, and ultimately of sex and gender. By refusing to compare women to men, by reasoning from the gender expression rather than sex-specificity of abortion, and by focusing on rights of mothering in maternity, the communications introduced critical breaks in the sex and gender binaries of reproductive subjectivity.

[62] M. Chandler, 'Queering Maternity' (1999) 1 *Journal of the Association for Research on Mothering* 21–32; M. Murray, 'The Networked Family: Reframing the Legal Understanding of Caregiving and Caregivers' (2008) 94 *Virginia Law Review* 385–455; D. Fontana and N. Schoebaum, 'Unsexing Pregnancy' (2019) 119 *Columbia Law Review* 309–368.

[63] CEDAW, Preamble and Arts. 2(f) and 5.

[64] Article 17 of the ICCPR protects the right to respect of both privacy and family, and under Article 23, protection of the family, includes 'the right to found a family implies, in principle, the possibility to [or not to] procreate'. HRC, General Comment No. 19 (E/C.12/GC/19) (1990), para. 5.

[65] L. Smyth, *Abortion and Nation: The Politics of Reproduction in Contemporary Ireland* (Aldershot: Ashgate, 2005); R. Fletcher, 'Reproducing Irishness: Race, Gender and Abortion Law' (2005) 17 *Canadian Journal of Women and the Law* 365–404.

3. States of Law: Childbirth and the Gender Hierarchy

In international human rights law, the preoccupation with gender as hierarchy creates a particular subject–state relation. In reproduction, women are treated as inherently vulnerable by virtue of their embodiment, and the nation-state is empowered to protect them from any social disadvantage or inequality premised upon it. This subject–state relation is central to two childbirth communications under the CEDAW, *Maria de Lourdes da Silva Pimentel* v. *Brazil*[66] and *S. M. F.* v. *Spain*.[67] When read together, however, these communications reveal a more complex account of gender and state power enacted through the reproductive body and its subject, thereby breaking the conventional subject–state relation of human rights law.

In *Maria de Lourdes da Silva Pimentel* v. *Brazil*, the author brought the communication on behalf of her daughter, Alyne da Silva Pimentel Teixeira, a Brazilian national of African descent, who died of obstetric complications while seeking care. When Alyne da Silva first presented at the health centre six months pregnant, staff misdiagnosed and mistreated an intrauterine foetal death, ignoring her complaints and sending her home. When she returned, they failed to induce labour, to remove the afterbirth and placenta, and her condition worsened. When Alyne da Silva required transfer to a hospital, the centre refused to send its only ambulance, and when she was eventually transferred, she was left unattended for twenty-one hours in a hospital hallway until her death. On these facts, the committee concluded that Alyne da Silva had died from systemic neglect, a major cause of Brazil's high rate of maternal mortality.[68]

Brazil did not contest the tragedy of Alyne da Silva's death but asked why the communication was brought to the CEDAW Committee.[69] What did her death have to do with discrimination against women? Alyne da Silva died of haemorrhage after low-quality service provision. For the committee, however, the connection was obvious. Alyne da Silva died

[66] UN CEDAW Committee, *Maria de Lourdes da Silva Pimentel* v. *Brazil*, Communication No. 17/2008 (2011).

[67] UN CEDAW Committee, *S.F.M.* v. *Spain*, Communication No. 138/2018 (2020).

[68] *Pimental*, para. 7.6.

[69] *Pimental*, para. 4.7.

because she was a woman.[70] Women in childbirth are inherently vulnerable, and state neglect of this sexed difference translates into gender inequality. No further explanation is needed or given. The logic perhaps persuades on the basis of sex, but when applied to an intersectional analysis of discrimination on the basis of sex and race, it strains.[71] In its analysis, the committee treated being of African descent, like being a woman, as an inherent risk in childbirth, and as such, Alyne da Silva as a 'woman of African descent' was especially vulnerable and required protection. Brazil also did not contest the truth of Afro-Brazilian women's vulnerability in childbirth but detailed its policies to improve maternal care among them.[72] The committee appreciated the policy commitment but insisted that human rights law requires more. The policies must work, and Alyne da Silva's death showed their failure. Her death embodied the systemic failure of the Brazilian maternal care system, and in remedy, the committee exhorted the state to do more.[73]

Doing more, indeed doing too much, was the claim at the centre of *S. M. F.* v. *Spain*. After a low-risk pregnancy and early hospital admission, *S. M. F.* was subjected to multiple interventions: vaginal examinations, oxytocin to induce delivery, a lithotomy birth position, with instrumental extraction and episiotomy. She received no explanation of these interventions, nor was she given any opportunity to express her opinion on them. After birth, *S. M. F.* and her husband were separated from their new-born child, who was treated for an infection related to the excessive interventions.

The committee described the violations that *S. M. F.* suffered as the pathologization of natural labour through medical interventionism, and

[70] *Pimental*, para. 7.3. See CEDAW, Art. 12(2), whereby 'states parties shall ensure to women appropriate services in connection with pregnancy, confinement and the post-natal period', and citing the World Health Organization definition of maternal death as 'the death of a woman'.

[71] *Pimentel*, para. 7.7. See K. A. Appiah, 'Racisms', in H. LaFollette (ed.), *Ethics in Practice* (Cambridge, MA: Blackwell, 1997).

[72] *Pimental*, paras. 4.11–4.12.

[73] *Pimental*, paras. 7.6 and 8. See also CEDAW, General Recommendation No. 24 (A/54/38/Rev.1) (1999), paras. 26–27, describing the duty of state parties ensure women's right to safe motherhood and emergency obstetric services including by 'measures to reduce maternal mortality and morbidity, in general, and in vulnerable groups, regions and communities, in particular'.

used this heuristic binary throughout its analysis: bottle versus breast-fed, analgesic versus emotional support, placental removal versus delivery.[74] In the communication, the maternal body is naturalized in biological terms, neurological and hormonal, but also psychical, being of mind and soul in maternal love.[75] The interventions are then described as having alienated the author from this state through the pathologization of her body and its submission into male-gendered, techno-medical control, expressly characterized as a form of obstetric violence.[76] In remedy, the committee called on the state to protect women from such violence by ensuring their right to informed consent and the following of medical protocol.[77] According to the committee, the interventions were medically unnecessary and reflected an abandonment of the 'principles, obligations and duties that govern doctor–patient relations in any other field of medicine'.[78]

The childbirth communications thus run parallel in this subject–state relation of victim and protector, premised on an inherent vulnerability of women in childbirth. Much as the committee did not ask why women die in childbirth, it did not ask why women suffer violence in childbirth: why medically unnecessary interventions are practised in obstetrics, and why existing protocols against mistreatment fail. Rather, the committee appeared to accept the fate of women in reproduction, their vulnerability to violence and death, as something that needs no explanation, only remedy. This is the danger of constructing reproductive subjects solely by reference to their vulnerability.[79] It breeds an acceptance of that vulnerability rather than an instinct to understand it – specifically, to

[74] *S. F. M.*, para. 7.2. For a critique, see B. Mansfield, 'The Social Nature of Natural Childbirth' (2008) 66 *Social Science & Medicine* 1084–1094.

[75] *S. F. M.*, para. 2.8. *S. M. F.* described having 'to create the bond with my daughter the hard way, rationally, without the help of the complex natural neurological and hormonal mechanisms that make mothers fall in love with their newborn children'.

[76] *S. F. M.*, para. 7.3. CEDAW, General Recommendation No. 28 (CEDAW/C/GC/28) (2010), para. 19; CEDAW, General Recommendation No. 35 (CEDAW/C/GC/35) (2017), paras. 10, 19. R. Sifris, *Reproductive Freedom, Torture and International Human Rights: Challenging the Masculinisation of Torture* (London: Routledge, 2013).

[77] CEDAW, General Recommendation No. 24 (A/54/38/Rev.1) (1999), para. 15.

[78] *S. F. M.*, para. 3.10.

[79] R. Kapur, 'The Tragedy of Victimization Rhetoric: Resurrecting the "Native" Subject in International/Post-Colonial Feminist Legal Politics' (2002) 15 *Harvard Human Rights Journal* 1–38.

engage the pathological gender structures and relations of power that circumscribe the body in maternal death and violence.[80] The text and context of these communications, however, created an opportunity for such understanding even if the committee failed to pursue it.

In the facts of the communication, *S. M. F.* described 'going into hospital ... like going ... onto an assembly line; everyone does things to you in a mechanical way. The woman does nothing, but she comes out ... with a baby'.[81] The committee used this statement to support its gender analysis of women's subjugation through objectification in medicalized birth. Rather than turn the material metaphor into an abstraction, the committee could have recognized in the mechanization of the labouring body a connection to the social world, specifically the norms of capitalist production: standardized labour, routinized intervention and above all efficiency of time and resources.[82] Indeed, both childbirth communications are preoccupied with clock-time.[83] The agonizing neglect of Alyne da Silva over hours and days. The too early hospital admission of *S. M. F.* and her body rushed through labour. In each communication, the committee took notice of clock-time, but never related it back to any social context. Clock-time is a structural feature of modern obstetric practice within market economies, and the larger economization of social life.[84] The fixing of labouring bodies to clock-time is how these bodies become the objects of predictable production: 'the woman does nothing, but she comes out ... with a baby'.

[80] CEDAW, General Recommendation No. 35 (CEDAW/C/GC/35) (2017), para. 9: 'The term "gender-based violence against women" ... makes explicit the gendered causes and impacts of the violence; the understanding of the violence as a social rather than an individual problem'. See M. Sadler et al., 'Moving beyond Disrespect and Abuse: Addressing the Structural Dimensions of Obstetric Violence' (2015) 24 *Sexual and Reproductive Health Matters* 47–55.

[81] *S.F.M.*, para. 2.8.

[82] B. Bridgman Perkins, *The Medical Delivery Business: Health Reform, Childbirth, and the Economic Order* (New Brunswick, NJ: Rutgers University Press, 2008); B. S. Turner, *Regulating Bodies: Essays in Medical Sociology* (London: Routledge, 1992).

[83] W. Simonds, 'Watching the Clock: Keeping Time during Pregnancy, Birth, and Postpartum Experiences' (2002) 55 *Social Science and Medicine* 559–570. See B. Adam, *Timewatch: The Social Analysis of Time* (Cambridge: Polity Press, 1995).

[84] R. Behruzi et al., 'Understanding Childbirth Practices as an Organizational Cultural Phenomenon: A Conceptual Framework', *BMC Pregnancy and Childbirth*, 11 November 2013, https://bmcpregnancychildbirth.biomedcentral.com/articles/10.1186/1471-2393-13-205.

Phenomenological body theory specifically recognizes time and movement through it as a mode of restricted embodiment, the experience of being 'passively present' as both subject and object.[85] In this analysis, subject and object are not presented as categorical and oppositional, but as states-in-relation to ask how reproductive subjects become objects.[86] In childbirth, the pathological construction of risk and routinized interventions to control that risk prove critical to this transition from subject to object.[87] Contrary to the committee's views, the interventions that *S. M. F.* suffered were not aberrations of obstetric practice, but the routines of it. Most obstetrical interventions are not medically necessary, they are socially expedient: they keep labouring bodies on time.[88] In other words, the construction of risk and its management in childbirth reflect and maintain certain social norms. In this case, by subordinating labouring bodies to the routines of mass production, obstetrics as a field of medicine fulfils the social imperatives of capitalist life.[89] In this account of obstetric violence, gender is expressed not in the objectification of women's body, but in the rationalization of that objectification through the conception and management of risk. Labouring bodies are risky bodies, but it is this intersection of bodily and social risk that uniquely engages the biopolitics of reproduction.[90]

[85] M. M. Burke, 'Gender as Lived Time: Reading *The Second Sex* for Feminist Phenomenology of Temporality' (2018) 33 *Hypatia* 111–127, citing S. de Beauvoir, *The Second Sex* (London: Vintage, 1997); I. M. Young, *'Throwing like a Girl' and Other Essays* (New York: Oxford University Press, 2005); I. M. Young, 'Pregnant Embodiment: Subjectivity and Alienation' (1984) 9 *Journal of Medicine and Philosophy* 45–62.

[86] A. Balsamo, *Technologies of the Gendered Body: Reading Cyborg Women* (Durham, NC: Duke University Press, 1996).

[87] D. Lupton, 'Risk and the Ontology of Pregnant Embodiment', in D. Lupton (ed.), *Risk and Sociocultural Theory* (Cambridge: Cambridge University Press, 2014); L. Fordyce and A. Maraësa (eds.), *Risk, Reproduction, and Narratives of Experiences* (Nashville, TN: Vanderbilt University Press, 2012).

[88] R. Davis-Floyd, 'The Technocratic, Humanistic and Holistic Paradigms of Childbirth' (2011) 75 *International Journal of Gynecology & Obstetrics* 5–23.

[89] E. Grosz, *Volatile Bodies: Toward a Corporeal Feminism* (Bloomington: Indiana University Press, 1994); R. Longhurst, *Maternities: Gender, Bodies and Space* (New York: Routledge, 2008).

[90] CEDAW, General Recommendation No. 24 (A/54/38/Rev.1) (1999), para. 6: 'While biological differences between women and men may lead to differences in health status, there are societal factors that are determinative of the health status of women and men and can vary among women themselves.'

While the capitalist social relations of Western Europe are a context perhaps too close to the human rights system itself to be the subject of its analysis, the committee has edged closer to the biopolitics of childbirth in other communications.[91] *A. S.* v. *Hungary* is one of the first human rights communications on the sterilization of women as part of eugenic state policy.[92] Its author, A. S., was a Roma woman subjected to involuntary sterilization during an emergency caesarean section. In labour with heavy bleeding, A. S. was taken to hospital where foetal death was diagnosed, and an emergency caesarean section advised. While on the operating table, A. S. was asked to sign a consent form for the surgery which included a barely legible note: 'I firmly request my sterilization.'[93] Within seventeen minutes of A. S. arriving at the hospital, the caesarean section was performed, the foetus and placenta removed, and her fallopian tubes tied. Only upon discharge did A. S. learn that she was sterilized. Clock-time again figured prominently in the analysis. The committee emphasized that seventeen minutes was an implausible time frame for the delivery of health care in accordance with medical standards, and on this basis, declared A. S. a victim of sex discrimination.[94] Its analysis was premised on the gender hierarchy and women's vulnerability to violence in childbirth – a vulnerability compounded by A. S.'s ethnic identity.[95] In remedy, the committee again called on the state to intervene and to protect women by ensuring their right to informed consent, and the following of medical protocol.

In A. S., the committee largely followed a conventional gender analysis, treating both sex and ethnicity as risk factors of individual vulnerability.[96] Yet in an important departure from this convention, the committee also engaged ethnicity in relation to social rather than biological reproduction, or reproduction in the family versus the health care setting. A. S. and her

[91] CESCR, General Comment No. 3 (E/1991/23) (1990), para. 8, describing how human rights law neither requires nor precludes any particular form of government or economic system, but is neutral, expressing 'no need for or desirability of a socialist or a capitalist system'.

[92] CEDAW, *A. S.* v. *Hungary*, Communication No. 4/2004 (2006). See CEDAW, General Recommendation No. 35 (CEDAW/C/GC/35) (2017), para. 18, describing forced sterilization as a form of gender-based violence.

[93] *A. S.*, para. 2.2. [94] *A. S.*, para. 11.3.

[95] See R. Sifris, 'The Involuntary Sterilisation of Marginalised Women: Power, Discrimination, and Intersectionality' (2016) 25 *Griffith Law Review* 45–70.

[96] CEDAW, General Recommendation No. 35 (CEDAW/C/GC/35) (2017), para. 12, describing ethnicity/race as an aggravating factor of gender-based violence.

partner lived in accordance with traditional Roma customs, where having children is central to the value system of Roma families.[97] The involuntary sterilization thus deprived A.S. of her right to decide freely on the number and spacing of children, grounding a distinct human rights violation in matters of family relations.[98] Although only A. S. and not her husband was named a victim of this violation, it nonetheless reflected an understanding of maternity as something of value not only to the individual, but to households and communities.[99] As in the abortion communications, however, the committee never reached the biopolitics of Roma reproduction in the Hungarian nation-state, or the ethno-gendered relations that structured its violence. While all human rights communications begin by naming its authors as 'of' a nation-state, rarely do they engage its reproductive subjects.

The forced sterilization of Roma women as a systemic practice across Central and Eastern Europe, which intensified towards the end of communism and into the newly formed democratic states, had an express political purpose of building 'healthy nations'. The practice was rooted in a belief that the social and economic hardships of a deeply racist society stemmed not from the political oppression of Roma people, but from some inherent pathology.[100] Once again obstetrics figured prominently in the practice, with the routine use of involuntary sterilizations premised on the specious risk of future uterine rupture.[101] In other words, the political pathologization of Roma reproduction was embedded into obstetric practice, with the well-being of patient and society merged in the assessment of risk and its management.

[97] *A. S.*, para. 2.4; [98] *A. S.*, para. 11.4; CEDAW, Art. 16(1)(e).

[99] CEDAW, General Recommendation No. 24 (A/54/38/Rev.1) (1999), para. 28, recognizing the intersection between the right to health and other rights that have a bearing on women's health.

[100] G. Albert and M. Szilvasi, 'Intersectional Discrimination of Romani Women Forcibly Sterilized in the Former Czechoslovakia and Czech Republic' (2016) 19 *Health & Human Rights* 23–34; V. Sokolová, *Cultural Politics of Ethnicity: Discourses on Roma in Communist Czechoslovakia* (Stuttgart: Ibidem, 2008).

[101] C. Cahn, *Human Rights, State Sovereignty and Medical Ethics: Examining Struggles around Coercive Sterilisation of Romani Women* (Leiden: Brill-Nijhoff, 2014). For a description of the relationship of medicalization and state expansion, see also A. M. Stern, 'Responsible Mothers and Normal Children: Eugenics, Nationalism, and Welfare in Post-revolutionary Mexico, 1920–1940' (2002) 12 *Journal Historical Sociology* 369–397.

In this analysis, obstetric violence is again shown as not merely repressive but productive in the 'marking and making of bodies' much as in the childbirth assembly line.[102] Roma women came to embody the nation-state and its racist ideologies in their very reproductive subjectivity, a kind of state violence which human rights law often fails to acknowledge, but not always.[103] *In J. D. et al.* v. *Czech Republic*, the Human Rights Committee under the International Covenant on Civil and Political Rights considered a communication brought by six Roma women who claimed that Czech law violated their human rights by requiring victims of forced sterilization to pursue civil remedies.[104] While deeming the communication inadmissible for failure to exhaust domestic remedies, the committee nevertheless recognized that these women had no hope of succeeding in a civil claim because of the nature of the violation they suffered. Forced sterilization deprived its victims not only of their reproductive capacity but rendered them sterile as legal subjects, the violence of the state enacted through and embodied in them.

Gender as a structure of nation-making and state-formation thus makes the reproductive subject of human rights law vulnerable in a different, but still embodied way. Such state violence shapes subjectivity itself by inscribing pathology onto the body and inhering vulnerability within it. In *Pimentel* v. *Brazil*, while recognizing the vulnerability of Afro-Brazilian women in childbirth, the committee did not historicize this vulnerability against the ideological role of Black maternity in the making of modern Brazil as a 'racial democracy'.[105] While sterilization was promoted to

[102] S. D'Cruze and A. Rao, 'Violence and the Vulnerabilities of Gender' (2204) 16 *Gender and History* 495–512.

[103] M. Foucault, *Society Must Be Defended: Lectures at the College de France 1975–1976* (New York: Picador, 2003); M. Foucault, *History of Sexuality*, 4 vols. (New York: Vintage, 1990), vol. 1.

[104] Human Rights Committee, *J. D. et al.* v. *Czech Republic*, Communication No. 102/216 (2019). See C. Cahn, 'Justice Delayed: The Right to Effective Remedy for Victims of Coercive Sterilization in the Czech Republic' (2017) 19 *Health and Human Rights* 9–22; S. Marks, 'The Romani Minority, Coercive Sterilization, and Languages of Denial in the Czech Lands' (2017) 84 *History Workshop Journal* 128–148.

[105] C. Roth, *A Miscarriage of Justice: Women's Reproductive Lives and the Law in Early Twentieth-Century Brazil* (Palo Alto, CA: Stanford University Press, 2020); K. Caldwell, *Negras in Brazil: Re-Envisioning Black Women, Citizenship, and the Politics of Identity* (New Brunswick, NJ: Rutgers University Press, 2007). Contrast: *Report of the Working Group of Experts on People of African Descent on Its Mission to Brazil*, UN Doc. A/HRC/45/44/ (2013).

reduce Black reproduction and whiten the 'Brazilian race', the scientific racism of Black reproductive pathology also entered the routines of maternal care as a culture of condemnation, a reason to blame Black mothers for their own failure to survive.[106] When Alyne da Silva arrived at the health centre, rather than inquire into her condition, the doctors dismissed it as symptomatic of a woman who had never received prenatal care, a woman responsible for her own ill-health.[107] When she lay dying in the hospital corridor, pale with blood on her mouth and clothes, her mother alone took notice. The health system appeared to accept Alyne da Silva's fate as a Black mother – and, in the most tragic turn of the communication, perhaps so did she. Women sometimes wait until the onset of labour or critical need to enter the health care system, fearful of it and their fate within it.[108] They participate in their own neglect, conditioned by a health care system to keep quiet and to silently endure, and, as such, reproductive risk and vulnerability becomes a subjective response to its systemic violence.

When read through body theory, the childbirth communications reveal that maternity as a state ideology is a subject–state relation, the complex and intersectional nature of which cannot be expressed in any simple hierarchical form. The subjects of these communications break convention by embodying the gender structures and relations of the state, its violence shaping their very subjectivity. In other words, reproductive pathology as reproductive subjectivity, or the way that embodied state violence shapes the subjectivity of its victims, profoundly challenges the subject–state relation of human rights law.

[106] S. De Zordo, 'Programming the Body, Planning Reproduction, Governing Life: The "(Ir-) Rationality" of Family Planning and the Embodiment of Social Inequalities in Salvador Da Bahia (Brazil)' (2012) 19 *Anthropology & Medicine* 207–223; C. Misago et al., 'From "Culture of Dehumanization of Childbirth" to "Childbirth as a Transformative Experience": Changes in Five Municipalities in North-East Brazil' (2001) 75 *International Journal of Gynecology & Obstetrics* 67–72.

[107] *Pimental*, para. 2.7.

[108] C. Mccallum and A. P. dos Reis, 'Childbirth as Ritual in Brazil: Young Mothers' Experiences' (2005) 70 *Ethnos: Journal of Anthropology* 335–360; N. Berry, 'Who's Judging the Quality of Care? Indigenous Maya and the Problem of "Not Being Attended"' (2008) 27 *Medical Anthropology* 164–189. See B. Schwartz, 'Waiting, Exchange, and Power: The Distribution of Time in Social System' (1974) 79 *American Journal of Sociology* 841–870.

4. Futures of Law: Assisted Reproduction and the Subject-State

When reproductive subjectivity is released from the binary constructs of sex and gender, embodiment becomes a resource rather than disadvantage, and international human rights law faces a new challenge in asking what limits if any attach to it. The infinite multiplication and reassembly of body parts and processes is the present-future of technoscientific reproduction, which human rights law has already recognized as 'blurring the boundaries between the physical, digital and biological worlds . . . chang[ing] not only society and human behaviour, but even human beings themselves'.[109]

This future subject-state of reproductive rights is central to the radical claims of *S. C. and G. P.* v. *Italy*, a communication on assisted reproduction under the International Covenant on Economic, Social and Cultural Rights.[110] S. C. and G. P., a woman and man, received in vitro fertilization (IVF) services at a private clinic in Italy to assist with having a child. In IVF, embryos are created in a laboratory, from which cells can be tested for genetic conditions, before being transferred into the uterus for implantation. Except for one, all the authors' embryos were untestable or tested for multiple osteochondromas, a hereditary condition, and the remaining embryo was deemed of 'average quality' with a low chance of success. S. C. declined to have this embryo transferred into her uterus, but the clinic informed her that Italian law prohibited the revocation of consent to transfer after fertilization. S. C. felt compelled to have the transfer and suffered a miscarriage. The remaining embryos were cryopreserved, and the authors requested their surrender from the clinic to donate for use in scientific research. The clinic refused, again citing a prohibition in Italian law against embryo research. The authors claimed multiple human rights violations, including a novel claim under the right to participate in and to enjoy the benefits of scientific progress.

Following convention, the committee framed its analysis in terms of women's bodily vulnerability in reproduction and focused on the coercive care to which S. C. was subjected in the forced transfer of the embryo into her uterus, calling on the state to protect women's informed consent under

[109] CESCR, General Comment No. 25 (E/C.12/GC/25) (2020), para. 72.

[110] CESCR, *S. C. and G. P.* v. *Italy*, Communication No. 22/2017 (2019).

the rights to health and equality.[111] It thus folded assisted reproduction easily into convention, naturalizing reproductive vulnerability in a woman's body without attention to social constructions of risk, including by the design of reproductive technologies that apply more invasively to female-sexed bodies.[112] Moreover, the committee recognized no violation of G. P.'s right to decide and exercise control over his body – that is, over the embryo as bodily material – although he too was denied the right to withdraw consent to its implantation. In the committee's analysis, the right of bodily integrity attached only to bodies and not their parts.

Assisted reproduction, however, raises the spectre of subjectivity in reproductive parts and materials, taken from and used outside bodies, in acts of creation and donation, across the sex binary and outside the heterosexual family.[113] This does not make assisted reproduction sexless, rather body materials are often re-gendered (for example, sperm are treated as male and ova as female) in their technoscientific uses.[114] Nonetheless, as technology reconfigures how people *do* reproduction with their bodies, the sex/gender of reproduction is challenged, and new subjectivities are forged.

In this respect, the communication is unique in naming a man, G. P., as an author, and thus as a reproductive subject of law.[115] In a separate claim

[111] *S. C. and G. P.*, paras. 10.1–10.3. See CESCR, General Comment No. 14 (E/C.12/2000/4) (2000), para. 34; CESCR, General Comment No. 22 (E/C.12/GC/22) (2016), para. 56, describing coercive medical treatments as an interference with an individual's freedom to control their own bodies.

[112] CESCR, General Comment No. 25 (E/C.12/GC/25) (2020), para. 33: State parties must 'ensure access to modern and safe forms of assisted reproductive technologies, and other sexual and reproductive goods and services, on the basis of non-discrimination and equality'. See I. van der Ploeg, '"Only Angels Can Do without Skin": On Reproductive Technology's Hybrids and the Politics of Body Boundaries' (2004) 10 *Body & Society* 153–181; M. C. Inhorn and D. Birenbaum-Carmeli, 'Assisted Reproductive Technologies and Culture Change' (2007) 37 *Annual Review of Anthropology* 177–234.

[113] R. Rapp, 'Reproductive Entanglements: Body, State, and Culture in the Dys/Regulation of Child-Bearing' (2011) 78 *Social Research* 693–718; M. Strathern, *Reproducing the Future: Anthropology, Kinship, and the New Reproductive Technologies* (New York: Routledge, Chapman & Hall, 1992); C. Thompson, *Making Parents: The Ontological Choreography of Reproductive Technologies* (Cambridge, MA: MIT Press, 2006).

[114] E. Martin, 'The Egg and the Sperm: How Science Has Constructed a Romance Based on Stereotypical Male–Female Roles' (1991) 16 *Signs* 485–501; R. Epstein, 'Space Invaders: Queer and Trans Bodies in Fertility Clinic' (2005) 21 *Sexualities* 1039–1058.

[115] This committee was also the first to recognize both men and women as potential victims of sex discrimination and gender inequality. CESCR, General Comment No. 16 (E/C.12/

under the right to health, the committee reasoned that because Italian law did not clarify whether consent to an embryo transfer could be withdrawn after fertilization, the couple would not attempt treatment again and were thus denied access to care in violation of the right.[116] Not only did this analysis de-sex reproductive care, but it also recognized men as no less vulnerable to reproductive harm than women. The gender-diverse reproductive subjects speculated in the abortion communications thus became real in a couple seeking to create a pregnancy, rather than to end one.

The committee was less willing, however, to entertain the authors' more radical claims. Specifically, in the denial of access to care, the authors claimed that Italy had frustrated their *reproductive intention* in violation of the 'right to freely decide the number, spacing and timing of children'.[117] In *A. S.* v. *Hungary*, the CEDAW Committee endorsed an almost identical claim, although the violation was tied to bodily violence in forced sterilization. In this communication, the committee was unwilling to even consider the prospect of disembodied subjectivity – that is, reproductive subjectivity not as an embodied state, but as a state of intention.[118]

This right of reproductive intention anchored the authors' most radical claim, specifically that Italy's prohibition on embryo donation had slowed down scientific research on hereditary multiple osteochondromas, and thereby affected their right to conceive a child.[119] In other words, the authors claimed the right to participate in and enjoy the benefits of scientific progress as a reproductive right. If S. C. could withdraw her consent to use an embryo in her body and avoid reproduction, why could S. C. and G. P. not use their bodily materials for scientific research in the quest for the 'elusive embryo' of their reproductive future.[120]

The committee declared the claim inadmissible, reasoning that it was simply too speculative to see S. C. and G. P. as victims of the prohibition on

GC/22) (2005), para. 14: 'Gender affects the equal right of men and women to the enjoyment of their rights.'

116 *S. C. and G. P.*, paras. 11.1–11.4. See CESCR, General Comment No. 14 (E/C.12/2000/4) (2000), para. 8; CESCR, General Comment No. 22 (E/C.12/GC/22) (2016), para. 5, on the right to health includes both freedoms and entitlements, specifically access to health care services.

117 *S. C. and G. P.*, para. 3.10.

118 *S. C. and G. P.*, para. 11.3.

119 *S. C. and G. P.*, paras. 3.1-3.3.

120 G. Becker, *The Elusive Embryo: How Women and Men Approach New Reproductive Technologies* (Berkeley: University of California Press, 2000).

embryo research, and that mere donation was no real form of participation.[121] The committee's views are rigid and unimaginative, separating both scientists who do science from the public who benefit from it, and reproductive research from its applications.[122] Most importantly, the committee ignored how people who use assisted reproduction see it, and specifically how they see themselves in relation to their embryos and what happens to them. It is not uncommon for people to feel connected to donated embryos and, more so, connected because of their 'double reproductive value' – that is, the embryos having been created in the context of assisted reproduction, but also in having a reproductive future.[123] In their perception that embryo donation for research may advance fertility care, the authors saw donation as part of family building, even an act of mothering towards future healthy children. Such speculative maternity based on genetic histories and legacies, and the blurred generational time of technoscientific reproduction, are entirely outside the conventions of reproductive rights law.[124] Yet for the authors, these ideas are woven into the subjectivity of reproductive intention.

In the committee's analysis, however, all the human rights that attach to the use of the embryo in assisted reproduction were extinguished in the crossover of its donation for research.[125] These subjects of law had no continuing interest in the embryo as a research object. This stark line again reveals the radical nature of the authors' claim, namely in its multiple challenges to the binaries of human rights law: present versus future, subject versus object. In the childbirth communications, the objectification

121 *S. C. and G. P.*, paras. 6.1–6.20.

122 Contrast to CESCR, General Comment No. 25 (E/C.12/GC/25) (2020). See S. Jasanoff (ed.), *States of Knowledge: The Co-Production of Science and the Social Order* (Berkeley: University of California Press, 2004).

123 S. Franklin, 'Embryonic Economies: The Double Reproductive Value of Stem Cells' (2006) 1 *BioSocieties* 71–90; S. Parry, '(Re)Constructing Embryos in Stem Cell Research: Exploring the Meaning of Embryos for People Involved in Fertility Treatments' (2006) 62 *Social Science & Medicine* 2349–2359.

124 E. Fox Keller, *The Century of the Gene* (Cambridge, MA: Harvard University Press, 2000); C. Novas and N. Rose, '*Genetic Risk and the Birth of the Somatic Individual*' (2000) 29 *Economy and Society* 485–513.

125 C. Williams et al., 'Human Embryos as Boundary Objects? Some Reflections on the Biomedical Worlds of Embryonic Stem Cells and Preimplantation Genetic Diagnosis' (2008) 27 *New Genetics and Society* 7–18; G. Laurie, 'Liminality and the Limits of Law in Health Research Regulation: What Are We Missing in the Spaces In-Between?' (2016) 25 *Medical Law Review* 47–72.

of reproductive subjects was the essence of the human rights violations. Body theory that deals with technoscience, however, negotiates a different relationship between these states, questioning the assumption that people need to be protected from technological objectification, but also in the figure of the cyborg, paying attention to how people use technology to produce subjectivity through objectification.[126] The experience of mechanizing bodies, turning them into objects, need not be violent. Indeed, S.C. and G.P. did not merely accept being an object, they wanted to actively participate in making their bodies into objects of scientific research.

Moreover, if the authors do not have an interest in their bodily material as objects of scientific research, then who does? The Italian state had an obvious interest given that it enacted the law on assisted reproduction, including the prohibition on embryo research. S.C. and G.P. pursued their reproductive rights within the heterosexual family, and thus presented no threat to this gendered institution of the nation-state.[127] Yet had the facts been different, and the reproductive intentions of the authors destabilized the family structure, the committee may have been forced to engage with the Italian law and its embedded norms about the 'proper way to have a child'.[128] Indeed, the Italian law originally allowed only adults of different genders and fertile age, who were married or living together, to engage in assisted reproduction.[129] Such an analysis of the gender norms of the law, like that undertaken in the abortion communications, may have eventually

[126] See D. Haraway, *Simians, Cyborgs, and Women: The Reinvention of Nature* (London: Free Association Books, 1991); S. Franklin, 'The Cyborg Embryo: Our Path to Transbiology' (2006) 23 *Theory Culture Society* 167–189; C. Thompson, 'Ontological Choreography: Agency through Objectification in Infertility Clinics' (2016) 26 *Social Studies of Science* 575–610; J. A. Gupta and A. Richters, 'Embodied Subjects and Fragmented Objects: Women's Bodies, Assisted Reproduction Technologies and the Right to Self-Determination' (2018) 5 *Journal of Bioethical Inquiry* 239–249.

[127] V. S. Peterson, 'Sexing Political Identities/Nationalism as Heterosexism' (1999) 1 *International Feminist Journal of Politics* 34–65. See also L. Mamo, *Queering Reproduction: Achieving Pregnancy in the Age of Technoscience* (Durham, NC: Duke University Press, 2007).

[128] J. A. Robertson, 'Protecting Embryos and Burdening Women: Assisted Reproduction in Italy' (2004) 19 *Human Reproduction* 1693–1696.

[129] I. Riezzo et al., 'Italian Law on Medically Assisted Reproduction: Do Women's Autonomy and Health Matter?' (2016) 16 *BMC Women's Health* 1–7.

reached the law itself as a gendered expression of 'Italian national identity based on a heteropatriarchal model of family relations'.[130]

Italy also enacted these prohibitions against an active commercial market in reproductive materials as global commodities, the social context of the fertility clinic in the communication. Reproductive technologies have created the possibility to disaggregate and reassemble the body at the cellular or molecular level, and to make these fragments (cells, tissues, genes) ever more productive.[131] This growing capital value of reproduction on a global scale and its destabilizing and gendered effects on reproductive labour and family structures has powerfully reshaped the biopolitical power of the nation-state and the subjectivity of those within it.[132] Thus, as the childbirth communications engaged the histories of reproductive subjectivity in the nation-state, this communication engages its futures.

5. Conclusion

Theoretical writing on reproduction often contemplates the meaning of the word itself, and its association with ideas of 'creation'. This sense of the word holds true in law. By bringing their bodies before the law, the reproductive subjects of human rights law continue to test its limits and to create new forms of subjectivity from the microbiological to the socio-political.

The body has always been central to reproductive rights but was historically essentialized as of the female sex and thus of women alone. When human rights law took on the concept of gender, this body was left unchallenged. Rather, gender captured the social disadvantage and inequality that women as compared to men suffered by virtue of their

[130] P. Hanafin, *Conceiving Life: Reproductive Politics and the Law in Contemporary Italy* (Leiden: Taylor & Francis, 2007); P. Hanafin, 'Rights, Bioconstitutionalism and the Politics of Reproductive Citizenship in Italy' 17 *Citizenship Studies* 942–955. See also C. Robcis, *The Law of Kinship: Anthropology, Psychoanalysis, and the Family in France* (Ithaca, NY: Cornell University Press, 2013).

[131] C. Waldby and R. Mitchell, *Tissue Economies: Blood, Organs, and Cell Lines in Late Capitalism* (Durham, NC: Duke University Press, 2006).

[132] M. Murphy, *Seizing the Means of Reproduction: Entanglements of Feminism, Health, and Technoscience* (Durham, NC: Duke University Press, 2012); C. Waldby and M. Cooper, 'The Biopolitics of Reproduction: Post-Fordist Biotechnology and Women's Clinical Labour' (2008) 23 *Australian Feminist Studies* 57–73.

embodied vulnerability. Human rights law called for this gender hierarchy of sexed reproduction to be dismantled and empowered the nation-state to do so.

Through body theory, the chapter has explored different constructions of the reproductive subject of international human rights law that break with these conventions – that is, the sexed category of 'women' as the reproductive subject of law, and the subject–state relation of gender as hierarchy that it sustains. In the abortion communications, abortion rights of gender diversity in bodily identity and expression, and rights to health care and social support in the recognition of reproduction as a biosocial phenomenon introduced critical breaks in the binaries of human versus social reproduction and maternity versus motherhood. In the childbirth communications, a more complex and intersectional account of gender in the structures and relations of state power enacted through the reproductive body and its subject break the conventional subject–state relation of human rights law. Gender as a structure of nation-making and state-formation makes the reproductive subject of human rights law vulnerable in a different way: the violence of the state inscribed onto the body, and thereby shaping the subjective experience of it. In the assisted reproduction communication, the radical claims of disembodied subjectivity and reproductive futures – that is, subjectivity in reproductive material and parts used outside sexed bodies in scientific research and global economies, but with gendered effects on reproductive labour and family structures within nation-states – appear to demand entirely new constructions of the human subject of human rights law.

By construction of gender and law, the reproductive body in human rights law is proving no longer a woman's alone, but a site of diverse and fluid identity and expression, a site of social resistance and relations, and a political site par excellence. Indeed, when taken together, these case studies on the reproductive subject of human rights law reveal that when the sex binary and gender hierarchy are challenged, all manner of binary thinking breaks down: subject and object, nature and machine, present and future. When reproduction is freed from such thinking, the body becomes truly procreative.

The Caring Subject 7

Jonathan Herring

1. Introduction

The vision of the self promoted by the law is of an isolated, independent, self-sufficient, autonomous man. Far from the reality of our vulnerable, caring, relational selves. The rights the law tends to protect are well suited for the legal self: those of autonomy, privacy and self-determination. They are unsuited for the reality of our existence in which autonomies are mixed; meaning is found in sharing experiences; and flourishing is discovered in the mingling of our lives. The legal self privileges particular activities, those traditionally seen as the world of men, and downplays the importance of caring, traditionally seen as the world of women. This sidelining of care, and the aggrandising of what is labelled 'economically productive', helps sustain and reinforce patriarchal oppression of women.

Feminist care ethics has promoted the caring self as a profound challenge to the legal conception.[1] It places at its heart the practice of care.

[1] Leading works on the ethics of care include: C. Gilligan, *In a Different Voice* (Cambridge, MA: Harvard University Press, 1982); J. Tronto, *Moral Boundaries* (Abingdon: Routledge, 1993); S. Sevenhuijsen, *Citizenship and the Ethics of Care* (Abingdon: Routledge, 1998); N. Noddings, *Starting at Home: Caring and Social Policy* (Berkeley: University of California Press, 2002); E. F. Kittay, *Love's Labour: Essays on Women, Equality and Dependency* (Abingdon: Routledge, 1999); R. Groenhout, *Connected Lives: Human Nature and an Ethics of Care* (New York: Rowman and Littlefield, 2004); V. Held, *The Ethics of Care* (Oxford: Oxford University Press, 2006); D. Engster, *The Heart of Justice: Care Ethics and Political Theory* (Oxford: Oxford University Press, 2007); J. Bridgeman, *Parental Responsibility, Young Children and Healthcare Law* (Cambridge: Cambridge University Press, 2009); J. Herring, *Caring and the Law* (Oxford: Hart, 2013;S. Collins, *The Core of Care Ethics* (Basingstoke: Palgrave, 2015); M. Barnes, T. Brannelly, L. Ward and N. Ward, *Ethics of Care: Critical Advances in International Perspective* (Bristol: Policy Press, 2015); R. Harding, R. Fletcher and C. Beasley, *Revaluing Care in Theory, Law and Policy* (Abingdon: Routledge, 2016); C. Rogers, *Intellectual Disability and Being Human: A Care Ethics Model* (Abingdon: Routledge, 2016); R. Harding, *Duties to Care* (Cambridge: Cambridge University Press, 2017); J. Herring, *Law and the Relational Self* (Cambridge: Cambridge University Press, 2019).

Care is essential to our survival; it is at the heart of our lives, at the core of our meaning, and is the ultimate good. Yet care is often invisible to the law. The injured pedestrian can receive compensation for their lost wages, but not the loss of an ability to care; the welfare recipient is encouraged to find paid employment – their care work counts for nothing; the GDP of a country is loudly trumpeted by the government, but there is silence about the levels of care provided.

Our law reports are replete with cases about making, losing and claiming money. They are set in the office, the boardroom or the casino. Rarely do the nappy changing table, the bedpan or the care home feature prominently. Our law graduates are well trained to advise well-heeled business-people on their rights of autonomy, freedom of contract and presumption of innocence. They would be ill equipped to advise the welfare recipient, the exhausted mother of a disabled child or the care home resident with dementia. The values the law seems to promote and the nature of the self they promote is anathema to them.

This chapter will start by arguing that the self is in its nature caring, vulnerable and relational.[2] Caring is essential to human survival and should be at the heart of the law. From our earliest days, caring relations are central to our physical health, emotional well-being and psychological identity.[3] However, the law fails to value care, and this chapter will explore some of the reasons for that, and ways that the law could do more to value care. The chapter will then, by way of example, focus on the issues of parenthood and the work–life balance.

2. The Caring Self

Everyone is vulnerable. As Catriona Mackenzie, Wendy Rogers and Susan Dodds explain: 'To be vulnerable is to be fragile, to be susceptible to wounding and to suffering; this susceptibility is an ontological conditional of our humanity.'[4] There is an extensive literature on the meaning of

[2] Herring, *Law and the Relational Self.*

[3] D. Engster, 'Care in the State of Nature: The Biological and Evolutionary Roots of the Disposition to Care in Human Beings', in D. Engster and M. Hamington (eds.), *Care Ethics and Political Theory* (Oxford: Oxford University Press, 2015).

[4] W. Rogers, C. Mackenzie and S. Dodds, 'Why Bioethics Needs a Theory of Vulnerability' (2012) 5 *International Journal of Feminist Approaches to Bioethics* 11–32 at 12.

vulnerability and it is not possible to do it justice here.[5] One basic definition is as follows:

> P is vulnerable if the following three factors are present:
>
> 1. P faces a risk of harm.
> 2. P does not have the resource to be able to avoid the risk of harm materializing.
> 3. P would not be able to adequately respond to the harm if the risk materialized.[6]

Vulnerability is commonly discussed in the media and by politicians. But when it is discussed, it comes with heavily negative connotations. Particular groups are defined as vulnerable and in need of care and protection. By contrast, the claim of universal vulnerability theorists is that vulnerability is an inevitable part of the whole human condition. And as a result care is an inevitable part of the human condition. If we are all vulnerable then our caring relationships are essential to our survival. Yet, similarly, our caring relationships are part of what makes us vulnerable. The concept of universal vulnerability is, therefore, integral to the claim of the caring self.

Martha Fineman has done more than anyone to develop the concept of universal vulnerability, and she explains it in this way:

> The vulnerability approach recognizes that individuals are anchored at each end of their lives by dependency and the absence of capacity. Of course, between these ends, loss of capacity and dependence may also occur, temporarily for many and permanently for some as a result of disability or illness. Constant and variable throughout life, individual vulnerability encompasses not only damage that has been done in the past and speculative harms of the distant future, but also the possibility of immediate harm. We are beings who live with the ever-present possibility that our needs and circumstances will change. On an individual level, the concept of vulnerability (unlike that of liberal autonomy) captures this present potential for each of us to become dependent based upon our persistent susceptibility to misfortune and catastrophe.[7]

[5] F. Sherwood-Johnson, 'Constructions of "Vulnerability" in Comparative Perspective: Scottish Protection Policies and the Trouble with "Adults at Risk"' (2013) 28 *Disability & Society* 908–918.

[6] J. Herring, *Vulnerability, Childhood and the Law* (Berlin: Springer, 2018), 21.

[7] M. Fineman, 'The Vulnerable Subject: Anchoring Equality in the Human Condition' (2008) 20 *Yale Journal of Law & Feminism* 1–71.

Society has built up a wide range of structures and forms of assistance which disguise the vulnerability of the so-called able bodied. The truth is that we rely on others and social provision for survival. Commonly the facilities used to deal with the vulnerabilities of others are highlighted, while overlooking the accommodations everyone needs to deal with their vulnerabilities. No one can get up to the seventh floor of a building without an accommodation. You might need stairs or you might need a lift, but you need something to assist you to get there. The provision that is given will enable some, but not others, to reach the seventh floor. We all need public provisions to survive.

It is because we are vulnerable beings that care is central. We all have needs and the meeting of needs in caring relationships is a universal experience. As Wendy Holloway argues, 'care is the psychological equivalent to our need to breathe unpolluted air'.[8] There will be few, if any, stages during anyone's life when they are not in caring relationships. Eva Feder Kittay, Bruce Gennings and Angela Wassuna explain:[9] 'People do not spring up from the soil like mushrooms. People produce people. People need to be cared for and nurtured throughout their lives by other people, at some times more urgently and more completely than at other times.' Clearly much more could be said about ethics of care,[10] but the focus of this chapter will not be unpacking its approach, but outlining its significance for lawyers.

3. The Challenges for the Law in Responding to the Caring Self

In this section the reasons why the law has struggled to find an effective way of recognizing and valuing care will be explored. Currently the law does not value care. We can see that at a practical level and by way of legal theory. Carers UK[11] reports a wide range of statistics indicating the disadvantages that carers suffer in the United Kingdom, including:

[8] W. Holloway, 'Introducing the Capacity to Care', in W. Holloway (ed.), *The Capacity to Care: Gender and Ethical Subjectivity* (Abingdon: Routledge, 2006).

[9] E. F. Kittay, B. Jennings and A. Wassuna, 'Dependency, Difference and the Global Ethic of Longterm Care' (2005) 13 *Journal of Political Philosophy* 433–455.

[10] See the literature at n. 1.

[11] Cares UK is a charity representing carers in the United Kingdom.

- 72% of carers ... said they had suffered mental ill health as a result of caring.
- 61% said they had suffered physical ill health as a result of caring.
- 8 in 10 people caring for loved ones say they have felt lonely or socially isolated.
- ... 600 people give up work every day to care for an older or disabled relative.[12]

Similar challenges to informal carers are found across Europe. The United Nations Economic Commission for Europe found: 'There are also significant hidden costs of informal care to carers. These include the opportunity costs of lost earnings, careers and pension entitlements, as well as the health consequences of the physical and psychological burden experienced.'[13]

Three primary issues will now be identified as to why the law has struggled to recognise and value care.

A. The Individualized Understanding of the Self

At the heart of the explanation for why the law fails to respond effectively to care is, as already mentioned, the understanding of the self at the heart of the law.[14] The law and many ethical theories assume that we are competent, detached, independent people who are entitled to have our rights of self-determination and autonomy fiercely protected.[15] These key rights protect the individual from interference from others. Further, the individualized notion of the self, as bounded and self-contained, encourages the promotion of self-reliance and independence. The self should be directing their efforts to doing all they can do to maximize personal gain.[16] On such an approach, rather than enhancing the self, caring endangers the self.[17] No one can, in fact, survive without the practical, emotional and psychological support of others. This means that legal interventions designed to restore a person's self-sufficiency will work to the disadvantage of those who care.

[12] Carers UK, Facts about Carers, www.carersuk.org/news-and-campaigns/press-releases/facts-and-figures.

[13] UNECE, *The Challenging Roles of Informal Carers* (Brussels: UNECE, 2019).

[14] Herring, *Law and the Relational Self*, ch. 2.

[15] Herring, *Vulnerable Adults and the Law*, ch. 2.

[16] L. Code, *What Can She Know? Feminist Theory and the Construction of Knowledge* (New York: Cornell University Press, 1991), 77–78.

[17] C. Willett, E. Anderson and D. Myers, 'Feminist Perspectives on the Self' (*Stanford Encyclopedia of Philosophy*), https://plato.stanford.edu/entries/feminism-self/.

A good example of this is financial orders in the event of a divorce, where the United Kingdom Supreme Court has explained: 'The ultimate objective is to give each party an equal start on the road to independent living.'[18] Yet such a goal makes no sense in cases where the couple have children or other heavy caring responsibilities. First, except in rare cases where the caring responsibilities are equally shared post-separation, the parties cannot be on an 'equal start' as the additional caring responsibilities will hinder that party's engagement in the workplace. Second, except in rare cases where the caring responsibilities have been equally shared during the relationship, the party who has undertaken the bulk of caring responsibilities will have suffered severe setbacks to their abilities to promote their career and gain the experience to have high-paid employment, while the other will have. We can only pretend that post-separation the parties can have an equal start if we ignore the care work.[19]

A law based around the caring subject would be highly alert to the importance and impact of care. It would recognize that we are ignorant, vulnerable, interdependent individuals, whose strength and reality is not in our autonomy, but in our relationships with others. It would ensure that legal interventions are built around the maintenance and preservation of caring relationships, rather than the image of individual person.

B. The Difficulties in Defining Care

A major problem facing those writing about care is providing a definition of care. That creates a problem for lawyers. Without a satisfactory definition, legal responses are difficult to formulate. Often cited in the ethical literature is the definition of care offered by Joan Tronto and Berenice Fischer:[20] 'A species of activity that includes everything we do to maintain, continue and repair our "world" so that we can live in it as well as possible. That world includes our bodies, ourselves and our environment.' This is in many ways an admirable definition, but it is hard to see it being used in a

[18] *Miller* v. *Miller; McFarlane* v. *McFarlane* [2006] UKHL 24, para. 144.

[19] E. Gordon-Bouvier, 'The Open Future: Analysing the Temporality of Autonomy in Family Law' (2020) 31 *Child and Family Law Quarterly* 1–23.

[20] J. Tronto and B. Fisher, 'Toward a Feminist Theory of Caring', in E. Abel and M. Nelson (eds.), *Circles of Care: Work and Identity in Women's Lives* (Albany, NY: SUNY Press, 1990).

legal context. First, its terms are so vague and potentially over-inclusive that it would lead to legal interventions that are inadequately targeted. Second, legal definitions have to be susceptible to evidence produced in court. The kinds of issues raised in Tronto and Fischer's definition seem to be the kind that are hard to prove.

It is interesting that two prominent legal discussions of care have advocated an approach which relies on 'markers of care'. These do not provide a definition of care, but rather indicators that care is taking place. The greater the number and extent of these markers, the closer the activity is to the core concept of care. I have suggested the markers of meeting needs, respect, responsibility and relationality.[21] Caracciolo di Torella and Masselot advocate the use of four such markers:[22] constant ongoing responsibilities; absence of choice; financial, physical and emotional costs; and emotionally sensitive personal connection. This kind of approach is not unknown in the law; it is found, for example, in the definition used by the European Court of Human Rights in relation to terms such as torture and family life. There, the court has avoided a traditional definition of these terms, but rather provided a list of factors which indicate that torture or family life are present. Traditionally, however, law has relied on bright-line definitions, which are susceptible to proof in courts, to target interventions.

C. The Breadth of the Topic

A third challenge facing legal interventions in relation to care is the breadth of the topic. Eugenia Caracciolo di Torella and Torella Masselot have called for an EU-level policy on care.[23] However, they acknowledge the enormous challenges this would face, given the vast number of areas of law that would need to be addressed. Very broadly speaking, these can be divided into three areas. First, in cases between individuals, they include personal law, such as the law on families, succession, medicine and employment. Care becomes relevant where as a result of undertaking care work one party has lost out and another party has gained. Here we do see

[21] Herring, *Caring and the Law*, ch. 2.

[22] E. Caracciolo di Torella and A. Masselot, *Caring Responsibilities in European Law and Policy* (London: Routledge, 2020), ch. 1.

[23] Ibid., 50.

the law providing some recognition to care work. A good example is in family law. In the English decision of *White* v. *White*,[24] Lord Nicholls developed the 'starting point' that on divorce a couple's assets should be shared equally. The justification for this was that each party had contributed equally to the marriage and 'There should be no bias in favour of the money-earner and against the home-maker and the child-carer'. In saying this, he rejected the previous case law which had, broadly speaking, been based on an assumption an employed spouse had earned their money, but on divorce could be required to meet the needs of the childcaring spouse. Such an approach did not value the care as such, but was focused on enforcing the promise in the 'marriage contract' that the parties should financially support each other. Financial orders on divorce are one of the few areas in which care is explicitly valued in English law. It is, however, strikingly limited. It is only a valuing of care within marriage, and there is no valuing of care for relationships outside that context, even though the carer may have contributed to the relationship as much as a spouse. Further, the care is valued in terms of wealth created by the other spouse, typically the husband. So the financial value attached to care provided to a millionaire's family will be worth significantly more than the care provided to an impoverished family. This reflects the difficulties the law has in valuing things that are not connected to economic productivity.

A second area of the law which interacts with care is where the state undertakes care, be that though education, medicine or social provision. The law has struggled to regulate the provision of care. In England there is a widespread acceptance that social care is inadequate and while there is a political consensus that something needs to be done to improve its provision, politicians have struggled to find any way forward. The legal difficulties are manifested in the provisions of the Care Act 2014, which provide for the use of 'personal budgets'. Under these, individuals in need are given money by the state in order to buy the necessary care. There is much political gain in such an approach because if there is a failure in social care the individual can be blamed for failing to use their budget appropriately. The approach is based on defining care in terms of tasks for which a sum of money can be given. This, however, ignores the relational and social significance of care. This 'marketization of care', necessary as

[24] [2000] UKHL 54.

the only way the law values things, denudes care of its emotional and social significance.[25]

The third interrelation of law and care might be areas which do not directly involve care but directly impact on it, such as the damages awarded in the law of tort or employment law protection. The leading case in England on tort law damages and care is *Hunt* v. *Severs*.[26] The House of Lords explained that if X injures A and as a result B (A's partner) has to give up work to care for A then no damages can be claimed by B. Damages can be claimed by A for the cost of care, as assessed on the 'market value' and these can be required to be held on trust for B. But B does not have a recognized loss and has no remedy in their own right, and the sum is limited to what the care would cost on the open market. In *Decoy* v. *Doxford*,[27] a woman who required care due to a range of medical conditions sued a company that caused the death of her husband. She was being cared for by relatives and so a 25 per cent reduction was given. No explanation was given for the reduction. It seems had she used professional carers the full sum could have been retained. Colin McEachran QC, in his assessment of the law, complains that informal care is 'grossly undervalued by the courts'.[28] The cases reflect the fact that care by women in particular tends to be seen as 'being as normal as breathing 'and simply 'taken for granted'.[29] It can only be rendered assessable by the courts if analogized with a paid care giver. We see here again the difficulties the law has in valuing care outside a marketized system. This reflects the general approach in English civil law that damages are only awarded for economic loss. As Eugenia Caracciolo di Torella and Annick Masselot put it: 'Care and care-work are difficult to monitor and to measure under traditional account methods. Accounting requires proof that the work has been done and that is has been done with high quality. However, care-work includes

[25] J. Herring, 'Personal Budgets: Holding onto the Purse Strings for Fear of Something Worse', in T. Feiler, J. Hordern and A. Papanikitas (eds.), *Marketisation, Ethics and Healthcare: Policy, Practice and Moral Formation* (London: Routledge, 2019).

[26] [1994] 2 All ER 385. [27] [2009] EWHC 1598 (QB).

[28] Quoted in Law Commission, *Damages for Personal Injury*, Report 262 (London: Law Commission, 1999), para. 3.84.

[29] C. Smart, 'Losing the Struggle from Another Voice' (1995) 18 *Dalhousie Law Journal* 173–195 at 177.

many dimensions that are not easily quantifiable in numbers, including love, trust and diplomacy.'[30]

As can be seen from this brief summary, a wide range of cases involve care, but also bump up against other important public policy concerns. Trying to acknowledge care within tort law would need a rethinking of the whole basis of damages in tort; rethinking 'personal budgets' involves a major political issues around levels of taxation and the provision of public services. And this is without seeking to factor in the ways that gender, disability, race, sexual orientation, class, age, ethnicity etc., and intersections between these identities interface with care, creating particular disadvantages in particular contexts.[31]

4. Law and the Caring Self

This section will focus on what a legal system that sought to promote caring might look like.

A. Promoting Care

Under an ethic of care, caring would become the most highly valued activity in society. Care is what gives meaning and value to a life. Caring relationships would be seen as fulfilling an essential societal obligation. Those missing out on providing care should be seen as having been deprived of an important good. Social support systems would encourage and enable caring relationships.[32] Damages under tort law would recognize interference with care work as a loss equal to interference with paid work. Employment law would recognize the right to combine paid work and care and require employees to make appropriate provision to enable a worker to meet their caring responsibilities.

The understanding of care would not be limited by the context or formal relationship between the parties. So while traditionally there has been

[30] Caracciolo di Torella and Masselot, *Caring Responsibilities in European Law and Policy*, 50.

[31] See also discussion of theories of recognition: M. Iser, 'Recognition' (*Stanford Encyclopedia of Philosophy*), https://plato.stanford.edu/archives/sum2019/entries/recognition/.

[32] O. Hankivsky, *Social Policy and the Ethic of Care* (Vancouver: University of British Columbia Press, 2004).

acknowledgement of care within the employment market (e.g. a paid nanny or child-minder), care work in other contexts, especially in the home, has been rendered invisible, particularly if it is undertaken outside marriage. This has in particular meant much of the care work of women has counted for nothing. This includes not just the standard examples of mother caring for children, but also care outside the norm: care in 'families of choice';[33] care for older parents; and care between friends.

Caring involves the actual giving of care, and the giving of care effectively.[34] Here it is useful to draw on the distinction drawn by many care writers between caring *about* and caring *for*.[35] Many people know someone who claims to care about all manner of things, but does not seem to put those feelings into practice. That is not genuine caring.[36] This is particularly significant given the unequal distribution of care within many opposite-sex households. On average, while fathers may care as much *about* their children as mothers, the caring *for* children is undertaken by mothers. On the other hand, this broader definition of care is wide enough to include things that do not fall into the paradigmatic image of care and could include everything from simply being with someone or arguably even offering sexual services. However, the interests in the state are particularly involved where the care meets the 'needs' of another.[37] Daniel Engster defines care as 'everything we do directly to help individuals to meet their vital biological needs, develop or maintain their basic capabilities, and avoid or alleviate unnecessary or unwanted pain and suffering, so that they can survive, develop, and function in society'.[38]

At a conceptual level, two tools in particular are used in legal policy currently to devalue care. The first is the concept that care work is a 'private' matter. That the state needs to be concerned with the public world of employment and government affairs. What happens in individuals'

[33] S. Marvel, 'The Evolution of Plural Parentage: Applying Vulnerability Theory to Polygamy and Same-Sex Marriage' (2015) 64 *Emory Law Journal* 2047–2087.

[34] A. Barnes, 'Am I a Carer and Do I Care?' (2004) 7 *Medicine, Health Care and Philosophy* 153–161.

[35] Tronto, *Moral Boundaries*, 127–134.

[36] K. Lynch, 'Love Labour as a Distinct and Non-Commodifiable Form of Care Labour' (2008) 55 *Sociological Review* 550–570.

[37] S. Clark Miller, 'Need, Care and Obligation' (2005) 57 *Royal Institute of Philosophy Supplement* 137–160.

[38] Engster, *The Heart of Justice*, 28–29.

homes should be private and no concern of the state.[39] The second is the idea of choice. Autonomy is highly prized in the law.[40] Individuals choose to care and do so out of love, aware that its rewards are not financial. The state should respect that choice and not seek to interfere in personal decisions through the legal regulation of care.

These powerful concepts of privacy and autonomy are, however, rejected, at least in their standard forms, by those who promote a caring law. It should be a primary responsibility of the state to meet the needs of those citizens who cannot provide for themselves. By describing care work as private and a choice, the state is given a 'free ride' by not compensating, or recognizing the value of, the work of those who fulfil the state's responsibility. This leaves mothers and those involved in care pauperized. It gives rise to a structural debt owed by society to carers which 'must be recognized, and payment accomplished, through policies and laws that provide both some economic compensation and structural compensation to caretakers'.[41] As Martha Nussbuam has written: 'Any real society is a caregiving and care-receiving society, and must therefore discover ways of coping with these facts of human neediness and dependency that are compatible with the recipients and do not exploit the caregivers. This ... is a central issue for gender justice.'[42]

This kind of approach would require a radical rethinking of state support for carers. This would include ensuring that those undertaking care in the home are at the very least not placed into poverty and that they receive welfare payments that acknowledge the value of their contributions. It would also mean the state offering practical support such as alternative care provision (respite care) so that those giving care can have a break.[43] It would require a rethinking of labour law so that employees are given rights to enable them to combined paid employment with caring responsibilities. Indeed, labour law needs to recognize caring work as work. As Judy Fudge explains: '[F]eminist labour law scholars have emphasized the importance of including caring and domestic labour, whether paid or unpaid,

[39] This is well captured in C. Pateman, *The Sexual Contract* (Cambridge: Polity Press, 1988).

[40] C. Foster, *Choosing Life, Choosing Death: The Tyranny of Autonomy in Medical Ethics and Law* (Oxford: Hart, 2009).

[41] M. Fineman, *The Autonomy Myth* (New York: New Press, 2004).

[42] M. Nussbaum, 'Capabilities as Fundamental Entitlements' (2003) 3 *Feminist Economics* 1–43 at 41.

[43] For details see Herring, *Caring and the Law*, ch. 3.

performed in a private household within the domain of labour law, and have been at the forefront of grappling with the specific dynamics governing affective or embodied labour.'[44] She adds that this would mean:

If unpaid, but socially necessary, reproductive work is considered to be as valuable as paid labour to individual and social development, employers would not be able to design jobs based on the assumption that it is the worker's private and individual responsibility to adapt their caring responsibilities to the temporal requirements of the job. Instead, working-time norms would be designed on the assumption that all workers engage in domestic labour for others and women would no longer be expected to shoulder the economic burden of unpaid care work. Similarly, if unpaid care work is considered to be as valuable as paid work, benefits provided to workers on maternity and parental leave would no longer be just a proportion of the worker's wage but equivalent to it.[45]

B. Intermingled Interests

Under the traditional legal image of the individualized self we understand each other primarily as individuals. Hence, a legal case is seen as a weighing up of the rights and claims of each of the two parties and deciding which person has the strongest. By contrast, if we understand ourselves as essentially caring, then it is our relationships which should be key. That, in fact, matches onto human experience. People understand themselves in terms of their relationships. They do not seek to promote only their own interests, not because they are 'selfless', but because their interests are tied up with the interests of others. They cannot seek to promote their own interests with no attention paid to others. If good things happen to those they are in a positive relationship with then that is good for them.[46] In relationships of caring and dependency, interests become intermingled. We do not break down into 'me' and 'you'. As Virginia Held puts it:

Care should not be understood as self-sacrifice. Egoism versus altruism is the wrong way to interpret the issues. Yes, the interests of care giver and care receiver will sometimes conflict, but for the most part we do not pit our own interests

[44] J. Fudge, 'Feminist Reflections on the Scope of Labour Law: Domestic Work, Social Reproduction, and Jurisdiction' (2014) 22 *Legal Studies* 1–23.

[45] Ibid. [46] J. Downie and J. Llewellyn, *Being Relational* (Vancouver: UBC Press, 2011).

against those of others in this context. We want what will be good for both or all of us together. We want our children and others we care for to do well along with ourselves, and for the relations between us to be good ones. If we are the recipients of care we want our care givers to do well along with us.[47]

This is legally significant in a number of ways.[48] A prominent example arises where the law is required to make an order which is in the best interests of an individual. This occurs when, for example, the law is required to make an order concerning a child or an adult lacking capacity. We can see this in English law, with the well know paramountcy principle in section 1(1) of the Children Act 1989:[49] This states:

When a court determines any question with respect to –

the upbringing of a child; or

the administration of a child's property or the application of any income arising from it,

the child's welfare shall be the court's paramount consideration.

The reference to 'paramount consideration' has been subject to quite some academic debate,[50] but it is generally taken to mean that the courts should focus on the welfare of the child, and not consider the interests of adults.[51] So in a family case if the interests of a parent favour solution A and the interests of a child favour solution B, then solution B must be chosen. Indeed, that seems to be the position even if solution B slightly favours the child but is very harmful to the parent.

However, a growing body of writing challenges this approach. It is impossible to isolate the interests of children from those of their parents in this way. The lives and interests are entwined. I have recommended an approach I labelled relationship-based welfare, which argues that children's best interests can only be understood within the context of the relationships they live in. As care includes emotional care, the well-being

47 V. Held, 'Care and Human Rights', in R. Cruft, M. Liao and M. Renzo (eds.), *Philosophical Foundations of Human Rights* (Oxford: Oxford University Press, 2015).

48 Herring, *Law and the Relational Self.*

49 J. Herring, 'Farewell Welfare' (2005) 27 *Journal of Social Welfare and Family Law* 159–181.

50 J. Herring, 'The Human Rights Act and the Welfare Principle in Family Law – Conflicting or Complementary?' (1999) 11 *Child and Family Law Quarterly* 223–245.

51 J. Eekelaar, 'Beyond the Welfare Principle' (2002) 14 *Child and Family Law Quarterly* 237–252.

of the parent is a vital aspect of that. That involves looking at what has happened in the relationships to date and what will happen in the future. It will acknowledge the care work that has been provided in the past and the value of that care.[52] Even if it was possible to separate the interests of the child, none of us would wish to be raised or cared for in a way that meant every decision was made solely in terms of our welfare. We would not want decisions made that placed enormous burdens on our carers in order to promote our welfare, maybe just the tiniest bit. We would accept that decisions might be made which on a particular occasion were not in our best interests, but which were part of a fair give and take in the relationships. All caring relations involve a complex interplay of dependencies and vulnerabilities. As Fine and Glendinning argue:

> Recent studies of care suggest that qualities of reciprocal dependence underlie much of what is termed 'care'. Rather than being a unidirectional activity in which an active care-giver does something to a passive and dependent recipient, these accounts suggest that care is best understood as the product or outcome of the relationship between two or more people.[53]

So the individualized understanding of the self which is used when the law assesses best interests fails to account for the relational nature of our selves and of our lives. It would be better if each person's needs and rights were considered in the context of their relationships, rather than on the basis of individualized selves. Children should be raised to care, as well as to be cared for.[54]

C. A New Right/Duty to Care

As mentioned earlier, the prominence given to the legal rights of autonomy and privacy reflect assumptions about the nature of the self. An ethics-of-care approach would challenge the traditional legal tools of rights and responsibilities. Ngaire

[52] The failure to take into account care has meant that children's welfare has been used as a justification for diminishing the interests of women and other disadvantaged groups. H. Reece, 'The Paramountcy Principle: Consensus or Construct' (1996) 8 *Current Legal Problems* 267–304.

[53] M. Fine and C. Glendinning, 'Dependence, Independence or Inter-dependence? Revisiting the Concepts of "Care" and "Dependency"' (2005) 25 *Ageing and Society* 601–621 at 616.

[54] J. Herring, 'Children Care', in B. Clough and J. Herring (eds.), *Disability, Care and Family Law* (London: Routledge, 2021).

> Naffine sums up the case for the relational self, saying we should think of human beings as inseparable from their relations. The guiding idea is that we are formed through relations – the mother–child bond provides an obvious one – and that we move through life within, and more importantly as, a great shifting constellation of relations. Within relations we become what we are as persons; here, we must make sense of our lives, which in turn must be understood by scholars who wish to explain us. There is never a full separation between persons, and indeed, human beings draw their very identity from their relations. When they work well, relations are not only formative (and unavoidable) but also conducive to human autonomy and to the flourishing of the individual. It follows that the role of law is to regulate relations rather than to ward them off . Law's job is to ensure that they run smoothly and that they neither oppress nor harm us.[55]

The law's individualized approach starts with individuals and determines what rights they have, while an ethic-of-care approach starts with caring relationships and asks what interventions would promote those relationships. Legal interventions, rights and interests are not designed to protect individuals per se, so much as upholding and maintaining networks of relationships of care. As Tove Pettersen explains, at the heart of most ethical theory is a core value: 'deontology accentuates rights; the theories of justice emphasize justice; and the utilitarian tradition values the society's overall well-being'.[56] For ethics of care the core value is care. It is, therefore, essential to have a sufficient definition of care.

Ethics of care emphasize the importance of responsibilities within caring relationships.[57] Indeed, many care ethicists claim that responsibilities should be the primary ethical tool, with rights playing a subordinate role. The classic liberal perspective is that one is 'born free' and that any responsibilities one takes must be in some sense voluntarily assumed. However, for the ethics-of-care approach, with its starting point being that people are relational, the supposition is that there will be responsibilities for others. We are born into relationships which carry responsibilities. So, the central legal or ethical question on a given issue should not be 'do I have a right to do X?'; the question should be 'what is my proper

[55] N. Naffine, 'The Liberal Legal Individual Accused: The Relational Case' (2014) 29 *Canadian Journal of Law and Society* 123.

[56] T. Pettersen, 'The Ethic of Care: Normative Structures and Empirical Implications' (2011) 54 *Health Care Analysis* 51–73.

[57] S. Collins, *The Core of Care Ethics* (Basingstoke: Palgrave, 2015).

obligation within the context of this relationship?'[58] Under this vision, rights primarily exist to enable people to carry out their responsibilities.[59] And the role of the law should primarily be to encourage and enable people to fulfil their responsibilities to each other, rather than enforce their rights. This is not to say that rights are unimportant. Rather it is to recognize their proper role: to enable us to exercise our responsibilities; rather than to protect our individual interests. Hence it is valuable to recognize, for example, a right to care, which entitles a person to legal claims from the state and others to enable them to meet their caring responsibilities.

Having considered some of the wider issues around the caring self, I will consider two particular issues. The first is the issue of parenthood and the second is work–life balance.

5. Parental Status and Parental Rights

An understanding of the caring self has much to teach us about the nature of parenthood in law and in practice.

A. Parenthood in Law

In this discussion, the law in England will be used, although the issues discussed are raised in all jurisdictions. The legal determination of who is the parent of a child is significant because parenthood is a status with legal and social significance. Parenthood in English law has traditionally been understood in biological terms. In simple terms the father is the man whose sperm produced the child; and the mother is the woman whose egg did. Prior to the advent of DNA and other biological testing, presumptions were used as to who was the biological parent (e.g. that the woman who gave birth to the child was the mother and that the husband of the woman who gave birth was the biological father). In effect, this gave a special privilege to marriage. It was hard to rebut the presumption of parenthood for husbands (in effect it would need to be shown the husband was living away from the wife at the time of the conception). Unmarried partners

[58] Held, *The Ethics of Care.*

[59] J. Herring, 'Compassion, Ethic of Care and Legal Rights' (2017) 13 *International Journal of Law in Context* 158–178.

were not presumed to be parents, although they could seek to prove paternity (typically by demonstrating they stayed overnight with the mother at the time of the conception). Although the presumption in effect privileged marriage, officially it was the biological link that was key, rather than marital status per se. That was made clear by the fact that the language of presumption was used in relation to husbands and the fact the courts were willing to rebut that presumption when there was sufficient evidence to do so. This marked out the position in England from other jurisdictions, such as France, where it was the marital relationship itself which bestowed parenthood on the husband. The French approach does seem to portray a particularly patriarchal assumption about marriage: that the father could claim 'ownership' over all the family 'assets'.

The use of the presumptions are still very much part of English law, although the advent of DNA testing has made it easier to determine biological truth, rather than relying on presumptions of genetic connection, as the law used to do. Technology has also meant that the law has departed from the biological model of parenthood in some cases, most notably in cases of assisted reproduction. Hence under the Human Fertilisation and Embryology Acts 1990 and 2008, egg and sperm donors are not treated as parents of a child, despite the biological link, and partners of the mother can be treated as parents, even without a genetic link. However these are seen as exceptions to the general rule,[60] which emphasizes the importance of the genetic link.[61]

I would argue that the emphasis on biology or marriage as the marker of parenthood is misconceived. Caring for a child should generate the privileged parental position, not a mere biological connection. The allocation of parenthood is a fine example of how the caring self and women's labour is side-lined in favour of a property-based or status-based approach.

Returning to the argument that parenthood should be allocated on the basis of a caring relationship, Judith Masson helpfully distinguishes parenting by doing and parenting by being.[62] She explains: 'Parenting by doing acknowledges the reality of looking after children by recognising

[60] *AB* v. *Leeds Teaching Hospitals NHS Trust* [2003] EWHC 1034.

[61] For more detail on the legal allocation of parenthood see A. Margaria, *The Construction of Fatherhood* (Cambridge: Cambridge University Press, 2019), ch. 1.

[62] An interesting link might be made with the reasoning of Boltanski that a foetus acquires legal status through the will of the mother, rather than biology. L. Boltanski, *The Foetal Condition* (Bristol: Polity Press, 2013).

adult–child relationships. Parenting by being reflects a wish to identify for the child and the state people with responsibility for the child, regardless of the practical role they are playing or want to play in the child's life.'[63] Parental status on this view should be earned by the care of and dedication to the child, something not shown simply by a biological link. It is the changing of the nappy; the wiping of the tear; and the working out of maths together that makes a parent, not the provision of an egg or sperm. It is an approach which recognizes and foregrounds the value of care. I suggest several reasons why this is the correct approach for the law to take.

First, we should give parental status to the person who is best placed to meet the responsibilities and use the rights of being a parent. In other words, the person who it would be in best interests of the child to be described as parent. That will be the person who knows the child best; the person who is caring for the child day to day. This explains also why it might make sense for a genetic father to be obliged to pay child support (that will benefit the child), but not to be given the parental authority to make decisions concerning the child (if he does not know the child well, the father making decisions will not benefit the child)

Second, parenthood is a responsibility that should be earned. A blood tie may be no more than a brief sexual encounter and is an insufficient basis for asserting claims over a child.[64] As Barbara Bennett Woodhouse claims, there is a danger that the law is 'intent on securing children for adults who claim them' rather than 'seeking to provide adults for children who need them'.[65]

Third, it is desirable for the legal definition of parenthood to match the child's understanding of who their parents is. This is likely to be the person who is carrying out the parental role in the child's life. This is particularly important in relation to disputes over custody. In many jurisdictions in recent years there has been a move towards 'joint custody', where a child

[63] J. Masson, 'Parenting by Being; Parenting by Doing – In Search of Principles for Founding Families', in J. Spencer and A. du Bois-Pedain (eds.), *Freedom and Responsibility in Reproductive Choice* (Oxford: Hart, 2006).

[64] J. Wallbank, '(En)Gendering the Fusion of Rights and Responsibilities in the Law of Contact', in J. Wallbank, S. Choudhry and J. Herring (eds.), *Rights, Gender and Family Law* (Abingdon: Routledge, 2009).

[65] B. Bennett Woodhouse, 'Hatching the Egg: A Child-Centered Perspective on Parents' Rights' (1993) 14 *Cardozo Law Review* 1747–1820 at 1814.

spends an equal amount of time with both parents after divorce. The evidence suggests that this can be an effective response where a child has been equally raised by parents before the separation, its use in cases where, typically, the mother has been the primary carer, can fail to recognize the care work of the mother and the role she has played in the child's life.

Fourth, the current approach of the English law is based on the heterosexual married model. The requirement that a child has one father and one mother reinforces that as a norm for parenthood. A good example of this is that under the Human Fertilisation and Embryology Act 1990 when a woman attends a clinic and becomes pregnant using donated sperm, if she has a male partner he will be recognized as the father, but if she has a female partner, the partner will be recognized as a 'second parent'. This strikingly demonstrates the difficulty the law has with a child having, for example, two mothers. As we depart from the assumption that the traditional heterosexual model is the primary game in town and focus on the caring relationships with the child, new vistas of what it means to be a parent are opened up.[66] It means there is no problem in recognizing that in a same-sex relationship a child can have two mothers or two fathers, both of equal standing; something impossible if biology is emphasized. We can also start to recognize the network of people that can play a role in a child's life. This includes recognition of the extent to which children care for other children.

So, an understanding of the caring self reveals that our understanding of parenthood should shift from focusing on blood ties to focusing on the caring relationship between child and adult. Rights should flow from the relationship with the child, not the blood tie. As a result, we should move away from the idea that a child can have only one parent. Further, in terms of legal rights, a range of adults might, depending on the context of their particular relationship, have a say in certain areas of the child's life. But the extent and nature of those rights will depend on the relationship.

B. Parenthood in Practice

At the heart of law governing parenting is the idea of 'parental responsibility': the duty on parents to promote the well-being of children.

[66] F. Kelly, *Transforming Law's Family: The Legal Recognition of Planned Lesbian Families* (Vancouver: University of British Columbia Press, 2011).

However, according to many voices in the media we are experiencing a 'crisis in parenting' and it is mothers who bear the brunt of this. In her book *The Parent Trap*, Maureen Freely argues that parents are now terrified that they are failing in their responsibilities to their children:

> Never have the odds against good-enough parenting been greater. The standards of performance are rising, just as more mothers are being pushed into work. The definitions of neglect and abuse are growing, and now extend to include cohabitation and marriage breakdown. In the present climate, to speak in public as a good-enough parent is to invite someone else to point out how abysmally we've failed. . . . This makes us an insecure and biddable constituency, quick to apologise for our faults and slow to point out where our masters could do better, and the government has taken advantage of our weaknesses to consolidate its power.[67]

This bleak picture of parenthood is reinforced by talk of a 'crisis of childhood', with children portrayed as being robbed of their childhood through a range of harmful changes, from which parents should protect their children, be that dangers on the internet or body image issues or obesity. Because women undertake the bulk of childcare it is on mothers that these burden fall and has impacted on women's careers and well-being. As the UK parliamentary briefing explained, although there have been improvements, women still undertake the bulk of childcare: 'In 1961 the amount of time fathers spent caring for pre-schoolers was 12 to 15 per cent of the time spent doing so by mothers; by 2017 it was almost half, meaning that for every hour a mother devotes to caring for a young child a father now devotes, on average, 30 minutes.'[68]

It is not just because women undertake the bulk of childcare that these protective burdens fall on mothers, but also because of the assumptions that mothers are naturally caregivers, with the mother–child bond being elevated as sacrosanct to the well-being of the child.[69] This has led to mothers being unfairly blamed for the challenges children face. As Linda Fentiman explains:

> During the past three decades there has been a growing emphasis – by doctors, the media, government officials, and prosecutors – on the 'risks' that mothers pose to

67 M. Freely, *The Parent Trap* (London: Virago, 2000), 13, 201.

68 Women and Equality Committee, *Fathers and the Workplace* (London: Hansard, 2018).

69 C. McGlynn, *Families and the European Union: Law, Policy and Pluralism* (Cambridge: Cambridge University Press, 2006), 23.

their children's health. Mothers – and pregnant women – are increasingly seen as exclusively responsible for all aspects of the children's health and well-being. At the same time, the enormous impact of poverty, genetics, environmental toxins, fathers, government and private institutions on children's health is largely ignored.[70]

This emphasis on the responsibility for parents (in effect mothers) for the behaviour of children has been reflected in the law. This is most obvious in the removal of children into state care where parents are deemed inadequate. Further, increasingly, authoritarian measures have been used against parents who were seen to be causing anti-social and criminal behaviour by not supplying sufficient levels of parenthood.[71] A good example from England is Parenting Orders (Magistrates' Courts (Parenting Orders) Rules 2004,[72] which allowed magistrates to require parents to sign parenting contracts, parenting programmes, or even to attend a residential parenting course. And it is typically mothers, and especially working class mothers, who bear the brunt of this responsibility.

This has all contributed to mothers feeling that responsible parenting involves acquiring and following the advice of experts.[73] Hence we have hyper-parenting where parents are going to excessive lengths to make the child the best possible child. Alvin Rosenfeld and Nicole Wise explain: 'This is happening because many contemporary parents see a parent's fundamental job as designing a perfect upbringing for their offspring, from conception to college. . . . That is why the most competitive adult sport is no longer golf. It is parenting.'[74] This is a harmful image of parenting, which reduces it to the doing of work or the performance of tasks. It means the child is too readily seen as the product of parental labour.[75] Indeed, it can mean that

[70] L. Fentiman, *Blaming Mothers* (New York: New York University Press, 2017), 3.

[71] V. Gillies, 'From Function to Competence: Engaging with the New Politics of Family' (2011) 16 *Sociological Research* 11–32. These arose in the context of a set of legal interventions designed to tackle 'anti-social behaviour', most infamously the 'anti-social behaviour order'. Anti-Social Behaviour, Crime and Policing Act 2014.

[72] Statutory Instrument 2004 No. 247.

[73] F. Furedi, 'It's Time to Expel the "Experts" from Family Life', *Spiked*, 12 September 2011, www.spiked-online.com/newsite/article/11067#.Vqg1liorLIU.

[74] A. Rosenfeld and N. Wise, *The Over-Scheduled Child: Avoiding the Hyper-Parenting Trap* (London: St Martin's Press, 2001).

[75] J. Herring, 'Vulnerability and Medical Decisions Concerning Children', in I. Goold, C. Auckland and J. Herring (eds.), *Parental Rights, Best Interests and Significant Harms* (Oxford: Hart, 2019), which is drawn on in this section.

mothers will constantly fail as the expectations over extra classes and lessons constantly increase, and the dangers, be it of diet, online material or self-harm, are seen to increase.

The model of parenthood is based on a premise that adults/parents are competent, self-sufficient and independent; while children are dependent, passive and require the support of parents for survival. It downplays the concept of childhood agency or responsibility is lost. The powerlessness of parenthood gets no look-in. It fails to recognize that parenting is about relationships. Children care, mould, control, discipline and cajole their parents, just as parents do their children. The misdeed of a parent seeking to engineer or hyper-parent their child is not just that the parent is seeking to impose a particular view of what is a good life on their child, although that is wrong. It is the error of failing to be open to change as an adult; failing to learn from children, failing to see that the things you thought were important are, in fact, not. It is failing to find the wonder, fear, loneliness, anxiety, spontaneity and joy of children, and to refine them for oneself.

The model of the parent who must ensure their child receives all possible advantages, and is constantly protected from any danger, reinforced by the law, is one that is overbearing, and falls primarily on mothers. It is a model that fails to recognize the mutually caring relationship between parent and child, and reduces it to tasks that can be monitored and measured.

6. Work–Life Balance

Many people find it a constant struggle to find a balance between work and family life, with family life suffering due to the demands of work, or career progression delayed when someone decides to focus on family responsibilities. Due to the unequal distribution of care work, this is a particular issue for women.[76] These issues are made all the harder for the 'sandwich generation' – a term used to refer to those who are caring for

[76] K. Backett-Milburn, L. Airey, L. McKie and G. Hogg, 'Family Comes First or Open All Hours? How Low Paid Women Working in Food Retailing Manage Webs of Obligation at Home and Work' (2008) 56 *Sociological Review* 474–493.

their children and parents at the same time.[77] It is not just a case of balancing work and care; it can be about balancing work and care and more care. With increasing hours of employment, a precarious job market and an intensification of what is expected of parents,[78] it is no wonder people find the balance impossible.

Fiona Williams provides a useful set of tools to start thinking about the key themes:

> Rather than care needs being fitted in to the traditional requirements of work, we can map people's work/life needs within three different but connected areas of their lives. First, there is personal time and space: what do we need for the care of self and maintenance of body, mind and soul (e.g. mobility/relationships/relaxation/life-long learning/spirituality)? Second, care time and space: what do we need to care properly for others? This would include, for example, child care and adult care provision; home care services; cleaning, laundry and food services; domiciliary services; kite marking for services; raising standards and reward for paid carers; direct payments for people receiving care/support; carer credits to protect pensions; state support for residential care costs. These would be underpinned by principles of accessibility, affordability, variety, choice, quality, flexibility and user control; they would be complemented by the removal of disabling barriers around space, time, organisations and the environment and a commitment to a caring, enabling environment – e.g. safe and accessible public spaces; safe, accessible, affordable transport. Third, there is work time and space: what do we need to enable us to gain economic self-sufficiency and balance these other areas? Included here are paid maternity and paternity leave; paid carers' leave for women and men; job-sharing; annualised hours/lifetime hours; work-based nurseries/breakfast clubs/holiday clubs; sabbaticals; part-time/flexible hours; shorter full-time hours; decent universal pensions with added protection for poorer and older pensioners.[79]

For all too many at the moment, it is the third category that takes up the energy.[80] Williams is right to list this as the third factor. But we need a lot

[77] E. Grundy and J. Henretta, 'Between Elderly Parents and Adult Children: A New Look at the Intergenerational Care Provided by the "Sandwich Generation"' (2006) 26 *Ageing and Society* 707–727. For further discussion, see R. Burke and L. Calvano, *The Sandwich Generation* (London: Edward Elgar, 2017).

[78] S. Hays, *The Cultural Contradictions of Motherhood* (New Haven, CT: Yale University Press, 2011).

[79] F. Williams, 'In and Beyond New Labour: Towards a New Political Ethics of Care' (2001) 21 *Critical Social Policy* 467–493 at 467.

[80] M. Daly, 'What Adult Worker Model? A Critical Look at Recent Social Policy Reform in Europe from a Gender and Family Perspective' (2011) 21 *Social Policy* 1–23.

of work on our current structures of employment practice and law to enable that to happen. They still seem stuck on the 'male breadwinner model' with the employee expected to have a partner at home meeting care needs and supporting their employment.

Media images when discussing the work/life balance typically portray a woman in a smart business suit, dropping off a child at childcare. This is far from the norm. More common are women seeking to combine childcare with low-paid, low-quality jobs[81] where earnings are largely used in paying for childcare.[82] In the United Kingdom, part-time workers earn 64 per cent of full-time male wage rates.[83]

Joan Williams has highlighted the concept of Family Responsibilities Discrimination (FRD). She has explained:

> FRD is discrimination against employees based on their responsibilities to care for family members. It includes pregnancy discrimination, discrimination against mothers and fathers, and discrimination against workers with other family care-giving responsibilities. While FRD most commonly occurs against pregnant women and mothers of young children, it can also affect fathers who wish to take on more than a nominal role in family caregiving and employees who care for aging parents or ill or disabled partners.[84]

As she emphasizes, those who perform care work, particularly care work which is outside the standard heterosexual married family unit, are severely disadvantaged in the workplace. FRD has the disadvantage of exerting strong pressure, perhaps especially on men, not to undertake significant degrees of care work, reinforcing the norm of the 'ideal' worker who is not encumbered by 'outside' responsibilities and is 'single-minded' in their devotion to their employer.[85] Those undertaking care, normally

[81] M. Selmi and N. Cahn, 'Women in the Workplace: Which Women, Which Agenda?' (2006) 13 *Duke Journal of Constitutional Law & Public Policy* 7–31.

[82] P. Barth, *Social Exclusion of Family Carers in Different Welfare State Regimes: A Comparison between Germany and Sweden* (Berlin: Grin, 2012).

[83] S. Himmelweit and H. Land, *Reducing Gender Inequalities to Create a Sustainable Care* (York: Joseph Rowntree Foundation, 2008).

[84] J. C. Williams and S. Bornstein, 'Evolution of "FReD": Family Responsibilities Discrimination and Developments in the Law of Stereotyping and Implicit Bias' (2008) 59 *Hastings Law Journal* 1311–1389.

[85] L. Trimble O'Connor and E. Cech, 'Not Just a Mothers' Problem: The Consequences of Perceived Workplace Flexibility Bias for All Workers' (2018) 61 *Sociological Perspectives* 808–829.

women, are 'mommy-tracked'[86] into less demanding roles within the workplace and denied promotion, reflecting the perception they are less committed to their jobs.

However, removing FRD will be of limited benefit unless there is equal sharing of childcare and other domestic work. As Alice Margaria writes: 'To achieve a good work–family balance, the goal of equal participation of women in paid employment needs to be tied to equal participation of men in the home.'[87] There are tools available to assist those struggling with balancing these pressures.[88] The EU has, for example, produced policy documents seeking to improve the provision of childcare.[89] The use of tax credits[90] has slightly improved the position of those in low-paid part-time jobs, making them a little more financially worthwhile. The Working Time Directive goes some way towards tackling the long-hours culture in employment.[91] These might make it easier for someone to combine employment and care. But the sums of money available is highly limited. However, to some extent these measures are seeking to mitigate the disadvantages of, rather than challenge, the 'ideal worker' image, which pressurizes couples into prioritizing the career of one of the partners (who can remain an 'ideal worker'), while the career of the other takes a hit.

A key moment in work/family balance arises around the birth of a child. Decisions made at this time about care of the child and careers can have consequences for the rest of the couple's lives. Most countries recognize this by granting parental leave, designed to enable a parent to take up short-term care of the new-born, while retaining their job. Traditionally the laws granting leave have been gendered with the focus on 'maternity leave' and no, or more limited paternity leave. This reflects the assumption

[86] Ibid.

[87] A. Margaria, '"New Fathers" and the Right to Parental Leave', in R. Harding, R. Fletcher and C. Beasley (eds.), *Revaluing Care in Theory, Law and Policy* (London: Routledge, 2019).

[88] J. Heymann, 'Can Working Families Ever Win?' (1 February 2002) *Boston Review*, https://bostonreview.net/forum/jody-heymann-can-working-families-ever-win.

[89] Council Recommendation 92/241/EEC 31 March 1992 on childcare, OJ 1992 No. L123/16; European Commission Recommendation 2013/112/EU 20 February 2013, Investing in children: Breaking the Cycle of Disadvantage, OJ 2013 No. L59/5.

[90] Tax credits in the United Kingdom are a form of welfare payment or deduction of taxes normally given to those on low wages. J. Wiggan, 'Managing Time: The Integration of Caring and Paid Work by Low-Income Families and the Role of the UK's Tax Credit System' (2010) 36 *Policy Studies* 631–651.

[91] OJ 1993 No. L307/18.

that the bulk of childcare will be undertaken by women. Many states now offer parental leave that can be taken up by either parent. In *C. D.* v. *S. T.*,[92] and *Z.* v. *A Government Department*,[93] the European Court of Justice held that EU law does not require the payments due under maternity or adoption leave to be paid to a mother who has received a child under a surrogacy arrangement. The court linked maternity leave to having gone through with a pregnancy, rather than recognizing the burden of care for a new-born. The links with adoption leave appeared even stronger, but in this case the applicant had not adopted the child. This seems to limit the recognition of care to cases where there is a legally recognized bond between the child and the parent.

Broadly across Europe parental leave can be divided into four different models:

- Maternity leave: a job-protected period of leave restricted to employed mothers; particularly focused on the time around childbirth, which typically comes with income support.
- Paternity leave: A job-protected period of leave restricted to employed fathers. This is often for a shorter period of time, and is sometimes accompanied by a form of income support.
- Parental leave: a job-protected period of leave which can be taken by either parent.
- Home-care leave: this is a period of leave normally granted after parental leave, enabling a parent to provide care at home, often until the child is two or three years old.

These period of leave are normally backed up by a form of income support, which can come from employers, the state or a combination of the two. Some seek to match incomes earned during employment, although often they are lower.

Across Europe, the take-up of parental leave by fathers is low. Research suggests that gender norms, concerns about the impact on their reputation at work, lack of flexibility in the workplace, and the lack of compensation are all linked to the low take-up by fathers.[94] One study found that where

[92] Case 167/12, [*C. D.* v. *S. T*] [2014] EUECJ C-167/12.

[93] Case 363/12, [*Z.* v. *A Government Department*] [2014] EUECJ C-363/12.

[94] Eurofound, *Promoting Uptake of Parental and Paternity Leave among Fathers in the European Union* (Luxembourg: Publications Office of the European Union, 2019).

the leave can be taken by either parent, only 2 per cent of men take the leave.[95] It is notable that some jurisdictions (e.g. Iceland) have gone so far as to require couples to share parental leave (or not to use it) in an attempt to increase uptake.[96] But in the majority of European countries, where the use of parental leave is heavily gendered, this has significant impact on women's employment. There can be a significant impact on women's career progression where leave of more than one year is taken.[97] The failure to share parental leave means that it is more likely that women will take a longer period of leave and the negative assumptions around taking parental leave are perpetuated.

The EU Work–Life Balance Directive (EU) 2019/1158 was passed in 2019 in an attempt to tackles these issues. In Recital 11 it is acknowledged that the 'current Union legal framework provides limited incentives for men to assume an equal share of caring responsibilities' and that the 'lack of paid paternity and parental leave in many Member States contributes to the low take-up of leave by fathers'. The directive was passed with the following aims:

- better supporting a work–life balance for parents and carers,
- encouraging a more equal sharing of parental leave between men and women, and
- addressing women's underrepresentation in the labour market.[98]

The directive requires that fathers be given at least ten working days of paternity leave, compensated at minimally the level of sick pay, and ensuring four months parental leave, of which two months cannot be transferred between parents. The potential significance of this reform is limited by the fact that the level of income granted during parental leave is to be determined by member states. Without a good level of income, take-up is likely to be low. The directive also requires the introduction of five days' leave per year for carers to provide personal care or support to a

[95] C. Miani and S. Hoorens, *Single Parents and Employment in Europe* (Brussels: European Commission, 2014).

[96] J. van Belle, *Paternity and Parental Leave Policies across the European Union* (Santa Monica, CA: Rand, 2016).

[97] O. Thévenon and A. Solaz, 'Labour Market Effects of Parental Leave Policies in OECD Countries' (2013) 141 *OECD Social, Employment and Migration Working Papers* 1–67.

[98] EU Work–Life Balance Directive (EU) 2019/1158 (on work–life balance for parents and carers), OJ 2019 No. [1158].

relative, although it comes with no right to income support. Again, take-up of this potentially helpful provision will be low if few people can afford it. There is also the 'right to request flexible working arrangements' for carers and working parents of children up to eight years old, although a right *to request* flexible arrangements are far weaker than a right *to* flexible arrangements. A further concern is that:

> [P]arental rights are still premised on the assumption of a two-adult family, as they are limited to caring relationships resembling the nuclear family. Indeed, the Directive does not take into consideration the needs of other families, such as single parents, reconstituted families or extended families, which could benefit from measures providing for longer leave or the ability to choose a person with whom care responsibilities may be shared.[99]

One of the difficulties that governments can face in producing regulation on this area is that a complex range of policies can conflict. In some countries, child welfare arguments are used on the assumption that it is better for a child in early life to be cared for by a parent – some might believe specifically a mother – rather than using childcare. There may be concerns about the impact of parental leave on the job market, particularly the financial burden for employers of the cost of parental leave and concerns that employers may be reluctant to employ people they believe will take parental leave. There are also demographic issues: whether the state wishes to encourage or discourage births. In considering these competing arguments, much depends on whether the promotion of gender equality is given sufficient priority to overcome these concerns.

Perhaps the overarching problem with these legal interventions is that the EU interventions have been largely 'ad hoc'.[100] There is a failure to develop an overarching policy towards care. As Eugenia Caracciolo di Torella and Annick Masselot write, what we need is

> for the EU to take leadership in this area; to place care firmly on the agenda and ultimately to devise a policy and normative framework. This can only be done by promoting and valuing the caring relationship, by adopting a more proactive

[99] E. Chieregato, 'A Work–Life Balance for All? Assessing the Inclusiveness of EU Directive 2019/1158' (2020) 36 *International Journal of Comparative Labour Law and Industrial Relations* 59–80.

[100] Caracciolo di Torella and Masselot, *Caring Responsibilities in European Law and Policy*, 3.

approach to rebalancing the relationship between paid and unpaid work for carers, and by protecting carers against discrimination and unfavourable treatment at work.[101]

The strong hold of the 'male breadwinner model' on employment structures and law, and the increase in entry of women into employment, has caused the 'global care chain'.[102] This concept, introduced by Arlie Hochschild, describes how dual-earning families in the West sought to make up for childcare difficulties by finding carers from developing countries.[103] Sometimes these women themselves hired women to care for their own children. Hochschild suggested that this created 'a series of personal links between people across the globe based on the paid or unpaid work of caring'.[104] With her co-authors she explains:

> A Sri Lankan nanny may leave her children in the care of her sister and a nanny in Colombo, for example, and take up the paid care of twin sons of an upper-middle-class couple in Los Angeles, the wife of whom gives, as a personnel officer, her 'care' to a multinational company. Meanwhile, the second nanny (who may come from a rural village outside Colombo) may leave her youngest children in the care of her 15-year-old daughter and leave a sickly mother in the care of a neighbor.[105]

She describes how the care deficit in developed countries is not resolved by better sharing of care between men and women, but by turning to women in developing countries to take on that role, often itself creating a care deficit in her family. The existence of these care chains lays bare the paucity of the 'male breadwinner model' of employment, which only operates in dual employment families by buying in a 'wife' for the couple. It also reveals that care is a scarce resource and the extent to which burdens of caring go unrecognized. Of course, the 'care chain' model must not be used in a simplified way, ignoring the fact that not all domestic migrant carers are mothers or even women; and can operate in a variety of

101 Ibid., 3.

102 N. Yeates, *Globalizing Care Economies and Migrant Workers: Explorations in Global Care Chains* (Basingstoke: Palgrave MacMillan, 2009).

103 P. Nadasen, 'Rethinking Care: Arlie Hochschild and the Global Care Chain' (2017) 45 *Women's Studies Quarterly* 124–128.

104 A. Hochschild, 'Global Care Chains and Emotional Surplus: Rethinking Care Values', in W. Hutton and A. Giddens (eds.), *On The Edge: Living with Global Capitalism* (London: Jonathan Cape, 2000), 131.

105 L. Widding Isaksen, S. Uma Devi and A. Russell Hochschild, 'Global Care Crisis a Problem of Capital, Care Chain, or Commons?' (2008) 52 *American Behavioral Scientist* 405–425.

forms of relationship. Nevertheless, one of the impacts of this care market is to reinforce the rhetoric of women as 'natural carers'. As Ethel Tungohan notes. 'exporting female care' uses 'stereotypes on female "docility" and female "compliance" to market their nationals to prospective employers abroad; [and] concurrently used rhetoric concerning female sacrifice and piety to encourage the labour migration of women'.[106]

7. Conclusion

We are vulnerable, interdependent individuals, whose strength and reality are not in our autonomy, but in our relationships with others. Caring is essential for our own individual well-being and flourishing of society. Caring provides joy, value and meaning for life. However, the law and public policy de-emphasizes care. It is undervalued and little acknowledged. Most carers receive no financial compensation and bear the economic costs alone. Those who are in employment generally receive the minimum wage. It is women who by and large lose out as a result.

The law is based on an image of the independent, self-sufficient man and arms him with rights designed to protect his so-called freedom. Many feminists have called for a rethinking of this approach. Currently the law's image of the self fails women. As Jennifer Nedelsky explains:

> The selves to be protected by rights are seen as essentially separate and not creatures whose interests, needs, and capacities are mutually constitutive. Thus, for example, one of the reasons women have always fit so poorly into the framework of liberal theory is that it becomes obviously awkward to think of women's relation to their children as essentially one of competing interests to be mediated by rights.[107]

We need a legal system that starts with a norm of interlocking mutually dependent relationships, rather than an individualized vision of rights. Legal interventions should not be designed to protect individuals per se, so much as upholding and maintaining networks of caring

[106] E. Tungohan, 'Reconceptualizing Motherhood, Reconceptualizing Resistance' (2013) 15 *International Feminist Journal of Politics* 39–51.

[107] J. Nedelsky, *Law's Relations* (Oxford: Oxford University Press, 2008), 15.

relationships. Rather than the law promoting people's freedom from responsibility, the focus should be on how the law can enable people to fulfil their responsibilities. Instead, we need to centre caring relationships at the heart of the law. It is in and through care that our selves are created. It is in and through care that our lives flourish.

Part III

Communities

The National Subject 8

Melany Toombs and Kim Rubenstein

1. Introduction

This chapter affirms the feminist impetus of this collection by reflecting on power relations in society and their impact on law and law's regulation. An acute site for this inquiry is in the state itself, and the state's determination of its own membership. It is the thesis of this chapter that the national subject, the legal citizen,[1] is a space in which gender, sexuality and race keenly interact with the everyday lives of individuals. An appreciation of this point is often overlooked. While the language of citizenship is often gender neutral, it often 'perpetuat[es] the invisibility of women' as citizens.[2] Margaret Thornton examines the civil status of women as citizens in the early years of the twentieth century to 'illustrate the peripheral civil status of women as citizens' and, therefore, questions the full membership consequences of citizenship.[3]

Whether or not the state bestows upon an individual the formal legal status of citizen, and enables the person to become a 'legal subject', reflects normative orders of gender, race and law. Citizenship legally identifies who is 'in' or 'out' of the political community and the consequences of being in or out are significant. This chapter highlights how the granting and withdrawing of citizenship by the state is shaped by power relations reflecting norms and attributes identified by the state as desirable. These include a subject born in the state, who has connection to the territory and,

[1] The term 'citizen' is mostly used in domestic contexts and 'national' generally directs us to the international context. Here we refer to 'citizens' to capture all who are identified as legal subjects of the state.

[2] L. Ackers, 'Women, Citizenship and European Community Law: The Gender Implications of the Free Movement Provisions' (1994) 11 *Journal of Social Welfare & Family Law* 391–406 at 392.

[3] M. Thornton, 'Embodying the Citizen', in M. Thornton (ed.), *Public and Private: Feminist Legal Debates* (Oxford: Oxford University Press, 1995), 198.

for newcomers, conforms to the cultural and moral norms of the governing populace.

A vast swathe of theory has identified and critiqued what citizenship represents. Bosniak's *Citizenship Denationalised* sets out citizenship as four disparate concepts: 'citizenship as a legal status', 'citizenship as a system of rights', 'citizenship as a form of political activity' and 'citizenship as a form of identity and solidarity'.[4] The state uses citizenship for the regulation of membership within this political community, as identification allows the state to regulate rights and benefits given to those members.[5] For Marshall,[6] citizenship is a 'status bestowed on those who are full members of a community' and is endowed with 'rights and duties'.[7] Alternatively, Waters encapsulates citizenship as a 'set of normative expectations specifying the relationship between the nation-state and its individual members' which also establish members' rights and obligations.[8] While not discussed here, citizenship has demonstrable benefits, often relating to presence within a territory, protection by the state, suffrage and social and economic rights.[9]

As such, citizenship and its legal status are central to the 'politics of belonging', or the politics of who belongs and 'who is to be excluded'.[10] The absence of a transnational uniform approach to deciding citizenship

[4] L. Bosniak, 'Citizenship Denationalized' (2000) 7 *Indiana Journal of Global Legal Studies* 447–509. Turner identifies four types of citizenship, based on the 'active' or 'passive' development of citizenship and the relation of private and public sectors within civil society. B. S. Turner, 'Outline of a Theory of Citizenship' (1990) 24 *Sociology (Oxford)* 189–217.

[5] S. H. Legomsky, 'Why Citizenship?' (1994) 35 *Virginia Journal of International Law* 279–300.

[6] Owen's concept of 'civic marginalisation' examines migrant access to national citizenship, rights and duties of the national citizen and the state's duties to the citizen.

[7] T. H. Marshall, 'Citizenship and Social Class', in D. Held (ed.), *States and Societies* (Oxford: Basil Blackwell, [1950] 1983), 253; D. Owen, 'Citizenship and the Marginalities of Migrants' (2013) 16 *Critical Review of International Social and Political Philosophy* 326–343.

[8] M. Waters, 'Citizenship and the Constitution of a Structured Social Inequality' (1989) 30 *International Journal of Comparative Sociology* 159–180 at 160.

[9] J. Shaw, *The People in Question: Citizens and Constitutions in Uncertain Times* (Bristol: Bristol University Press, 2020), 152.

[10] N. Yuval-Davis, 'Belonging and the Politics of Belonging' (2006) 40 *Patterns of Prejudice* 197–214 at 205; L. Morrice, 'British Citizenship, Gender and Migration: The Containment of Cultural Differences and the Stratification of Belonging' (2017) 38 *British Journal of Sociology of Education* 597–609 at 597.

acquisition and removal indicates the involvement of differing normative expectations about what a 'desirable' citizen looks like. Extensive literature documents the existence and salience of normative frameworks, which are societal expectations of behaviour or beliefs that can shape, be refined by or be opposed to existing laws.[11] While laws introduce their own norms, they take place in a context of existing social norms and expectations of what citizenship law aims to achieve.[12] The ideal of citizenship aims to afford everyone equality and dignity.[13] However, citizenship models rely on a distinction between individuals who have sufficient qualities to secure their standing as fully fledged community members and those who do not.[14]

Law delineates the prerequisites to achieving the status of citizen. While there has been some denial of the normative force of the law, significant theory canvasses the way that legal structures and legislation construct and enact ideas about the world.[15] Law is used by the state to act as a regulator of membership and determines who is entitled to membership. We adopt Slawner's aphorism that 'legal definitions of citizenship always incorporate what is considered to be desirable activity'.[16] As Young argues, the public law of gender is 'constituted, legislated and regulated'.[17] In synthesizing the insights of Fraser and Honneth,[18] Young tracks the manner in which law creates harms (for example, to gender justice) through its processes of 'recognition, redistribution and representation'

[11] T. R. Tyler, *Why People Obey the Law* (New Haven, CT: Yale University Press, 1990); E. Carbonara, 'Law and Social Norms', in F. Parisi (ed.), *The Oxford Handbook of Law and Economics*, 1st ed. (Oxford: Oxford University Press, 2017); E. A. Posner, *Law and Social Norms* (Cambridge, MA: Harvard University Press, 2000).

[12] Carbonara, 'Law and Social Norms'.

[13] A. Green, 'Three Models of Political Membership: Delineating "The People in Question"' (2020) 41(2) *Oxford Journal of Legal Studies* 565–583.

[14] Ibid., at 9; Shaw, *The People in Question*, 155.

[15] K. Young, 'Introduction: A Public Law of Gender?', in K. Rubenstein and K. Young (eds.), *The Public Law of Gender: From the Local to the Global* (Cambridge: Cambridge University Press, 2016), 5; J. K. Cogan, 'Noncompliance and the International Rule of Law' (2006) 31 *Yale Journal of International Law* 189–210; R. E. Scott, 'The Limits of Behavioral Theories of Law and Social Norms' (2000) 86 *Virginia Law Review* 1603–1647.

[16] K. Slawner, 'Uncivil Society: Liberalism, Hermeneutics, and "Good Citizenship"', in K. Slawner and M. E. Denham (eds.), *Citizenship after Liberalism* (New York: Peter York, 1998), 83.

[17] Young, 'Introduction: A Public Law of Gender?', 1.

[18] N. Fraser and A. Honneth, *Redistribution or Recognition? A Political-Philosophical Exchange* (London: Verso, 2003).

across multiple levels of society.[19] While the reasons for the absence of gender equality are complex, law 'continues to constitute, or insulate' various gender-based harms such as 'sexual violence, insecurity, and poverty'.[20]

Legal structures reproduce norms relating to gender and race, for example through the utilization of distinct legal categories. Different types of laws deal with citizenship, including citizenship acquisition laws, international family law, statelessness case law, different countries' responses to terrorist offences and citizenship removal laws. Williams and Shaw examine the norms, identities and politics that are espoused by states' constitutions.[21] Institutions including the United Nations also enshrine the normative orders of gender and law in international relations and procedure.[22] Ultimately, we write this chapter conscious of how 'law is normative, prescriptive, and it demands justification'.[23]

Inside the normative frameworks espoused by law are the normative frameworks of gender, which similarly inform what is considered a desirable national subject. More specifically, gendered expectations shape what is required of a person to be given citizenship and avoid citizenship removal. As Young articulates, gender is a powerful force that, while 'based on perceived differences between the sexes . . . has served to organise social relations' in a range of ways worldwide.[24]

What is considered desirable in a national subject is highly gendered. As will be noted in this chapter, literature by Yuval-Davis and others introduced the concept of women as the 'biological reproducers of the nation'.[25]

[19] Young, 'Introduction: A Public Law of Gender?', 126. [20] Ibid., 3.

[21] S. H. Williams, 'Customary Law, Constitutional Law, and Women's Equality', in K. Rubenstein and K. Young (eds.), *The Public Law of Gender: From the Local to the Global* (Cambridge: Cambridge University Press, 2016); Shaw, *The People in Question*, 23–26.

[22] L. Chappell, '"Governing Victims": Redress and Gender Justice at the International Criminal Court', in K. Rubenstein and K. Young (eds.), *The Public Law of Gender: From the Local to the Global* (Cambridge: Cambridge University Press, 2016).

[23] Young, 'Introduction: A Public Law of Gender?', 1383. [24] Ibid., 7.

[25] N. Yuval-Davis, 'Gender and Nation' (1993) 16 *Ethnic and Racial Studies* 621–632; N. Yuval-Davis, 'Women as Biological Reproducers of "the Nation"' (1996) 19 *Women's Studies International Forum* 17–24; N. Yuval-Davis, F. Anthias and J. Campling, *Woman, Nation, State* (Basingstoke: Macmillan, 1989); L. London and N. Yuval-Davis, 'Women as National Reproducers: The Nationality Act (1981)', in Formations Editorial Collective, *Formations on Nations and People* (London: Routledge & Kegan Paul, 1984); A. Kristol and J. Dahinden, 'Becoming a Citizen through Marriage: How Gender, Ethnicity and Class Shape the Nation' (2020) 24 *Citizenship Studies* 40–56, at 49.

As such, women's bodies have become sites of nation-building as they are seen as responsible for reproducing the 'national stock', in particular by birthing 'new members who conformed to ethnicized and racialized representations of the nation'.[26] Loyalty to family is another 'desirable' and highly gendered quality of national subjects. Research by Choo identifies the extra and yet informal thresholds demanded not of migrant husbands but of migrant wives in South Korea, who 'had to highlight their love for their husbands and prove their commitment to marriage and family to refute the suspicion that they were 'fake wives''.[27] The institutions of family and marriage in particular are some of the primary pathways through which women acquire citizenship, which raises questions about women's genuine 'autonomy' and ability to acquire citizenship in their own right.[28] Further, this chapter draws on extensive literature on the expectations of desirable national subjects built around normative ideas on 'sexual citizenship' – in particular, expectations on women to avoid immoral sexual activity.[29] Norms surrounding race also inform how the state constructs a desirable national subject. Many theorists explore how gender and 'social markers' such as race, sexuality, class and the legalization process 'intersect social experiences'.[30]

Drawing upon this rich material, this chapter examines to whom states grant citizenship and from whom it is withdrawn and illustrates how normative expectations of a desirable citizen are constructed by conceptions of law, gender, race and sexuality. Granting citizenship is predicated on birth, descent or acquisition via marriage or migrant application; however, these categories in turn are only bestowed on those people considered desirable citizens. Withdrawing citizenship refers to the

[26] N. Yuval-Davis, 'Nationalist Projects' (2003) 40 *Narodna umjetnost – Hrvatski časopis za etnologiju i folkloristiku* 9–36 at 13; Kristol and Dahinden, 'Becoming a Citizen through Marriage', at 29.

[27] H. Y. Choo, 'The Cost of Rights: Migrant Women, Feminist Advocacy, and Gendered Morality in South Korea' (2013) 27 *Gender & Society* 445–468 at 461.

[28] Ibid., at 464; J. S. O'Connor, A. S. Orloff and S. Shaver, *States, Markets, Families* (Cambridge: Cambridge University Press, 1999).

[29] D. T. Evans, *Sexual Citizenship: The Material Construction of Sexualities* (London: Routledge, 1993).

[30] O. Salcido and C. Menjívar, 'Gendered Paths to Legal Citizenship: The Case of Latin-American Immigrants in Phoenix, Arizona' (2012) 46 *Law & Society Review* 335–368 at 336; E. Crenshaw, 'Cross-National Determinants of Income Inequality: A Replication and Extension Using Ecological-Evolutionary Theory' (1992) 71 *Social Forces* 339–363.

removal of citizenship through marital denaturalization or terrorism-stripping. Withdrawing citizenship demonstrates who the state considers is an undesirable citizen and thus no longer worthy of citizenship status.

2. Granting Citizenship

The construction of the national subject hinges upon who the state deems to form part of the national citizenry, whether by birth, descent, acquisition through marriage or migration. These avenues are each highly gendered, sexualized and racialized by the intersecting expectations of 'desirable citizens'. First, citizenship is determined in many cases by place of birth, prompting debate about the seemingly unjust opportunities for the 'undesirable' children of migrants to be made citizens. Second, there have been highly gendered changes to citizenship by descent over the last century, as states have either preserved or moved away from bloodline- and ethnicity-based citizenship, depending on whom they wished to include. Third, acquiring citizenship by marriage demands that applicants morally, sexually and racially conform to the state's expectations. Both descent and marriage are areas in which women in particular are expected to subject themselves to the governance of the state or subsidiary institutions such as the family, at the expense of their own legal agency. Fourth, the procedures facilitating acquisition via migration reproduce states' expectations of the model citizen which are often deeply gendered.

The doctrine of *ius sanguinis* (by blood or descent) has had significant impact on citizenship throughout Western Europe and is most closely associated with Germany.[31] The 1990s saw a movement away from the 'right of blood' and concept of a German people tied together by ethnic and cultural identity, towards the French *ius soli* or 'right of territory'.[32] *Ius soli* and *ius sanguinis* were each tied to historical changes, such as the French Revolution and internal migration of ethnic and socio-economic groups

[31] D. Sainsbury, 'Gender Differentiation and Citizenship Acquisition: Nationality Reforms in Comparative and Historical Perspective' (2018) 68 *Women's Studies International Forum* 28–35 at 29.

[32] D. Göktürk, D. Gramling and A. Kaes (eds.), *Germany in Transit: Nation and Migration 1955–2005* (Berkeley: University of California Press, 2007), 1–20; D. Gramling, 'The New Cosmopolitan Monolingualism: On Linguistic Citizenship in Twenty-First Century Germany' (2009) 42 *Die Unterrichtspraxis* 130–140 at 130–131.

within nineteenth-century Germany.[33] They are thought of as the 'civic' and 'ethnic' models respectively.[34] *Ius sanguinis* has a distinctive approach to immigration as it does not naturally include immigrants.[35] Rather than the French 'political-affirmative' concept of the nation, where membership is 'determined by the deliberate affiliation with the state', *ius sanguinis* relied on a 'Common language, culture, and history' or 'ethnocultural' approach.[36]

A. Birth

Birth is a central aspect of the 'gendered reproduction of the nation', as women '"reproduce" the nation' by birthing new citizens.[37] From a security perspective, Lubhéid documents how the childbearing abilities of women are seen as 'a threat to the sovereignty of the nation-state'.[38] Altering who is allowed citizenship by birth provides a legislative arena in which the state can exclude 'undesirable' citizens and 'reaffirm its means of governance and its power to control borders', in a time when sovereignty is otherwise compromised by globalization.[39] Citizenship through birth is a way for the state to ensure through law that the 'right' individuals are subject to the 'right' state.

Many countries have grappled with birthright citizenship, with the United States being a well-known example of citizenship by birth being protected by its constitution. In Ireland, a highly politicized debate occurred surrounding citizenship by birth, culminating in a referendum.

33 M. Künkler and T. Stein, 'Citizenship and the Concept of Nationality [1995]', in E. Böckenförde, M. Künkler and T. Stein (eds.), *Constitutional and Political Theory: Selected Writings*, 1st ed. (Oxford: Oxford University Press, [1995] 2017), 318.

34 R. Brubaker, *Citizenship and Nationhood in France and Germany* (Cambridge, MA: Harvard University Press, 1992); C. Finotelli and M. C. La Barbera, 'When the Exception Becomes the Rule: The Spanish Citizenship Regime' (2013) 10 *Migration Letters* 245–253 at 245.

35 Künkler and Stein, 'Citizenship and the Concept of Nationality', 318.

36 Ibid., 320–321.

37 S. Garner, 'Babies, Bodies and Entitlement: Gendered Aspects of Access to Citizenship in the Republic of Ireland' (2007) 60 *Parliamentary Affairs* 437–451 at 444.

38 E. Lubhéid, 'Childbearing against the State?' (2004) 27(4) *Women's Studies International Forum*, 335–349 at, 344–345.

39 Garner, 'Babies, Bodies and Entitlement', at 448; S. Garner and A. Moran, 'Asylum and the Nation-State: Putting the "Order" Back into "Borders" in Australia and the Republic of Ireland', in A. Lentin and R. Lentin (eds.), *Race and State* (Newcastle: Cambridge Scholars Press, 2006), 101–120.

The initial provisions in Ireland reflected a statutory adoption of the common law principle of *jus soli* – citizenship by place of birth. At common law, birth within the sovereign's dominion only conferred nationality if the person owed allegiance to the monarch. The debate in Ireland was sparked by women from developing nations obtaining citizenship for their babies and residence for themselves through *ius soli*, or births on Irish soil.[40] Migrants were suspected of 'birth tourism' or intentionally birthing children in affluent, Western nations to secure citizenship benefits such as social welfare.[41] Garner links the emergence of concerns over migrant citizenship with Ireland's transition to a 'country of immigration', economic growth and relative civil peace prior to the early 2000s.[42] Up until the Citizenship Act of 2004, any child born on Irish soil acquired Irish citizenship and their parents obtained residence.[43] In 2003 the Minister for Justice, Equality and Law Reform, Michael McDowell, challenged this precedent through the cases of a Czech couple and Nigerian couple who resisted deportation on the grounds that they had birthed children in Ireland.[44] The minister pushed for a referendum to formally amend the Citizenship Act in 2004.[45] Passing with 80 per cent of votes, amendments included a three-year residency requirement for the parents of 'Irish Born Children' (IBCs) before the child would receive citizenship.[46]

Citizenship through birth raises questions of who has control over a woman's body or her unborn child. Garner sets out the bizarre inversion of pro-life arguments that is found in the citizenship referendum 'Yes' campaign.[47] While the rights of an unborn future Irish citizen are not to be affected in any way, the referendum 'Yes' campaign sought to ensure that the nationality of an IBC's parents would delay the IBC's right to citizenship.[48] Applying a racial lens, 'by re-legislating "them" away from access',

40 Garner, 'Babies, Bodies and Entitlement', at 438.

41 J. A. Harrington, 'Citizenship and the Biopolitics of Post-Nationalist Ireland' (2005) 32 *Journal of Law and Society* 424–449; J. M. Mancini and G. Finlay, '"Citizenship Matters": Lessons from the Irish Citizenship Referendum' (2008) 60 *American Quarterly* 575–599.

42 Garner, 'Babies, Bodies and Entitlement', at 437.

43 Ibid., at 438. Entitlements confirmed by the Supreme Court's 1989 'Fajujonu' ruling.

44 Ibid., at 438. Claims following this point were considered on a case-by-case basis.

45 Ibid., at 439.

46 Ibid., at 439. Referendum held on 11 June 2004. The amendment received an 80 per cent backing of the voters on a 62 per cent turnout, and was enshrined in the Citizenship Act 2004 (enacted 1 January 2005).

47 Ibid., at 444.

48 Ibid.

the 'bad' genes are 'provisionally kept out of the national gene pool'.[49] The state thus excluded babies' bodies from membership of the state 'via the racialised bodies of their parents (particularly those of their mothers)'.[50] This excludes the bodies both 'in physical space and in the national imaginary' as the 'gender-mediated discourse constructs the children of non-national women as queue-jumping competitors for resources'.[51]

Pressures to amend the Citizenship Act surrounded the 'increasing pressure [that] had been placed on the Irish maternity system by an "influx" of non-national women attempting to take advantage of ius soli'.[52] The media circulated reports of droves of foreign women arriving in the late stages of pregnancy without medical records or with HIV.[53] Garner describes the perception that these female immigrants made 'the difference between viable and overburdened services', so the 'incentive' for birthing children in Ireland needed to be removed.[54] Increasing hostility against immigrants and perceptions of resource scarcity meant that pregnant women from non-EU states were seen as 'jeopardising the quality of care given to authentic national mothers'.[55] IBCs were even described as 'cuckoos in the Irish nest'.[56]

Debate surrounded the belief that the benefits of citizenship should be reserved exclusively for people with 'social, historic or cultural links to Ireland', as described by one pro-'Yes' senator.[57] The IBC 'loophole' was seen as 'threatening the integrity of Ireland's immigration system' by facilitating a more expeditious path to residence.[58] Senator Minihan roused fears that IBCs could pass on citizenship to their own descendants even if they never reside in Ireland by virtue solely of being born in Ireland.[59] This disparaging language is in stark contrast to the characterization of people in Boston or Melbourne who claim Irish citizenship

[49] Garner harnesses a Foucauldian lens. Ibid., at 446. See also I. Tyler, 'Designed to Fail: A Biopolitics of British Citizenship' (2010) 14 *Citizenship Studies: Design and Citizenship* 61–74.

[50] Garner, 'Babies, Bodies and Entitlement', at 448. [51] Ibid., at 448. [52] Ibid., at 439.

[53] Ibid., at 440. The minister cited the misleading figure of 60,000 births to non-Irish women in 2003. Ibid., at 439.

[54] Ibid., at 440. [55] Ibid., at 443.

[56] Ibid., at 443. The Chen decision embodied the 'citizenship tourism' that motivated the Citizenship Act amendments. Ibid., at 442. In this case, a pregnant Chinese national was refused UK residency but was advised by her lawyer to travel to Ireland to secure citizenship for her child and residence for herself. Ibid., at 442.

[57] Ibid., at 439. [58] Ibid., at 439–440. [59] Ibid., at 441.

through their grandparents, evidencing the hierarchization of Western states.[60] The disparity between these responses evidences the desire of the state to bestow citizenship only on the 'right' people for the 'right' reasons. In another instance of legislative responses to 'fly-in-fly-out' babies, 2020 amendments to US State Department regulations deny temporary visas if it is decided that the '"primary purpose" of travel is to obtain US citizenship for a child by giving birth in the United States'.[61] However, the rule does not apply to thirty-nine predominantly European countries, which provides a clear line between the cultural 'us' and 'them' in state policy.[62]

B. Descent

Citizenship by descent overtly includes or excludes people from citizenship. Descent is shaped by norms that seek to promote ethnically and culturally homogenous national populations as well as norms positioning women's status in relation to men. The cases of Morocco and Jordan demonstrate the influence of patrilineal frameworks in determining women's status, while South Sudan and Nepal reveal acute consequences for women and children where they cannot pass on citizenship to their children in the same manner as men.

Perceiving women as part of a male household underpins the denial of their independent citizenship status. This is central to the identification of how gender and law interact in making women subject to various state and local institutions. Citizenship laws in Morocco and Jordan are both informed by patrilineality (the 'legal processes of transmitting citizenship through paternal lineage') and patriarchy ('male right/rule through family law').[63] Many states 'legally define the *family* as the basic unit of society', with men situated as the head of the household through 'legal notions of marriage as a sexual contract mandating men's control over women',

60 Ibid., at 441.

61 K. Atwood, G. Sands and J. Hansler, 'US Issues New Rules Restricting Travel by Pregnant Foreigners, Fearing the use of "Birth Tourism"', CNN, 24 January 2020, https://edition.cnn.com/2020/01/23/politics/us-new-rules-restricting-travel-fearing-birth-tourism/index.html.

62 Ibid.

63 A. A. Mitra, 'Woman in the Body Politic: Gendered Citizenship and Islamic Jurisprudence' (2019) 3 *Undergraduate Journal of Global Citizenship* 1–20 at 2.

guardianship laws and divorce laws.[64] The fact that 'women are brought into the nation-state as appendages of husbands and fathers' shapes women's rights to pass on citizenship.[65] The influence of French and Spanish colonial administrations in Morocco drew citizenship laws more in line with the 'right-of-blood descent' in order to 'distinguish settler colonials from "natives"'.[66] Significantly, since 2007 all Moroccan women have been able to pass on citizenship to their children, regardless of whom the women are married to.[67]

In many cases, the ability of mothers to pass on citizenship is informed by the intersection of law, religion and colonization in the construction of the female citizen. Throughout much of British history the male head of the household was the 'representative of the marriage relation' so it was considered 'incompatible' for women also to be considered citizens.[68] Jordan was heavily influenced by the British nationality laws, enshrining 'descent through paternal blood' or the transmission of nationality through the identity of the father through the 1928 Jordanian Nationality Law and retaining this concept post-independence in the 1954 Nationality Law. Jordanian women cannot transfer their citizenship to their children unless the father is stateless or unknown, a status that affects 89,000 women (married to foreign men) and leaves 360,000 children stateless if the fathers are from countries that do not grant citizenship by descent.[69] As Mitra describes, 'women are legally constructed not as equal citizens, but rather as actors deeply embedded within a patrilineal social structure'.[70] Conceptions of marriage, duty to the family and duty to the state form part of a complex web of Islamic jurisprudence that underpins gendered citizenship laws.[71] Against calls to modify these citizenship laws, advocates for the present structure have referenced Qur'anic verses that one should 'call [children] by [the names

[64] Ibid., at 3.

[65] S. Joseph, 'Gender and Citizenship in Middle Eastern States' (1996) 26 *Middle East Report* 4–10

[66] Mitra, 'Woman in the Body Politic', at 7. [67] Ibid., at 7.

[68] U. Vogel, 'Is Citizenship Gender Specific?', in U. Vogel and M. Moran (eds.), *The Frontiers of Citizenship* (New York: St. Martin's Press, 1991), 59.

[69] Mitra, 'Woman in the Body Politic', at 8. [70] Ibid., at 8.

[71] K. Ali, *Sexual Ethics and Islam: Feminist Reflections on Qur'an, Hadith, and Jurisprudence* (Oxford: Oneworld, 2006), 36.

of] their fathers; it is more just in the sight of Allah'.[72] Jordanian leaders cited these principles of Islamic marriage and divorce law when opting out of provisions of the Convention on the Elimination of all Discrimination Against Women (CEDAW) in 1980 that would have mandated equal citizenship laws.[73]

Reliance on paternal descent has distinctly adverse impacts on women and children, particularly where documentation and paternal identity are in issue. The Convention on the Rights of the Child and CEDAW enshrine the right of all children to a nationality status at birth (regardless of the sex of the parent) and the right for women and men to pass on their nationality to their children respectively.[74] Yet in 2019, twenty-five states still possess laws denying 'women the right to pass their nationality to their children on an equal basis with men'.[75] The UNHCR highlights the consequences which 'leave children stateless', severely restricting their access to welfare and exposing them to discrimination.[76] Statelessness epitomizes dire consequences of being denied the status of citizen. Without citizenship, one is without a place in the legal hierarchical system – or, more starkly, one is further below the lowest status one can possibly be. Statelessness affects at least 3.9 million people worldwide and dramatically increases the risk of trafficking, abuse and detention.[77] Examples include South Sudan following its independence from Sudan in 2011. Sudanese mothers were unable to pass on their citizenship to their children.[78] Despite Sudan being a signatory to the 2017 Brazzaville Declaration on Eradication of Statelessness in the Great Lakes Region, thousands of children became stateless if their South Sudanese fathers did not possess adequate documentation to prove their citizenship.[79] This occurred even where the

[72] Qur'an 33:5, Mitra, 'Woman in the Body Politic', at 9–10.

[73] Sura 33, Verse 5, Mitra, 'Woman in the Body Politic', at 11.

[74] UNHCR, 'Urgent Action Needed to Reform Gender Discriminatory Nationality Laws Causing Childhood Statelessness', 22 August 2019, www.unhcr.org/en-au/news/press/2019/8/5d5e63d9456/urgent-action-needed-reform-gender-discriminatory-nationality-laws-causing.html. Also relevant is the 1957 United Nations Convention on the Nationality of Married Women (entered into force 1958).

[75] UNHCR, 'Urgent Action Needed'. [76] Ibid. [77] Ibid.

[78] M. Elfatih Elnaiem, *Sudanese Mother Wins Citizenship for Her Children after Seven-Year Legal Struggle*, UNHCR, 6 March 2020, www.unhcr.org/en-au/news/stories/2020/3/5e612b894/sudanese-mother-wins-citizenship-children-seven-year-legal-struggle.html.

[79] Ibid.

children possessed Sudanese birth certificates, removing their ability to complete their education unless they registered as non-citizens, to access healthcare or to find opportunities for employment.[80] Likewise, in Nepal a child may be granted full citizenship by descent if their father is Nepali, or if their mother is Nepali and their father is unknown, but may only receive naturalized (*angikrit*) citizenship status if their mother is Nepali and their father is foreign.[81]

Ultimately, citizenship by descent sets up and affirms norms surrounding women's dependent or independent status and norms surrounding 'desirable' citizens that have racial overtones. These norms often result in the inclusion of ethno-culturally similar people through patrilineal legal avenues.

C. Acquisition: Naturalization

Having examined citizenship by birth and descent, we now turn to citizenship acquisition through other means, often collectively identified as 'naturalization'. The term naturalization itself speaks to the normative underpinning of citizenship – to turn someone into a member makes them 'natural' – moving them from 'unnatural' or 'other' or 'outside' to 'natural', 'member', 'insider'. Each of the following categories of acquisition through marriage, or migration broadly, and the provision of citizenship testing to complete the process, highlight gendered and racialized expectations of the future acceptable citizen. The law provides significant room for decision-makers to exercise their discretion, allowing for gender, racial and religious bias to permeate decisions.

D. Acquisition through Naturalization: Marriage

Perceptions of gender, sexuality and race are heavily entwined in the state's construction of citizenship acquisition through marriage.

[80] Ibid.

[81] A. Pradhan, Nepal's Unequal Citizenship Law, *Nepali Times*, 19 December 2020, www.nepalitimes.com/banner/nepal-waits-for-an-unequal-citizenship-law/ This policy is also motivated by the open border between India and the Terai region of Nepal with the goal of insulating the Nepali nation from India. For citizenship in Nepal, see S. Tamang, *Gender, State and Citizenship in Nepal* (Ann Arbor, MI: ProQuest Dissertations Publishing, 2000).

Naturalization policies (re)produce the constitution of the state by acting as gatekeepers to who can become a citizen.[82] The process of facilitated naturalization in Switzerland hinges on the recommendations (for or against naturalization) of caseworkers.[83] Crucially for this analysis, these recommendations are imbued with the state's assumptions about 'desirable and undesirable' future citizens.[84] These acquisition processes demand that applicants sexually, morally and racially conform to the state's expectations.

It is important to acknowledge the structural limitations of citizenship regimes that 'leav[e] few pathways open for migration, other than by "marriage"'.[85] Different migration streams, including domestic workers and tourism, have also contributed to these citizenship acquisition trends.[86] Historically, structural forces such as wartime service produced phenomena such as the Australian 'bridal train' of 'war brides', who married US troops and migrated to the United States.[87]

Naturalization through marriage reveals the biases and presumptions of decision-makers, and thus the normative hierarchies that underpin citizenship policy. The report produced by the Swiss State Secretariat of Migration for each applicant incorporates information about the applicant's criminal, social and financial situation, as well as recommendations by local bureaucrats following a personal interview.[88] Buffat highlights the

[82] Kristol and Dahinden, 'Becoming a Citizen through Marriage', at 40.

[83] Recommendations inform the State Secretariat for Migration's reports on applicants.

[84] D. Fassin and S. Mazouz, 'What Is It to Become French? Naturalization as a Republican Rite of Institution' (2009) 50 *Revue Française de Sociologie* 37–64; Kristol and Dahinden, 'Becoming a Citizen through Marriage', at 40; L. Brace, 'Reflections on the Good Citizen', in B. Anderson and V. Hughes (eds.), *Citizenship and Its Others, Migration, Diasporas and Citizenship* (Basingstoke: Palgrave Macmillan UK, 2015), www.palgrave.com/de/book/9781137435071; J. A. Geddes and A. Favell (eds.), *The Politics of Belonging: Migrants and Minorities in Contemporary Europe* (Aldershot: Ashgate, 1999); C. Fischer and J. Dahinden, 'Gender Representations in Politics of Belonging: An Analysis of Swiss Immigration Regulation from the 19th Century until Today' (2017) 17 *Ethnicities* 445–468.

[85] P. Statham, S. Scuzzarello, S. Sunanta and A. Trupp, 'Globalising Thailand through Gendered "Both-Ways" Migration Pathways with "the West": Cross-Border Connections between People, States, and Places' (2020) 46 *Journal of Ethnic and Migration Studies* 1513–1542 at 1513.

[86] E.g. tourism pathways between Asian and Western states. Ibid., 1513.

[87] R. Arrowsmith, *All the Way to the USA: Australian WWII War Brides* (self-published, 2013).

[88] Kristol and Dahinden, 'Becoming a Citizen through Marriage', at 42.

formal and informal rules and normative logics that shape the exercise of discretionary powers.[89] Caseworkers 'assess applicants on the basis of gendered, racialized and ethnicized ascriptions, [that] rely on representations of (un)desirable citizens'.[90] The model citizen is thus a compilation of their state-accessed information, as well as questions about 'their identity and life trajectory', relationships and the extent to which they have integrated into society, which is where biases and racial prejudices have the most effect.[91]

Citizenship acquisition through marriage is tied closely to 'sexual citizenship', or normative expectations delineating the 'boundaries of immorality and illegality'.[92] Kristol and Dahinden track how Swiss naturalization caseworkers act as gatekeepers to citizenship based on what they deem to be acceptable marriages.[93] The caseworkers determine whether couples undergo further questioning, based on 'whether their marriage is a "true" one and the spouses are integrated'.[94] Considerations include a large age gap, intention to separate, contact with prostitution or living apart.[95] Caseworkers describe difficulty 'see[ing] a romantic story' in cases where couples do not have any common hobbies, friends or travels.[96] These

[89] A. Buffat, 'When and Why Discretion Is Weak or Strong: The Case of Taxing Officers in a Public Unemployment Fund', in P. Hupe, M. J. Hill and A. Buffat (eds.), *Understanding Street-Level Bureaucracy* (Bristol: Policy Press, 2015).

[90] Kristol and Dahinden, 'Becoming a Citizen through Marriage', at 41. [91] Ibid., at 42–43.

[92] Evans, *Sexual Citizenship*, 8. Literature surrounding sexuality and migration documents the discrimination that frequently faces couples in homosexual, polyamorous or diverse relationships. F. Anthias and N. Yuval-Davis, *Racialized Boundaries: Race, Nation, Gender, Colour, and Class and the Anti-Racist Struggle* (London: Routledge, 1992); M. A. White, *Intimate Archives, Migrant Negotiations: Affective Governance and the Recognition of 'Same-Sex' Family Class Migration in Canada* (Ottawa: ProQuest Dissertations Publishing, 2011); N. Mai and R. King, 'Love, Sexuality and Migration: Mapping the Issue(s)' (2009) 4 *Mobilities* 295–307. See broader literature on sexuality and political asylum. J. Millbank, 'Fear of Persecution or Just a Queer Feeling?' (1995) 20 *Alternative Law Journal* 261–265; J. Millbank, 'From Discretion to Disbelief: Recent Trends in Refugee Determinations on the Basis of Sexual Orientation in Australia and the United Kingdom' (2009) 13(2–3) *International Journal of Human Rights* 391–414; A. Miller, 'Gay Enough? Some Tensions in Seeking the Grant of Asylum and Protecting Global Sexual Diversity', in B. Epps, K. Valens and B. Johnson-Gonzales (eds.), *Passing Lines: Sexuality and Immigration* (Cambridge, MA: Harvard University Press, 2005).

[93] Kristol and Dahinden, 'Becoming a Citizen through Marriage', at 42.

[94] Ibid., at 43. Couples must have been married for three years and resided in the country for five years to apply. This is much less onerous than the regular acquisition route which requires ten years' residence and navigation through three levels of government.

[95] Ibid., at 44. [96] Ibid., at 45.

discourses form part of a broader normative framework of what 'proper citizens' and 'proper marriages' are.[97] Swiss-facilitated naturalization revolves around the 'formal criteria of intention "to found a family" and sexual fidelity'.[98] Naturalization decisions have been investigated for review where children born out of wedlock within two years of naturalization suggested the presence of extra-marital relationships.[99] Swiss citizens do not face such scrutiny, while non-citizen spouses are 'seen as illegitimate reproducers of the cultural and national group' if they do not conform to traditionalist expectations of sexual citizenship.[100] Citizens and their non-citizen family members face pressure to 'perform intimate citizenship' in meeting these expectations.[101]

Caseworkers arguably reproduce colonial and racial hierarchies by boxing applicants into cultural groups and associating them with the assumed practices of their origin state.[102] Interviewed caseworkers drew on Western conceptions of marriage for love, and were sceptical of marriages between citizens and non-citizens.[103] Often suspicious of people from outside the European Union conducting 'sham marriages', caseworkers openly asserted that people from within the EU had no interest in sham marriages as they already benefited from rights to live and work in European countries.[104] Assumptions tied to race and gender are amplified by class hierarchies.[105]

97 S. Bonjour and B. de Hart, 'A Proper Wife, a Proper Marriage: Constructions of "Us" and "Them" in Dutch Family Migration Policy' (2013) 20 *European Journal of Women's Studies* 61–76; L. Block, '"I'm Not Entitled to Be Married in Germany? Am I German or Am I Not?" Narratives and Discursive Strategies of Citizen Sponsors in the German Spousal Migration Context' (2021) 28 *Identities* 56–73 at 59. Bonjour and De Hart track the way that citizen sponsors attempt to demonstrate integration in normative frameworks relating to family and citizenship. S. Bonjour and B. de Hart, 'Intimate Citizenship: Introduction to the Special Issue on Citizenship, Membership and Belonging in Mixed-Status Families' (2020) 28 *Identities* 1-17.

98 Kristol and Dahinden, 'Becoming a Citizen through Marriage', at 45.

99 Ibid., at 45.

100 Ibid., at 45.

101 Bonjour and de Hart, 'Intimate Citizenship'.

102 E. W. Saïd, *Orientalism* (New York: Pantheon Books, 1978); S. Hall, 'The West and the Rest: Discourse and Power', in S. Hall and B. Gieben (eds.), *Formations of Modernity* (Cambridge: Polity Press, 1992); Kristol and Dahinden, 'Becoming a Citizen through Marriage', at 46.

103 Kristol and Dahinden, 'Becoming a Citizen through Marriage', at 45.

104 Ibid., at 45–46.

105 S. Mazouz, 'The Value of Nation' (2019) 37 *French Politics, Culture and Society* 139–161 at 155; Kristol and Dahinden, 'Becoming a Citizen through Marriage', at 49. Applicants

Moreover, women are viewed as 'less legitimate vehicles [than men] for transmitting Swiss citizenship to their foreign spouses'.[106] Swiss women marrying non-citizen men are 'presented as passive, as victims, rather than as active citizens' .[107] This is accompanied by 'moral panic about foreigners stealing "our" women' through fraudulent marriages.[108] This 'logic of control over women's intimate relationships' eventuates in mixed marriages being seen as illegitimate avenues for non-citizen men to gain Swiss citizenship.[109] Inversely, non-citizen women are depicted as 'victims of poverty or as disadvantaged', with marriage to a Swiss male as their chosen mechanism to achieve 'upward social mobility'.[110] This 'better life' is contingent on traditional Swiss ideals of marriage and childbearing, which means that non-citizen women are preferred over non-citizen men, particularly if they marry 'second-rate' Swiss men who are otherwise unlikely to find Swiss partners, and if they conform to traditional, family-oriented gender roles.[111]

Female naturalization applicants are subjected to particularly rigorous evaluation of moral character. Choo emphasizes the gendered morality applied in the 'two feminized sectors of migration – cross-border marriage and sexual commerce'.[112] Women have long been viewed as 'mothers and as morally suspect subjects'.[113] For women, their moral standing is often

from the foreign elite were asked less questions partially due to their 'economic contribution[s]'.

[106] Kristol and Dahinden, 'Becoming a Citizen through Marriage', at 50.

[107] Ibid., at 50; S. Scheel, 'Appropriating Mobility and Bordering Europe through Romantic Love: Unearthing the Intricate Intertwinement of Border Regimes and Migratory Practices' (2017) 5 *Migration Studies* 389–408.

[108] Kristol and Dahinden, 'Becoming a Citizen through Marriage', at 50; Scheel, 'Appropriating Mobility and Bordering Europe'.

[109] Kristol and Dahinden, 'Becoming a Citizen through Marriage', at 51.

[110] Ibid., at 50.

[111] Ibid., at 50. Inversely, groups such as the Immigration Widows Campaign emphasized how racialized prejudices caused the 'foreign husbands issue'. J. Bhabha, F. Klug, S. Shutter and Women, Immigration and Nationality Group, *Worlds Apart: Women under Immigration and Nationality Law* (London: Pluto Press, 1985), 1. While women from Western states such as Australia could sponsor their husbands with ease, women from states such as India experienced significant difficulty in their foreign husbands immigrating, such that each woman is 'forced to choose between her husband and her home'. Bhabha et al., *Worlds Apart*, 1.

[112] Choo, 'The Cost of Rights'.

[113] D. Cook Martin, 'Soldiers and Wayward Women: Gendered Citizenship, and Migration Policy in Argentina, Italy and Spain since 1850' (2006) 10 *Citizenship Studies* 571–590.

tied with their conformance to approved forms of sexuality, reproduction and kinship.[114] Kim, Khawaja and Eivers emphasize the centrality of good character in evaluating the citizenship applications of South Korean marriage migrants.[115]

E. Acquisition through Naturalization: Naturalization Requirements and Citizenship Tests

With countries moving away from the explicitly gendered citizenship models around marriage, many countries claim that migration and citizenship procedures are now 'gender neutral'. Yet these apparent gender-neutral laws are interpreted through 'gendered meanings' and social structures.[116] The evidence that applicants must assemble for their applications carries expectations of a model woman, migrant and national subject. Migrants seeking citizenship are required to 'put themselves under the microscope' by 'compiling a dossier of documents that fully establishes their identity and traces their trajectory from birth to the moment of application'.[117] Some theorists have tracked how the development of gender-equality issues and politics on a domestic and international scale have shaped these requirements of migrant citizenship acquisition.[118]

In particular, citizenship tests are structures combining racial beliefs with disadvantages experienced by women. Several European countries introduced citizenship testing as part of a 'citizenship turn' during the 2000s, where public and governmental discourse shifted its focus towards naturalization.[119] This shift was accompanied by increasingly stringent

[114] Anthias and Yuval-Davis, *Racialized Boundaries*.

[115] H. Kim, N. G. Khawaja and A. Eivers, 'Stress and Support: The Dual Role of the Migrant Community in the Acculturation of Korean Migrant Families in Australia' (2020) 30 *Journal of Community & Applied Social Psychology* 103–116.

[116] Salcido and Menjívar, 'Gendered Paths to Legal Citizenship', at 336.

[117] H. McAvay and R. Waldinger, 'Accelerating the Passage to Citizenship: Marriage and Naturalization in France', UCLA: International Institute, 2021, https://escholarship.org/uc/item/27j043hc.

[118] Sainsbury links this to 'two-level games', demonstrating the interconnectedness of domestic immigration policy and gender policy. Sainsbury, 'Gender Differentiation and Citizenship Acquisition'; Mazouz, 'The Value of Nation', at 143–144.

[119] B. Byrne, 'Testing Times: The Place of the Citizenship Test in the UK Immigration Regime and New Citizens' Responses to It' (2017) 51 *Sociology* (Oxford) 323–338 at 324.

requirements, such as a longer period of residency prior to applying for citizenship.[120] Citizenship tests represent another obstacle that can leave women and low-income migrants in 'limbo' as 'denizen[s]', or permanent residents who are still 'alien[s]'.[121]

From October 2013, the United Kingdom removed the English for Speakers of Other Languages (ESOL) option, which had formerly allowed citizenship applicants to progress their English to the requisite standard through a recognized institution.[122] The replacement of this option with the more rigorous 'Life in the UK' test stemmed from the alleged 'failure' of multiculturalism and movements towards streamlining a cohesive national culture.[123] Literature identifies citizenship tests as a process of 'exclusive-inclusion',[124] which espouses normative expectations of the ideal, new citizen and excludes the 'anti-citizen'.[125] Despite governmental emphasis on it not being a test of 'Britishness', the new test requires potential citizens to behave as a 'super citizen' or 'demonstrate extra commitment' to acquire extra knowledge about the United Kingdom.[126] These barriers act as a 'silent and largely invisible filter' which privileges migrants from affluent, Westernized nations who possess analogous cultural knowledge and can afford further educative preparation.[127]

Data from the UK Home Office demonstrates the disproportionate effects of changes to the citizenship test on applicants from

[120] Ibid., at 324.

[121] T. Hammar, *Democracy and the Nation State: Aliens, Denizens and Citizens in a World of International Migration*, Research in Ethnic Relations series (Aldershot: Avebury, 1990), 598; B. S. Turner, 'We Are All Denizens Now: On the Erosion of Citizenship' (2016) 20 *Citizenship Studies* 679–692.

[122] Morrice, 'British Citizenship, Gender and Migration', at 599.

[123] Ibid., at 599; A. Lentin and G. Titley, *The Crises of Multiculturalism: Racism in a Neoliberal Age* (London: Zed Books, 2011); R. Grillo, 'An Excess of Alterity? Debating Difference in a Multicultural Society' (2007) 30 *Ethnic and Racial Studies* 979–998 at 980.

[124] J. Turner, 'Testing the Liberal Subject: (In)Security, Responsibility and "Self-Improvement" in the UK Citizenship Test' (2014) 18 *Citizenship Studies* 332–348.

[125] I. Barbero, 'Orientalising Citizenship: The Legitimation of Immigrant Regimes in the European Union' (2012) 16 *Citizenship Studies* 751–768.

[126] Byrne, 'Testing Times', at 328; E. Badenhoop, 'The Evocation of "Super Citizens" in British and German Citizenship Ceremony Speeches', in 'Contested Migration Regimes – European Perspectives and Beyond' of the European Sociological Association's Research Network 35, 'Sociology of Migration' midterm conference, Goethe University, Frankfurt am Main, 13–14 November 2014.

[127] Morrice, 'British Citizenship, Gender and Migration', at 606.

'non-English-speaking, low-income countries and countries with low literacy rates'.[128] Although there is no information on gendered pass rates of citizenship tests, these countries have incredibly low literacy rates, with even lower rates for the female population.[129] Likewise, female partner and domestic worker migrants from Bangladesh, Somalia and Afghanistan were the most heavily reliant on the ESOL programme.[130] Finally, changes to fees for citizenship tests and applications raised concerns that it would make it disproportionately more difficult for 'women and low-paid workers' to prepare and apply for citizenship, as these groups previously relied on eligibility for concession fees.[131]

The notion of literacy forming the basis for civic participation is problematic for women and reinforces hierarchies based on access to education.[132] The 2005 Global Campaign for Education explicitly avows that literacy forms the basis for the 'development of active citizenship'.[133] The 'literacy-for-citizenship' campaigns stem from a concern for female education and civic participation, but can function as a prerequisite for participation.[134] New literature proposes that rather than the linear progression of literacy to citizenship, citizenship rights can provide an important avenue towards female further education.[135]

Preparing for citizenship tests is challenging for many migrant women. Access to information in their home countries is frequently in the public

[128] Ibid., at 601. Data from 2005–2010 and 2014. While pass rates for Canada, the United States and Australia remained high, and dropped a little for states such as India and Ghana, pass rates for Somalia, Bangladesh and Afghanistan dropped significantly following the 2013 changes. Ibid., at 602.

[129] Morrice, 'British Citizenship, Gender and Migration', at 602.

[130] Ibid., at 603; B. Ryan, *Integration Rules in Immigration and Nationality Law: The Case of the United Kingdom*, UK Country Report for the INTEC Project: Integration and Naturalisation Tests: The New Way to European Citizenship, 2010, www.ru.nl/publish/pages/621216/ukdef.pdf.

[131] S. Hubble and S. Kennedy, *Changes to Funding for English for Speakers of Other Languages (ESOL) Courses*, 2011, https://researchbriefings.files.parliament.uk/documents/SN05946/SN05946.pdf.

[132] A. Rogers, 'Women, Literacy and Citizenship: A Critique' (2007) 53 *International Review of Education* 159–181 at 160.

[133] Ibid., at 160.

[134] M. Arnot and J. A. Dillabough (eds.), *Challenging Democracy: International Perspectives on Gender, Education and Citizenship* (London: Routledge Falmer, 2000).

[135] K. Fuwa, 'Relationship between Adult Education and Citizenship' (2001) 4 *Journal of Adult and Continuing Education* 1–4 at 2.

domain, controlled and reserved for men.[136] Many women leave home to work as domestic workers instead of finishing their schooling.[137] Lower literacy levels in migrant domestic workers are heavily intertwined with their experiences navigating information and applying for citizenship.[138] Morrice criticizes that 'Liberal citizenship regimes treat migrants as a homogeneous group', and fail to recognize women's distinct difficulties applying for citizenship.[139]

The expectations espoused by citizenship tests do not align well with the experiences of many migrant women. The handbook for the UK citizenship test focuses on 'liberal western modes of citizenship' which emphasize the concept that 'all can and should participate in the public sphere on an equal basis'.[140] Membership of a state carries expectations of participation in the workforce and community, for example through volunteering.[141] This conception fails to appreciate why female migrants may have difficulty finding employment or volunteering, such as language, caring responsibilities, transport and discrimination.[142] Migrant women may not 'recognise their own civic labour in the citizenship ideals promoted'.[143] The handbook describes practices in secular and individualistic terms and ignores 'family, kinship, ethnic and community groups [as] key sites of

[136] Rogers, 'Women, Literacy and Citizenship', at 161; M. Wahiduzzaman, 'The Role of Mass Media in Non-formal Education in Bangladesh with Special Reference to Radio and Television', PhD thesis (University of Nottingham, 2005).

[137] A. North, 'Domestic Work, Learning and Literacy Practices across Transnational Space' (2018) 27 *International Studies in Sociology of Education: Special Issue: Migration, Borders, and Education: International Sociological Inquiries* 217–238 at 217.

[138] Ibid. This is analogous to the difficulty many migrants experience in obtaining health information. A. A. Gele, K. S. Pettersen, L. E. Torheim and B. Kumar, 'Health Literacy: The Missing Link in Improving the Health of Somali Immigrant Women in Oslo' (2016) 16 *BMC Public Health* 1134–1134. Migrant women were also more likely than men to be unemployed and socially less integrated.

[139] Morrice, 'British Citizenship, Gender and Migration', at 604; E. Kofman, 'Contemporary European Migrations, Civic Stratification and Citizenship' (2002) 21 *Political Geography* 1035–1054; S. Castles and J. Miller, *The Age of Migration*, 4th ed. (Basingstoke: Palgrave MacMillan, 2009).

[140] The *Life in the UK* handbook: Home Office, *Life in the United Kingdom: A Guide for New Residents*, 3rd ed (London: TSO, 2013), cited in Morrice, 'British Citizenship, Gender and Migration', at 604; P. Coare and R. Johnston, *Adult Learning, Citizenship and Community Voices: Exploring Community-Based Practice* (Leicester: NIACE, 2004).

[141] Home Office, *Life in the United Kingdom*.

[142] Morrice, 'British Citizenship, Gender and Migration', at 604.

[143] Ibid., at 604.

agency and participatory citizenship for migrant women'.[144] Religious groups are a central point of connection and participation for many migrant women.[145] These and contributions to the home are not reflected in the examples espoused by the handbook, which is reflective of the ways in which the contributions of female migrants and women in general fail to be considered when determining civic hierarchies more broadly.

Migrant citizenship acquisition is laced with gendered and racialized expectations of the model citizen. The 'linguistic assimilation interviews' of the French Naturalization Office consider applicants' cultural assimilation.[146] Caseworkers query the applicants' level of education within the French educational system, use of the French language, choice of schools for their children and links to their origin countries to assess where their allegiances lie.[147] If a female applicant wears a veil (noting that in several contexts, women are more likely to act as visual repositories of religion and culture) or a male applicant is bearded, the caseworkers are mandated to mention this in a specific box on their interview record.[148] This question allegedly assesses whether applicants align with 'French customs' but is in practice used to identify visual signs of practising Islam.[149] Some

[144] Ibid., at 605; H. Ralston, 'Citizenship, Identity, Agency and Resistance among Canadian and Australian Women of South Asian Origin', in E. Tastsoglou and A. Dobrowolsky (eds.), *Women, Migration and Citizenship: Making Local, National and Transnational Connections* (New York: Routledge, 2016); E. Tastsoglou, 'Gender, Migration and Citizenship: Immigrant Women and the Politics of Belonging in the Canadian Maritimes', in E. Tastsoglou and A. Dobrowolsky (eds.), *Women, Migration and Citizenship: Making Local, National and Transnational Connections* (New York: Routledge, 2016); L. Williams, 'Agency and Citizenship in Cross-Border Marriages', in M. Abraham, E. Ngan-ling Chow, L. Maratou-Alipranti and E. Tastsoglou (eds.), *Contours of Citizenship: Women, Diversity and Practices of Citizenship* (New York: Routledge, 2010). For specific analysis of the intersection of religion and migration in UK communities, see T. Modood, *Still Not Easy Being British: Struggles for a Multicultural Citizenship* (Stoke on Trent: Trentham Books, 2010); J. Zavos, 'Negotiating Multiculturalism: Religion and the Organisation of Hindu Identity in Contemporary Britain' (2009) 35 *Journal of Ethnic and Migration Studies* 881–900.

[145] Morrice, 'British Citizenship, Gender and Migration', at 605; M. Moosa-Mitha, 'A Difference-Centred Alternative to Theorization of Children's Citizenship Rights' (2005) 9 *Citizenship Studies* 369–388; M. Moosa-Mitha, 'Social Citizenship Rights of Canadian Muslim Youth: Youth Resiliencies and the Claims for Social Inclusion' (2009) 31 *Arab Studies Quarterly* 121–140.

[146] Mazouz, 'The Value of Nation', at 139.

[147] State schools are perceived as signalling 'deeper integration'. Mazouz, 'The Value of Nation', at 141.

[148] Ibid., at 141. [149] Ibid.

caseworkers reportedly believe that a veil indicates that a female applicant will know little to no French and will consider hesitation or stumbling as confirmation of their unsuitability for citizenship approval.[150] Mazouz noted that 'most candidates . . . make an effort to be well dressed' for their interview, choosing 'dark, discreet colours'.[151] Some female applicants, particularly North African women, blow-dry or straighten their hair.[152] For these women, 'presenting "well" involves attempting to erase a racialized phenotypic marker'.[153]

Officials' perspectives on applicants' countries of origin influence the success of migrant citizenship applications.[154] The French Conseil d'État presents acquiring citizenship as not a 'right' but a 'favour' for migrants.[155] Caseworkers made frequent references to the democratic governance of Western states, in contrast with the 'political regimes' of applicants' home states.[156] Decision-makers sometimes assume that women occupy subordinate positions, through 'associations of gender constructs with characteristics and behaviors that end up positioning women as dependents and men as breadwinners'.[157] This at times excludes women from citizenship on the assumption that they will burden the state financially.[158] Women face heightened scrutiny of their sexual histories, a gendered dynamic of the citizenship acquisition process that ties in with race and morality.[159] While other literature expands upon concepts of behaviours that are 'prohibited' by the state, these prejudices are further heightened in the

[150] Ibid., at 147–148. Caseworkers can only officially justify their referral or denial based on the applicant's level of French, which sees the applications of some women with veils adjourned regardless of their French proficiency. Ibid., at 148–149.

[151] Ibid., at 148–149.

[152] Ibid., at 154; L. Frader, 'From Muscles to Nerves: Gender, "Race", and the Body at Work in France, 1919–1939' (1999) 44 *International Review of Social History* 123–147.

[153] Mazouz, 'The Value of Nation', at 154. [154] Ibid., at 150. [155] Ibid., at 144.

[156] Ibid., at 150.

[157] Salcido and Menjívar, 'Gendered Paths to Legal Citizenship', at 335; S. Castles and A. Davidson, *Citizenship and Migration: Globalization and the Politics of Belonging* (Basingstoke: Macmillan, 2000).

[158] Salcido and Menjívar, 'Gendered Paths to Legal Citizenship', at 338. Examples include the US naturalization system where emphasis on the family nuclear unit views single women critically.

[159] V. Jackson, 'Feminisms and Constitutions', in K. Rubenstein and K. Young (eds.), *The Public Law of Gender: From the Local to the Global* (Cambridge: Cambridge University Press, 2016); J. Nagel, *Race, Ethnicity, and Sexuality: Intimate Intersections, Forbidden Frontiers* (New York: Oxford University Press, 2003).

case of LGBTQI+ migrants and refugees.[160] French caseworkers expressed assumptions that women in polygamous marriages 'accept polygamy because they would not even think of opposing it' and that women with many lovers themselves were exceptions to the norm.[161]

3. Withdrawing Citizenship

A. Introduction

Gender, sexuality and race are entwined in determining not only who is granted citizenship, but from whom citizenship is removed. The processes of marital denaturalization and citizenship-stripping in relation to terrorism are areas in which gender, sexuality, race and law together create distinctive and often marginalized experiences. For centuries, marital denaturalization has epitomized a normative order where women's citizenship and identity as subjects are contingent on the husband's nationality. Similarly, women who have had their citizenship stripped on account of links to terrorist activity are often treated not as individuals but as undesirable agents of their male partners.

B. Marital Denaturalization

The removal of women's citizenship based on the nationality of their husbands demonstrates the construction of the national subject based on perceived allegiance to the state through marriage. Marital

[160] Jackson, 'Feminisms and Constitutions'; A. Dobrowolsky and E. Tastsoglou (eds.), *Women, Migration and Citizenship: Making Local, National and Transnational Connections* (New York: Routledge, 2016); S. Castro-Gómez, 'Ciencias sociales, violencia epistémicay el problema de la "invención del otro"' [The Social Sciences, Epistemic Violence and the Problem of 'Invention of the Other'], in E. Lander (ed.), *La colonialidad del saber: eurocentrismo y ciencias sociales. Perspectivas Latinoamericanas* [Eurocentrism Modern Knowledges, and the 'Natural Order of Global Capital'] (Buenos Aires: Clacsopp, 2000); E. Luibheid and L. Cantú, '*Queer Migrations: Sexuality, U.S. Citizenship, and Border Crossings*', conference proceedings (Minneapolis: University of Minnesota Press, 2005, and ProQuest Ebooks); R. Lewis, 'Deportable Subjects: Lesbians and Political Asylum' (2013) 25 *Feminist Formations* 174–194; R. Terrell, 'To What Extent Does Australian Judicial Decision-Making Authorise and Legitimatise Abusive Administrative Decision-Making Practices in the Context of Refugee Claims Based on Sexuality?', Supervised Research Paper (Canberra: Australian National University, 2019).

[161] Mazouz, 'The Value of Nation', at 152.

denaturalization draws on normative orders where women leave their homes, families and nations to marry into the contexts of their husbands, with the expectation that they leave their former identities and loyalties behind.

The US 1907 Expatriation Act illustrates the construction of female denaturalization as contingent on women's decisions to be subject to the state and status contingent on that of their husbands. This Act decreed that women who married non-citizens 'shall take the nationality of their husband', albeit with the option to resume US citizenship if the marriage ended.[162] In the Supreme Court case of *MacKenzie* v. *Hare*,[163] the justices argued that this did not represent forced denaturalization (which would be inconsistent with the US Constitution) but was 'voluntary expatriation' as women married knowing the consequences of their actions. Kerber describes the extreme disloyalty of American-born women who married non-citizen men, in contrast to American-born men who subsumed non-citizen women under their citizenship 'umbrella' and thus escaped criticism.[164] Ultimately, removing a woman's citizenship on account of her husband's nationality demonstrates a 'refusal to treat a woman as a citizen in her own person' and 'den[ies] her the status of an adult'.[165]

Moreover, the 1922 Cable Act ensured that women did not automatically resume their premarital citizenship upon their marriage ending.[166] To restore citizenship, a woman had to 'petition for naturalization' even if she had never left the country during her marriage to a non-citizen.[167] A particular difficulty emerged through the Bill's 'abolition of automatic naturalization by marriage'.[168] Women from states such as Canada were

[162] An Act in Reference to the Expatriation of Citizens and their Protection Abroad, 1907.

[163] *Mackenzie* v. *Hare et al., Board of Election of San Francisco* (1915) 239 US 299 [311].

[164] T. B. Brown, 'That Time American Women Lost Their Citizenship because They Married Foreigners', NPR, 17 March 2017, www.npr.org/sections/codeswitch/2017/03/17/520517665/that-time-american-women-lost-their-citizenship-because-they-married-foreigners.

[165] C. Macmillan, 'The Nationality of Married Women', Pamphlet (Nationality of Married Women Pass the Bill Committee, January 1931, Supplement, April 1932); H. Irving, 'What Is a Citizen?', Legal Studies Research Paper No. 16/90, 2016, 1–2, 41; C. Macmillan, 'Nationality of Married Women: Present Tendencies' (1925) 7 *Journal of Comparative Legislation and International Law* 142–154.

[166] C. L. Bredbenner, *A Nationality of Her Own: Women, Marriage, and the Law of Citizenship* (Berkeley: University of California Press, 2018), 101.

[167] Ibid., 101. [168] Ibid.

expatriated upon marrying a US citizen, but did not automatically become US citizens, and thus became stateless.[169] In a shocking nexus of race and gender, new immigration rules in 1924 meant that 'native-born women of colour' could be barred from re-entry into the United States, their birth country, if they had lost their citizenship through marriage and had left the country.[170] These steps illustrate the seriousness of perceived betrayal of the home state through marriage to a non-citizen, the assumption that a woman's primary allegiance is to her husband and that her connection to the state is mediated through her connection to her husband.

British 'alien widows' demonstrate a distinctively female experience of being excluded from being a national subject. In industrial and maritime areas such as South Shields, intermarriage was prevalent due to the influx of male migrants.[171] This led to many women losing their British nationality upon marrying migrants, without even leaving their home country. The 1870 Naturalisation Act held that a woman was the subject of the same state as her husband.[172] Campaigns to restrict immigration inadvertently made it more difficult for expatriated women to regain British citizenship.[173] Until she applied for naturalization after a husband's death (as divorce was virtually unavailable), a married woman 'remained femme couverte in British law, legally obliterated, a nonperson. Marriage erased a woman's civil existence: her legal personhood resided in her husband'.[174]

The process of applying for naturalization was particularly difficult for women because they lacked the credentials available to men and were held to higher standards of character and respectability. Between 1870 and 1902, all successful applicants for naturalization were men.[175] In the

[169] Ibid., 101. The House Committee on Immigration and Naturalization reasoned that women who became stateless would be motivated to relieve themselves of the 'embarrassment of being without a country' and so would resolve their situation of their own accord. Ibid., 101–102.

[170] Ibid., 98.

[171] L. Tabili, 'Outsiders in the Land of Their Birth: Exogamy, Citizenship, and Identity in War and Peace' (2005) 44 *Journal of British Studies* 796–815 at 801.

[172] Status known as coverture. *Parliamentary Debates* (Commons), vol. 200 (1 April 1870), col. 1130, and vol. 200 (25 April 1870), col. 1741.

[173] Tabili, 'Outsiders in the Land of Their Birth', at 803.

[174] Ibid., at 802–803. Admittedly, these women were still entitled to social benefits. Ibid., at 802.

[175] Ibid., at 804.

mid-twentieth century the state reduced application costs, but intensified 'Scrutiny of women's character, "respectability", and prospective loyalty to the state'.[176] Women lacked commercial, political and military ties to the public sphere so had to rely on their personal, familial and neighbourhood networks.[177] Many women mobilized kin to provide their required character references or cited their sons' military service as evidence of their loyalty to Britain.[178] Between 1903 and 1945 approximately thirty-six women from the South Shields port area were successfully renaturalized out of the thousands of women who lost their citizenship.[179] In stark contrast, thousands of non-citizen men were granted British citizenship despite 'tenuous claims' to residing in Britain.[180]

The US and UK marital denaturalization laws expelled women from the citizenry if they married non-citizen men. While it was possible to reapply for citizenship, the process penalized women for their alleged rejection of state allegiance, instead privileging male networks and participation in the state. This phenomenon was supposedly repudiated by the 1957 UN Convention on the Nationality of Married Women, but is still present in twenty-five countries today.[181]

C. Citizenship-Stripping for Terrorism

The phenomenon of citizenship-stripping is another arena where states exclude those whom they perceive as undesirable. Tied in with

[176] Ibid., at 808.

[177] Ibid., at 809. Alien widows had to produce two character witnesses. Ibid., at 808–809. Women did not have 'direct links to the state via public sphere practices such as work, property, and military service' so had to rely on the 'fruits of personal, kin, neighborhood, and work networks' to evidence their loyalty to Britain. Ibid., at 809–811.

[178] Ibid., at 811.

[179] Ibid., at 796. There were an estimated 30,000 British-born alien women in the United Kingdom in 1922. Public Record Office (PRO), 'Census of Aliens in the UK, 1915–1924', Home Office Aliens Department HO45/11522/287235. Ibid., at 796.

[180] Ibid., at 796.

[181] UNHCR, *Background Note on Gender Equality, Nationality Laws and Statelessness*, 2020, www.refworld.org/pdfid/5f0d7b934.pdf; H. Irving, 'The Impact of Marital Denaturalisation', in *Citizenship, Alienage, and the Modern Constitutional State: A Gendered History* (Cambridge: Cambridge University Press, 2016); R. Govil and A. Edwards, 'Women, Nationality and Statelessness: The Problem of Unequal Rights', in A. Edwards and L. van Waas (eds.), *Nationality and Statelessness under International Law* (Cambridge: Cambridge University Press, 2014).

Islamophobia and assumptions about women's agency, citizenship-stripping in relation to terrorist activities affects women in distinctive ways. While stereotypes of the 'Arab terrorist' are primarily associated with men, their wives face stereotypes associated with being failed mothers and agents of their husbands.[182]

Citizenship-stripping is underpinned by an 'integrationist narrative' emphasizing security through a shared national identity.[183] The 2015 Australian citizenship-stripping provisions sought to ensure the compatibility of Australian citizenship with the 'shared values of the Australian community',[184] providing for automatic loss of Australian citizenship in legislated contexts, without any discretion.[185] Citizenship cancellations have primarily affected men based on links to criminal or gang-related activities.[186] Further, a 2020 Australian High Court case examining the state's power to deport two Indigenous men who were not formally Australian citizens having been born outside Australia to one parent who was not Australian (and not obtaining citizenship by descent) arose through the government using their non-citizenship status and criminal activity as grounds for expelling undesirable individuals. However, the Court held that Indigenous Australians could not be deported even if they did not have formal citizenship due to their '"special" connection to the country').[187]

[182] L. Volpp, 'The Citizen and the Terrorist' (2002) 49 *UCLA Law Review* 1575–1600 at 1575.

[183] N. Kapoor and K. Narkowicz, 'Unmaking Citizens: Passport Removals, Pre-Emptive Policing and the Reimagining of Colonial Governmentalities' (2019) 42 *Ethnic and Racial Studies: ERS Open* 45–62 at 52.

[184] The Parliament of the Commonwealth of Australia, Explanatory Memorandum, Australian Citizenship Amendment (Citizenship Cessation) Bill 2019.

[185] The Explanatory Memorandum to the 2019 legislation explains the role of the 2015 legislation in protecting the Australian community.

[186] K. Hoang and S. Reich, 'Managing Crime through Migration Law in Australia and the United States: A Comparative Analysis' (2017) 5 *Comparative Migration Studies* 1–24; 'PM Pushes Back against Islamic State Bride's Plea to Come Home', *The New Daily*, 14 March 2019, https://thenewdaily.com.au/news/people/2019/03/14/pm-islamic-state-bride-australia/.

[187] K. Rubenstein, 'A Surprise Judgment from a Conservative Court', *The Canberra Times*, 12 February 2020, www.canberratimes.com.au/story/6625520/a-surprise-judgment-from-a-conservative-court/; High Court of Australia, *Love* v. *Commonwealth of Australia; Thoms* v. *Commonwealth of Australia* [2020] HCA 3 [391] (Edelman J).

A salient result of citizenship-removal is statelessness, which is highly gendered in its nature and effects.[188] The criteria for stateless people and refugees to be granted asylum generally align with men's experiences – for example, direct political persecution – whereas women's persecution is often less visible or caused by association with men involved in conflict.[189] The UN Division for the Advancement of Women recognized in 2003 that women are often 'invisible' to asylum programmes as they have scarce public presence, are listed as part of family units rather than as individuals and their documentation (if any) may be held by male family members.[190] Absence of citizenship status also makes women more vulnerable to human trafficking. Citizenship status combined with cultural and language barriers mean that women may find it difficult to escape situations where their agency and mobility are compromised.[191]

The stark reality of being removed from the national citizenry stems from norms and expectations about gender, race and religion that are woven tightly through the fabric of law. Marital denaturalization and citizenship-stripping in relation to terrorism are both areas in which norms surrounding gender have consistently operated to women's disadvantage, and at times in exceedingly punitive ways. In both cases, women's identity and citizenship status are tied to their husband's nationality and criminal or non-criminal activity.

4. Conclusion

In thinking about power relations in society and their impact on law and law's regulation through the state over citizenship, the question through the feminist lens and impetus of this collection must be who those citizens

[188] European Institute for Gender Equality, *Stateless Women*, 2021, https://eige.europa.eu/thesaurus/terms/1393.

[189] J. Greatbach, 'The Gender Difference: Feminist Critiques of Refugee Discourse' (1989) 1 *International Journal of Refugee Law* 518–527.

[190] K. Newland, 'Seeking Protection: Women in Asylum and Refugee Resettlement Processes', Presented at the United Nations Division for the Advancement of Women, Expert Consultation on Migration and Mobility and How This Movement Affects Women, Malmo, Sweden, 2–4 December 2003, www.un.org/womenwatch/daw/meetings/consult/CM-Dec03-EP8.pdf.

[191] J. A. Reid, 'Exploratory Review of Route-Specific, Gendered, and Age-Graded Dynamics of Exploitation: Applying Life Course Theory to Victimization in Sex Trafficking in North America' (2012) 17 *Aggression and Violent Behavior* 257–271 at 257.

should be? Under Neuman's concept of bilateral liberalism, the state 'considers all applicable costs and benefits in deciding to whom to offer citizenship'.[192] Some argue that there is a causal relationship between the criteria for citizenship (such as birth on that state's soil or parentage) and whether those individuals will predictably constitute good, productive members of the state.[193] Alternatively, academia has set out the significant utility to naturalizing foreign aliens who have committed to the state they live in.[194] There is arguably great advantage to a uniform legal approach to immigration restrictions – for example, a class that 'can be defined by reference to specific physical characteristics and events' such as permanent residence for a specific period rather than being defined in relation to the 'legal abstraction' of citizenship.[195] A more prescriptive legal approach would help prevent statelessness by reducing the number of cases where it is unclear where individuals fit.[196]

Instead, presently, the national subject, the citizen, is identified in law based on what the state deems desirable. Even with 'gender neutral' legal orders, citizenship law has allowed a plethora of gender-related and racial stereotypes to go unchallenged due to the large room for discretion that the law allows and which privileges the state over the individual's human rights. As such, this chapter has highlighted how the differing legal approaches regarding to whom citizenship is granted and withdrawn by the state is neither gender nor race neutral. In many instances it is the interaction of these normative frameworks that produces uniquely problematic forms of marginalization for women through law. Examples include the characterization of the female wives of accused terrorists who are damned not only based on their perceived repudiation of national allegiances, but their failure to conform to hierarchies of family and motherhood.

It is important to note how this chapter has primarily examined gender in relation to women. This is due to the 'disproportionate harm to women

[192] Legomsky, 'Why Citizenship?', at 283. [193] Ibid., at 291.

[194] C. Gathmann, 'Naturalization and Citizenship: Who Benefits?' (2015) 125 *IZA World of Labor*, https://wol.iza.org/uploads/articles/125/pdfs/naturalization-and-citizenship-who-benefits.pdf; Legomsky, 'Why Citizenship?', at 281.

[195] Legomsky, 'Why Citizenship?', at 289.

[196] UNHCR, *Nationality and Statelessness: A Handbook for Parliamentarians*, Handbook for Parliamentarians, no. 11, 2005, www.un.org/ruleoflaw/files/Nationality%20and%20Statelessness.pdf.

caused by gendered laws and assumptions, on a sheer numbers basis'.[197] Weaving in insights from feminist critical theory, which 'focuses on the existence of power, domination, and exploitation', and postmodern or post-structural theory, which 'urges reconsideration of "objectivity"',[198] we do identify some instances where aspects of citizenship law are particularly tied to male characteristics (for example, certain types of labour relating to migrant citizenship acquisition around men as breadwinners). We also explore to a limited extent the gendered implications of citizenship processes for LGBTQI+ people.

Ultimately, the national subject, the citizen, is a legal space in which gender, sexuality and race keenly interact with the everyday lives of individuals. This is due to the fact that the inherently hierarchical nature of citizenship of the state is fundamentally about power relations in society, which are wrapped up, through law, with gender and race. Case studies and trends such as those explored in this chapter suggest the need to make citizenship law's granting and removal of citizenship more transparent. While it is beyond the scope of this chapter, initiatives such as transnational migration agreements represent tangible opportunities to work safely and holistically towards the fair treatment through law of every person wherever they reside. Systems promoting dignity and opportunities for people will not only reflect their inherent worth but will be beneficial for both the individual and the state or territory where they are based. States that aim to have clear, accessible and transparent citizenship law systems in order to provide forums for migrant and stateless people to find a sense of belonging, as well as avenues for all people in the territory to contribute their skills and ideas towards the societies that welcome them, will benefit all concerned.

[197] Young, 'Introduction: A Public Law of Gender?', 7.

[198] S. Brisolara, 'Feminist Theory: Its Domains and Applications', in D. Seigart and S. Brisolara (eds.), *Feminist Evaluation: Explorations and Experiences: New Directions for Evaluation*, vol. 96 (New York: Guilford Press, 2014), 15–16.

9 The Familial Subject

Fernanda G. Nicola and Ann Shalleck

1. Introduction: The Familial Subject

Lawyers, judges and scholars often see the domain of the family as distinctive, namely as affective rather than instrumental, sharing rather than distributive, distinguished from the functioning of both the state and the market by its altruism, intimacy and sacredness. They also often consider family law as exceptional, as occupying a distinctive domain and operating differently than its private law counterparts such as contracts, torts and property law or its public ones such as criminal, administrative and constitutional law.[1] We begin from the premise, however, that the law that regulates and shapes the experiences and situations of members of a family arises, too, in these other domains. Family law encompasses not just the rules and doctrines associated with the formation, operation and dissolution of families (traditional family law) but also laws of the market and the state that regulate and shape the definition and operation of families.[2]

[1] J. Halley and K. Rittich, 'Critical Directions in Comparative Family Law: Genealogies and Contemporary Studies of Family Law Exceptionalism' (2010) 58 *American Journal of Comparative Law* 753–775 at 754–755.

[2] For example, scholars of gender across disciplines have analysed the ideology of separate spheres as it operates across family, market and state. From the early stages of gender studies, scholars have been documenting these dynamics. See for a documentation of the trial of Ann Hibbins in 1640 for disputing the quality and cost of carpentry work done on her home rather than leaving the matter to her husband's purview, e.g., N. F. Cott et al. (eds.), *Root of Bitterness: Documents of the Social History of American Women*, 2nd ed. (New York: E. P. Dutton and Company, 1972), 11–16. Within feminist legal theory, see F. E. Olsen, 'The Family and the Market: A Study of Ideology and Legal Reform' (1983) 96 *Harvard Law Review* 1497–1578. Authoritative legal texts, too, have recognized the ideology of separate spheres, while according it different legal significance over time. See, e.g., *Bradwell* v. *Illinois*, 83 US 130, [141] (1872) (Bradley J concurring), agreeing that denying a married woman admission to the bar was proper because women belong in the domestic

Inside the family unit, the division of duties within a marriage, differences in notions of mothering and fathering, the allocation of power, wealth and authority within the patriarchal family, and the experience of violence within the family are all heavily gendered. Similarly, in the market, gender infuses many employment practices instrumental to familial decision-making, such as job definition and segregation, the treatment of care work, unequal pay, the meaning and consequences of entry into and exit from employment, and job mobility. In addition, within state regulatory regimes, gender assumptions are built into the structures of social welfare benefits, including housing, food and childcare, income supplements, mechanisms of family surveillance, the meaning of child neglect, support for those with disabilities, and the provision of healthcare. Thus, gender ideologies within market operation and state regulation, along with the law of the family, shape the family choices that individuals make. When the view of family law and the family as exceptional – distinct from market and state – predominates, politicians, jurists and policymakers alike use this exceptionalism to secure vast latitude in advancing through the law of the family their ideological agendas.[3]

In contrast, social scientists across disciplines have been less constrained by family law exceptionalism. They have developed extensive understanding of how the construction and operation of families around gender, particularly at the intersection with race and class, connect to the operation of the market and the policies of the government. For example, they have shown how the modern family maintains 'patriarchal bargains'[4] by wrapping them in an ideology of romantic marriages.[5] Notions like domesticity help maintain separate spheres within the family in which female homemakers with dependent children become dependent on male

sphere; *Orr* v. *Orr*, 440 US 268, [279–280] (1979), determining that a statute's validity cannot rely on outdated notions of gender roles.

3 See F. G. Nicola, 'Family Law Exceptionalism in Comparative Law' (2010) 58 *American Journal of Comparative Law* 777–810, A. Shalleck, 'Introduction, Comparative Family Law: What Is the Global Family? Family Law in Decolonization, Modernization and Globalization' (2011) 19 *American University Journal of Gender, Social Policy and the Law* 449–458; F. G. Nicola, 'Intimate Liability: Emotional Harm, Family Law, and Stereotyped Narratives in Interspousal Torts' (2013) 19 *William and Mary Journal of Race, Gender, and Social Justice* 445–510.

4 See D. Kandiyoti, 'Bargaining with Patriarchy', 2 *Gender and Society* 274–290.

5 See S. Coontz, *Marriage, a History: From Obedience to Intimacy or How Love Conquered Marriage* (New York: Viking Press, 2005).

breadwinners, even as increasing numbers of women participate in the job market, in which women receive unequal pay.[6] Feminist economists have shown the instability of the patriarchal-capitalist bargains negotiated between male factory owners and union workers for a 'family wage' when subjected to the pressures of deindustrialization and globalization, and the consequences for families that could no longer support stay-at-home mothers.[7] Social scientists have disputed whether the diffusion of the nuclear family after the Second World War served to justify the imperialism of Western industrial societies.[8] Sociologists and political scientists have documented the staggeringly high rates of poverty for children and for unmarried mothers in the United States through much of the post-Second World War era and analysed its relationship to the economic fragility of families, and to meagre and punitive gendered and racialized social welfare policies.[9]

This chapter seeks to show how family law, broadly understood in conjunction with gender ideology and social norms, has co-produced the familial subject through different visions of family life. The familial subject changes according to the ideological and doctrinal shifts constituting different images of the family through which legislators, judges and policymakers articulate family law reforms over time. The familial subject

[6] See Z. Eisenstein, 'Developing a Theory of Capitalist Patriarchy', in Z. R. Eisenstein (ed.), *Capitalist Patriarchy and the Case for Socialist Feminism* (New York: Monthly Review Press, 1979), 5 and 30. See generally J. Stacey, 'The Family Is Dead, Long Live Our Families', in N. Holmstrom (ed.), *The Socialist Feminist Project* (New York: Monthly Review Press, 2002), 90.

[7] See H. Hartmann, 'Capitalism, Patriarchy, and Job Segregation by Sex', in Z. R. Eisenstein (ed.), *Capitalist Patriarchy and the Case for Socialist Feminism* (New York: Monthly Review Press, 1979), 206.

[8] Compare W. J. Goode, *World Revolution and Family Patterns* (New York: Free Press of Glencoe, 1963), with A. J. Cherlin, 'Goode's "World Revolution and Family Patterns": A Reconsideration at Fifty Years' (2012) 38 *Population and Development Review* 577–607, and the latter's book review, J. Aldous, 'Book Review' (2000) 62 *Journal of Marriage and Family* 856–858.

[9] M. Abramovitz, 'Still under Attack: Women and Welfare Reform', in N. Holmstrom (ed.), *The Socialist Feminist Project* (New York: Monthly Review Press, 2002), 216; M. Abramowitz, *Regulating the Lives of Women: Social Welfare Policy from Colonial Times to the Present* (Boston, MA: South End Press, 1988). For a review of the growth of right-wing family values movements in the 1980s and 1990s, see J. Stacey, 'Families against "The Family": The Transatlantic Passage of the Politics of Family Values' (1998) 89 *Radical Philosophy*, www.radicalphilosophyarchive.com/issue-files/rp89_commentary_familiesagainstthefamily_stacey.pdf, 2.

is like a prism that has at least three different faces. The first face is the ideological one, in which gender and social theories, ranging from radical to cultural feminism, from liberal to queer theories of sexuality, from traditional to libertarian concepts of the, shape different legal images of the family and its members. A second face lies in legal regimes that regulate and shape the experiences and situations of members of a family, law that arises both within the traditional doctrines regarding the formation, operation and dissolution of families and the laws of the market and the state. The role of law in constructing the familial subject is stark with regard to race and gender, where for centuries law totally or partially stripped people of legal subjectivity.[10] The third face of the familial subject remains embedded in the world and its political economy. Family members experience their lives in families at the intersection of class, race and gender[11]. through the operation of social norms and governmental institutions, which are structured in relationship to the market and legal regimes that overlap with or encompass traditional family law.[12]

All three faces shape the prism of the familial subject and these components produce different legal images of the family. In highlighting these different legal images, we analyse two doctrinal fields: same-sex marriage and child support. We first show how the sexual and natural family imaginaries shaped the legal and political struggles around same-sex marriage across the Atlantic. We then evaluate how child support regimes reflect and shape legal images of the economic family in the United States and Europe, while accommodating conservative or progressive social values regarding family life. We show how state intervention through laws regulating child support fuelled and reflected diverging neoliberal or social

[10] See T. W. Hunter, *Bound in Wedlock: Slave and Free Black Marriage in the Nineteenth Century* (Cambridge, MA: Belknap Press of Harvard University Press, 2017); G. Perrone, '"Back into the Days of Slavery": Freedom, Citizenship, and the Black Family in the Reconstruction-Era Courtroom' (2019) 37 *Law and History Review* 125–161; R. A. Lenhardt, 'Marriage as Black Citizenship?' (2015) 66 *Hastings Law Journal* 1317–1364; L. F. Edwards, *Gendered Strife and Confusion: The Political Culture of Reconstruction* (Champaign: University of Illinois Press, 1997); D. Green, 'Ain't I . . . ?: The Dehumanizing Effect of the Regulation of Slave Womanhood and Family Life' (2018) 25 *Duke Journal of Gender Law and Policy* 191–220; M. A. Burnham, 'An Impossible Marriage: Slave Law and Family Law' (1987) 5 *Law and Inequality* 187–226.

[11] See M. R. Marella, 'Critical Family Law' (2011) 19 *Journal of Gender Social Policy and Law* 721–754 at 723.

[12] See J. Halley, 'What Is Family Law? A Genealogy Part I' (2011) 23 *Yale Journal of Law and Humanities* 1–109.

welfare visions of a familial subject, both deeply infused with their own visions of gender and race.

Western family law has coalesced in a way that encompasses different visions of the family that are ideologically manipulable and historically context-dependent. Protected in the privacy of the domestic sphere, the familial subject has oscillated between the sexual and the natural family in equating same-sex relationships with the paramount notion of heterosexual marriage or rejecting this equivalence. The familial subject has also oscillated between welfarist and market liberalization approaches underlying child support regimes that reflect different visions of the economic family, which, in all its manifestations, has become detached from the sexual family. Rooted in contested social values over the role of the state in the economic life of the family, both visions of the economic family enlist punitive practices that devalue relationships within families that are poor, of colour, unmarried, or of non-conforming sexual identities.

As a result, grounded in family law exceptionalism, judges, lawyers and scholars have, through different visions of the family, created new room for ideological struggles that displace careful assessment of the existing hierarchies, dependencies, economic inequality and subordination by gender and race that shape the situated character of the familial subject.

2. The Evolution of Western Family Law between the State and the Market

Historically, family law has served to shape the identity of nation-states, especially since the nineteenth century. With its encasement in civil codes in Europe, the family became the locus of where traditional Catholic values rather than non-Western religious ones of the new nation coalesced.[13] In the United States, racial exclusion from the identity of the nation was expressed at the founding through the inability of slaves to marry or to

[13] See D. Kennedy, 'Savigny's Family/Patrimony Distinction and Its Place in the Global Genealogy of Classical Legal Thought' (2010) 58 *American Journal of Comparative Law* 811–841. Tsoukala shows how Ottoman family law regimes in Greece were set aside in the founding of Greece as a modern Catholic Orthodox Western nation. P. Tsoukala, 'Marrying Family Law to the Nation' (2010) 58 *American Journal of Comparative Law* 873–910.

have parental rights to their children.[14] Racial restrictions on marriage continued in many states, not just those that had been slaveholding, long after the end of slavery and the dismantling of Jim Crow. Until 1967 when the Supreme Court acted in *Loving* v. *Virginia*[15] to overturn state prohibitions on interracial marriage, the family remained a site where avowed racial privilege defined the values of the state.[16]

With the expansion of financial capitalism and the greater involvement of the state in the economy throughout the twentieth century, modern family law began to take on form, changing from the law of domestic relations to contemporary family law.[17] It also developed from a system of diverging state laws to an increasingly unified system,[18] sometimes through efforts at creating uniform rules among states, as in the case of the Uniform Marriage and Divorce Act,[19] and sometimes through the interventions of US federal law, as in the case of laws governing state intervention into the parent–child relationship[20] and state regulation of child support and paternity.[21] These efforts began in earnest in the post-Second World War era with rapid economic growth and political agendas to achieve public policy goals through regulating the organization and operation of families. Within these strategies, jurists and politicians maintained family law as a distinctive sphere to situate contested social values as expressions of familial relations rather than opposing approaches to economic distribution.

[14] D. C. Goring, 'The History of Slave Marriage in the United States' (2006) 39 *John Marshall Law Review* 299–347 at 302–304 and 304 fn. 20. See generally Lenhardt, 'Marriage as Black Citizenship?'; Hunter, *Bound in Wedlock*.

[15] 388 US 1 (1967).

[16] N. F. Cott, *Public Vows: A History of Marriage and the Nation* (Cambridge, MA: Harvard University Press, 2000), 4. Racial exclusion, marginalization and inequities continue to the present throughout the operation of family law. See, e.g., D. Roberts, *Shattered Bonds: The Color of Child Welfare* (London: Civitas Books, 2009).

[17] Halley, 'What Is Family Law?'.

[18] See, e.g., L. H. Elrod, 'Epilogue: Of Families, Federalization, and a Quest for Policy' (1999) 33 *Family Law Quarterly* 843–864 at 846–851.

[19] Uniform Marriage and Divorce Act, Arts. 101–506 (National Conference of Commissioners on Uniform State Laws 1970).

[20] E.g., Adoption Assistance and Child Welfare Act of 1980, Pub. L. No. 96-272, 94 Stat. 500; Adoption and Safe Families Act of 1997, Pub. L. No. 105-89, 111 Stat. 2115. See E. Stein, 'Uniformity and Diversity in a Divided-Power System: The United States' Experience' (1986) 61 *Washington Law Review* 1081–1102 at 1093–1096.

[21] Social Services Amendments of 1974, Pub. L. No. 93-647, 88 Stat. 2337 (1975).

In the United States during the 1960s, the government sought to extend economic opportunity and alleviate the suffering and expand the power of poor people through diverse forms of federal social welfare programmes and funding, the development and expansion of poverty law, and the creation of community anti-poverty offices, known collectively as the War on Poverty.[22] It also sought to remove racial barriers to access to benefits that characterized the New Deal programmes.[23] Intense social and political battles ensued that resulted in compromises.[24] In return for receiving economic aid to care for children, poor mothers and fathers were subjected to increased government surveillance and repeated efforts to conform to dominant norms of marriage and work, through punishing unmarried cohabitation, and stigmatizing the single parenthood of women and the inability of men to provide for their families.[25] In this bargain, government welfare policies entrenched the vision of the male breadwinner and female caregiver as the proper site for financial and social responsibility for children, whatever the actual material circumstances of the people receiving welfare. Non-conforming mothers and fathers were treated as failures. In the sphere of social welfare law and policy, an ideal marital family served as the foil for the deviant and racialized woman-

[22] See J. F. Handler, *The Poverty of Welfare Reform* (London: Yale University Press, 1995), 32; J. F. Handler and Y. Hasenfeld, *We the Poor People: Work, Poverty, and Welfare* (London: Yale University Press, 1997), 32–33; J. F. Handler and Y. Hasenfeld, *Blame Welfare, Ignore Poverty and Inequality* (Cambridge: Cambridge University Press, 2006), 3 and 166–174; D. Pearce, 'Welfare Is Not for Women: Why the War on Poverty Cannot Conquer the Feminization of Poverty', in L. Gordon (ed.), *Women, the State, and Welfare* (Madison: University of Wisconsin Press, 1990), 273. As part of the War on Poverty, Congress enacted the Economic Opportunity Act of 1964, Pub. L. No. 88-452, 78 Stat. 508.

[23] J. Quadagno, *The Color of Welfare: How Racism Undermined the War on Poverty* (Oxford: Oxford University Press, 1994); D. C. Miller, *Women and Social Welfare: A Feminist Analysis* (New York: Praeger, 1990), 33–34; M. Minow, 'The Welfare of Single Mothers and Their Children' (1994) 26 *Connecticut Law Review* 817–842 at 824–825. For a review of L. Gordon, *Pitied but Not Entitled: Single Mothers and the History of Welfare* (Cambridge, MA: Harvard University Press, 1994), and Quadagno, *The Color of Welfare*, see D. E. Roberts, 'Welfare: Yesterday and Today' (1995) 24 *Contemporary Sociology* 1–3.

[24] Handler and Hasenfeld, *Blame Welfare*, 3 and 166–174; Miller, *Women and Social Welfare*, 31; M. J. Bailey and N. J. Duquette, 'How Johnson Fought the War on Poverty: The Economics and Politics of Funding at the Office of Economic Opportunity' (2014) 74 *Journal of Economic History* 351–388.

[25] Miller, *Women and Social Welfare*, 33; Handler, *The Poverty of Welfare*, 23–34. See also Gordon, *Pitied but Not Entitled*.

headed family in need of welfare benefits,[26] increasing in ideological significance as opposition to welfare programmes grew.[27]

At the same time, in Europe, economic and political imperatives to achieve governmental or market integration outcomes created increasing pressures toward gender equality, while preserving the family as a distinctive site for the expression of national and social values.[28] Even when the European Communities project aimed to displace domestic borders with the purpose of creating a single market, Christian Democrat politicians and jurists alike anchored family law regimes into national legal traditions, thereby preventing supranational EU law from governing legal issues related to the family.[29]

By the mid-1980s, during the Reagan–Thatcher era, family law served to counter or supplement the creation of markets in governments' right-wing liberalizing endeavour in both Europe and the United States. One aspect of this neoliberal development is that in certain aspects of their lives as members of families, legal subjects experienced greater liberties within the family.[30] For example, with the liberalization of the free movement of workers and citizens in the EU, the creation of a more liberal family law regime in the member states followed.[31] Greater convergence across the Atlantic led to the widespread acceptance of no-fault divorce[32] and increasing recognition of reproductive rights regimes as a cornerstone of

[26] See Handler and Hasenfeld, *We the Poor People*, 27–33; Handler and Hasenfeld, *Blame Welfare*, 3–4 and 171–177; Pearce, 'Welfare Is Not for Women', 271–272; L. E. White, 'No Exit: Rethinking "Welfare Dependency" from a Different Ground' (1993) 81 *Georgetown Law Journal* 1961–2002 at 1966–1968; M. A. Fineman, 'Dependencies', in N. J. Hirschmann and U. Liebert (eds.), *Women and Welfare: Theory and Practice in the United States and Europe* (New Brunswick, NJ: Rutgers University Press, 2001), 23 and 32–33.

[27] Roberts, 'Welfare: Yesterday and Today', at 2; Minow, 'The Welfare of Single Mothers', at 823.

[28] See P. Tsoukala, 'Household Regulation and European Integration: The Family Portrait of a Crisis' (2015) 63 *American Journal of Comparative Law* 747–799.

[29] See A. Trabucchi, *Cinquant'anni nell'esperienza giuridica* (Padova: CEDAM, 1988).

[30] See C. Powell, 'Gender Indicators as Global Governance: Not Your Father's World Bank' (2016) 17 *Georgetown Journal of Gender and the Law* 777–807.

[31] See B. Stark and J. Heaton (eds.), *Routledge Handbook of International Family Law* (Abingdon, Oxon: Routledge, 2019); K. Boele-Woelki et al., *Principles of European Family Law Regarding Divorce and Maintenance between Former Spouses* (Cambridge: Intersentia, 2004).

[32] See M. Rheinstein, 'Trends in Marriage and Divorce Laws of Western Countries', in M. B. Sussman (ed.), *Sourcebook in Marriage and the Family* (San Francisco, CA: Houghton Mifflin, 1968).

liberal equality against gender paternalism.[33] Similarly, law regarding family formation and organization became increasingly fluid, permitting more varied choices and legal statuses accomplished through contractual regimes.[34] From cohabitation to alternative family formations such as de facto or equitable parenthood that exemplified new forms of legal parenthood detached from biology or marriage, or the law of non-marriage, these new social and legal realities have often run up against moralizing and stigmatizing by social conservatives.[35]

While neoliberal economic policy fostered the expansion of certain spheres of personal freedom within the family, it also produced increased economic regulation of family life. For instance, in the United States, the assumption that single mothers of young children who received welfare should not just be caregivers but should also be in the workforce grew in prominence.[36] Also, federal child support regimes, which had originally been aimed at relieving governments of welfare obligations for economic support of poor families, were expanded to reallocate between parents not receiving welfare the financial burdens of caring for children.[37] The federal collection regime to secure and enforce child support expanded to assist

[33] See R. B. Siegel, 'Dignity and the Politics of Protection: Abortion Restrictions under Casey/Carhart' (2008) 117 *Yale Law Journal* 1694–1800.

[34] See M. M. Ertman, *Love's Promises: How Formal and Informal Contracts Shape All Kinds of Families* (Boston, IL: Beacon Press, 2015).

[35] See A. Antognini, 'Against Nonmarital Exceptionalism' (2018) 51 *UC Davis Law Review* 1891–1972; M. J. Higdon, 'Constitutional Parenthood' (2018) 103 *Iowa Law Review* 1483–1541.

[36] Minow, 'The Welfare of Single Mothers', at 823–826; Miller, *Women and Social Welfare*, 37; L. A. Williams, 'The Legal Construction of Poverty: Gender, "Work" and the "Social Contract"' (2011) 22 *Stellenbosch Law Review* 463–481.

[37] C. Solomon-Fears, *The Child Support Enforcement Program: A Legislative History*, Congressional Research Service, R44423, 2016; Child Support Enforcement Amendments of 1984, Pub. L. No. 98-378, 98 Stat. 1305, codified at 42 USC 651, 657, 658, 666: 'Section 451 of the Social Security Act is amended by ... assuring that assistance in obtaining support will be available under this part to all children (whether or not eligible for aid under part A) for whom such assistance is requested'; 42 USC 666 on interception of tax refunds: 'for the purpose of enforcing a support order under any State plan approved under this part'; 42 USC 658 on incentive payments: 'In order to encourage and reward State child support enforcement programs which perform in a cost-effective and efficient manner to secure support for all children who have sought assistance in securing support, whether ... or not they are eligible for aid to families with dependent children ... and regardless of the economic circumstances of their parents'; 42 USC 657, requiring states to continue child support services to families terminated from the welfare rolls without charging an application fee.

middle-class and divorced women who were encumbered in their market participation. Governments loath to regulate markets directly welcomed social policies rooted in changing economic allocation within the family as a way to foster women's participation in the labour force in the face of the gendered division of labour within the family. Advocacy organizations concerned about gender equity mobilized to enlist the child support system to moderate the consequences for women of an increasingly harsh market for families, exacerbated by neoliberal policies.[38]

By the 1990s, economic conditions and state economic support for families became ever more tenuous, not just for the poor, but for increasing segments of the population.[39] In the European Union although family law remained an area of competence of the member states, the procedural rules applying in cross-border cases to European couples led to the increasing harmonization of family law regimes.[40] With the EU enlargement towards

[38] J. E. Crowley, 'The Gentrification of Child Support Enforcement Services, 1950–1984' (2003) 77 *Social Service Review* 585–604. See Oversight Hearing on Child Support Enforcement before the Subcommittee on Select Education of the House Committee on Education and Labor, 98th Cong. 67–77 (1983), statement of Judith Avner, Staff Attorney, National Organization for Women Legal Defense and Education Fund and National Center on Women and Family Law; Hearings on Potential Inequities Affecting Women before the Senate Committee on Finance, 98th Cong. 80, 103, 118, 255 (1983), testimony on behalf of the American Association of University for Women, National Organization for Women Legal Defense and Education Fund, National Women's Law Center, and Women's Legal Defense Fund; Hearing on Child Support Enforcement Program Reform Proposals before the Senate Committee on Finance, 98th Cong. 211 (1984), testimony on behalf of the National Women's Law Center; Hearing on Child Support Enforcement Legislation before the Subcommittee on Public Assistance and Unemployment Compensation of the House Committee on Ways and Means, 98th Cong. 128, 354 (1983), testimony on behalf of the National Women's Law Center, Women's Legal Defense Fund, and twenty-eight other organizations. For a review of A. H. Beller and J. W. Graham, *Small Change: The Economics of Child Support* (London: Yale University Press, 1993), and D. J. Hernandez, *America's Children: Resources from Family, Government and the Economy* (New York: Russell Sage Foundation, 1993), see C. Pateman, *The Sexual Contract* (Cambridge: Polity Press, 1988). See also M. Garrison, 'Child Support and Children's Poverty' (1994) 28 *Family Law Quarterly* 475–508.

[39] Professor Melinda Cooper uses Clinton's Personal Responsibility and Work Opportunity Reconciliation Act of 1996, Pub. L. No. 104–193, 110 Stat. 2105, as an example to show the alliance between neoliberalism and social conservatives. M. Cooper, *Family Values: Between Neoliberalism and the New Social Conservatism* (New York: Zone Books, 2017), 101–109. See also L. Adler, *Gay Priori: A Queer Critical Legal Studies Approach to Law Reform* (Durham, NC: Duke University Press, 2018).

[40] See M. Antokolskaia, 'Harmonisation of Substantive Family Law in Europe: Myths and Reality' (2010) 22 *Child and Family Law Quarterly* 397–421.

Eastern and Central Europe, neoliberal economic policies made it increasingly difficult for poor and middle-class families to obtain state-sponsored or -funded economic support as they faced increasingly insecure market-based conditions for safeguarding the welfare of family life and the well-being of working women.[41] In the United States, family members experienced increasing regulation of family life. Family law provided mechanisms for minutely controlled redistribution of income within a family, largely divorced from the gendered and racialized operation of markets.[42] The alliance between neoliberal and neoconservative economic policy expanded monitoring and surveillance of families, beginning with those dependent upon the state for economic sustenance.[43]

As family law became an important site for increased liberalization regarding social norms and practices of family life, it also became the site for growing conflicts regarding those changes. For instance, in the EU, states retained the ability to implement greater social welfare measures for the family as they retained through their liberal constitutional orders the ability to recognize a plurality of religious practices in family law.[44] Despite the different meanings of equality in the American and the European contexts,[45] the universalist justifications for same-sex marriage, which have revolved around notions of individual privacy and human dignity, coalesced with LGBTQ+ strategies into the human rights

[41] See K. Rittich, *Recharacterizing Restructuring: Law, Distribution and Gender in Market Reform* (Berlin: Springer, 2002).

[42] See Williams, 'The Legal Construction of Poverty'; Minow, 'The Welfare of Single Mothers', at 834–838. Stein highlights the originality of this cooperative federalism between state and federal governments in family law. Stein, 'Uniformity and Diversity'. For a criticism of the apolitical views of Europeans on cooperative federalism, see E. Delaney, 'From Dual to Cooperative Federalism: The Changing Structure of European Law' (2010) 41 *Publius: The Journal of Federalism* 349–359, reviewing R. Schútze, *From Dual to Cooperative Federalism: The Changing Structure of European Law* (Oxford: Oxford University Press, 2009).

[43] Handler, *The Poverty of Welfare*, 60–62 and 89–90; D. E. Roberts, 'The Value of Black Mothers' Work' (1994) 26 *Connecticut Law Review* 871–878; D. L. Chambers, 'Fathers, the Welfare System, and the Virtues and Perils of Child-Support Enforcement' (1995) 81 *Virginia Law Review* 2575–2605.

[44] See S. Mancini (ed.), *Constitutions and Religion* (Cheltenham: Edward Elgar, 2020).

[45] See I. Isailovic, 'Same Sex but Not the Same: Same-Sex Marriage in the United States and France and the Universalist Narrative' (2018) 66 *American Journal of Comparative Law* 267–315.

movements.[46] The vision of the sexual family as a private sphere in the home, protected from government intrusion, has emerged prominently in the European Convention on Human Rights and its jurisprudence on same-sex marriage.[47] As early as 2001, legislatures in the Netherlands and Belgium introduced same-sex marriage, with Spain following soon after, in 2003. However, when confronted with the opportunity to create a universal right of marriage for same-sex couples, the European Court of Human Rights (ECtHR) declined to do so, even though it created a positive obligation for the states to recognize and protect same-sex couples.[48] In doing so, the ECtHR left to the states the flexibility to reconcile religious norms with the legal definition of marriage. By contrast, in the United States – where, beginning in 2004, some states had legalized same-sex marriage through court rulings, legislation or popular direct votes – the Supreme Court legalized same-sex marriage throughout the country with its 2015 ruling in *Obergefell*, leaving very little ability for the states to depart from it.[49]

While *Obergefell* equalized, at least in a formal sense, access to civil marriage, the case also downplayed all those forms of partnership that do not amount to marriage.[50] *Obergefell*'s exaltation of marriage created new tensions with many other Supreme Court cases that, over the last fifty years, have offered tentative constitutional protections for non-marriage

[46] See D. Paternotte and M. Tremblay (eds.), *The Ashgate Research Companion to Lesbian and Gay Activism* (London: Routledge, 2015).

[47] See Art. 8, European Convention on Human Rights, opened for signature 4 November1950, CETS No. 5, guaranteeing the right to respect for private life, family life, home and correspondence.

[48] See *Oliari* v. *Italy*, App. Nos. 18766/11 and 36030/11, 174-186 (21 July 2015), http://hudoc.echr.coe.int/eng?i=001-156265. For a comment, see S. Ragone and V. Volpe, 'An Emerging Right to a "Gay" Family Life? The Case Oliari v. Italy in a Comparative Perspective' (2018) 17 *German Law Journal* 451–485; L. Hodson, 'Sexual Orientation and the European Convention on Human Rights: What of the "L" in LGBT?' (2019) 23 *Journal of Lesbian Studies* 383–396.

[49] See *Miller* v. *Davis*, 123 F. Supp. 3d 924 (ED Ky. 2015), granting an injunction against a county clerk who, following the *Obergefell* decision, announced that her office would refuse to issue marriage licences to any couples in order to avoid granting licences to same-sex couples, vacated as moot, *Miller* v. *Davis*, No. 15-44-DLB, 2016 WL 11695944 (ED Ky. 18 August 2016).

[50] M. Murray, 'Obergefell v. Hodges and Nonmarriage Inequality' (2016) 104 *Californian Law Review* 1207–1258 at 1210.

and non-marital families.[51] As Melissa Murray explained, the Court's ruling in *Obergefell* might be understood as effectively foreclosing the possibility of greater protections for situations that fall outside marriage.[52] In *Obergefell*, the Supreme Court promoted marriage as the 'unique' normative ideal for intimate life. In encouraging marriage so vigorously, *Obergefell* went beyond the idea of simply favouring marriage over potential alternatives; it gestured toward the repudiation of the jurisprudence of non-marriage and its aspirations for non-marital equality.[53] From a familial subject standpoint, marriage was now firmly enshrined and regulated as part of the sexual rather than the economic family.

3. From Racial Emancipation in *Loving* to the Sexual Family in *Obergefell*

More than fifty years ago, the Supreme Court ruled unanimously, in *Loving* v. *Virginia*, that laws prohibiting interracial marriage or anti-miscegenation laws were unconstitutional.[54] Academics have described *Loving* as 'a case about law ceding to the power of love in the face of astonishing harassment and bigotry endured by interracial couples'.[55] Rather than celebrating love, the Warren Court's opinion stated that Virginia's laws against interracial marriage were unconstitutional since they represented measures designed to 'maintain White Supremacy'.[56]

[51] See, e.g., *Lawrence* v. *Texas*, 539 US 558 (2003); *Moore* v. *City of East Cleveland*, 431 US 494 (1977). Moore can be seen as a ruling aimed at a more pluralistic regime of relationship recognition in which marriage exists alongside a range of non-marital alternatives.

[52] Murray, 'Obergefell v. Hodges and Nonmarriage Inequality', at 1239.

[53] *Obergefell*, 576 US [656] (emphasis added).

[54] *Loving* v. *Virginia*, 388 US 1 (1967).

[55] O. K. Obasogie, 'Was Loving v. Virginia Really about Love?', *The Atlantic*, 12 June 2017, www.theatlantic.com/politics/archive/2017/06/loving-v-virginia-marks-its-fiftieth-anniversary/529929; L. C. McClain, 'Prejudice, Constitutional Moral Progress, and Being "On the Right Side of History": Reflections on Loving v. Virginia at Fifty' (2018) 86 *Fordham Law Review* 2701–2715.

[56] *Loving*, 388 US [11]:

> There is patently no legitimate overriding purpose independent of invidious racial discrimination which justifies this classification. The fact that Virginia prohibits only interracial marriages involving white persons demonstrates that the racial classifications must stand on their own justification, as measures designed to maintain White Supremacy. We have consistently denied the constitutionality of measures which restrict the rights of citizens on account of race. There can be no doubt that restricting

Indeed, when *Loving* was decided, Virginia had passed two relevant provisions: the Racial Integrity Act[57] and the Sterilization Act,[58] highlighting Virginia's concern with interracial love and underlining that the white race was in danger of being weakened by 'inferior traits'. At the time of *Loving*, marriage was seen by the Supreme Court justices as an opportunity to create racial emancipation through moral progress.[59] However, critical race scholars have shown the failures of the judicial integrationist ideal of the Warren court,[60] as the notion of 'racial agency' was lost in favour of abstract constitutional principles.[61] In practice, the decline of marriage among African Americans, for a variety of socio-economic reasons,[62] demonstrates that the current supremacy of marriage for structuring families, as opposed to cohabitation, has heavily penalized poor and racialized communities.[63]

In *United States* v. *Windsor*,[64] the Supreme Court, following its Fourteenth Amendment jurisprudence,[65] held that a section of the Defense of Marriage Act (DOMA),[66] which defined marriage at the federal level as exclusively a relationship between one man and one woman, was unconstitutional for stigmatizing those entering into a same-sex marriage.[67] But *Windsor* did not eliminate the mobility paradox of what happens to a same-sex couple legally married in one state when residing in another state that does not recognize same-sex marriage, entailing the

the freedom to marry solely because of racial classifications violates the central meaning of the Equal Protection Clause.

57 Preservation of Racial Integrity Act, 1924 Va. Acts 534, invalidated by *Loving* v. *Virginia*, 388 US 1 (1967).

58 Virginia Sterilization Act, 1924 Va. Acts c. 394 (repealed 1974).

59 See McClain, 'Prejudice, Constitutional Moral Progress'.

60 D. A. Bell Jr, 'Serving Two Masters: Integration Ideals and Client Interests in School Desegregation Litigation' (1976) 85 *Yale Law Journal* 470–516.

61 See S. Foster, 'Race, Agency, and Equal Protection: A Retrospective on the Warren Court', in H. N. Scheiber (ed.), *Earl Warren and the Warren Court: The Legacy in American and Foreign Law* (Lanham, MD: Lexington Books, 2007), 77.

62 On evidence that Black couples paid more taxes than their white counterparts in the United States, see D. A. Brown, *The Whiteness of Wealth: How the Tax System Impoverishes Black Americans – and How We Can Fix It* (New York: Crown, 2021).

63 See Lenhardt, 'Marriage as Black Citizenship?'; R. A. Lenhardt, 'The Color of Kinship' (2017) 102 *Iowa Law Review* 2071–2107.

64 570 US 744 (2013).

65 See *Romer* v. *Evans*, 517 US 635 (1996); *Lawrence* v. *Texas*, 539 US 558, 578 (2003).

66 Defense of Marriage Act (DOMA), Pub. L. No. 104–199, 110 Stat. 2419 (1996), invalidated by *United States* v. *Windsor*, 570 US 744 (2013).

67 *Windsor*, 570 US [774-775].

loss of tax, inheritance and a multitude of other legal benefits for spouses. This paradoxical situation was resolved by judicial fiat in 2015 by *Obergefell* v. *Hodges*. In the summer of 2013, Jim Obergefell and John Aurthur, partners for twenty years, travelled from their home in Ohio, where same-sex marriage was illegal, to Maryland, a state that had legalized same-sex marriage. Arthur was terminally ill, so the pair had chartered a medical flight and were married on the tarmac at Baltimore/Washington International Airport. After Arthur's death, Ohio refused to list Obergefell as the surviving spouse on Arthur's death certificate, and Obergefell sued to have their marriage recognized by Ohio.[68]

As Obergefell was legally married in Maryland but not in Ohio, the Supreme Court could have addressed this mobility paradox through the Privileges and Immunities or the Full Faith and Credit Clauses in the Constitution, which guarantee that all US citizens are afforded the same rights. Instead, Justice Kennedy framed the question around the right to marry as a fundamental right that must also be guaranteed to same-sex couples.[69] Differently from *Loving*, generally seen as a story about romantic love,[70] but tackling more urgent antiracist goals, in *Obergefell*, the Supreme Court fully embraced the importance of romantic love as central to its vision of the marital privacy and companionship of the sexual family.[71]

If *Loving* constitutes a relevant case concerning racial intimacy,[72] *Obergefell* seems much more related to how the right to marry allows structuring care and addresses individual alienation through the nuclear family by focusing disproportionately on individual dignity rather than social equality. Some commentators explained that *Obergefell* represented

[68] See M. S. Rosenwald, 'How Jim Obergefell Became the Face of the Supreme Court Gay Marriage Case', *Washington Post*, 6 April 2015, www.washingtonpost.com/local/how-jim-obergefell-became-the-face-of-the-supreme-court-gay-marriage-case/2015/04/06/3740433c-d958-11e4-b3f2-607bd612aeac_story.html.

[69] *Obergefell*, 576 US [675].

[70] See, e.g., A. Kerr, 'Love Wins', *Women Advance*, 17 June 2019, www.womenadvancenc.org/2019/06/17/love-wins.

[71] *Obergefell*, 576 US [667]. In Justice Kennedy's words, '[m]arriage responds to the universal fear that a lonely person might call out only to find no one there. It offers the hope of companionship and understanding and assurance that while both still live there will be someone to care for the other'. *Obergefell*, 576 US [667].

[72] H. Lau, From *Loving* to *Obergefell*: Elevating the Significance of Discriminatory Effects (2018) 25 *Virginia Journal of Social Policy & the Law* 317–329.

a 'fundamental rights' reasoning, relying primarily on the Fourteenth Amendment's Due Process clause, as well as repeatedly emphasizing the concept of individual dignity.[73] Others pointed out how the ruling was likely to have negative repercussions for those who, by choice or by circumstance, live their lives outside of marriage.[74] Indeed, *Obergefell* established equal access to marriage based on the idea that marriage represents the most profound, dignified and fundamental institution that individuals may enter in their lives. By comparison, however, alternatives to marriage appeared to be less profound, less dignified and less valuable,[75] yet constituted the realities of those racialized, poor and vulnerable subjects[76] not included as perfect plaintiffs advocating for the sexual family.[77]

To some commentators, the consequences that may result from *Obergefell* are that it forecloses the possibility of further developing the jurisprudence to provide robust constitutional protections for life outside marriage,[78] and it leaves those non-marital families constituted by poor, racialized and vulnerable subjects in a constitutionally precarious position.[79] Even though *Obergefell* deals with equal access to marriage for same-sex couples, it implicitly underwrites the inequality of non-marital families, a consequence that has led scholars to call it the jurisprudence of non-marriage.[80]

[73] K. Yoshino, 'A New Birth of Freedom? Obergefell v. Hodges' (2015) 129 *Harvard Law Review* 147–179.

[74] N. D. Polikoff, 'Ending Marriage as We Know It' (2003) 32 *Hofstra Law Review* 201–232; M. Warner, 'Beyond Gay Marriage', in W. Brown and J. Halley (eds.), *Left Legalism/Left Critique* (Durham, NC: Duke University Press, 2002), 260; A. P. Harris, 'From Stonewall to Suburbs? Toward a Political Economy of Sexuality' (2006) 14 *William & Mary Bill of Rights Journal* 1539–1582; Adler, *Gay Priori*, 61.

[75] Murray, 'Obergefell v. Hodges and Nonmarriage Inequality'.

[76] M. Albertson Fineman, 'Vulnerability and Inevitable Inequality' (2017) 4 *Oslo Law Review* 133–149.

[77] See K. M. Franke, 'The Politics of Same-Sex Marriage Politics' (2006) 15 *Columbia Journal of Gender and Law* 236–248 at 239.

[78] See C. G. Joslin, 'The Gay Rights Canon and the Right to Nonmarriage' (2017) 97 *Boston University Law Review* 425–488; K. T. Matsumura, 'A Right Not to Marry' (2016) 84 *Fordham Law Review* 1509–1588.

[79] Murray explains that in a footnote of his dissenting opinion, Justice Thomas criticizes the majority for its assertion according to which 'marriage confers "nobility" on individuals', referring to *Obergefell* v. *Hodges*, 576 US 644, [735, n. 8] (2015). Murray, 'Obergefell v. Hodges and Nonmarriage Inequality', at 1257.

[80] Murray, 'Obergefell v. Hodges and Nonmarriage Inequality', at 1258.

4. Oscillating between the Sexual and the Economic Family in *Coman*

In 2018 the European Court of Justice (ECJ) in its *Coman*[81] ruling fell short of the general requirement to establish same-sex marriage in all twenty-seven member states, as established in all fifty states by the US Supreme Court in *Obergefell.*[82] However, just like the Supreme Court, the ECJ was called upon to interpret when state family law is in conflict with European free movement rights bestowed on EU citizens.[83] The parallel with *Obergefell* thus lies not so much in the comparison with the due process or equal protection jurisprudence but as the functional analogy of removing the barriers to free movement for same-sex couples from one state to another. For this reason, scholars have celebrated *Coman* as part of a more general development of extending the recognition of same-sex marriage by granting to same-sex spouses moving to a different state in the EU the right of residence irrespective of whether that member state has recognized same-sex marriage.[84] In contrast to *Obergefell*, the ECJ framed the issue presented in *Coman* as a question of internal market law, rather than a circumstance involving fundamental rights and human dignity,[85] thus, allaying some of the concerns of the member states that vehemently

[81] Case C-673/16, *Coman* v. *Imigrări*, ECLI:EU:C:2018:385 (5 June 2018).

[82] *Obergefell*, 576 US [680-681].

[83] Art. 21(1) of the Treaty on the Functioning of the EU (TFEU), stating that '[e]very citizen of the Union shall have the right to move and reside freely within the territory of the Member States, subject to the limitations and conditions laid down in the Treaties and by the measures adopted to give them effect', Consolidated Version of the Treaty on the Functioning of the European Union Art. 21(1), 26 October 2012, 2012 OJ (C 326/47) 57.

[84] S. Peers, 'Love Wins in the CJEU: Same Sex Marriages and EU Free Movement Law', *EU Law Analysis*, 5 June 2018, http://eulawanalysis.blogspot.com/2018/06/love-wins-in-cjeu-same-sex-marriages.html; A. Tryfonidou, 'An Analysis of the ECJ Ruling in Case C-673/16 Coman: The Right of Same-Sex Spouses under EU Law to Move Freely between EU Member States', NELFA, January 2019, http://nelfa.org/inprogress/wp-content/uploads/2019/01/NELFA-Tryfonidou-report-Coman-final-NEW.pdf.

[85] Article 9 of the Charter of Fundamental Rights of the European Union (EUCFR) states: 'The right to marry and the right to found a family shall be guaranteed in accordance with the national laws governing the exercise of these rights'. Art. 9, Charter of Fundamental Rights of the European Union, 2000 OJ (C 364) 1, 10. This provision, laid down in Article 1 of the EUCFR, played a relevant role in domestic Constitutional Courts in relation to cases concerning the rights of same-sex couples. The ECJ preferred instead to make reference only to Article 7 of the Charter, about the respect for private and family life.

opposed same-sex marriage.[86] In its reasoning, the court analysed the case mostly from the perspective of the right to freedom of movement of EU citizens so that it oscillated from the sexual towards the economic family.[87]

In 2002, Relu Adrian Coman, who held both Romanian and US citizenships, met Robert Clabourn Hamilton, a US national, in New York. They started a relationship and, after several years of cohabitation, Coman decided to leave the United States to work as a parliamentary assistant at the European Parliament in Brussels, where the couple married in 2010. Such a marriage was not possible in Romania, as the country offers neither marriage nor partnership for same-sex couples.[88] Following several years of a long-distance relationship, the couple decided to settle in Romania, where Coman applied for a residence-permit for his husband based on his right of family reunification.[89] When the couple requested information from the Romanian authorities on the procedure and conditions under which Hamilton could obtain the right to reside lawfully in Romania as Coman's husband, they were informed that Hamilton did not have such a right. Under the Romanian Civil Code,[90] marriage between persons of the same sex is not recognized,[91] and the Romanian authorities refused to

[86] Article 7 of the Charter of Fundamental Rights of the European Union states that '[e]veryone has the right to respect for his or her private and family life, home and communications', 2000 OJ (C 364). However, similarly to its reproductive rights jurisprudence, the *Coman* court relied on the free movement of its citizens, rather than their fundamental rights. See S. Hennette Vauchez, 'The Society for the Protection of Unborn Children v. Grogan: Rereading the Case and Retelling the Story of Reproductive Rights in Europe', in F. Nicola and B. Davies (eds.), *EU Law Stories: Contextual and Critical Histories of European Jurisprudence* (Cambridge: Cambridge University Press, 2017), 393.

[87] Case C-673/16, *Coman* v. *Imigrări*, ECLI:EU:C:2018:385, 25, 28, 41, 47, 51 (5 June 2018), relying on Council Directive 2004/38, Art. 3, 2(2)(a), 7 2004 O.J. (L 158) 77, entitled 'on the right of citizens of the Union and their family members to move and reside freely within the territory of the Member States'.

[88] D. Kochenov and U. Belavusau, 'Same-Sex Spouses: More Free Movement, but What about Marriage?' (2020) 57 *Common Market Law Review* 227–242.

[89] Directive of the European Parliament and of the Council on the right of citizens of the Union and their family members to move and reside freely within the territory of the Member States, 2004/38, 2004 OJ (L 158) 77 [hereinafter Council Directive 2004/38].

[90] Tryfonidou, 'An Analysis of the ECJ Ruling in Case C-673/16 Coman', at 1–2.

[91] Article 259(1) of the Romanian Civil Code states that marriage is 'the freely consented union between one man and one woman'. Codul civil al României [Civil Code], Art. 259 (Rom.). In addition, Article 277(1) of the Civil Code emphasizes that 'marriage shall be prohibited between persons of the same sex'. Finally, Article 277(4) states, even more

abide by the EU directive regulating the rights of free movement of European citizens.[92]

Supported by the LGBTQ organization Asociaţia ACCEPT, the couple filed an action before a Romanian tribunal, alleging that because the Civil Code did not recognize marriages between persons of the same sex entered into abroad, it infringed some of the provisions of the Romanian Constitution. The tribunal referred the matter to the Romanian Constitutional Court, which, considering both the EU and the Romanian constitutional frameworks, decided to submit a preliminary reference to the ECJ. The national court sought to clarify the conditions under which Hamilton could be granted the right to reside in Romania and whether EU law required the couple to move to gain recognition as married and, as such, to grant them family reunification rights.[93]

In its interpretation of Directive 2004/38, the ECJ held that the term 'spouse' within the meaning of the statue was gender neutral. Therefore, it could also cover a 'same-sex spouse of the Union citizens concerned'.[94] As a consequence, member states could not rely on their domestic provisions as justification for refusing to recognize in their territory a marriage concluded by a national with a citizen of the same sex in another member state.[95] The *Coman* case departs from the previous ECJ jurisprudence in which the rights of same-sex partners were mostly about equal treatment in the fields of employment and occupation.[96] It took a long time for a preliminary question on same-sex marriage and free-movement rights to arrive before the ECJ in Luxembourg because, in the case of same-sex couples consisting of two nationals from different European states, each

specifically, that 'marriages between persons of the same sex entered into or contracted abroad by Romanian citizens or by foreigners shall not be recognized in Romania'.

92 See Council Directive 2004/38.

93 Case C-673/16, *Coman* v. *Imigrări*, ECLI:EU:C:2018:385, 1–2 (5 June 2018).

94 Ibid., at 35. 95 Ibid., at 36.

96 See, e.g., staff cases: Joined Cases C-122 and 125/99 *P, D* v. *Council of the Eur. Union*, 2001 ECR I-4342; Case T-58/08 P, *Commission of the European Communities* v. *Roodhuijzen*, 2009 ECR II-3801. See in the field of employment, Case C-249/96, *Grant* v. *S.-W. Trains Ltd.*, 1998 ECR I-636; Case C-267/06, *Maruko* v. *Bühnen*, 2008 ECR I-1788; Case C-147/08, *Römer* v. *Hamburg*, 2011 ECR I-3645; Case C-267/12, *Hay* v. *Crédit agricole mutuel de Charente-Maritime et des Deux-Sèvres*, ECLI:EU:C:2013:823 (12 December 2013); Case C-443/15, *Parris* v. *Trinity Coll. Dublin*, ECLI:EU:C:2016:897 (24 November 2016).

spouse could independently claim their rights of free movement as an EU citizen. Conversely, with respect to family members who are non-EU citizens, like one of the spouses in *Coman*, Hamilton was allowed to invoke derived rights based only on his connection to an EU citizen. This makes the *Coman* case perfect strategic litigation.[97]

The *Coman* ruling offers much overdue legal certainty for married couples of the same sex. The focus on the economic family derives from the importance of freedom of movement that, if denied, would easily result in a set of serious inconveniences at the administrative, professional and private levels. These same concerns motivated the *Obergefell* litigation but, unlike the Supreme Court, the ECJ did not seize the opportunity to address the issue of marriage equality based on the rights protected in its own legal framework and fully embrace the sexual family. Nonetheless, the *Coman* ruling generated conflicting outcomes in some EU member states.[98] For example, in January 2019, the Lithuanian Constitutional Court established that provisions regarding freedom of movement of family members also applied to same-sex couples. Therefore, any refusal to issue a temporary residence permit to a same-sex spouse or partner could not be based solely on gender identity and/or sexual orientation.[99] A few months later, a Bulgarian Supreme Administrative Court refused to recognize a same-sex couple's union.[100]

In Western family law, the oscillation of same-sex marriage between the sexual and the economic family has become part of the regulation of both financial and intimate relationships that we associate with the familial

[97] A. Coman, 'Landmark Case from Romania Expands Possibilities for LGBT Rights', OpenGlobalRights, 5 March 2019, www.openglobalrights.org/landmark-case-from-romania-expands-possibilities-for-lgbt-rights.

[98] B. Sieverding, 'Presentation at Recognising Rainbow Families: Rainbow Families in Europe', *NELFA*, 18 June 2019, http://nelfa.org/inprogress/wp-content/uploads/2019/06/NELFA-presentation-18062019-final1.pdf.

[99] Ruling on the Compliance of Item 5 of Paragraph 1 of Article 43 of the Republic of Lithuania's Law on the Legal Status of Aliens with the Constitution of the Republic of Lithuania, Case No. 16/2016, Kt3-N1/2019 (Constitutional Court of the Republic of Lithuania, 11 January 2019).

[100] Should the case arrive before the European Court of Justice, this would be another opportunity for a ruling on same-sex marriage. I. Ivanova, 'The Supreme Administrative Court Refused to Recognize that Same-Sex Couples Are Entitled to Their Marriages Concluded Abroad', NELFA, 12 November 2019, http://nelfa.org/inprogress/wp-content/uploads/2019/12/Deystvie-PR-12112019-deniedmarriage.pdf.

subject.[101] At the same time, resistance to this transnational or federal governmentality of the family triggered by *Coman* and *Obergefell* has coalesced around entrenched traditional family values, from patriarchy to domination of men over women and children, now re-emerging in the agenda of authoritarian and illiberal democracies.[102] Not surprisingly, anti-same-sex marriage litigation has begun rapidly at least in the United States in the shadow of anti-abortion advocacy which has led to the overturning of a fifty-year precedent.[103] The success of social conservatives in undermining reproductive rights draws upon and elevates long entrenched precedents based in arguments in favour of traditional family values.[104]

5. The Social Conservative Narrative of the Natural Family

Family law rules are not only central to understanding how markets function; they also provide another alternative to the state as a way to shape the identity of a nation.[105] The neoconservative view of the ideal nuclear family is not connected to the idea of free markets, but rather to those social values that should be actively protected by the state. Social conservative lawyers, judges and politicians have set the family aside from the market and support welfare regimes controlling the shaping of family units that fit a particular white, heterosexual and male-headed vision of the family.[106] Although social conservatives and liberals seem to hold opposite values, they have found common ground in the ways they aim to regulate welfare and family

[101] See I. Isailovic, 'Gender Equality as Investment: EU Work–Life Balance Measures and the Neoliberal Shift' (2021) 46 *Yale Journal of International Law* 277–324.

[102] See Cooper, *Family Values*.

[103] *Dobbs* v. *Jackson Women's Health Org.*, 597 US __ (2022) (overruling *Roe* v. *Wade*, 410 US 113 (1973)).

[104] See D. NeJaime and R. Siegel, 'Revised Opinions in Obergefell v. Hodges (Concurring)', in J. M. Balkin (ed.), *What Obergefell v. Hodges Should Have Said: The Nation's Top Legal Experts Rewrite America's Same-Sex Marriage Decision* (London: Yale University Press, 2020), 112; D. NeJaime and R. Siegel, 'Religious Exemptions and Antidiscrimination Law in Masterpiece Cakeshop' (2018) 128 *Yale Law Journal Forum* 201–225; D. NeJaime and R. Siegel, 'Conscience Wars in the Americas' (2020) 5 *Latin American Law Review* 1–26.

[105] See Cooper, *Family Values*, 62; D. Kennedy, 'Three Globalizations of Law and Legal Thought: 1850–2000', in D. M. Trubek and A. Santos (eds.), *The New Law and Economic Development: A Critical Appraisal* (2006), 19 and 25–27.

[106] See J. Stacey, *In the Name of the Family: Rethinking Family Values in the Postmodern Age* (Boston, MA: Beacon, 1996).

regimes. While social conservatives have promoted state intervention as a necessary means to impose new patriarchal structures on a central social unit like the family, neoliberals have supported economic incentives to make the family more efficient, like the market.[107]

An emblematic case showing the social conservative intervention of the US Supreme Court in the family by elevating marriage above biology in shaping legal parenthood is *Michael H.* v. *Gerald D.*,[108] in which a married woman became pregnant with a child whose father was not her husband.[109] Based on an irrebuttable marital presumption, her husband was legally the child's father.[110] However, the child spent significant time and maintained a relationship with both of the fathers.[111] As the child grew up, the biological father had less access to the child and sued to obtain visitation.[112] Justice Antonin Scalia, writing the plurality opinion, expressed a desire to preserve the integrity of only the marital family unit using the historical specter of legitimacy, although it thoroughly discredited in contemporary American law.[113] While repeatedly emphasizing the importance of history and tradition, Justice Scalia also asserted that discussed the court could not provide a non-marital biological parent any legal recognition without taking away that fundamental right from the legally presumed parent.[114] Even though the child's attorney argued that the child had a fundamental interest in a relationship with both fathers,[115] the court held that the legal parents of the child were the married parents only, regardless of biology.[116]

In the European Union, the rise of populist governments after 2010, which embrace either progressive or conservative social values, has led the latter movements to put traditional family values at the centre of their agenda.[117] In the United States, socially conservative initiatives have included limiting or abolishing reproductive freedom; increasing the permissible scope of religiously based restrictions on individual behaviour that have consequences for family life and gender-affirming medical procedures for minors; the forced separation of immigrant children from parents and other family, with no legal process; and the exclusion of immigrant families from family-based social welfare programmes. The

[107] Cooper, *Family Values*. [108] 491 US 110 (1989). [109] Ibid., [113–114].
[110] Ibid., [113, 115 and 117]. [111] Ibid., [113–116]. [112] Ibid., [114–115].
[113] Ibid., [120 and 131]. [114] Ibid., [118 and 130]. [115] Ibid., [114–116 and 130–131].
[116] Ibid., [131–132].
[117] B. Bugarič, 'The Two Faces of Populism: Between Authoritarian and Democratic Populism' (2019) 20 *German Law Journal* 390–400.

retrenchment from supporting the sexual family as a site of certain types of non-economic liberty coincides with increasing economic right-liberalizing policies. These politics have exacerbated a neoliberal vision of the economic family, triggering great economic insecurity for poor, racialized and vulnerable families. These economic dynamics reinforce gender norms by entrenching conservative social values rooted in patriarchal structures in the construction of the narrative of the natural family. narrative oscillates between more welfarist or neoliberal visions of the economic family, thus making the familial subject a fundamental part of economic redistribution.

In 1997, the first World Congress of Families (WCF) took place in Prague and by 1999 its goal was seeking to 'unite and equip leaders, organizations, and families to affirm, celebrate and defend the natural family as the only fundamental and sustainable unit of society'.'[118] The WCF originates from Allan Carlson, a retired scholar and professor of history at Hillsdale College in Michigan and a former Reagan administration official.[119] Carlson's writings are about how sexual and feminist liberation brought on a demographic decline caused by the collapse of the traditional family pattern, affected, over time, by factors such as divorce, women in the workforce and homosexuality.[120] Carlson was a co-founder of the Howard Center for Family, Religion & Society, an organization aimed at researching the societal benefits of the natural family embedded in a religious culture and at creating continuity in the social order, while affirming the economic patterns sustaining a healthy home and family integrity.[121] Although its origins are traceable to the United States, the

[118] International Organization for the Family, 'Mission', https://profam.org/mission. See generally D. Buss and D. Herman, *Globalizing Family Values: The Christian Right in International Politics* (Minneapolis: University of Minnesota Press, 2003).

[119] A. C. Carlson, 'Biography', www.allanccarlson.com/about.

[120] See 'Demographic Winter: The Decline of the Human Family', Acuity Productions, 2008, www.youtube.com/watch?v=lZeyYIsGdAA (filmed at the 2007 WCF congress); see also R. Trimble, 'The Threat of "Demographic Winter": A Transnational Politics of Motherhood and Endangered Populations in Pro-Family Documentaries' (2013) 25 *Feminist Formations* (Special Issue) 30–54.

[121] R. J. Trimble, 'Conceiving a "Natural Family" Order: The World Congress of Families and Transnational Conservative Christian Politics', PhD dissertation (Ohio State University, ProQuest, 2014), 1, fn. 2, and 63; A. Carlson, '"Family Cycles" and the Future of Family Law' (2015) 29 *Brigham Young University Journal of Public Law* 431–470 at 432–433 (2015). See generally A. C. Carlson and P. T. Mero, *The Natural Family: Bulwark of Liberty* (New York: Routledge, 2009); A. Carlson, *Fractured Generations: Crafting a Family Policy for Twenty-First-Century America* (New Brunswick, NJ: Transaction Publishers, 2005).

Howard Center, through the International Organization for Family (IOF) and WCF, rapidly influenced different countries, providing transnational networking for global anti-LGBTQ+ forces, working to curtail reproductive rights across the world, and promoting the natural family narrative.[122]

Through the natural family vision, IOF endorses a strict conception of the family, based exclusively on the marriage between one man and one woman and their biological children.[123] The patriarchal vision of the organization endorses the division of gender roles, in which men are those in charge of guiding the choices of the family and women take care of children in the home – only this type of family can stop the so-called demographic winter and give new light to our era.[124] Relying on the natural family, this IOF ideology opposes marriage equality and reproductive rights as the expression of free market liberalism. However, it also denies the freedoms and guarantees of marriage to LGBTQ+ families, single and divorced parents, and same-sex parents raising children of other family members.[125]

The manifesto of the natural family focuses on the centrality of marriage and childrearing to freedom and is designed to liberate 'the whole world – including dying Europa – for light and life, for children'.[126] The natural family narrative aims at the marginalization of LGBTQ+ community members and at the erosion of women's reproductive rights through its strict adherence to heterosexual unions and binary gender roles.[127]

[122] Trimble, *Conceiving a 'Natural Family' Order*, 2–4 and 66; D. S. Browning, *Marriage and Modernization: How Globalization Threatens Marriage and What to Do About It* (Grand Rapids, MI: Eerdmans, 2003), 211–114.

[123] International Organization for the Family, 'Mission'; A. C. Carlson, 'The Family in America: Retrospective and Prospective', *The Natural Family*, 19 September 2009, https://thenaturalfamily.org/article/the-family-in-america; Trimble, *Conceiving a 'Natural Family' Order*, 67–68.

[124] Trimble, *Conceiving a 'Natural Family' Order*, 123–127 and 132–133.

[125] See Carlson and Mero, *The Natural Family*, 10–14; K. Fox and V. Di Donato, 'In Italy's City of Love, Global Far-Right Groups Join Forces under a "Pro-Family" Umbrella', CNN, 31 March 2019, www.cnn.com/2019/03/31/europe/verona-world-congress-of-families-intl/index.html. The US Supreme Court has allowed Catholic charities to discriminate based on their free exercise of religion against same-sex couples seeking to become foster parents, *Fulton* v. *City of Philadelphia*, 593 US ___ (2021).

[126] A. C. Carlson and P. T. Mero, 'The Natural Family: A Manifesto', 2007, www.worldcongress.pl/docs/en/pdf/the_natural_family.pdf, 11

[127] A letter coordinated by the WCF and signed by 120 religious leaders from 11 countries to contest the participation of the US embassy in the Prague Gay Pride celebration in August 2012. Letter by Pro-Family Leaders Worldwide Protesting Participation of the US Embassy

Not surprisingly, this socially conservative position has enlisted as a prominent ally the Vatican, with its long crusade against 'gender ideology'.[128]

The natural family narrative migrated from the United States to other continents and, particularly, throughout Europe.[129] By holding conferences in cities around the world, the WCF has become the most important vehicle for transferring the natural family narrative sponsored by the Howard Center beyond North America. The congresses are international public events that seek to proselytize political leaders and common people to exalt and protect the natural family against gender ideology.[130] European illiberal democracies such as Hungary and Poland together with authoritarian regimes such as Turkey have undertaken the legal battle to withdraw from the 2011 Council of Europe Convention on Preventing and Combating Violence against Women and Domestic Violence[131] (Istanbul Convention) and replace it with another international treaty protecting traditional families as the Convention on the Rights of the Family.[132]

The socially conservative and authoritarian turn in Western liberal democracies demonstrates that family law operates as a battleground for larger ideological stakes that oscillate between the sexual and the natural

in Prague "Gay Pride" Parade, 13 August 2012, https://web.archive.org/web/20130514211638/http://profam.org/docs/Prague_Letter.pdf.

128 See M. A. Case, 'Trans Formations in the Vatican's War on "Gender Ideology"' (2019) 44 *Signs: Journal of Women in Culture and Society* 639–664.

129 Human Rights Campaign Foundation, 'Exposed: The World Congress of Families – An American Organization Exporting Hate', 2015, https://assets2.hrc.org/files/assets/resources/WCF_Report_REV_6-17-15_FINAL_(1).pdf?_ga=2.86083480.1205949973.1627494109-257637163.1627494109, 8. Specifically, the Howard Center gained more influence in Russia through the Russian Orthodox Church and the Putin regime, and in Central and Eastern Europe, especially Ukraine, Poland and Hungary. Human Rights Campaign Foundation, 'Exposed', 6 and 12–14.

130 Ibid., 5 and 9. During the XIII edition of the WCF that took place in Verona, 20,000 people protested, reaffirming the inalienability of gay rights, the right of abortion, and divorce. A. Giuffrida, 'Christian Right Summit in Verona Draws Massive Protest', *The Guardian*, 30 March 2019, www.theguardian.com/world/2019/mar/30/christian-right-summit-in-verona-draws-massive-protest.

131 Convention on Preventing and Combating Violence Against Women and Domestic Violence, opened for signature 5 November 2011, CETS 210, https://rm.coe.int/168008482e.

132 'International Convention on the Rights of the Family', Ordo Luris Inst. for Legal Culture, 7 November 2018, https://en.ordoiuris.pl/pliki/INTERNATIONAL_CONVENTION_ON_THE_RIGHTS_OF_THE_FAMILY.pdf, 3. See C. Ciobanu, 'Poland Begins Push in Region to Replace Istanbul Convention with "Family Rights" Treaty', Balkan Insight: Reporting Democracy, 6 October 2020, https://balkaninsight.com/2020/10/06/family-rights-treaty.

family. As family law exceptionalism reminds us, the underlying economic forms of redistribution also oscillate between welfarism and neoliberalism. The change in visions of the family underlying different types of political economy permits lawyers, politicians and judges to undertake their ideological struggles under the rubric of family law reforms.

6. Divorcing the Right to Marry from Family Welfare: Child Support and Parentage in the Economic Family

Just as in *Obergefell*, *Zablocki* v. *Redhail*[133] demonstrates an oscillation between the sexual and the economic family, as well as between different visions of the economic family.[134] In *Zablocki*, the Supreme Court held that an unmarried non-custodial father of a minor child could not be barred from marriage based on an unfulfilled child support obligation to that child or the likelihood that the child would become a public charge.[135] Individuals characterized as having failed at their financial responsibilities to support children or are poor and unlikely to provide future financial support nonetheless maintain their sphere of liberty regarding the decision to marry.

This liberty co-exists with approval of severe economic constraints based in the market and state welfare policy, which belie the idea of individual failure. While the Supreme Court gave Redhail the right to marry, it affirmed the state child support regime that consigned him to economic vulnerability in the market.[136] Rooted in gendered and racialized conceptions of motherhood and fatherhood, economic responsibility for children, and dependency upon the state, the law of child support and parentage constructed Redhail's choices.

Mr Redhail, a sixteen-year-old high school student, and his girlfriend had a daughter while unmarried.[137] At the time of her birth, the mother

[133] 434 US 374 (1978).

[134] This US Supreme Court case is another in the line of Supreme Court cases beginning with *Loving* v. *Virginia* and culminating with *Obergefell* v. *Hodges* that made most restrictions on access to marriage unconstitutional.

[135] *Zablocki*, 434 US [389].

[136] See Handler, *The Poverty of Welfare*.

[137] See T. L. Brito et al., 'Chronicle of a Debt Foretold: Zablocki v. Red Hail (1978)', in M. A. Failinger and E. Rosser (eds.), *The Poverty Law Canon: Exploring the Major Cases* (Ann Arbor: University of Michigan Press, 2016), 232. This chapter discusses the case in light of

applied for and received government benefits through Aid to Families with Dependent Children (AFDC).[138] As part of establishing her eligibility, the mother had to assign to the county her right to child support from the father. The government instituted a paternity action against Redhail, a legal prerequisite to the child support action. Redhail admitted paternity, and, without the mother or father present,[139] the court adjudicated Redhail the father and entered a child support order of $109 per month under a legal standard of 'just and reasonable',[140] although he was a minor, unemployed and indigent. All parties agreed in the litigation leading to the Supreme Court's decision that Redhail was unable to pay any of the child support obligation. That obligation was not owed to and would not go to the mother and child. Based on the assignment, Redhail owed money to the government to reimburse it for the AFDC payment.

After about two years, Redhail, who remained unable to pay, was several thousand dollars in arrears. He wanted to marry a woman who was not the mother of his child, but was pregnant with another child of his.[141] Under the Wisconsin statute challenged in the Supreme Court,[142] the state denied him and the woman he wanted to marry a licence because he was too poor to support his child. From the entry of the child support order through the denial of the application to get married, Redhail was indigent and unable to fulfil the child support order. Even had he been able to pay the full amount, he would not have been able to meet the public charge component of the statutory requirement, as the AFDC payments exceeded the child support payments he would have had to make.

the context of the experience of urban American Indians, particularly those in Milwaukee, Wisconsin. Roger Red Hail – the correct spelling of his name – a member of the Oneida tribe, lived in Milwaukee, Wisconsin, with his mother and eight siblings, with a large extended family in their neighbourhood. The family was poor.

[138] Ibid., 240. [139] Ibid.

[140] *Redhail* v. *Zablocki*, 418 F. Supp. 1061, 1063 (ED Wis. 1976). The court also ordered that he pay birth expenses, already covered by Medicaid, as well as court costs and a fee for having a guardian ad litem.

[141] Brito et al., 'Chronicle of a Debt Foretold', 233.

[142] Wis. Stat. Arts. 245.10(1), (4), (5) (repealed 1978). The statute required that he demonstrate to a court that he had fulfilled existing child support obligations and that any children covered by the order 'are not then and are not likely thereafter to become public charges'. Any marriage entered into without compliance would be void and getting a licence without compliance would be subject to civil and criminal penalties. These provisions were upheld by the Wisconsin Supreme Court in *State* v. *Mueller*, 171 NW 2d 414 (Wis. 1969), a case interpreting the penalties under the statute.

The Supreme Court rejected state justifications of the marriage bar as a device to counsel people intending to get married to pay child support[143] or as a debt collection tool[144] because both failed to serve their purported purposes. It did, however, endorse the legitimacy of the state using its monitoring and enforcement powers when poor people failed to pay child support. The state could pursue mechanisms, no matter how draconian,[145] to enforce the child support order, even in Redhail's dire and seemingly hopeless economic situation driven by market conditions. The court protected only Redhail's right to marry.[146]

This scenario in *Zablocki* implicates a powerful and expansive legal structure at the intersection of traditional family law (child support and parentage) with social welfare law. Although child support law began as private law[147] (one parent suing another for child support, public primarily through criminal statutes punishing non-support in state courts or through incarceration as a remedy in civil proceedings), it has become almost entirely a creature of federal regulatory law through the linkage of federal welfare payments to the collection of child support from what are labelled absent parents. Federal law mandated states to pass child support and paternity laws consistent with federal requirements to receive federal funds for extensive and expensive child support enforcement and parentage establishment programmes.[148]

143 *Zablocki* v. *Redhail*, 434 US 374, [388–389] (1978).

144 The marriage bar failed to yield any actual payments. Ibid., [389–390].

145 For example, civil and criminal penalties or increased child support.

146 J. Carbone and N. Cahn, *Marriage Markets: How Inequality Is Remaking the American Family* (Oxford: Oxford University Press, 2014); M. Eichner, 'The Privatized American Family' (2017) 93 *Notre Dame Law Review* 213–266.

147 E. Katz, 'Criminal Law in a Civil Guise: The Evolution of Family Courts and Support Laws' (2019) 86 *The University of Chicago Law Review* 1241–1309.

148 The scope of the state's role in securing child support is enormous. It includes child support establishment (which includes identifying and locating parents, establishing legal parentage, and adjudicating a child support amount), collecting that amount, enforcing payment and making modifications as families change. It requires numerous legal tools, many of which take the legal form of requirements imposed by the federal government on the states. States must establish massive and expensive administrative and judicial mechanisms to accomplish the multiple purposes of the programme; pass relatively uniform state laws making the federal requirements matters of state law; and impose draconian penalties for non-payment of child support. The federally mandated state laws range from the establishment of paternity through greater uniformity in child support awards (child support guidelines), through integration of the judicial and administrative mechanisms needed for the operation of a child support legal regime. The federal

Modern federal welfare law began during the New Deal as payments first to widows and then to single mothers with the creation of Aid to Dependent Children (ADC), which expanded in scope in the late 1950s and 1960s to Aid to Families with Dependent Children (AFDC). While child support was not officially incorporated into welfare law until later,[149] efforts during the welfare liberalization in the 1960s were contested by conservative forces seeking to punish single mothers and blame absent fathers, no matter how poor they were themselves. Despite extensive empirical evidence to the contrary, the custodial mother was portrayed as black and irresponsible;[150] the non-custodial father as a deadbeat dad.[151]

From the beginning of federalized child support, the state tied welfare payments to enforcement of the child support obligation of the non-custodial parent, almost always the father.[152] The family was entitled to state support only when it had failed in its private obligation to support children. The mother had failed for not being married and not working, the father for not supporting the family. The state had the right/obligation to recoup from fathers welfare payments to mothers, reimbursement for having to assume what were seen as intra-family obligations. This concept of state responsibility for the welfare of citizens took the legal form of the

government also makes available to states federal mechanisms for finding and monitoring people and collecting child support debts. See Child Support Enforcement Amendments of 1984, Pub. L. No. 98-378, 98 Stat. 1305, codified at 42 USC 503, [601–603, 651–658, 664, 667, 670–671 and 1315]. See generally L. H. Elrod, 'The Federalization of Child Support Guidelines' (1990) 6 *Journal of the American Academy of Matrimonial Lawyers* 103–130.

149 Legislation regarding welfare, child support, and parentage were all located within Title IV of the Social Security Act, 42 USC 602(a)(26)(A) (1976). Welfare law was Part A of the Social Security Act, and child support and parentage law were Part D. Pub. L. No. 74-271, 49 Stat. 620 (1935). Handler and Hasenfeld, *We the Poor People*, 128–131.

150 See, e.g., K. M. Bridges, *Critical Race Theory: A Primer* (St. Paul, MN: Foundation Press, 2019), 407–436; K. M. Bridges, *Reproducing Race: An Ethnography of Pregnancy as a Site of Racialization* (Berkeley: University of California Press, 2011), ch. 6; E. M. Townes, 'From Mammy to Welfare Queen: Images of Black Women in Public-Policy Formation', in B. J. Brooten (ed.), *Beyond Slavery: Overcoming Its Religious and Sexual Legacies* (2010); P. Nadasen, 'From Widow to "Welfare Queen": Welfare and the Politics of Race' (New York: Palgrave Macmillan, 2007) 1 *Black Women, Gender and Families* 52–77.

151 See, e.g., L. S. Kohn, 'Engaging Men as Fathers: The Courts, the Law, and Father-Absence in Low-Income Families' (2013) 35 *Cardoza Law Review* 512–557; A. Cammett, 'Deadbeats, Deadbrokes, and Prisoners' (2011) 18 *Georgetown Journal on Poverty Law and Policy* 127–168.

152 Custody was not used to refer to legally established custody. Rather, the custodial parent was the one who was taking care of the child.

custodial parent's assignment of the right to child support to the state, executed as a condition for the receipt of benefits.[153] With this assignment, the custodial parent ceased to be the legally recognized subject regarding decisions involving child support. The state became the primary actor in establishing, enforcing and collecting child support payments.

In the late 1970s and 1980s, modifications to child support law expanded the power of the government to make extracting money from non-custodial parents more efficient and effective[154] and to extend government's reach over the establishment, collection and enforcement of child support even where the state paid no public benefits to families.[155] State child support agencies also began providing help in securing the transfer of funds between two parents where no one was on welfare.[156] Liberal and cultural feminists advocated these reforms as promoting gender equality within the family where non-custodial parents – usually fathers – were not shouldering their share of the costs of raising a child.[157] These changes were directed primarily towards helping middle-class and white families in which mothers had dual responsibilities to support themselves and their children economically and to care for those children.

These reforms presented a conceptual challenge to the child support regime as these families were not poor, temporarily or long-term, and the role of the state was not to remedy their failure. The goal became preventing future dependency upon the state, consistent with the neoliberal interest in maintaining the primary role of the family in caring for the economic dependency of all. Conservatives wanting to promote marriage and mandate market work, even if unavailable or inadequate, and to reinforce the moral position of the responsible family allied with feminists

[153] 42 USC 602(a)(26)(A) (1976).

[154] See, e.g., J. C. Murphy, 'Legal Images of Fatherhood: Welfare Reform, Child Support Enforcement, and Fatherless Children' (2005) 81 *Notre Dame Law Review* 325–386 at 350–352. See also Garrison, 'Child Support and Children's Poverty'; Handler and Hasenfeld, *We the Poor People*, 128–131.

[155] D. L. Hatcher, *The Poverty Industry: The Exploitation of America's Most Vulnerable Citizens* (New York: NYU Press, 2016); D. L. Hatcher, 'States Diverting Funds from the Poor', in E. Rosser (ed.), *Holes in the Safety Net: Federalism and Poverty* (Cambridge: Cambridge University Press, 2019), 151; D. L. Hatcher, 'Stop Foster Care Agencies from Taking Children's Resources' (2019) 71 *Florida Law Review Forum* 104–112.

[156] See n. 38.

[157] L. C. McClain, *The Place of Families: Fostering Capacity, Equality, and Responsibility* (Cambridge, MA: Harvard University Press, 2006), 60.

to strengthen the legal tools for child support collection.[158] These dynamics intensified from the 1990s into this century, beginning when Aid to Families with Dependent Children was reconstituted under President Clinton as Temporary Aid to Needy Families (TANF). TANF reduced payments, added work requirements, promoted marriage and punished parents for excessive procreation. The neoliberal commitment to solving poverty through the market completely overtook the welfarist vision of the economic family; neoliberals allied with social conservatives by supporting the natural family ideology.[159]

Even in its most progressive phase in the United States in the mid-twentieth century, support for children encompassed both a welfarist vision of economic support for poor families and socially conservative values regarding gendered division of labour within the family, the threat of single motherhood, racial stereotypes about different types of families, and the moral value of work within the market. This arrangement has increasingly been supplanted by an alliance of neoliberal reliance on the market with conservative commitment to the promotion of marriage as the way to address poverty. Thus, the oscillation between welfarist and neoliberal visions of the economic family has always coexisted with conservative values, particularly regarding marriage, race and work.

In Europe, this oscillation looks different. The welfarist approach to the economic family is strongest in the Scandinavian countries and other northern European countries such as Germany and the Netherlands, with social democratic traditions that support de-commodifying social services and providing state support for employment.[160] These countries often provide state-sponsored child support in the form of child subsidies to families for the care of children as part of their welfarist economic visions. However, Europe also offers a vision of the resurgence of the natural family as a model for child support that restricts access to abortion and encompasses anti-immigrant and nationalist ideology. Conservative populist or authoritarian regimes use payments for children to encourage motherhood by supporting families in which women remain at home rather than in the workforce,

[158] See n. 39 and accompanying text.

[159] M. Eichner, *The Free-Market Family: How the Market Crushed the American Dream (and How It Can Be Restored)* (Oxford: Oxford University Press, 2020); Handler and Hasenfeld, *We the Poor People*; Cooper, *Family Values.*

[160] G. Esping-Andersen, *The Three Worlds of Welfare Capitalism* (Princeton, NJ: Princeton University Press, 1990).

while espousing neoliberal policies that encourage privatization of state services, including resources for childcare.[161]

7. Conclusion: Deconstructing the Familial Subject

Legal theorists of gender, adopting various approaches within feminist legal theory – including liberal/formal equality, cultural/relational, intersectional, vulnerability, queer or postmodern perspectives – have engaged with reforms of family law, traditionally understood.[162] Some have increasingly come to consider, in different ways, the role of gender in its relationship to race, class or sexuality in constructing the familial subject.[163] While feminist theories have illuminated various facets of the debates about divorce, property distribution, custody, alimony, child support, parentage, child welfare or same-sex marriage, they have largely underappreciated questions raised by the role of law in the political economy of how social welfare and market functioning reflect and reinforce gendered and racialized stereotypes and experiences of the

[161] M. A. Orenstein and B. Bugarič, 'Work, Family, Fatherland: The Political Economy of Populism in Central and Eastern Europe' (2020) *Journal of European Public Policy*, www.tandfonline.com/doi/abs/10.1080/13501763.2020.1832557?journalCode=rjpp20; F. G. Nicola, 'Editorial, Another View of the Cathedral: What Does the Rule of Law Crisis Tell Us about Democratizing the EU?' (2018) 25 *Maastricht Journal of European and Comparative Law* 133–138.

[162] Gender scholars have sought to categorize feminist theories in overlapping ways. See M. Chamallas, *Introduction to Feminist Legal Theory*, 3rd ed. (New York: Wolters Kluwer Law & Business, 2013); N. Levit and R. R. M. Verchick, *Feminist Legal Theory*, 2nd ed. (New York: NYU Press, 2016); R. West and C. Grant Bowman (eds.), *Research Handbook on Feminist Jurisprudence* (Cheltenham: Edward Elgar, 2019). Other strands of feminist theory include critical race, socialist-feminist, dominance, pragmatic and post-colonial feminisms.

[163] See, e.g., Eichner, *The Free-Market Family*; McClain, *The Place of Families*; C. Huntington, *Failure to Flourish: How Law Undermines Family Relationships* (Oxford: Oxford University Press, 2014); Roberts, *Shattered Bonds*; M. Albertson Fineman, *The Neutered Mother, the Sexual Family and Other Twentieth Century Tragedies* (New York: Routledge, 1995); M. Albertson Fineman, *The Autonomy Myth: A Theory of Dependency* (New York: New Press, 2005); M. Albertson Fineman and I. Karpin (eds.), *Mothers in Law: Feminist Theory and the Legal Regulation of Motherhood* (Vancouver: University of British Columbia Press, 1995).

family.[164] Analysis of the distributional effects of family law reforms have largely focused on the role of family law rules in internal distribution within the family, for example in property division following divorce, and only in recent years addressed the differential impact of social policies on family functioning.[165] Concomitantly, feminist legal scholars have called for reforms of social policies or market practices to alleviate the burdens placed on families, most of which are experienced differentially based on class, race and sexuality.[166] Neither project, however, has fully engaged with how the law of the market and the law of the welfare state intersect with traditional family law rules to create or reinforce economic disparities among poor, racialized and non-marital families.[167]

The calls for family law reform have tended to view the family as exceptional, a discrete realm that may have distinctive legal tools to allocate resources within it, but whose many other social functions should be recognized by policymakers as deserving of support through state or market policy.[168] This framing leaves family law as a battleground open on the one hand to social conservatives seeking to place the blame for broader economic and social problems on the functioning of the modern family

[164] Boone reviews Eichner, *The Free-Market Family.* M. Boone, 'The Market Cannot Be Your Mother' (2021) 119 *Michigan Law Review* 1207–1221 at 1219–1221; Roberts, 'Welfare: Yesterday and Today'.

[165] Huntington, *Failure to Flourish.*

[166] Ibid.; Eichner, *The Free-Market Family*; Roberts, 'Welfare: Yesterday and Today' .

[167] After advocating for reform of the child welfare system for decades, Dorothy Roberts has begun work on a more thorough critique of what she and others now refer to as 'the Family Regulation System'. See D. Roberts, *Torn Apart: How the Child Welfare System Destroys Black Families – and How Abolition Can Build a Safer World* (New York: Basic Books, 2022); D. Roberts, 'Abolishing Policing Also Means Abolishing Family Regulation', *Imprint,* 16 June 2020, https://imprintnews.org/child-welfare-2/abolishing-policing-also-means-abolishing-family-regulation/44480; A. Cilia, 'The Family Regulation System: Why Those Committed to Racial Justice Must Interrogate It', *Harvard Civil Rights-Civil Liberties Law Review,* 17 February 2021, https://harvardcrcl.org/the-family-regulation-system-why-those-committed-to-racial-justice-must-interrogate-it.

[168] For a thorough discussion of the 'market/family dichotomy', see F. E. Olsen, 'The Family and the Market: A Study of Ideology and Legal Reform' (1983) 96 *Harvard Law Review* 1497–1578. A prominent example concerning social welfare law is D. E. Roberts, 'Prison, Foster Care, and the Systemic Punishment of Black Mothers' (2012) 59 *UCLA Law Review* 1474–1500. For a prominent counter-example likening policies of non-intervention in the family to a laissez faire approach to the free market, see F. E. Olsen, 'The Myth of State Intervention in the Family' (1985) 18 *University of Michigan Journal of Law Reform* 835–864.

and return to the logic of patriarchy.[169] On the other, gender equality reforms under the guise of neoliberal policies have justified uneven distributive outcomes burdening poor families, families of colour and non-marital families.[170]

This chapter sheds light on how the familial subject appears within this ideological battleground foregrounding visions of the sexual, economic and natural family while viewing as deviant poor, racialized, LGBTQ+ and non-marital families. If for historical and ideological reasons liberal and cultural feminist alliances have captured family law reforms along what we have characterized as sexual or economic family imaginaries, we also underlined how these alliances are ceding to increasing market pressures and socially conservative agendas that promote either neoliberal or natural imaginaries of the family. We suggest deconstructing the familial subject to analyse all sides of its prism. In doing so, we propose shifting the focus of scholars, advocates and jurists towards family law and its political economy as inevitably intertwined with class, sexual and racial hierarchies. The familial subject is in desperate need of this perspective to adequately address the distributive consequences of family law reforms for poor, racialized, LGBTQ+ and non-marital families.

[169] See G. Frankenberg and F. G. Nicola, 'The Logic of Patriarchy', *Verfassungsblog*, 1 July 2022, https://verfassungsblog.de/the-logic-of-patriarchy.

[170] See N. D. Polikoff, *Beyond (Straight and Gay) Marriage: Valuing All Families under the Law* (Boston, MA: Beacon Press, 2008); Franke, 'The Politics of Same-Sex Marriage Politics', at 239; K. Franke, *Wedlocked: The Perils of Marriage Equality* (New York: NYU Press, 2015); Murray, 'Obergefell v. Hodges and Nonmarriage Inequality'.

10 The Political Subject

Stéphanie Hennette Vauchez and Ruth Rubio-Marín

What is the 'political'? What rights, prerogatives and duties turn a person into a political subject? And to what extent is a gendered order, or are other systems of hierarchies contained in the legal definition of the political subject? The right to vote immediately comes to mind as an obvious candidate for illustrating this particular dimension of political rights, for it is well-established that, historically and across a wide range of countries, the very definitions of citizenship as a legal category has been based on the exclusion of a number of categories of people. Women were of course one of these categories, but also others who failed to fit the dominant model of the rational and independent (male) individual that classical political philosophy as well as modern legal systems had consolidated and promoted by the end of the eighteenth century. While this chapter addresses the right to vote as a crucial dimension of the legal construction of 'the political subject', it also adopts a wider perspective. This is achieved by adding a historical dynamic to the inquiry about the scope and contours of what has come to be defined as 'political' activity since the end of the eighteenth century (Section 1), and by viewing subsequent developments from the conquest of suffrage to more contemporary participatory rules seeking to challenge the foundational gender order enshrined in the definition of the political subject (Section 2) through a comparative lens.

To the extent that it constitutes a paradigmatic example, if not a foundational episode, of early European political modernity,[1] the exploration of the contents and contours of the 'political subject' usefully takes the French Revolution as a starting point. Such a historical perspective is all the more relevant with respect to the co-production hypothesis that structures the present volume, given that the legacy of the French

[1] C. Lucas (ed.), *The French Revolution and the Invention of Modern Political Culture*, 4 vols. (New York: Pergamon Press, 1987–1994), vol. 2; K. Offen, *European Feminisms 1700–1950: A Political History* (Palo Alto, CA: Stanford University Press, 2000).

Revolution can certainly be read as the interactive and reinforcing result of law and gender as normative orders in terms of political rights. The early revolutionary definition of 'the political' was indeed very much law-based: Citizenship as a modern legal category was not only invented,[2] it was also progressively defined and refined as encompassing the right to vote as well as other political rights – such as the right to bear arms, the right to assemble or express oneself and, to some extent, a corresponding set of responsibilities. Gender norms in turn played a very important role in the progressive shaping of the contents and contours of these political rights and citizenship duties. In fact, such norms are to a significant extent responsible for the profound 'paradox'[3] of early Western/European modernity that consisted of an apparent contradiction between the totem of universalism and the taboo of diminished forms of citizenship.[4]

Gender may be seen as having informed the then-in-formation category of 'the political' in at least two distinct ways. The first has to do with women's deprivation of the paramount right to vote, despite the actual importance of their political participation in the early years of the French Revolution: From the outset, despite the very partial regime of franchise created in the Revolution that effectively denied the right to vote to a number of individuals (including women) for their failure to meet standards of independence, women remained extremely politically active and continuously claimed a robust and multifaceted conception of their political rights, notwithstanding the fact that the right to vote did not feature prominently among those.[5] Another influence is present in the ways in which their political involvement was progressively curbed and policed, as a series of legal rules from 1793 onwards explicitly excluded them from the exercise of various political rights – a move that was only further strengthened and entrenched by Napoleonic laws and policies. These legal and political elements explain why 'the first five years of the French

[2] R. Brubaker, 'The French Revolution and the Invention of Citizenship' (1989) 7 *French Politics and Society* 30–49.

[3] J. W. Scott, *Only Paradoxes to Offer: French Feminists and the Rights of Man* (Cambridge, MA: Harvard University Press, 1996).

[4] G. Mazeau and C. Plumauzille, 'Penser avec le genre: trouble dans la citoyenneté révolutionnaire' (2015) 9 *La Révolution Française: Cahiers de l'Institut d'histoire de la Révolution française* 1–28.

[5] P. Barthélémy and V. Sebillotte-Cuchet, 'Sous la citoyenneté, le genre' (2016) 1 *Clio: Femmes, Genre, Histoire* 7–22.

Revolution constitute an unprecedented historical laboratory for the study of European gender politics'.[6]

As the chapter focuses on these two distinct legal moves by which women were implicitly denied franchise in 1789, and explicitly prohibited from all political activity in 1793–1795, the first section unearths the interaction between law and gender in the very shaping of a category of 'political subjectivity' in early European modernity. The denial of political franchise is first explained to be not so much an openly sex-based exclusion from 'the political', but rather one that was based on a (deeply gendered) notion of familial status. In that, the episode of the French Revolution is a clear example of the ways in which early political modernity created a distinction between the public and the private spheres[7] through a dialogical construction of both,[8] in which the family played a fundamentally public/political role in enabling the public while being conceptualized as the domain of the private. As such, revolutionary citizenship was profoundly gendered in its connection to family status and thereby to heterosexual norms and hierarchical dynamics. Section 1 continues by describing the further denial of political rights to women as a form of backlash against the types of activity and public involvement of revolutionary women, and their alleged failure to conform to the nurturing and reproductive roles that they were expected to assume as their gender-specific civic duty. Both these dimensions of the revolutionary articulation of 'the political subject' have a legal dimension and rest on a highly gendered articulation of separate social spheres (domestic versus public) whose enduring consequences in more recent times are analysed in Section 2.

Against this background, the chapter goes on to examine two of the most important sites of women's affirmation as political subjects in contemporary history with a focus on Europe (Section 2): First came the struggle for suffrage, and then the fight for participatory parity. We describe the fight for suffrage and the multiple ways in which the reality as well as the conceptual construct of the modern gender order being built

6 K. Offen, *Les féminismes en Europe 1700–1950* (Rennes: Presses Universitaires de Rennes, 2012), 89.

7 C. Pateman, 'Feminist Critiques of the Public/Private Dichotomy', in S. I. Benn and G. F. Gaus (eds.), *Public and Private in Social Life* (New York: St Martin's Press, 1983), 281.

8 S. Gal, 'A Semiotics of the Public/Private Distinction' (2002) 13 *Differences: A Journal of Feminist Cultural Studies* 77–95 at 80.

around the family shaped women's struggle for suffrage rights. This was an attempt to challenge dominant understandings of citizenship that deprived women's domestic concerns from political salience while it judged them unfit for those activities, like voting, that gradually came to epitomize political subjecthood. After assessing the limited transformative potential of the franchise in terms of allowing women to become decision-makers and to occupy positions of authority that would enable them to shape policies and communal norms, the chapter addresses women's contemporary fight for paritary participation, as well as for a broader disestablishment of gender roles, including in the private sphere. In so doing, the chapter shows how this struggle for participatory parity goes beyond the rights logic to represent an attempt to redefine the rules of democracy and representation in a manner that can better overcome the foundational sexual contract defining the modern political subject in inherently gender-biased ways.

1. Early European Political Modernity and the Gendered Genesis of Modern Political Rights

A. Implicit Gendered Exclusions from Suffrage

Citoyennes sans citoyenneté: The oxymoron coined by historian Dominique Godineau[9] captures the paradoxical situation in which women were placed by the invention of citizenship as a legal category.[10] *Citoyennes*, as they liked to call themselves, argued that they were included in the 1789 Declaration on the rights of man.[11] However, it was soon clear that they would be deprived of what now appears to be the core and primary dimension of citizenship, i.e., the right to vote, and the right to be elected.

The law of 22 December 1789 determining who had the right to vote created a basic distinction between 'active' and 'passive' citizens. The latter category encompassed those individuals whose fiscal contribution was

[9] D. Godineau, *Les citoyennes tricoteuses. Les femmes du peuple à Paris pendant la Révolution française* (Paris: Alinéa, 1988).

[10] R. Brubacker, 'The French Revolution and the Invention of Citizenship' (1989) 7 *French Politics and Society* 30–49.

[11] D. Godineau, 'Autour du mot citoyenne' (1988) 16 *Mots* 91–110 at 106.

inferior to the equivalent of three working days' worth of wages, and thereby barred them from any form of political participation. Further thresholds divided the category of active citizens, drawing distinctions based on property and wealth, and connections between these categories and domains of political participation (i.e., in local, departmental and/or national assemblies).[12] Considerations of property and wealth, of course, fed into the deeper philosophical concept of the citizen as an *independent* individual, meaning a self-sufficient person who does not need to rely on others or institutions, and the understanding that only such individuals were to exercise political rights. This understanding is sustained by a number of philosophical traditions. In the words of constitutional theorist and revolutionary political actor Siéyès, 'legitimate property ensures independence; one is a slave when one exists at the expense of another's property'.[13]

Yet, as Nancy Fraser has shown in her genealogical inquiry into the concept, independence was never based on economic status alone, but also encompassed socio-legal and political elements.[14] For women, it was their purported dependence on men within a patriarchal construct of the family that proved paramount. Independence – or rather, the perceived lack thereof – was thus the dominant rationale for the legal exclusion from citizenship of women, but also of others (servants, vagabonds and beggars, Jews and colonial subjects) who were deemed subject to external ruling powers incompatible with political franchise: their masters, their owners, their husbands. Together, they formed the de facto category of 'non-citizens'[15] created by the 1789 Act through its facially neutral wealth-based categories and thresholds.[16] In other words, for the purposes of the

[12] See J. Godechot, *Les institutions en France sous la révolution et l'empire* (Paris: PUF, 1985), 76.

[13] Cited by O. Le Cour Grandmaison, 'Les non-citoyens dans la Révolution française' (1989) 94 *L'Homme et la société* 19–32 at 21 [our translation].

[14] N. Fraser and L. Gordon, 'A Genealogy of Dependency: Tracing a Keyword of the US Welfare State' (1994) 19 *Signs* 309–336.

[15] Le Cour Grandmaison, 'Les non-citoyens dans la Révolution française'.

[16] The 1789 distinction between active and passive citizens was later abolished by the Law of 10 August 1792, but this did not result in the enfranchisement of previously excluded categories. At face value, the 1793 Constitution would also have enlarged enfranchised groups (for instance, it proclaimed the end of domesticity), but it was never applied. The Napoleonic empire and the monarchical restorations reinstated wealth-based suffrage systems that again excluded servants until the proclamation of universal male suffrage in 1848, the first constitutional text to detach citizenship from its former underpinning

present inquiry into the role of gender in the eighteenth century's initial legal definition of political rights, it is important to underline that this 1789 definition of the 'independent citizen' did not correlate directly or specifically to sex. In fact, no mention of 'women' is made in the 1789 Act.[17] The normative model of the 'independent citizen' that ultimately underlay it was, however, deeply gendered, as its true yardstick was family status and the specific role in a household, at a time when family and household roles were profoundly gendered, in both static (heteronormativity) and dynamic (hierarchy) terms.

The pioneering work of historians such as Anne Verjus, Jennifer Heuer and Suzanne Desan[18] details the complex ways in which revolutionary franchise was articulated around family status in this household-based understanding of the Republic: Family status constituted the real constitutive element of citizenship. Archival work has established that the taxonomies that structured the effective exercise of political franchise in revolutionary times were not sex-based. In particular, the study of a 1793 registrar shows that despite the sex-based labels of the three different categories under which voters are listed (men/women/children), the first column effectively listed heads of household (including widows, should they maintain an independent household), and servants (including male servants) were in fact registered as women.[19] Men and women were not defined in biological terms for the purpose of assessing their political subjectivity, but rather on the basis of their independent/dependent status in a society structured around the patriarchal family as the basic societal pillar. Accordingly, men who were not heads of their household were denied citizenship because they were deemed incapable of administering

requirement of independence. By then, only women remained excluded from the category of political subjects. A. Verjus, *Le cens de la famille: Les femmes et le vote (1789–1848)* (Paris: Belin, 2002). Women only gained the right to vote in 1944. See also P. Rosanvallon, *Le sacre du citoyen: Histoire du suffrage universel en France* (Paris: Gallimard, 1992).

17 E. Viennot, *Et la modernité fut masculine: La France, les femmes et le pouvoir, 1789–1804* (Paris: Perrin, 2016), 137.

18 Verjus, *Le cens de la famille*; J. Heuer, *The Family and the Nation: Gender and Citizenship in Revolutionary France 1789-1830* (Ithaca, NY: Cornell University Press, 2005); S. Desan, *The Family on Trial in Revolutionary France* (Berkeley: University of California Press, 2004).

19 S. Aberdam, *L'élargissement du droit de vote entre 1792 et 1795 au travers du dénombrement du comité de division et des votes populaires sur les Constitutions de 1792 et 1795*, cited in J. Heuer and A. Verjus, 'L'invention de la sphère domestique au sortir de la Révolution' (2002) 1 *Annales historiques de la Révolution française* 1–28 at 16.

their own selves, their families or their properties: '[N]ot all men were "naturally" men in the political sense given to that category.'[20] The primacy of family status over biological sex also explains the persistence of the occasional exercise of political and civil rights by some women – such as noblewomen, widows or otherwise unmarried women – well into the nineteenth century, even though women were predominantly conceived of as married women and thus politically as well as civilly represented by their husbands. The placement of women as well as servants and children in the domestic sphere was what assigned them a political status distinct from that of full active citizens, sealing their dependence on men while at the same time antagonistically presenting the family as an 'apolitical' construct dividing the world into two spheres, the public and the private, as domains defining the contours of men's and women's differentiated citizenship.

This enduring relevance of family status in the legal construction of citizenship, and accordingly in the very shape of the political sphere, was long obfuscated by the grand narrative of the French Revolution as an enterprise that not only proclaimed the principles of equality and individualism through the 1789 Declaration, but also sought to extend their authority to the government of the family. A number of early revolutionary legal reforms affecting the family had indeed started to implement that vision. In this vein, the 1791 Constitution defined marriage as a civil contract agreed upon by two individuals exercising their free and equal wills. Obligations of fidelity, common residence and duties of assistance between spouses disappeared from the revolutionary legislation defining marriage, making adultery no longer a criminal offence. Furthermore, divorce was legalized by the law of 20 September 1792 and could be obtained on a wide variety of grounds, including mere 'incompatibility of character'. The law of 7 March 1793 proclaimed all children born in marriage to be equal in terms of inheritance rights. Through these and other important reforms, early revolutionary legislation genuinely attempted to actively view the family through an egalitarian lens.[21]

[20] Verjus, *Le cens de la famille.*

[21] H. Fulchiron, 'La femme, mère et épouse dans le droit révolutionnaire', in M.-F. Brive (ed.), *Les femmes et la Révolution française*, 3 vols. (Toulouse: Presses Universitaires de Toulouse, 1989), vol. 1, 377.

Should reforms of the sort have continued to dominate and permeate into actual social practices, these revolutionary reforms in the field of family law might have weighed into the concept of citizenship and favoured the affirmation of an egalitarian paradigm for the political sphere as well. But they were instead short-lived: In fact, they helped trigger strong backlash that coalesced in the adoption of the 1804 Napoleonic Civil Code. This family code spread throughout Europe and its colonial domains[22] firmly entrenching the notion of the distinction between a socio-political sphere that could be governed by the revolutionary principle of individual will and contract, and a domestic sphere that ought to reflect and be governed by the 'natural order of things'.[23] Marriage was no longer defined as a civil contract between equals but became an institution that could only be annulled for a predefined set of reasons. Moreover, divorce was made illegal through an 1816 Act. As wives, women became subject to a number of duties, including duties of obedience and fidelity, that were asymmetric in that they did not apply to men. They were also obliged to reside in their husband's residence of choice, were no longer able to take responsibility for any kind of legal act, and lost legal capacity in a more general sense as well. In fact, the legal status of Frenchwomen became strikingly similar to what women had experienced in common law systems that for several decades had systematized and increased the severity of the medieval common law doctrine of coverture according to which husband and wife became one single person in marriage by virtue of a legal fiction.[24]

In sum, the French Revolution certainly invented a modern concept of citizenship, even if it failed to make it autonomous from pre-existing forms of social hierarchy and subordination that coalesced in the socio-political entity of the family. Therefore, the right to vote as it existed in revolutionary times remained determined by family status. This was crucial in allowing for the Napoleonic invention of family law to seal women's dependence on men, signalling the start of an ice age[25] for women's political subjecthood.

[22] B. Rodriguez Ruiz and R. Rubio Marin (eds.), *The Struggle for Female Suffrage in Europe: Voting to Become Citizens* (Leiden: Brill, 2012), esp. Introduction.

[23] Verjus, *Le cens de la famille.*

[24] W. Blackstone, *Commentaries on the Laws of England*, 4 vols. (Oxford: Clarendon Press, 1765–1769).

[25] Fulchiron, 'La femme, mère et épouse dans le droit révolutionnaire', 377 on 'glaciation napoléonienne'.

B. Explicit Gendered Exclusions from Broader Political Rights

Godineau's expression *citoyennes sans citoyenneté*[26] also captures the ways in which women established themselves as full and relevant actors of the political sphere at the time of the French Revolution despite not being generally granted the right to vote. This essential fact was long downplayed by dominant learned interpretations of European political modernity that converged in the notion that women had more generally been barred from *all* political rights as they had been deprived of the right to vote, and consequently had played no major political role. Fortunately, recent historiography has significantly challenged this narrative and complemented it with testimonies to the abundant political involvement of women in the Revolution. Indeed, recalling their participation is crucial, for only when it is considered in its full measure can the severe backlash that it helped trigger become visible and analysable. This is particularly relevant for the present chapter's objective to unearth the ways in which the very content and contours of 'political rights' as a category then in the making was gendered.

Historiography of the last decades has indeed documented the multifaceted ways in which early political modernity was not only a period of exclusion from political rights for women, but also one of emancipation and self-invention.[27] Women played an important and certainly active political role, so much so that some of their actions, such as the *Marche sur Versailles* of October 1789,[28] have even come to symbolize the Revolution. Women were major and active political actors in the Revolution. Since their political participation often meant that they had to bring along domestic work that they could not afford to interrupt or set aside, these politically active women were given the nickname of 'knitting women' ('les tricoteuses').[29] This label's blending of women's 'public' and 'private' forms

[26] Godineau, *Les citoyennes tricoteuses.*

[27] For an illuminating account, see S. Desan, 'Recent Historiography on the French Revolution and Gender' (2019) 52 *Journal of Social History* 566–574.

[28] After gathering in protest against a scarcity of bread in the capital, approximately 6,000 people (a majority of them women) marched to Versailles, where the royal family was established, on 5–6 October 1789. This important event is generally read as a weakening of royal authority, for not only did the crowd manage to cause the royal family return to Paris, thereby defining Paris as the centre of political power, the King also signed the 1789 Declaration of the Rights of Man and the Citizen.

[29] Godineau, *Les citoyennes tricoteuses.*

of participation shows that women saw no conflict between their various forms of contribution to the household and broader community, something which also explains the types of issues for which they mobilized during the Revolution: Women foregrounded issues that were central to their lives as caretakers in revolutionary politics. For instance, women initiated and took part in a number of demonstrations, riots and other forms of political action in relation to the cost of living, the availability of food and primary foodstuffs, and the cost of grain and hoarding. In spite of this, and precisely because they were led by women and foregrounded sustenance and care concerns, many of the causes and modalities of women's political action during the Revolution, as well as the venues in which they organized, tended to be perceived as 'sub-political' or 'a-political'.[30] Gender codes created the ontology of 'the political subject' and the meaning of 'politics', rather than any predefined notion of activities designed to influence society.

Women's active political involvement in the Revolution did not, however, operate on a gender-free, equal basis with that of their male counterparts. This is largely due to the fact that gendered imaginaries established not only the rights but also the duties expected from good revolutionary citizens. Men had the right, but were also expected, to bear arms in order to protect the nation. Women's primary duty was to offer offspring to the Republic. The exaltation of motherhood during the Revolution was vigorous, be it in iconography, folk practices or official political discourse. Jean-Jacques Rousseau's concept of a 'civic mother' certainly fed into a conception of female citizenship as motherhood. Revolutionary representative Saint-Just argued that whenever no children were born to couples that had been married for seven years, they ought to be deemed legally separated.[31] Procreation was indeed elevated as a republican duty, and celibacy was denounced as anti-patriotic. Breastfeeding was largely praised as well.[32]

[30] See for her notion of 'subaltern counterpublics', N. Fraser, 'Rethinking the Public Sphere: A Contribution to the Critique of Actually Existing Democracy' (1990) 25/26 *Social Text* 56–80.

[31] Le Cour Grandmaison, *Les citoyennetés en révolution*, 289.

[32] See for instance the symbolic revolutionary Unity Day celebrated on 10 August 1793, during which eighty-six elderly men from all parts of the country were invited to drink the milk flowing out of the breasts of Isis' statue. Mazeau and Plumauzille, 'Penser avec le genre'.

The gendered dimension of women's political role in revolutionary times also resulted from legal rules that actively kept women outside the realm of rights and duties that were deemed 'political' rather than 'domestic'. In particular, women were neither recruited for nor accepted in the national guard; they were not awarded the right to bear arms either, despite their forceful claims.[33] More significantly still, women ended up paying a high price for their enduring political involvement as the Revolution took a radical turn. By 1793, as the counter-revolutionary forces had grown stronger and progressively led to situations akin to civil war, the Reign of Terror began. When it became clear that women too were part and parcel of this radicalization process, their active role was increasingly problematized. Anxieties about women's political involvement culminated in a series of important legal rules passed between 1793 and 1795 that explicitly denied them political agency and rights in a broader sense.

Illustratively, on 31 October 1793, representative Fabre d'Eglantine spoke out against a prominent and radical female political club (the *Société des citoyennes républicaines révolutionnaires*): 'I have come to observe that these clubs are not composed of their brothers or sisters of young age, but of adventuresses of sorts, of stray knightesses, of emancipated girls, of female grenadiers',[34] thus depicting its members as out of control, dangerous and subversive. The next day, representative Amar came before the National Assembly with his famous report on women's political rights, in which he argued that their nature commanded that they remain in the home and refrain from any kind of political action. Two days later, Olympe de Gouges, who had published the famously subversive *Déclaration des droits de la femme et de la citoyenne* in 1791,[35] was guillotined. Such political discourses and actions conveyed highly gendered assumptions about how women ought (not) to behave, especially when in the public sphere. They also reflected dominant perceptions about the ethos of the public sphere and the arguably limited role of emotions within it. More problematically, they suggested forms of discipline for

[33] Since its creation in 1789, service in the national guard had been construed as a political right on a par with suffrage. All active citizens therefore had the right (and indeed the obligation) to bear arms and serve in the national guard.

[34] Cited by Le Cour Grandmaison, *Les citoyennetés en révolution*, 288.

[35] Olympe de Gouges, *Déclaration des droits de la femme et de la citoyenne*, 1791.

women, not only for defending certain causes, but also for breaking gender codes in doing so.

The instrument by which women's 'transgressions' were measured was largely based on the sexualization of women's political activism ('emancipated girls', 'stray knightesses'), and the use of derogatory terms that were ultimately taken to justify forms of policing and control. Dominique Godineau has documented this tendency of revolutionary political speech to amalgamate activist women and prostitutes as a way to contest women's very presence in the public space.[36] Clyde Plumauzille's specific investigation into the policing of prostitution during the Revolution also establishes that women who were found in obvious 'offence of independence', such as prostitutes, were immediately called to order for their transgression of gender norms.[37] Most telling in this respect is the fact that prostitutes were called 'public women' (*femmes publiques*).[38] As Elisabeth Sledziewski has it, 'political citoyennes remained activists and their irruption into the public space was often assimilated to an offence'.[39]

At any rate, these highly gendered norms pertaining to the role of women significantly found their way into important legal rules that explicitly excluded women from the enjoyment of political rights. A decree of April 1793 first officially excluded women from the army. On 23 May 1793, another legal rule established that women were no longer allowed to attend any form of political assembly. And a decree of 30 September 1793 forbade all female political clubs. As women nonetheless continued to take part in popular political action,[40] a further law of 23 May 1795 established that any public gathering of more than five women would lead to arrest.[41]

[36] Godineau, *Les citoyennes tricoteuses*, 268–269.

[37] C. Plumauzille, *Prostitution et Révolution: Les femmes publiques dans la cité républicaine, 1789–1804* (Paris: Champ Vallon, 2016), 15.

[38] Ibid.

[39] E. Sledziewski, 'La femme dans la législation révolutionnaire', in M.-F. Brive (ed.), *Les femmes et la Révolution française*, 3 vols. (Toulouse: Presses Universitaires de Toulouse, 1989), vol. 1, 411.

[40] Consider especially their role during the *journées de Prairial* in 1795, one of the last popular uprisings of the Revolution in Paris.

[41] The text's wording is of interest: '[A]ll women withdraw in their respective homes; those who … will be found in the street, in gatherings of more than five, will be dispersed by force and arrested until public tranquillity is restored in Paris.'

In her seminal work on women and the Revolution, Joan Landes considered that, 'by 1793, women were banned from active and passive participation in the political sphere',[42] and concluded that, in the end, 'the Republic was constructed against women, not just without them'.[43] Her analysis reinforces what this chapter has so far revealed about the content and contours of the very category of the 'political subject' then in the making. Women's progressive sidelining (implicit exclusion from the right to vote) and eventual exclusion (1793–1795 explicit exclusion from broader political rights), as well as the political construction of the domestic sphere as in antagonism with the public sphere, were indeed constitutive of the dynamic definition of 'the political' during the Revolution, rather than a mere side effect therefrom. As such, it appears that law and gender have co-produced the modern 'political subject' in ways that were inherently biased towards the exclusion of women, who came to be constructed to be precisely directly opposed to it.

2. Women's Reclaiming of the Political in Late European Political Modernity and Contemporary Times

A. The Struggle for and Conquest of Women's Suffrage

i. The Conceptual and Ideological Background of the Debate on Women's Suffrage

We have seen how the gendered norm of independence interacted with the early modern legal construction of the citizen in ways that excluded women from the political sphere as well as reinforced their legal dependence on men. In this way, gender norms and legal norms merged in creating the modern political subject, male, by definition, and the political sphere, male, by definition, in opposition to the domestic sphere, female,

[42] J. Landes, *Women and the Public Sphere in the Age of the French Revolution* (Ithaca, NY: Cornell University Press, 1988), 147. Later works have insisted that this view might have been too narrowly focused on the legal recognition of political rights and underestimated the ways in which women continued political action regardless. Yet it holds from a legal standpoint, as women successively lost the right to attend and participate in political gatherings, and to gather in groups of five and more.

[43] Landes, *Women and the Public Sphere*, 12.

by definition, as a sphere in which human necessity and dependence, rather than freedom and autonomy, were to be managed.

The allocation of men and women to separate spheres was both a reality and a 'self-reinforcing ideological construct supported by an entire legal architecture': 'the two converged in the creation of synergies accounting for the disassociation of men's and women's franchise'.[44] Indeed, women were often deprived of education, and means of economic self-sufficiency, including paid employment and professional opportunities similar to those of men. Women's relegation to the domestic sphere, where they were expected to devote themselves to the social and symbolic reproduction of the species, therefore allowed for a prediction of conservative, traditionalist and religiously affected political behaviour that women would likely exhibit were they to become enfranchised. This was in turn used as an argument for postponing female suffrage on strategic grounds even by many of those who supported the cause on principle. In Luxemburg, for instance, liberals opposed female suffrage because they thought that it would threaten their aspirations to limit the sovereign power of the Crown as well as the influence of the Catholic Church.[45] In Belgium, even though female suffrage was mainly supported by the Socialist Party for principled reasons at the turn of the century, the Socialists dropped the demand for female franchise in an attempt to unite anti-Catholic forces to break the political domination of the Catholic Party.[46]

Indeed, the appearance of the suffragist movement was to great extent a response to how dominant political parties from all political persuasions (meaning both conservative and progressive) shared in symbolically 'depoliticizing' women's vote – that is to say, in treating it as a minor or dispensable political issue. Other causes that were considered more politically relevant were systemically prioritized; and women who, against party lines, decided to organize separately, either within or outside political parties, were disciplined for being politically 'promiscuous' or 'disobedient', and in so doing, breaking gender codes. These became standard forms

[44] R. Rubio-Marín, 'The Achievement of Female Suffrage in Europe: On Women's Citizenship' (2014) 12 *International Journal of Constitutional Law – ICON* 4–34 at 9.

[45] See S. Kmec, 'Female Suffrage in Luxemburg', in Rodríguez-Ruiz and Rubio-Marin (eds.), *The Struggle for Female Suffrage in Europe*, p. 165.

[46] See P. Meier, 'Caught between Strategic Positions and Principles of Equality: Female Suffrage in Belgium', in B. Rodriguez Ruiz and R. Rubio Marin (eds.), *The Struggle for Female Suffrage in Europe: Voting to Become Citizens* (Leiden: Brill, 2012), 412.

of disrespect of women's political agency reflective of the depth to which gender hierarchies and women's misfit in the political domain had been normalized. In the United Kingdom, the Liberal government repeatedly disappointed women.[47] In Ireland, unionists as well as nationalists prioritized the home rule position over female suffrage despite women's obvious contributions to both fronts.[48] In Denmark, the Social Democratic Party never recognized an ideologically aligned women's organization (the Social Democratic Women's Suffrage Association) because of its cooperation with women not affiliated to the party.[49] In Sweden, women rebelled against their party of reference, in this case the Conservative Party, by founding a separate branch, but then had great difficulty in participating in suffragist associations that recruited members from the entire political spectrum.[50]

Yet nothing could stop women, who had always found ways to remain politically active, from fighting against their legal political erasure. Thus, partly as a reaction to the inaction of all other relevant actors, including political parties, and partly as an expression of dissatisfaction with the limited agenda of women's bourgeois associations at the time, suffragist organizations proliferated at the turn of the century, forming a suffragist movement with international ambitions.[51] The emergence of a newly

[47] See M. Hill, 'Divisions and Debates: The Irish Suffrage Experience', in B. Rodriguez Ruiz and R. Rubio Marin (eds.), *The Struggle for Female Suffrage in Europe: Voting to Become Citizens* (Leiden: Brill, 2012), 265, quoting from S. K. Kent, *Sex and Suffrage in Britain 1860–1914* (London: Routledge, 1990), at 54–55.

[48] See Hill, 'Divisions and Debates', 261.

[49] See C. Fiig and B. Siim, 'Democratisation of Denmark: Inclusion of Women in Political Citizenship', in B. Rodriguez Ruiz and R. Rubio Marin (eds.), *The Struggle for Female Suffrage in Europe: Voting to Become Citizens* (Leiden: Brill, 2012), 63.

[50] See L. Wängnerud, 'How Women Gained Suffrage in Sweden: A Weave of Alliances', in B. Rodriguez Ruiz and R. Rubio Marin (eds.), *The Struggle for Female Suffrage in Europe: Voting to Become Citizens* (Leiden: Brill, 2012), 248.

[51] This was, however, not the first expression of women's transnational coalition building. The Women's Christian Temperance Union (WCTU) was formed in the United States in 1874 as a conventional Protestant women's organization with a narrow moral reform focus, which went on to become a more ambitious and politically focused organization. In 1884, it led to the formation of the World's Women's Christian Temperance Union, which contributed greatly to Australia's and New Zealand's early winning of suffrage. See E. C. DuBois, 'Women Suffrage around the World: Three Phases of Suffragist Internationalism', in C. Daley and M. Nolan (eds.), *Suffrage and Beyond: International Feminist Perspectives* (New York: New York University Press, 1994), 265 and 256. Both the temperance and the suffragist movements show how women drew connections between the private and the public in their conception of their political struggles. Women's involvement in the

militant suffragism was influenced by the upsurge of socialist politics at the end of the nineteenth century, but it was ideologically and organizationally independent from it. This form of suffragism had its roots in England, but its branches spread out over much of the rest of the world, with the International Woman Suffrage Association being established between 1899 and 1902. Initially viewed as a working-class initiative, suffragist militancy ended up recruiting women from all walks of life, as it came to challenge dominant definitions of womanhood articulated around the separation of public and private spheres.[52]

The institutional characteristics and tactics of suffragist organizations varied. Even though most were independent organizations, many also had party connections, including some which took the form of branches of existing political parties. While most pursued suffrage through the means accorded by the political system, some were more radical in their methods – notably the suffragettes in the United Kingdom. They defended various forms of civil disobedience when necessary. Like the members of the Social and Political Union in Britain, they engaged in highly unconventional activities, which included arson and hunger strikes in prison, as expressions of what Mrs Pankhurst called a 'civil war' waged by women.[53]

In spite of this, internal tension was present within the women's movement. Some of it was related to either the reality or the ideological construct of the separate spheres. For instance, not all women agreed on the implications of women's domestic socialization when it came to assessing women's qualification for exercising the right to vote. Indeed, without necessarily endorsing essentializing understandings on women's distinctive nature, many enlightened feminists of the time shared the concerns of their male counterparts about the likeliness of women's regressive political behaviour, in causes such as limiting the powers of the church or of the monarchy. They feared that, if full voting rights were

temperance movement was fundamentally based on a struggle to counter the violence that women experienced in the household as a result of alcohol consumption by their husbands. As for the struggle for suffrage, connections were often drawn between the two spheres, alluding to the transformative potential of women's suffrage to strengthen their position in private life and eliminate men's domestic tyranny. See R. Siegel, 'The Nineteenth Amendment and the Democratization of the Family' (2020) 129 *Yale Law Journal Forum* 450–495 at 459.

[52] See DuBois, 'Women Suffrage around the World', 265.

[53] See Pankhurst, in M. Schneir (ed.), *Feminism: The Essential Historical Writings* (New York: Random House, 1972), 296.

granted before a certain degree of education and independence had been achieved, women could hold back the reforms envisioned in liberalism and modernity.[54]

In fact, among the women's associations that began to flourish in Europe in the mid-1850s, which were mostly led by educated, politically connected and bourgeois women, the priorities tended to lie with factors other than the lack of suffrage, such as access to education, employment and professional development, all of which were also necessary stepping stones for women's independence.[55] Similarly, the appeal to the right to vote as a paradigmatic expression of women's refusal to be confined to the private sphere could simply not be fully convincing to the women who, for reasons linked to class or race, could never 'afford' to devote themselves entirely to the sustenance of their household, and were reasonably more concerned with improving their working and existential conditions, and sought political empowerment as instrumentally connected to these goals.

It is important to understand that in a context of enforced dependency in the marketplace as well as in the family, the disagreement within and outside the women's movement was not only ideological. Many feared that political equality epitomizing women's independence would mean that women would need to let go of their 'protected dependent status', and that women would suffer even more under a 'formal equality status' that, while according them equal rights, still would not grant them equal opportunities. Moreover, that men could be asked to take on their due share of responsibility for household chores and childrearing was simply unthinkable for most. In this setting, many women, and not only conservative men, saw women's suffrage as a threat to the family order and their natural place in the polity. This explains why some went paradoxically as far as organizing against women's enfranchisement, making this their foremost political cause.[56]

[54] For the debate in Spain, see A. Aguado, 'Constructing Women's Citizenship: The Conquest of Suffrage and Women's Political Rights in Spain', in B. Rodriguez Ruiz and R. Rubio Marin (eds.), *The Struggle for Female Suffrage in Europe: Voting to Become Citizens* (Leiden: Brill, 2012).

[55] B. Siim et al., *Gendering Citizenship in Western Europe* (Bristol: Policy Press, 2007), 38.

[56] In Britain, e.g., women were active in the National League for Opposing Women's Suffrage, founded in 1908. See K. Cowman, 'Female Suffrage in Great Britain', in B. Rodriguez Ruiz and R. Rubio Marin (eds.), *The Struggle for Female Suffrage in Europe: Voting to Become Citizens* (Leiden: Brill, 2012), 275–276.

Interestingly, gender stereotypes and prevalent gender roles accounted not only for arguments against, but also those in favour of suffrage. Women fighting for women's suffrage often did not challenge women's roles as mothers, but rather the fact that motherhood disqualified women from voting or holding office. Certainly, arguments concerning women's caring nature and their role as mothers were most often relied upon by conservative political forces opposing female suffrage. Female suffrage was said to be politically contentious because it could undermine family harmony and generate social instability. Women were to be represented by the men as the heads of the family household instead.[57] Yet many of the arguments in support of female suffrage also explicitly alluded to women's distinct position or experience in the family, and to their caring nature as mothers, as something they could put at the service of the community, especially at a time when the legislative concern with social welfare was increasing to the benefit of the entire nation. In some contexts, the idea of patriotic motherhood was quite explicitly articulated, as when the first voice raised in favour of women's suffrage in Portugal (that of Domingos Borges de Barros, deputy of Baía, Brazil) on 22 April 1822 proposed the extension of voting rights to all women who were mother to six legitimate children.[58] Not all defences were framed in instrumental terms, however. A key dividing line separated egalitarian and 'maternalist' organizations of women. The former relied not so much on women's maternal values and caring approach to life, but on plainer considerations of justice endorsing the language of individual freedom and equality, as did the International Women Suffrage Association.[59]

What is interesting to note is that all conceptualizations of the 'political' that precede the generalization of women's franchise illustrate the importance of gender norms in the very shaping of what appears to be 'political rights'. First, women had considered that the eighteenth century's definition of political rights as essentially corresponding to franchise was too narrow, making them prioritize other claims. Later on, they would either

[57] R. B. Siegel, 'She the People: The Nineteenth Amendment, Sex Equality, Federalism, and the Family' (2002) 115 *Harvard Law Review* 947–1046 at 979.

[58] See M. L. Amaral and T. Anjinho, 'Winning Women's Vote: Female Suffrage in Portugal', in B. Rodriguez Ruiz and R. Rubio Marin (eds.), *The Struggle for Female Suffrage in Europe: Voting to Become Citizens* (Leiden: Brill, 2012), 483.

[59] See N. Berkovitch, *From Motherhood to Citizenship: Women's Rights and International Organizations* (Baltimore, MD: Johns Hopkins University Press, 1999), 26.

fear that they had actually more to lose than to gain from political franchise as long as it remained detached from other more pressing guarantees in terms of shared responsibilities for household chores, for instance, or conversely make a claim about their specific preparedness and legitimacy to vote because of their roles as mothers and carers.

ii. The Gendered Process and Account of Women's Enfranchisement

In most real-life scenarios, the conquest of women's suffrage, when resulting from bottom-up struggles, seems to have been the result of a combination of egalitarian and difference/maternalist arguments, both of which were strategically used by pro-suffragists.[60] This shows that the stakes were never just the question of women's access to political rights, but the very definition of what the necessary skills are for the meaningful exercise of such rights, a deeply gendered question which remains relevant to this day.

In any event, gender scripts ended up influencing not only the debates and narratives, but also the forms and extent of women's incorporation into the political, allowing for distinctions which meant the further entrenching of gender norms. Indeed, most European countries did not grant voting rights to all women at once. They were selective regarding the type of political participation that they gave access to, or the kinds of women to grant such access. This selection was done in ways that confirmed rather than challenged the separate spheres ideology. In some countries – including the United Kingdom, Sweden, Belgium, Denmark and Romania – women were granted the right to vote in local elections while still being excluded from parliamentary elections.[61] This is consistent with the fact that national voting was perceived as the primary sphere of politics, whereas local politics was often regarded as more closely related to the family and neighbourhood concerns with which women traditionally had been more involved. Women's participation in the latter could thus be seen as putting the caring and managing skills that they had

[60] C. Pateman, 'Three Questions about Womanhood Suffrage', in C. Daley and M. Nolan (eds.), *Suffrage and Beyond: International Feminist Perspectives* (New York: New York University Press, 1994), 337.

[61] Rubio-Marín, 'The Achievement of Female Suffrage in Europe', at 17.

developed in the private domain to public use, while still leaving the 'true public arena' to men.[62]

Furthermore, in many European countries, some women were put on a faster track to political rights than others. Independence or perceived independence was, as mentioned before, the crucial factor. This explains why both male and female slaves, domestics and (often racialized) colonized peoples encountered most obstacles in being perceived as candidates for citizenship rights.[63] Conversely, white women who paid taxes, owned property, headed their own household, were economically active and unmarried or widowed were among those often prioritized in this process of selective enfranchisement. In the United Kingdom, for instance, female suffrage was first granted to women with property,[64] while in Finland, Iceland and Sweden (though not in Denmark), unmarried and economically active women gained the vote before other groups.[65] It seems that functional closeness to manliness, measured in terms of both economic self-sufficiency and independent marital/family status, was the key consideration. Sometimes, political exclusion was also used as a gendered discipline tool for punishing the 'deviant', as in Belgium, where adulterous women 3 prostitutes were left disenfranchised for failing to live up to proper and gendered sexual codes.[66]

It is also worth noting that suffrage for women came earlier in societies or regimes with a less dominant tradition of separation of spheres, often linked to women's faster access to civil equality with men in the law. Notably, in Scandinavian countries, a strong connection seems to exist between the early achievement of civil equality in marital legal regimes and political citizenship rights.[67] Additionally, it has been pointed out that several of the countries to first grant women suffrage were mostly agrarian societies, as were Finland, Sweden and Denmark, illustrating that it was the lack of separation between the home and labour and employment that

[62] Pateman, 'Three Questions about Womanhood Suffrage', 339.

[63] See D. T. Goldberg, *The Racial State* (Malden, MA: Blackwell, 2002); C. W. Mills, *The Racial Contract* (Ithaca, NY: Cornell University Press, 1997).

[64] See Cowman, 'Female Suffrage in Great Britain', 273.

[65] See Fiig and Siim, 'Democratisation of Denmark'; Wängnerud, 'How Women Gained Suffrage in Sweden', 243.

[66] P. Meier, 'Caught between Strategic Positions and Principles of Equality: Female Suffrage in Belgium', in B. Rodriguez Ruiz and R. Rubio Marin (eds.), *The Struggle for Female Suffrage in Europe: Voting to Become Citizens* (Leiden: Brill, 2012).

[67] Siim et al., *Gendering Citizenship*, p. 31.

helped make the recognition of women as production sources more evident, thereby making the construct of the separate spheres less appealing.[68] In turn, the early granting of suffrage to women under socialist regimes, whatever voting rights might have been worth in these authoritarian states, sat well with the dominant ideological criticism of the bourgeois family, even though the promises of community sharing of housework and childcare did not prevent women from having to shoulder most of the reproduction costs in these countries either.[69]

Contrary to official doctrine, women have always departed from gender stereotypes and engaged politically in whatever happened to be the struggle of the day, as shown by the example of their involvement in the French Revolution discussed above. Telling in this regard is that the right to suffrage was a form of reward for women's other forms of political participation in quite a few countries. In several European countries, women won the right to vote during or immediately after the First World War; in some countries, women were actually rewarded for their active and direct contribution to the war effort.[70] Women's broader involvement in nationalist struggles similarly accelerated their access to suffrage in other jurisdictions. In Finland, for example, women successfully participated in the nationalist struggle against the Russian oppression, as well as the fight for the confirmation of the Finnish instead of the Swedish language, before being granted the right to vote.[71] Similarly, in Estonia, Latvia and Lithuania, female suffrage was in part related to the women's involvement in the nationalist struggle against the Russian Empire.[72]

[68] Ibid.

[69] J. Zollinger, *Two Paths to Women's Equality: Temperance, Suffrage and the Origins of Modern Feminism* (New York: Twayne Publishers, 1995), 11–12; H. Scott, *Women and Socialism: Experiences from Eastern Europe* (London: Alison & Busby, 1976), 212–213.

[70] See L. Garner, *Stepping Stones to Women's Liberty: Feminist Ideas in the Women's Suffrage Movement, 1900–1988* (London: Heineman Educational Books, 1984), ch. 7; B. S. Turner, *Citizenship and Capitalism: The Debate over Reformism* (London: Unwin Hyman, 1986), 60.

[71] See A. Korppi-Tommola, 'A Long Tradition of Equality: Women's Suffrage in Finland', in B. Rodriguez Ruiz and R. Rubio Marin (eds.), *The Struggle for Female Suffrage in Europe: Voting to Become Citizens* (Leiden: Brill, 2012), 47–48.

[72] See, respectively, H. Biin and A. Alby, 'Suffrage and the Nation: Women's Vote in Estonia'; A. Branta, 'Winning Women's Vote: Experiences from Latvia'; T. Birmontienė and V. Jurėnienė, 'The Development of Women's Rights in Lithuania: Striving for Political Equality', all in B. Rodriguez Ruiz and R. Rubio Marin (eds.), *The Struggle for Female Suffrage in Europe: Voting to Become Citizens* (Leiden: Brill, 2012).

Regardless, as was the case for the French Revolution, much of women's political engagement has been covered up by the way women's political subjecthood was historiographically constructed, including the dominant narratives on the history of women's access to voting rights. Thus, with a few exceptions (notably the cases of England and the United States), the achievement of suffrage at the turn of the century has been portrayed as the result of governments granting the vote to women in a calculated, top-down and self-interested manner. On the whole, it is presented as a conservative endeavour, as regards both the forces responsible for achieving votes for women and the impact that women's votes had on political life. Yet this portrayal has been shown to be largely unsubstantiated.[73] It obscures women's agency and fails to reflect the importance of women's broader political participation as well as women's suffrage movements, and their internationally organized contribution to fighting women's marginalization in the politics of each nation. In fact, women's determined efforts through the organized labour of feminist movements demanding the vote for women has been shown to be one of the factors that best accounts for why women were enfranchised sooner in some countries than in others.[74]

B. The Struggle for Participatory Parity

i. Narratives, Actors and Strategies in the Struggle for Gender Parity

International standards, world culture and isomorphism seem to have converged after the Second World War to facilitate the general consolidation of women's suffrage.[75] With decolonization and the reorganization of international politics as well as the consolidation of the international women's movement, national independence also became a major catalyst for universal franchise.[76] As a result, by the last quarter of the twentieth century, female suffrage had become fully integrated in the definition of

[73] In this regard, see DuBois, 'Women Suffrage around the World', 252, referring to Richard Evan's classic survey, *The Feminists: Women's Emancipation Movements in Europe, America, and Australasia, 1840–1920* (New York: Barnes & Noble, 1978).

[74] See F. O. Ramirez, Y. Soysal and S. Shanahan, 'The Changing Logic of Political Citizenship: Cross-National Acquisition of Women's Suffrage Rights' (1997) 62 *American Sociological Review* 735–745.

[75] Ibid. [76] Ibid.

what a modern democracy required. Yet modern democracies would remain markedly masculine when it came to the exercise of power and authority. The legal right to suffrage or to run for office were by themselves not sufficient to subvert the socially entrenched gender norms: Women remained systematically politically underrepresented in virtually every country of the world. After all, we must bear in mind that in Western societies the cultural hegemony of the nuclear family and family breadwinner model, and the separate-spheres construct on which it rested, peaked precisely in the years following the end of the Second World War, and that the inequalities linked to marital status in family codes were the last forms of discrimination to be addressed under the influence of second-wave feminism starting only in the 1970s. The fact remains that even in the handful of pioneer European countries where women had gained suffrage at the turn of the twentieth century, they had at best crossed the 20 per cent threshold in parliamentary seats by the 1960s, with representation stalling, if not decreasing, after the mid-1970s.[77]

In view of the persistence of women's underrepresentation, the turn of the century saw a new call for action and legal intervention: this time in the form of legislated gender quotas linked to notions of substantive equality and parity democracy.[78] This legislation wave that has expanded globally seeks to ensure either minimum thresholds or, increasingly, the equal representation of women not only in politics, but also in an ever larger set of domains of public and private authority and decision-making. Although such quotas are likely to be seen as mechanisms to guarantee women fairer opportunities when it comes to accessing positions of power, they can also be seen as legal tools of cultural transformation defying the construction of the modern political subject in ways that allow for overcoming its inherently male original conception, pushing for a renewed understanding of democracy that relies on the subversion and cultural disestablishment of traditional gender roles.

Once again, women's transnational mobilization and organization proved essential. At the global level, CEDAW compelled states to 'take appropriate measures to eliminate discrimination against women in the

[77] Rodriguez Ruiz and Rubio Marin (eds.), *The Struggle for Female Suffrage in Europe*, 40–41.

[78] See D. Dahlerup and L. Freidenvall, 'Quotas as a "Fast Track" to Equal Representation for Women: Why Scandinavia Is No Longer the Model' (2005) 7 *International Feminist Journal of Politics* 26–48.

political and public life of the countries' (Art. 7). However, it was the Beijing Declaration and Platform for Action, signed at the sixteenth plenary meeting of 15 September 1995 at the United Nations Fourth World Conference on Women, that came to epitomize a true breakthrough in its attempt to foreground women's inclusion in decision-making and empowerment as a democratic requirement, in all forms of public office as well as in civil society. It explicitly endorsed affirmative action as not only a legitimate but also a necessary remedy, linking women's access to decision-making to the notion of justice as well as democracy.[79]

In Europe, the 1997 Declaration on Equality between women and men as a fundamental criterion of democracy was adopted during the Fourth European Ministerial Conference on Equality between Women and Men in Istanbul. It soon became a reference for all those working to increase the participation of women in decision-making.[80] Legislation in European states followed, and was put at the service of this new understanding of democracy. By 2021, nine EU member states (Belgium, Croatia, France, Greece, Ireland, Italy, Poland, Portugal and Spain) have implemented legislated quotas, seeking either minimum thresholds or gender-balanced or paritary participation for their lower parliamentary chamber. Additionally, political parties in twenty EU countries have implemented voluntary gender quotas.[81] The European wave of gender quotas seeking women's increased participation in the legislature then started targeting other domains of decision-making, including civil service governing bodies, decision-making positions within universities, higher education and research institutions, the

[79] Fourth World Conference on Women, 'Beijing Declaration and Platform for Action,' Strategic Objective G1, 181.

[80] Even before, in 1989, a seminar on 'The democratic principle of equal representation' had taken place, in which the concept of parity was first discussed. Inspired by the emerging discourse on parity democracy, fourteen high-ranking female elected officials attending the first European Summit on Women in Power held in Athens in November 1992 signed the 'Athens Declaration' supporting gender parity in the representation and administration of nation states on 3 November 1992. Since the turn of the century, the balanced participation of women has remained a clear priority of the Council of Europe, with the Committee of Ministers adopting a Recommendation on 'The Balanced Participation of Women and Men in Political and Public Decision-Making' in 2003 (Rec. (2003)3, Committee of Minister of the Council of Europe, adopted on 12 March 2003 (831st Session).

[81] See www.quotaproject.org.

judiciary, and – most recently – professional sports organizations.[82] Moreover, Europe has since also become the global leader in the adoption of gender quotas for the corporate boards of publicly traded companies, with Belgium, France, Germany, Iceland, Italy, the Netherlands, Norway and Spain having adopted some form of gender-balance rules for corporate boards.[83] This domain expansion shows that, when it comes to the disestablishment of the gender order, a need has been felt to go beyond the narrowly conceived domain of 'the political' to reach every site and domain of authority and decision-making. This has entailed identifying the various domains within the state apparatus and in civil society from which women have traditionally been excluded as a result of being normatively confined to a 'private sphere' that was in fact limited to the domain of the family. At least in Europe, the expansion of gender quotas has to some extent also taken place in the context of narratives and policies seeking to incentivize men to take on their share of reproduction and care tasks. Therefore, it has been suggested that what we may be witnessing is a deeper challenge to the separation of spheres' tradition and the definition of masculinity and femininity that this separation helped entrench, as well as to the traditional manner in which democracies were constructed around such definitions.[84]

In terms of the actual politics underlying the adoption of parity measures, they have been unstructured, as politics tends to be. Not unlike what we saw happen in the struggle for suffrage, a combination of

[82] On gender quotas domain diffusion, see E. Lépinard, 'From Breaking the Rule to Making the Rules: The Adoption, Entrenchment and Diffusion of Gender Quotas in France' (2008) 4 *Politics, Groups and Identities* 231–245; P. Meier, 'Quotas for Advisory Committees, Business and Politics: Just More of the Same?' (2008) 35 *International Political Science Review* 106–128; E. Lépinard and R. Rubio-Marín, 'Completing the Unfinished Task? Gender Quotas and the Ongoing Struggle for Women's Empowerment in Europe', in E. Lépinard and R. Rubio-Marín (eds.), *Transforming Gender Citizenship: The Irresistible Rise of Gender Quotas in Europe* (Cambridge: Cambridge University Press, 2018).

[83] See M. Teigen, 'Gender Quotas on Corporate Boards: On the Diffusion of a Distinct National Policy Reform', in F. Engelstad and M. Teigen (eds.), *Firms, Boards and Gender Quotas: Comparative Perspectives* (Bingley: Emerald, 2012).

[84] See E. Lépinard and R. Rubio-Marín, 'Assessing the Transformative Potential of Gender Quotas for Gender Equality and Democratic Citizenship', in E. Lépinard and R. Rubio-Marín (eds.), *Transforming Gender Citizenship: The Irresistible Rise of Gender Quotas in Europe* (Cambridge: Cambridge University Press, 2018), 450–456.

arguments stemming from egalitarian and difference feminism have been at work in many of the countries where quotas are being adopted. Furthermore, discourses in favour and against the adoption of gender quotas also combined strategic and principled reasoning, allowing for alignment with each country's pre-existing and idiosyncratic gender regimes.[85] And, as for the conquest of suffrage, women have often not been able to rely exclusively on existing structures, such as mainstream political parties, but have needed specific women-led forms of activism, especially in countries where (even left-wing) political parties proved unwilling to change.

In those countries, women's autonomous organizations ended up playing a much more important role in the belated adoption of gender quotas. In Sweden, women's organizations reacted to the decrease in female representation following the 1991 legislative elections by forming a network called *Stödstrumporna* (the Support Stockings), which threatened to create a women's party, a strategy that proved effective in convincing traditional political parties to place more women on their lists.[86] In Greece, it was mostly women lawyers who mobilized outside political parties to create momentum in the public sphere for a constitutional revision of the definition of gender equality, a revision which proved instrumental in passing gender quota laws.[87]

Finally, in line with the struggle for suffrage again, women's organizations fighting for gender quotas have also depended on multilevel governance and transnational networks to pursue their goals. Yet women's agencies and other actors of state feminism, non-existent in the time of the struggle for suffrage, have also played an important role, particularly in quota diffusion, sometimes forming alliances with women's organizations and letting others take the lead, especially in places where the movement's mobilization was largely missing.[88]

[85] On France's chaotic path to parity, see J. W. Scott, *Only Paradoxes to Offer. French Feminists and the Rights of Man* (Cambridge, MA: Harvard University Press, 1996).

[86] See L. Freidenvall, 'Gender Equality without Legislated Quotas in Sweden', in E. Lépinard and R. Rubio-Marín (eds.), *Transforming Gender Citizenship: The Irresistible Rise of Gender Quotas in Europe* (Cambridge: Cambridge University Press, 2018), 380–381.

[87] See D. Anagnostou, 'The Protracted Struggle for Gender Quotas in Greek Politics: Constitutional Reform and Feminist Mobilization in the EU Context', in E. Lépinard and R. Rubio-Marín (eds.), *Transforming Gender Citizenship: The Irresistible Rise of Gender Quotas in Europe* (Cambridge: Cambridge University Press, 2018), 167–171.

[88] Lépinard and Rubio-Marín, 'Completing the Unfinished Task?', 24–26.

ii. The Law as Friend and Foe of Gender Parity

The narrative so far seems to suggest that, where political parties and other actors did not self-impose promotional measures, the law has come to the rescue in the many countries in which various kinds of legislative quotas were adopted, often as a result of women's mobilization and under the auspices of transnational actors endorsing gender-balanced representation. The story is, however, more complex: In many European countries, high-order law, i.e., constitutional law, was in fact a stumbling block to the adoption of such legislation when such first-order law was interpreted as committed to formalistic notions of legal equality, more compatible with gender neutrality than with gender quotas, and/or traditional conceptions of democracy linked to general and unitary representation and full respect for political party autonomy. Fortunately, different forms of constitutional amendment have been passed to overcome or prevent such hurdles, allowing new (more substantive) understandings of equality or new visions of democratic legitimacy (as requiring gender-balanced participation) to affirm themselves in an increasing number of European countries, including Portugal, Slovenia, France, Italy, Belgium and Greece.[89]

An overarching commitment to formal notions of gender equality in France reinforced by the country's espousal of a Republican universalist conception of citizenship, for example, explains the strength of the constitutional resistance not only against the adoption of political quotas, but also against any further extension of quotas to other domains such as that of corporate governance. Indeed, France is unique in that almost every attempt to expand parity beyond elective functions taking place during the 2000s was met with resistance by both the Constitutional Council and the *Conseil d'Etat* (the highest administrative court). This situation persevered even after the first constitutional reform enabling the adoption of political quotas had taken place, precisely because the reform was interpreted as a

[89] See R. Rubio-Marín, 'Women's Political Citizenship in New European Constitutionalism: Between Constitutional Amendment and Progressive Interpretation', in H. Irving (ed.), *Gender and Constitutions* (Cheltenham: Edward Elgar, 2017). This was, however, less the case in countries in other parts of the world where quotas have been adopted more recently under evolving human rights standards and evolved notions of democratic legitimacy and, more importantly, under constitutions that were already drafted with clauses sanctioning the legitimacy of positive measures to ensure women's representation. See R. Rubio Marín, *Global Gender Constitutionalism and Women's Citizenship: A Struggle for Transformative Inclusion* (Cambridge: Cambridge University Press, 2022), ch. 3, section on parity democracy.

narrow exception to the dominant norm of formal equality. A second constitutional reform was therefore necessary that would allow for a better response to women's systematic underrepresentation in all sites of decision-making power and thereby in the 'public sphere' of the gender order relegating women to motherhood and care.[90] But even in some countries, such as Italy, that are also generically committed to substantive equality in their constitutions, and thus allow or even expect public powers to remove societal obstacles to the meaningful enjoyment of rights by disempowered groups, constitutional reform was necessary in order for political quotas for women to be covered. This has to do with quotas being seen as affecting not only women's (or men's) political or equality rights but also the country's overall political system of representation.[91] Only in some cases, such as Spain, has a general constitutional clause expressing commitment to substantive equality (Art. 9.2) been interpreted as providing sufficient constitutional grounds to allow for gender quotas when these were challenged before the Constitutional Court.[92] Debates are ongoing in Germany about whether a similar commitment to substantive gender equality under the German Basic Law would be sufficient to give coverage to promotional measures seeking to guarantee gender-balanced representation.[93]

In any event, the necessary constitutional amendment processes to enshrine either more generic substantive equality clauses or more specific clauses enabling legislative quotas, have sometimes been bottom-up (as in Austria, Germany and Greece) and sometimes top-down (as those taking place in Portugal and Italy, where women's groups never engaged in the quota struggle actively). A variety of actors haven taken the initiative in

[90] See E. Lépinard, 'The French Parity Reform: The Never-Ending Quest for a New Gender Equality Principle', in E. Lépinard and R. Rubio-Marín (eds.), *Transforming Gender Citizenship: The Irresistible Rise of Gender Quotas in Europe* (Cambridge: Cambridge University Press, 2018), 62–93.

[91] See A. Donà, 'Eppur si Muove: The Tortuous Adoption and Implementation of Gender Quotas in Conservative Italy', in E. Lépinard and R. Rubio-Marín (eds.), *Transforming Gender Citizenship: The Irresistible Rise of Gender Quotas in Europe* (Cambridge: Cambridge University Press, 2018), 186–215.

[92] See Blanca Rodríguez-Ruiz and Ruth Rubio-Marin, 'The Gender of Representation: On Democracy, Equality and Parity' (2008) 6 *International Journal of Constitutional Law* 287–316 at 296–300.

[93] See L. K. Davidson-Schmich, *Gender Quotas and Democratic Participation: Recruiting Candidates for Elective Offices in Germany* (Ann Arbor: University of Michigan Press, 2016).

both scenarios, such as political parties (as in Portugal and Italy) but also women's groups. As with other forms of affirmation of women's political agency, the constitutional reform processes had a contagion effect, with the French reform affecting Belgium and Italy, and the reforms in Austria, Germany and Portugal affecting those in Greece. In the latter, the reform campaign explicitly referred to a constitutional tradition in the making, shared by many EU member states and expressed in the growing number of national constitutions guaranteeing substantive equality, and incorporating positive action provisions. Not surprisingly, the narrative in support of constitutional amendments included arguments based on international and European laws and policies in support of women's empowerment in most of these countries.

3. Conclusion

What this chapter has sought to establish is therefore that the 'political subject' as it exists in various countries is one facet of the legal subject's existence that has been profoundly shaped by the interaction of law and gender. At all historical junctures of the legal delineation of what the concept of political rights encompasses, gender norms have played an essential role. Women's assertion of their political agency has encouraged them to engage in a historical struggle to conquer political rights, including in a sense broader than the one delineated in early political modernity, as here exemplified by women's involvement in the French Revolution. Furthermore, it encouraged them to fight for actual political representation, a struggle that is ongoing, as exemplified by the more recent global conquest of parity measures. Interestingly, historiography has only recently foregrounded women's agency in early revolutionary struggles as well as in later efforts to achieve suffrage or parity. The importance of women's persistent reliance on transnational networks is also noteworthy given that they have not been able to rely on existing and male-dominated structures, such as mainstream political parties, to advance their claims.

This chapter also addresses the path dependency of the contemporary delineation of what counts as political rights. Such delineation is traced back to the late eighteenth century's legacy of the distinction between separate private and public spheres, and the restricted access to the latter, only allowing entry to those individuals who met the gendered norm of independence. Later legal rules effectively backed these foundational conceptions, using them as justifications for the denial of equal political rights and duties to women (franchise, jury service, military, etc.). They also further entrenched women's dependence on men, in particular as family law turned women into legal minors. Because of this, every struggle women have fought to conquer equal legal status must be seen as an affirmation of their political agency. Only later in the twentieth century have these gender and legal norms been challenged, and laws progressively been subjected to reform processes, first leading to gender-neutral legal orders and, more recently, to norms explicitly supporting the adoption of promotional measures – especially in the form of gender quotas and parity measures.

Women's struggle for political agency has thus always relied on a challenge to the very shape and substance of what had come to represent the political domain. Sometimes, it has entailed doing politics in ways that openly contested the public/private divide: the temperance movement as connected to gender violence; the suffrage movement as linked to improving conditions of women at home; the parity movement as seeking to disestablish gender roles in public and private spheres. In the ongoing tug of war over the very definition of 'the political', backlash against and resistance to women's affirmation of political agency has largely been based on the reaffirmation of the gendered public/private divide. Just as the French Revolution repressed women who engaged in political action, so were suffragists opposed in the name of women's domestic roles. Contemporary forms of resistance and backlash against gender equality provide a modern iteration. Some of these forms are expressed in the name of the traditional family, and can accordingly be read as a reaction against women's growing empowerment as they conquer more and more sites of power and decision-making. Other forms of resistance focus on the displacement of contested sites of power, as increasing numbers of such sites are asked to live up to parity standards. In other words, the delineation of the political seems to be a never-ending, continuously gendered process.

Index